Bridging Liberalism
and Multiculturalism in
American Education

Rob Reich

Bridging Liberalism and Multiculturalism in American Education

THE UNIVERSITY OF CHICAGO PRESS

Chicago & London

Rob Reich is assistant professor of political science at Stanford University.

The University of Chicago Press, Chicago 60637
The University of Chicago Press, Ltd., London
© 2002 by The University of Chicago
All rights reserved. Published 2002
Printed in the United States of America

11 10 09 08 07 06 05 04 03 02   1 2 3 4 5
ISBN: 0-226-70736-9 (cloth)
ISBN: 0-226-70737-7 (paper)

Library of Congress Cataloging-in-Publication Data

Reich, Rob.
   Bridging liberalism and multiculturalism in American education / Rob Reich.
      p. cm.
   Includes bibliographical references (p.) and index.
   ISBN 0-226-70736-9 (cloth : alk. paper) — ISBN 0-226-70737-7 (pbk. : alk. paper)
   1. Multicultural education—United States.   2. Liberalism—United States.
   3. Civics—Study and teaching—United States.   I. Title.

LC1099.3 .R44 2002
370.117'0973—dc21

                                                                    2001052270

CONTENTS

ACKNOWLEDGMENTS

This is a book about philosophy and education, and in my view few things are as important as these activities. One of them, however, is love. Heather Kirkpatrick's unsurpassable love, energy, and confidence in me have brought to my life a joyousness without which not much else seems possible. To her I dedicate this book. *Brennende Liebe.*

Writing is a solitary endeavor, but philosophy and education proceed through human interaction and dialogue. I am grateful to the following individuals for the many conversations that have shaped and challenged my thinking: Harry Brighouse, Larry Cuban, Elisabeth Hansot, Russell Hardin, Heather Kirkpatrick, Meira Levinson, Steve Macedo, Nel Noddings, Susan Moller Okin, Denis Phillips, Debra Satz, John Tomasi, David Tyack, and Susan Verducci. I owe a special debt to Eamonn Callan and David Nyberg, both of whom offered unflagging support and read the entire manuscript at a late date. I must also single out Mark Brilliant, friend and interlocutor nonpareil.

Portions of this book were presented at seminars at Brown University's departments of education and political science, Stanford University's School of Education, political science department, and Center on Adolescence, and at annual meetings of the American Political Science Association and the American Educational Research Association. I thank the participants in these seminars. Sections of chapter 3 were developed for a conference (and forthcoming volume) on cosmopolitanism and collective identity, hosted by Walter Feinberg and Kevin McDonough at McGill University. I am grateful to New York University Press for permission to reproduce portions of "Testing the Boundaries of Parental Authority over Education: The Case of Homeschooling," in *NOMOS 43: Moral and Political Education,* ed. Stephen Macedo and Yael Tamir (New York: New York University Press, 2001).

Intellectual dialogue is indispensable when writing, but so too is institutional support. During the conception and completion of this book I received financial support from the Stanford School of Education and the Stanford University Lieberman Fellowship. The Stanford Humanities Center provided the ideal intellectual environment during the writing of the first draft; a grant from Al Camarillo and the Center for Comparative Studies in Race and Ethnicity relieved me from one quarter of teaching so I could complete the final draft.

For their help and many excellent suggestions, I am indebted also to John Tryneski, Anne Ford, Nick Murray, and two anonymous reviewers for the University of Chicago Press. Anne Wood, an exceptional undergraduate student, offered numerous improvements to the text, especially in chapter 6, and offered superb assistance with the index. Thanks also to Li Sa Ng.

Other friends and colleagues made contributions and offered necessary encouragement: Chris Barbic, Kate Bickert, Nandini Gandhi, Kay Moffett, Mitch Neuger, Russell Shaw, Shira Stutman, Rami Wernik, and Anna Yusim.

My parents have followed the writing of this book with a mixture of pride and curiosity. I thank them, and my sister Cristie and brother Stephen, with love and admiration.

Finally, I wish to thank my high school teachers, Russ Irving and John Graf, for first showing me that a life of the mind was a life worth leading.

INTRODUCTION

I first began thinking about questions of liberalism, multiculturalism, and education during the two years I worked as a sixth grade teacher in a public elementary school in Houston, Texas, in the early 1990s. The school confronted the familiar litany of problems besetting many urban schools: abysmal test scores, low teacher morale, and a series of ineffective administrators who shuffled through the principal's office. Like most new teachers, I wanted to make a difference in the lives of my students. And, as all new teachers quickly discover, my ambitions exceeded my abilities. In response, I turned to my more experienced colleagues for help and signed up for whatever professional development opportunities the school or district offered.

In the informal conversations in the teachers' lounge, in formal training sessions run by colleagues, and in official professional development programs, I found that one of the central topics of discussion was the importance of multiculturalism. This was a topic with which I was already familiar, for talk about multiculturalism was becoming increasingly popular in the mainstream press and on college campuses. When I talked with my colleagues in Houston and participated in teacher training programs, the term was ubiquitous. Our classrooms and our school were to be multicultural. Our lessons and our pedagogy were to be multicultural. The lunch menu and school assemblies were to be multicultural. This was so because our students, their families, the city as a whole, and indeed the entire country were multicultural.

I agreed with all this, and I am sure that if someone had asked me if I was a proponent and practitioner of multicultural education, I would have replied, "Of course." Then, as now, the rhetoric of multiculturalism exerted a kind of inexorable gravitational pull. It was impossible to be against it, for that would imply that you were in favor of monoculturalism, or that you were opposed to diversity.

But as the school year progressed, I realized that I didn't really understand what multiculturalism or multicultural education was. So many things were packaged under its name, from the innocuous to the completely transformative. Was adjusting the school menu to include a variety of ethnic foods a part of the same reform idea as renovating the school curriculum to include the history and literature of cultural minorities? Was making Black History month a visible feature of the school building in February or celebrating *Cinco de Mayo* a corollary to culturally sensitive pedagogy? Moreover, I wondered about the fact that while the city of Houston was multicultural, my school was not a place of great diversity, whether measured by socioeconomic status, race, or ethnicity. Almost all the students were Latino and came from families who occupied the lowest rungs of the socioeconomic ladder. When I thought about it, I found that neither I nor any of my colleagues could articulate a clear and coherent idea of multiculturalism. It was something we all spoke of, but we couldn't say exactly what it was.

Caught up in the daily struggles of learning to be a better teacher, committed to the idea that an equal opportunity to attain an excellent education is a matter of social justice, I didn't spend much time then reflecting on the meaning of multiculturalism. Only later, when I enrolled in graduate school to study issues involving democracy and education, did I begin thinking more seriously about multiculturalism, especially its relation to questions of social justice. What is the history of cultural diversity in American schools, and how did it affect educational policy? How should public schools in a liberal democracy treat the cultural identities of their youngest citizens? What is the place of ethnocentric or religious schools in a liberal democracy? Over time, I began to ask some fundamental questions about the intersection of political theory and education. In a culturally diverse society, what ought to be the civic aims of schooling? Is there a tension between cultivating citizenship and honoring and respecting social diversity? What is the appropriate balance of authority over the education of children? Should we educate children to be autonomous? This book is my attempt to make some sense of the confusion I first felt as a teacher about multiculturalism and the proper aims of education. The book speaks, I hope, to educators and educational policymakers, and to scholars in political theory who have written about the purposes of education in a culturally diverse liberal democracy.

ASTONISHINGLY, little more than a decade ago, in 1988, the Nexis database of major American newspapers records not a single reference to "multiculturalism." In 1994, however, there were more than 1,400 references, and in 1997 there were thousands. The term has become commonplace; from scholarly books and journals to daily newspapers and monthly magazines, to workplace and household conversations, *multiculturalism* has won a rapid and broad incorporation into our national consciousness and vocabulary.

But debates over multiculturalism only seem new. *Multiculturalism* is a new word applied to an old issue. In the early twentieth century, at the time of John Dewey and Horace Kallen, the idea went by the term *cultural pluralism*. In the nineteenth century, Tocqueville, the famous sojourner in the United States, observed of the American scene, "Picture to yourself . . . a society which comprises all the nations of the world—English, French, German: people differing from one another in language, in beliefs, in opinions; in a word a society possessing no roots. . . . What is the connecting link between these so different elements? How are they welded into one people?"[1] Indeed, even prior to the Revolutionary War, Americans were dealing with the challenges of living in a polity composed of vastly different people from many diverse cultures. As historians often remind us, the United States has *always* been a multicultural society.[2] Despite the lack of reference to it in 1988, there is nothing especially novel about the general phenomenon of multiculturalism.

What *is* new in the debate over multiculturalism is the way in which it is taken to be antithetical to the political philosophy central to most modern democracies: classical liberalism. Liberalism, especially contemporary liberal theory, emphasizes autonomy, individual rights, the freedom to develop and revise a life plan, and the need for civic education and a common political identity to provide unity in a diverse society. In contrast, common formulations of multiculturalism are often skeptical of, or reject outright, these liberal values. Whereas liberals stress autonomy and individual identity, multiculturalists often build theory and policies from inherited or ascribed group identities;[3] whereas liberals focus on individual rights and the equality of persons, multiculturalists often focus on group rights and the equality of groups;[4] and whereas liberals emphasize the need for civic education and a common political identity, multiculturalists often reject the view that a common culture is the necessary cement of a society.[5] But as Will Kymlicka points out, a long history of liberals held liberalism to support or entail beliefs, like the provision of group rights, that we now associate with multiculturalism.[6] Liberalism and multiculturalism today constitute something of a dualism. It need not be this way, for liberalism and multiculturalism do not, historically or of logical necessity, stand at loggerheads.

Historians have been for the most part quicker to document, interpret, and address the tensions between liberalism and multiculturalism than philosophers.[7] Only within the past ten years have philosophers begun to weigh in on the issues.[8] Historians and philosophers alike, however, all too often gloss over a crucial fact: the venue in which multicultural issues have been most vociferously debated in America is the field of education. Schools, in many ways, have always served as the battleground for "culture wars," though this is particularly true for the debate in the 1980s and 1990s.[9] Beginning with nineteenth-century debates between Catholics and Protestants over the place of the Bible in public schools, the schoolhouse has been caught in the cross-fire of broader cultural conflicts, from controversies over bilingualism at the turn of the century, to the Americanization and acculturation campaigns in the 1920s, debates about busing and desegregation in the 1970s, and finally contemporary debates about multicultural curricula, ethnocentric schools, common values across cultures, and the decline of civic capacity.

In the past few years, several political theorists have written about civic education in liberal democracies. This is, in my view, a welcome development, for educational questions have long resided at the center of some of the classical works of political theory. Plato, Aristotle, and Rousseau, for example, all saw education as absolutely central to politics and wrote extensively on the subject. John Stuart Mill, John Locke, and John Dewey all recognized that a theory of liberalism required a corresponding and complementary theory of education. Dewey, in fact, thought that if education means the formation of fundamental habits of the mind, then "all philosophy may even be defined *as the general theory of education.*"[10] In the United States, the Founding Fathers were well aware of the importance of education, making repeated calls for common schools as a means of creating an enlightened citizenry.[11] Viewed from the vantage point of the history of philosophy, it is a strange anomaly that many contemporary liberal theorists are largely silent about the educational presuppositions and implications of liberalism.

Among the most influential of those contemporary theorists who have addressed questions of education are Eamonn Callan and Stephen Macedo. In *Creating Citizens*, Callan provides a friendly criticism of Rawlsian liberalism, arguing that the liberal state justly attempts to foster a set of civic skills and allegiances in all citizens in order to ensure the endurance of ideals of equality and freedom.[12] Stephen Macedo's recent book, *Diversity and Distrust*, argues for the transformative aims of schooling in a liberal state, so that diversity may be properly shaped and restrained for civic purposes.[13] I am sympathetic to the main thrust of Callan's and Macedo's work, which is that schools in a liberal society properly attempt to cultivate in children certain civic virtues and dispositions. Yet when these authors focus on multiculturalism, they are mostly concerned with questions about *religious* diversity, specifically religious fundamentalism, as opposed to broader forms of cultural diversity. Neither Callan nor Macedo fully incorporates an analysis of both liberal and multicultural theory while grounding the work within the history and institutions of schooling.

In this book, I examine liberalism and multiculturalism within the historical and institutional context of American education. I aim to articulate a liberal theory of multicultural education that incorporates the insights of both liberalism and multiculturalism, and takes seriously the history of schooling. My goal is to outline and defend the civic purposes of education in a liberal society characterized by wide cultural diversity.

My motivation for developing a liberal theory of multicultural education is threefold. First, I find that political theorists often ignore the historical context in which their theories are to be applied, and even more often they ignore the educational presuppositions and implications of their theories. The most prominent defender of contemporary liberalism, John Rawls, and the most prominent defender of multiculturalism, Will Kymlicka, as well as many of those who have commented on their respective theories, say little about the role of schools in a society governed by their principles of justice. Contemporary theorists, generally speaking, seem to assume that the persons populating a given political territory are all fully functioning, autonomous adults, upon whom certain rights and responsibilities of citizenship are conferred, and in whom civic values, habits, beliefs, and group attachments and loyalties already reside. They are largely and strangely silent about the civic role of schools, gesturing, at best, to some educational prescriptions that seem to flow from the principles of justice they defend.

Second, the educators and educational policymakers who might be expected to take up questions about the appropriate aims of education have instead focused their attention almost exclusively on increasing academic achievement in the service of economic ends. At the top of the agenda are concerns about how to prepare workers for the changing and increasingly global economy. According to an influential report in 1983, the United States is "a nation at risk." If not worried about the economic competitiveness of Americans, policymakers point to the failure of schools and call more frequently for abandoning "government schools" and privatizing education through vouchers or charter schools. Lost amid this clamor is recognition that public schools have served, and continue to serve, an important civic role in the United States. Indeed, the formation of publicly funded common schools was justified largely in terms of the role they would play in creating citizens, not workers.

And third, while theorists and educational practitioners alike say little about the civic ends of schools, social scientists continue to accumulate evidence documenting the decline of civic engagement in America, the fraying of the social fabric. A recent report aptly titled "A Nation of Spectators" shows a steady decline in civic health since 1960.[14] Or, as Robert Putnam puts it, the past generation has witnessed "the strange disappearance of civic America."[15] While schools certainly cannot play a solitary savior's role in restoring civic engagement—too many other factors are implicated in the decline—one would think that the warnings of the social scientists might provide new reasons to reconsider and perhaps reinvigorate the role of schools in creating an active and engaged citizenry.

The time is ripe, then, I believe, for work on the civic purpose of schooling that at once locates itself in the broader debates of political philosophy and recognizes the historical context in which it is to apply. Political theory and educational theory are intertwined. This means that liberal and multicultural theorists cannot simply spell out the educational implications of their theories, as if these were prescriptions deduced from the theories. They must instead recognize how liberal and multicultural theories depend upon educational *presuppositions,* so that the theories may be realized in practice. Similarly, this means that educators cannot simply defend a range of educational practices and policies, as if these had no civic importance or meaning beyond the classroom or schoolhouse. They must instead recognize how their policies and practices connect to (and support or undermine) the political framework in which education is embedded. Civic education must, in my opinion, be consistent with the political principles of the larger society (indeed, it may be instrumental in their realization) and show an awareness of the history of schooling. In developing a liberal theory of multicultural education I therefore operate largely within contemporary political theory, tapping necessary resources of current work in history and multicultural education. The liberal theory of multicultural education that I defend is my attempt to link together political theory, educational theory, and educational history.

I HOPE to accomplish two main tasks in this book. The first is theoretical and primarily addresses political theorists; the second is political and primarily addresses policy analysts and educators. First, by examining contemporary liberal and multicultural theories, I take up the issues involved in delineating the state's interest in and the legitimate boundaries of civic education. Among the questions I consider are the following: What are the educational presuppositions and implications of particular theories? How does the cultivation of liberal values in schools affect cultural identities? When does civic education become an *illiberal* imposition of liberal values, overriding the interests and perhaps the rights of cultural groups or parents? Should the state encourage all citizens to be autonomous, either for civic or personal reasons? Should certain groups, such as homeschoolers or the Amish, be exempted from regulations governing such things as attendance and curricula?

The second, more practical, task outlines in broad form a pedagogical approach to liberal multicultural education and some legal and policy implications that flow from such a theory. I consider the following relevant questions: Should children's interests in education be added to the usual calculus of state's interests and parents' interests? How—if at all—should the liberal state regulate private and religious schools and homeschooling? What pedagogical strategies make sense for teaching students about cultural diversity and differences?

My main theoretical argument is that in order to construct a liberal theory of multicultural education, liberals and multiculturalists each must concede important claims to the objections of the other. Liberals like John Rawls, on the one hand, must give up the frequent assertion that liberalism can be neutral to the various ways and ends of life pursued by citizens. The multicultural insight is that the liberal state is in no way neutral to cultural groups. Furthermore, nowhere is this more visible than in both educational history and the requirements of liberal theory. Liberals should not promote schools that attempt, as they have done in the past, to impose a narrow cultural uniformity on citizens. They must likewise avoid promoting a school system and civil society that purport to be neutral when they should in fact be partial to the value of autonomy. From a multicultural perspective, liberals must allow for the expression and cultivation of cultural diversity in schools and should own up to and defend their partiality to the substantive value of autonomy.

Proponents of multiculturalism like Will Kymlicka, on the other hand, must avoid placing an interest in the sustenance and integrity of cultural groups above the freedom and equality of the individuals within, especially children. Once again, the problems are most visible in the educational policies that follow from multicultural theories. Rights to separate schooling or exemptions from education, for example, have the potential to undermine the development of civic virtues, such as autonomy and mutual respect, that are fundamental to the legitimacy and stability of the liberal state. Moreover, multicultural theorists often justify their principles by reference to the autonomous choices of adults, without recognizing that respecting the autonomy of adults to affiliate themselves with cultural communities should not result in allowing adults to educate their children in any manner they see fit. From a liberal perspective, multiculturalists should take care to assure that all children are provided an education that fosters their autonomy, which in turn contributes to their participation as equal citizens in the public sphere and facilitates a capacity to form, revise, and pursue a conception of the good, be it similar or dissimilar to that of their parents and cultural group, in the private sphere.

A liberal theory of multicultural education avoids, then, the fallacy of liberal neutrality common among liberal political theorists and the false fixity of cultural identity common among multiculturalists. It describes a civic education that properly insists on teaching students the substantive liberal value of autonomy, which is not culturally neutral; it teaches students nevertheless to recognize and respect the variety of cultural groups that have contributed to the nation's history and are present among the citizenry. In accepting and defending autonomy as a central value, liberal multicultural education takes lines of cultural identity to be permeable, broad (extending beyond race and ethnicity), and multiple, treating individuals as capable of choosing identities as well as inheriting them and as capable of negotiating among different identities as well as possessing but one. At bottom, a liberal theory of multicultural education attempts not to ascribe any particular cultural identity to a student but to treat the student as an unfinished, evolving, and prospectively self-governing person, the possession neither of the state nor of his or her parents.

Outline of the Book

Chapter 1 presents a historical look at multicultural conflict in schools in the United States, showing how tensions between the struggle to respect cultural diversity and efforts to secure civic unity have always been present. The phenomenon of multiculturalism is nothing new. From the particulars of U.S. history, I turn to the abstraction of political theory, where in recent years the simple fact of cultural diversity has played an increasingly larger role. In chapter 2 I examine contemporary liberal political theory from the perspective of multiculturalism, arguing that, as the liberal state asks all citizens to be autonomous, liberal claims to neutrality cannot be maintained. Chapter 3 turns the tables, so to speak, as I examine contemporary multicultural political theory from the perspective of liberalism. Here I show that the multicultural interest in protecting and sustaining the sanctity of cultural groups often comes at the price of overlooking the interests of children in becoming autonomous.

Because the concept of autonomy figures heavily in the theorizing of both liberals and multiculturalists, I devote chapter 4 to a sustained examination of what it means to be autonomous. I define and defend a minimalist conception of autonomy which is neither so minimal that it will be promoted or accepted by all cultural groups, or achieved effortlessly by all people, nor so exacting that it will be rejected as a broad-based, overly comprehensive, moral ideal unsuited to serve as the basis of a liberal, pluralist society. Minimalist autonomy, as I shall claim, both underwrites and constrains cultural diversity in a liberal society, and therefore mediates between liberal theory and multicultural theory.

In chapter 5 I outline and defend the liberal theory of multicultural education I have just described. The theory posits fostering minimalist autonomy as a central educational aim that is promoted by an education that exposes children to and engages them intellectually with diverse cultural beliefs, values, and traditions. In the process, I argue against liberals who believe that neutrality must stand as a central strand of liberal thinking; on the contrary, I believe that autonomy is crucial to liberal concerns, the holding of which in turn obviates the possibility of neutrality. I also argue against multiculturalists who believe that the fixity or primacy of group identity stands as the central strand of multicultural thinking; on the contrary, I believe that a commitment to minimalist autonomy is consistent with a deep concern for cultural diversity, in particular for cultural minorities.

Chapter 6 takes up the question of how authority over the education of children should be distributed in a liberal society. Almost all who write on this subject discuss one or both of the following U.S. court cases: *Wisconsin v. Yoder*, concerning the rights of Amish parents to exempt their children from mandatory attendance laws beyond the eighth grade, and *Mozert v. Hawkins County Board of Education*, concerning the rights of religiously motivated parents to opt their children out of certain parts of a public middle school curriculum. I attempt to move the discussion beyond the odd fixation on *Yoder* and *Mozert* by examining the increasingly popular phenomenon of homeschooling in the United States. Should the liberal state regulate homeschooling, the arrangement that gives parents the greatest control over the education of children? If so, how should it do so? Building on a liberal theory of multicultural education, I argue that the state should permit but vigorously regulate homeschooling because a function of any school environment, including any homeschool, must be to teach children about values and beliefs other than those they are likely to encounter within their homes.

Finally, in chapter 7 I examine the pedagogical and policy implications of liberal multicultural education. Multicultural education scholars have written extensively about pedagogical reforms, and I canvass this literature in order to contrast my recommendations with their prevailing conclusions. Rather than aiming at so-called cultural congruity in teaching, I argue that teachers should aim at developing the evaluative capacities of students through a process that is at heart hermeneutical—a broadening of their interpretive and evaluative capacities. As for policy implications, I consider how a liberal theory of multicultural education simultaneously aims to shape educational policymaking—setting boundary conditions to permissible forms of schooling and regulating all others—while leaving ample room for parental discretion over the education of their children. I also examine the implications of liberal multicultural education for three of the most prominent trends in contemporary school reform—vouchers, charter schools, and the small school movement.

While my approach to the questions and problems of education in a culturally diverse liberal society is informed by the practice of education—by both my own experience as a teacher and the history of education in America—I am first and foremost a political theorist in these pages. I am under no illusions, however, that any amount of philosophizing can resolve all issues, particularly those concerning specific pedagogical or policy recommendations. While I hope this work will provide a framework within which issues of civic education for a multicultural citizenry can be profitably discussed, I strongly believe that the particularities of many schoolhouse issues must be decided at the local level. This is no weakness of philosophy, but an honest and pragmatic admission that those with expertise and knowledge of local contexts are better suited to make decisions, given a defensible framework, than philosophers without such expertise and knowledge. While I would not go so far as to agree with Richard Rorty that philosophy is irrelevant to education, I do not believe a philosophical theory of liberal multicultural education furnishes a complete blueprint for all educational practice. Seen in this light, the absence here of a detailed plan, ready for implementation, about how to educate children represents not an oversight, but a virtue—proper philosophical humility.

A NOTE ON TERMINOLOGY: *LIBERALISM, MULTICULTURALISM, AND CULTURE*

In common conversation, *liberalism* is the antonym of *conservatism*. In recent years, to be a "liberal" has taken on a pejorative meaning, damning for most prospective public officeholders. My invocation and use of *liberalism* refers, however, to the historical meaning of the word that hearkens back to political philosophers such as Locke and Mill and continues through contemporary philosophers such as John Rawls and Ronald Dworkin. Both the liberals and conservatives in the former sense share commitments to the basic beliefs of what could be called "classical liberalism." Classical liberals stress the overriding importance of the ideals of individualism, freedom, and equality, which manifest themselves politically in, for example, individual rights, the separation of church and state, guaranteed freedom of expression, formal equality under the law, and so on. As mentioned earlier, classical liberals also typically emphasize autonomy, the freedom to develop and revise a life plan, and the need for an informed citizenry capable of critical thinking so that political participation can be effective. When I use the word *liberalism,* I mean this historical and philosophical tradition of liberalism, whose more specific details will become plain in the following pages.

The potential confusion about the word *liberalism* is small when compared to the potential confusion provoked by the word *multiculturalism.* As I quickly learned while teaching in Houston, people use the word *multiculturalism* in multiple ways. It is important to distinguish between two general usages: *descriptive* multiculturalism, denoting the demographic coexistence of various cultures within a single society; and *normative* multiculturalism, denoting a moral ideal or specific political agenda. In the former case, the word *multiculturalism* describes a fact—the fact of cultural diversity. In the United States, that fact is proven in unspoken testimony every day when thousands of schools and workplaces fill up with students and staff of vastly different backgrounds who are the bearers of many different cultural traditions and values. In this descriptive sense, multiculturalism exists whether we want it to or not. Descriptive multiculturalism is analogous to what political philosophers call "the fact of pluralism" or "value pluralism." As most eloquently articulated by John Rawls, the fact of pluralism means that the "good" cannot come prior to the "right," because society will not share any substantive view of the good life. The descriptive fact of multiculturalism and the diverse and even incommensurable values that are spread among many cultures militate against the state espousing and promoting any single conception of the good. The claim is not that different values correspond tidily with different cultures—this is clearly false—but that cultures are in part defined by their promotion of a set of values, a *nomos,* that other cultural groups may not share. As Joseph Raz says, "Multiculturalism arises out of a belief in value pluralism, and in particular in the validity of the diverse values embodied in the practices which constitute the diverse and in many ways incompatible values of different societies."[16]

In the latter, normative usage, *multiculturalism* has an unmistakable moral undertone to it, an implication that certain policies must follow from the plain fact that many different cultures exist within a common political boundary. This is the idea that being a multiculturalist requires social and political change, like promoting a multicultural curriculum or agitating for multicultural accommodations, laws, and policies. Normative multiculturalism constitutes social critique or reconstruction.

This initial division, however, is still unsatisfactory. For within the normative usage of the term, a broad range of positions makes it difficult to distill any coherent meaning from the word. In political theory, we find Will Kymlicka and Joseph Raz defending multiculturalism as a liberal corollary, and a group from Chicago elaborating "critical multiculturalism" as a skeptical response to liberalism.[17] Within the field of education, we find Molefi Kete Asante, a passionate defender of Afrocentric schooling, and Diane Ravitch, a vigorous critic of ethnocentric schools, both declaring themselves in favor of multiculturalism.[18] We find multiculturalists like Gary Nash, author of the embattled national history standards, who believe a core curriculum is necessary, and other multiculturalists, like Anthony Appiah, who reject it, holding that there need be no common civic culture to weld society together, much less as a common course of study.[19] So many varied positions and so many people of different political temperaments have gathered themselves under the banner of multiculturalism that one hardly knows what the normative usage means anymore.

I will use the phrase *liberal multicultural education* or *liberal theory of multicultural education* when referring to the theory I aim to defend in these pages. When I refer in general to *multiculturalism* or *multiculturalists*, I almost always mean it in the normative sense. I attempt as far as possible to describe or attribute specific beliefs or positions to their authors. But in order to help clarify matters, it might help to indicate my general impression of what people mean by *multiculturalism* and *multicultural education*. For the purposes of this work, I understand the term *multiculturalism* to represent a theory or position that emphasizes diversity over sameness, recognition of difference over homogenizing similarity, the particular over the universal, the group over the individual, race and ethnicity over, say, class and gender, and cultural identification rather than cultural affiliation. I understand most people to use the phrase *multicultural education* to represent an approach to education that emphasizes learning about and celebrating a child's home culture, learning about and recognizing the cultures of others, an expanded curriculum that incorporates contributions of minority groups, and an expanded repertoire of pedagogical strategies designed to reach students of diverse cultural backgrounds. While this may not accurately describe the views of some people who would claim to be advocates of multiculturalism or multicultural education, I do not think it unrepresentative or unfair. What is important for my purposes here is not that we define once and for all what multiculturalism or multicultural education mean, but that the distinction between liberal multicultural education and other multiculturalisms can be made clear.

If defining multiculturalism is more difficult than defining liberalism, determining the meaning of *culture* is still more problematic. Raymond Williams says of this vexing concept that "culture is one of the two or three most complicated words in the English language."[20] So complicated is the term that some have begun to call for its abandonment. In a recent article, for example, Roger Just finds that "nowadays the concept of culture may well have outlived its usefulness in anthropology, but as a folk concept it has proved alarmingly successful. Culture is no longer an academically imposed classification, but a popularly espoused and politically potent one."[21]

Following most work in political theory, I employ the more popular usage of the word, which refers to the supposedly distinctive *Weltanschauungen* of various groups of people. Yet even the meaning of the folk concept is stunningly indeterminate, spanning a long continuum of broad to narrow scope, depending on how large the relevant group happens to be. It ranges from a macro-context, such as "Western culture" or "Western civilization" in the way Samuel Huntington uses it in his *Clash of Civilizations* (in which case the United States is monocultural),[22] to more familiar contexts, such as African-American culture, Latino culture, Jewish culture, or deaf culture, and to micro-contexts, such as the culture of Silicon Valley or the culture of football hooligans. Each context is a plausible area of study, I suppose, but to make sense of each other when we use the word *culture,* we need to specify the scope of our usage. So, simply stipulating my usage, I mean generally something in the middle range of this spectrum, something akin to what John Rawls means by a "comprehensive doctrine"—a set of values that inform our life as a whole, contributing to each person's social identity and prescribing or giving guidance on ideals of personal character as well as of friendship and family. A culture creates a *nomos,* or a set of norms that pervade a person's life, and defines, as some say, a "way of life." Such a definition, I should note, expands the colloquial use of *culture* in the U.S. media, in which its reference is almost exclusively to racial and ethnic groups. Describing a way of life, *culture* can refer also to religious, regional, and socioeconomic groups.

Let me be clear that this definition of culture points to an "ideal type" more than anything objectively real in the world. Though many have tried, it is simply futile to engage in cultural cartography; culture does not correspond necessarily with specific plots of soil or borders. There are no fixed and distinct boundaries of cultural groups, whose edges, if one must use a spatial metaphor, are more like the areas between climatic regions than like the lines drawn between states. Moreover, the culture of a group, however it is specified, is not fixed in time like some eternal Platonic form. Cultures, like all organic things, evolve, shift, grow, stagnate, and decay. One must always bear in mind, therefore, that to speak of African-American or Anglo-American culture, for example, is to refer to an ideal and not a material reality amenable to exact inventory and specification. Cultures not only resist precise elaboration but inevitably change over time.[23]

A Short History of Cultural Conflict in American Education

> [You] cannot dedicate yourself to America unless you become in every re-
> spect and with every purpose of your will thorough Americans. You cannot
> become thorough Americans if you think of yourselves in groups. America
> does not consist of groups. A man who thinks of himself as belonging to a
> particular national group in America has not yet become an American, and
> the man who goes among you to trade upon your nationality is no worthy
> son to live under the Stars and Stripes.
>
> President Woodrow Wilson, "Message to Newly Naturalized Citizens"

In a highly charged atmosphere of intolerance for racial and ethnic minorities, a widely respected educator entered an impassioned plea in a national
magazine for respect and tolerance of those from other cultures. Arguing that
Americans were a people "international and interracial in [their] make-up,"
he concluded that "the genuine American, the typical American, is himself a
hyphenated character." Addressing his thoughts to other educators, he wrote,
"[T]he American is himself Pole-German-English-French-Spanish-Italian-
Greek-Irish-Scandanavian-Bohemian-Jew- and so on. . . . And this means at
least that our public schools shall teach each factor to respect every other, and
shall take pains to enlighten all as to the great past contributions of every
strain of our composite make-up."[1] These are sentiments that any educator
would recognize today as a standard salvo in the debate over multiculturalism. Yet these words were written in 1916 by John Dewey, just one year after
President Wilson's message to newly naturalized citizens. Worried about the
Americanization campaigns sweeping across the land, Dewey, along with
other intellectuals of the era, sought to defuse the tension by begging for
greater understanding of America as a place of multiple cultural composition.

If the academic and popular press is to be believed, culture wars currently
wrack America anew. No fewer than ten major books appearing in the 1990s

make the militaristic image of cultural war a central feature of their titles alone.[2] Most of the books, and certainly popular opinion in the press, convey the message that the phenomenon of multiculturalism is responsible for setting off and fueling the culture wars. Moreover, the books all note that education functions as the central battleground for the culture wars.

To most of its proponents and critics, multiculturalism and multicultural education are taken to be novel developments. Judging by the usage of the term, one understands how such a conclusion might be drawn. The Lexis database of major American newspapers records nary a reference to multiculturalism in 1988, but over 1,400 in 1994.[3] Today, the term is ubiquitous, employed by academics and laypersons alike.

But multiculturalism and debates over it only appear to be new. As Dewey's words imply, multiculturalism is in fact a new word applied to an old issue, an issue that dates back, at least, to the founding period of America. In 1782, for example, the French immigrant Hector St. John Crevecoeur marveled at the confluence of people from different European nations, asking most famously, "What then is the American, this new man?" This chapter aims to introduce the philosophical and political interest in multiculturalism, and in the process provide an antidote to the historical amnesia that plagues current discourse over multiculturalism and, in particular, multicultural education.

Multiculturalism is notoriously difficult to define. The term connotes both a descriptive and demographic fact—the existence of multiple cultures within a common political structure. And it connotes a normative and intellectual ideal—the idea that by virtue of the fact of cultural diversity, certain policies or programs that tolerate, recognize, or, more strongly, actively support cultural groups must follow. Historians attest to the fact of descriptive multiculturalism in the United States—it has always been a land of diverse ethnic, racial, and religious composition. The normative understanding of multiculturalism, however, is generally taken to be an argument against the uniform assimilation of cultural groups to some common, usually white, mainstream norm. In this work, I will understand multiculturalism to refer to its normative, and more controversial, usage. I argue here that even a casual glance at history reveals how normative multiculturalism and multicultural conflict have been evident in American education since its very inception.

Multicultural conflict, as reflected in questions about the ability of a common school to accommodate students of diverse cultural backgrounds, punctuates the history of American education dating back to the beginning of public schooling in the mid-nineteenth century. To substantiate this claim, I examine three different periods of intense cultural conflict in American education: first, the battles in the nineteenth century between Protestants and Catholics over the Protestant bias of the common schools; second, the clashes at the turn of the century between German immigrants and American nativists over instruction in the German language; and third, the fight in the 1910s and 1920s over Americanization campaigns and immigrant children in the public schools.

I hope primarily to correct the misunderstanding that multiculturalism is something novel by showing the roots of the current debates in the past. But I also wish to use history as a guide, suggesting what the multicultural conflicts of the past have to tell us today, comparing the ways in which previous multicultural conflicts may have differed from those of today. There are, I believe, important lessons to be learned from the history of multiculturalism.

Though portrayed in sometimes cataclysmic terms today, the debate over multiculturalism can be viewed as another episode in the ever-present tension between common values and pluralism in America. There have always been demographic cultural differences in American society; and education—even in its most strenuous aspirations to inculcate unity—has had to cope with social diversity. In short, schools have always been diverse and simultaneously tried to transmit common values. At one level, then, contemporary conflicts over multiculturalism represent business as usual, for conflicts over cultural divisions in society are endemic to the history of American common schooling. At another level, however, today's conflicts are not business as usual, for they attest to the increasingly liberal and inclusive context for resolving or handling such conflicts. Seen through the lens of history, we find that while the current conflagration over multiculturalism and multicultural education may revisit in many important aspects previous debates about the place of religion, language, race, and ethnicity within the schoolhouse, the twentieth century's broader acceptance of tolerance for diversity and its greater emphasis on inclusion within civic institutions offer a comparatively less incendiary environment with reduced dangers of outright cultural oppression or denigration.

Catholics and the Common School Crusaders

Because contemporary debates about multiculturalism focus on racial and ethnic group cultures to such a great degree, it may be easy to forget that the most significant cultural differences in the nineteenth century were religious.[4] Yet political clashes between Protestants and Catholics were common, and in the case of education, they revealed the limits of whom the common school crusaders were willing to include within the public schools.

The strict separation of church and state has become such a common feature of American life in the twentieth century that it is now difficult to imagine the deep Protestantism that colored the arguments of the common school founders and, ultimately, the curriculum of the public schools they helped to develop. As David Tyack and Elisabeth Hansot note in their study of public school leaders, the common school crusaders in the 1840s, 1850s, and 1860s were "largely Protestant in religion and Anglo-Saxon in ethnic background, [and] they shared a common religious and political conception of the role of public education in shaping a Christian nation."[5] For these crusaders, the private and charity schools of the early decades of the 1800s would be replaced by common, publicly funded schools that would teach Christian and republican virtue, ideals that at the time were closely tied up with prevailing conceptions of good citizenship.[6]

The unabashedly religious impulse behind the movement to create public schools was reflected in the diversity of Protestant sects represented among its leaders. Though the Protestant leaders initially quarreled internally, split by sectarian differences about the proper type of religious instruction for schools, there eventually emerged what historians Carl Kaestle and David Tyack call a pan-Protestant consensus.[7] Protestant clergy united in a millennial vision of America as God's chosen country and agreed to teach the Protestant, or King James, version of the Bible without comment. Teaching the Bible without comment made it possible for the common school promoters to present schools as nonsectarian. Horace Mann, for example, the archetypal common school crusader, recommended allowing the Bible to "speak for itself" and championed common schools as a means to transmit a common virtue among diverse citizens.

So integral to the crusaders was the pan-Protestant orientation that reading the Protestant Bible was assumed to be a required part of any school curriculum. Those who objected were often subjected to insult and ridicule. An editorial in the Massachusetts' *Common School Journal*, for example, lambasted immigrants who objected to Bible reading:

> The English Bible, in some way or other, has, ever since the settlement of
> Cambridge, been read in its public schools, by children of every denomi-
> nation; but in the year 1851, the ignorant immigrants, who have found
> food and shelter in this land of freedom and plenty, made free and plen-
> tiful through the influence of these very scriptures, presume to dictate to
> us, and refuse to let their children read as ours do, and always have done,
> the Word of Life. The arrogance, not to say impudence, of this conduct,
> must startle every native citizen, and can not but hope that they will im-

mediately take measures to teach these deluded aliens, that their poverty and ignorance in their own country arose mainly from their ignorance of the Bible.[8]

The aliens to whom the editorial refers were most certainly Irish Catholics. To the ever-increasing number of Catholics flooding America's shores, however, the Protestant cast of common schools was an outright affront. As immigration from Ireland, and, to a lesser degree, Germany, brought thousands of Roman Catholics to America each year, the voices of protest rose dramatically. Some immigration statistics illustrate the rapidity of the Catholic arrival in America and give a hint as to the proximate cause of the coming culture clash between Protestants and Catholics in the mid-nineteenth century. In 1820 there were 200,000 Catholics in America, up from 35,000 in 1790. But in the next decade 200,000 more arrived from Europe, and then, fleeing the Irish Potato Famine in 1845–47, another 780,000 came ashore in the next decade. By 1850 there were over 2 million Catholics in America, still a small minority of the total population, but large enough to make the Catholic Church the largest religious body in the land.[9]

It is difficult to imagine today the cultural gulf that separated Protestants and Catholics. Religiously, of course, Protestants rejected the Catholic insistence on Papal authority, especially as reflected in interpretation of scripture. But the spiritual and worldly authority of the Pope had political implications as well. Many Protestant Americans were deeply suspicious of Catholic immigrants, even in the founding period, worrying that Catholics' loyalty to the Pope in Rome called into doubt their allegiance to a fledgling nation. Popery seemed the antithesis of the freedom American institutions were designed to protect. Lawrence Fuchs notes that, before 1800, South Carolinians burned the Pope in effigy, Marylanders levied a double land tax on Catholics, and seven state constitutions banned Catholics from holding public office.[10] The flood of immigrants in the coming years only inspired more fear among the overwhelmingly Protestant populace. In the 1830s and 1840s, blood ran in the streets of Philadelphia when more than a dozen people were killed during the "Bible riots," clashes between Protestants and Catholics over the choice of scripture to be used in public schools. And though no one was killed, deep political conflict between Catholics and Protestants also rent New York City, Boston, Cincinnati, Chicago, and San Francisco.

Due to such outright discrimination, Catholics were attuned to the suspicions of Protestants early on. Seeing no opportunity for acquiring an education in publicly funded schools that would not undermine the Catholic faith, in 1829 Catholic bishops decreed that Catholics should start separate schools.[11] Even so, Catholics still pressed to be included in the emerging common school movement. In 1840 the American Catholic hierarchy denounced the Protestant bias of the common schools.[12] But such criticism only aroused the ire and suspicion of Protestants more. As Tyack notes, "When Catholics sought successfully to eject the Protestant Bible from the common school, Protestants thought that they were attacking the very basis of American institutions. When they demanded the removal of biased textbooks, citizens and school officials thought Catholics were trying to control the curriculum."[13]

The pan-Protestant school reformers were for the most part unconciliatory. Kaestle finds only scattered successes of Catholic protest, places where Bible reading was not mandatory or scriptural choice was made an option.[14] But overall, neither the common school founders, nor the administrators of the nascent educational system, nor political or judicial leaders made significant concessions to Catholics. Thomas James's survey of judicial decisions found that "the courts of the nineteenth century sided with the Protestant majority and its values in almost every case."[15] In the 1850s in New York a Catholic student was beaten and expelled from a public school when he refused to read from the King James Bible. And in Maine in the same decade, the State Supreme Court decided that public school officials could rightfully compel all students to read from the Protestant Bible.[16] The nativist Know-Nothing, or American Party was organized in the 1850s with a central platform of excluding immigrants and, in particular, Roman Catholics. In 1856, 104 members of Congress, seven governors, and eight U.S. Senators were Know-Nothing members.[17] The National Teachers Association declared in 1869 that "the Bible should not only be studied, venerated, and honored as a classic for all ages, people, and languages . . . but devotionally read, and its precepts inculcated in all the common schools of the land."[18] The successor of the NTA, the National Education Association, would continue for several decades to attack Catholics for seeking to deprive America's children of proper moral training based on the Bible.[19]

In a short time and across many states, then, it became clear to Catholic leaders that the common schools would not be hospitable environments for Catholic children. So, in tandem with continuous objection to the Protestant bias in common schools, Catholic leaders pursued state support for their own schools. Catholics paid taxes like any other citizens and therefore public schools should accommodate them, they argued. Failing that, public funds should support their own schools. Despite state sanction of the Protestant

Bible in public schools, courts and politicians rejected this plea on the basis that state support of Catholic schools would constitute state endorsement of religion, contrary to the First Amendment. Bishop John Hughes, for example, pursued this separatist strategy in New York City in the 1840s and 1850s. But, as Ravitch notes, "Between the Trustees of the Public School Society and the Catholic clergy, there was an unbridgeable cultural gulf."[20] The legislature and the courts received his request no more favorably.

Finding this cultural gulf unbridgeable, then, many Catholics resolved to construct, with whatever meager funds were available, their own alternative system of public education. The separatist strategy became official policy in 1884, when a formal decree of the Third Plenary Council of Baltimore made it mandatory for every Catholic church to erect a school near to the church structure and compelled parents to send their children to Catholic schools.[21] The cultural gap between the pan-Protestant common school crusaders and the ever-increasing number of Catholics in America resulted, therefore, in the formation of the Catholic school system, which expanded rapidly in the 1880s and 1890s. Already in 1890 the parochial school system enrolled more than six hundred thousand students, making it the largest alternative to public schools in the country.[22] The rise of compulsory education laws in the late nineteenth century and the early twentieth century led to renewed conflict between Protestants and Catholics. Finally, in 1925, the Supreme Court held in *Pierce v. Society of Sisters* (268 U.S. 510) that parents could not be forced to send their children to public school and therewith gave constitutional standing to all private schools. The clash between the culture of Protestantism and the culture of Catholicism turned out to be so endemic—so incommensurable, one might say—in the sphere of public schools, that an entire alternative school system arose out of the conflict. On the multicultural question of how public schools could accommodate religio-cultural diversity in the mid-nineteenth century, the clash of Protestants and Catholics was irreconcilable.

GERMANS AND BILINGUAL EDUCATION

German immigrants and their settlement in the Midwest created the atmosphere for the next major multicultural conflict in education. Rather than the religious beliefs of the immigrants, however, this conflict centered around ethnicity and language. The crux of the controversy was the German immigrants' desire to educate their children in German. Few people today recognize the roots of contemporary battles over bilingual education in this earlier period of American history.

As it is today, language maintenance was an issue of central importance to ethnic groups settling in the United States. As Tyack notes, "To many immigrants, it was vital to assert the value of their culture by teaching their language to their children—after all they paid taxes and deserved a say in the curriculum."[23] For the German immigrants who made up more than a quarter of the foreign-born population between 1850 and 1900, ethnic pride in the world-renowned achievements of German culture made German-language instruction an immediate issue for public schools.[24]

Initially, public schools generally accommodated the demands of the German immigrants. In 1840, for example, the Ohio legislature passed a provision that required school boards to teach in German if seventy-five freeholders requested it in writing. Germans successfully lobbied the St. Louis school board to provide German-language instruction in 1864. William Torrey Harris, a well-known Hegel scholar and the superintendent of St. Louis schools, wrote to his board of education in 1874 that it was in the "interest of the entire community here that the German shall cultivate his own language while he adopts English as his general means of communication."[25] In 1872 Oregon legalized entirely monolingual German schools. By 1900 there were more than 230,000 children learning regular subject matter in German in elementary schools.[26]

By the turn of the century, however, a groundswell of opposition to German bilingual instruction arose in many midwestern cities. Louisville, St. Louis, and St. Paul ceased offering German instruction in their elementary schools in the 1880s and 1890s.[27] In 1889 the Edwards law in Illinois and the Bennett bill in Wisconsin required students statewide to attend public or private school where English was the main language of instruction.

But it was the xenophobia associated with World War I, and fear of Germans in particular, that impelled many more states to restrict or ban German instruction from public and private schools. This was the era in which many states passed compulsory school attendance laws, many of which contained provisions prescribing English as the language of instruction. In 1903, for example, fourteen states legislated that instruction be carried out in English. By 1923, the number of states requiring English in schools had grown to thirty-four.[28] Yet legislatures did not limit their intolerance of the German language to the schoolhouse. Fishman reports that many states forbade the use of German at public meetings, over the telephone, or on the streets. German speakers were regularly harassed and even beaten for speaking in their native tongue.[29]

Unlike the robust protest of Catholics against the Protestant bias of common schools, German immigrants did not resist English-only policies with great vigor. Perhaps German-Americans feared inflaming anti-German feeling as a result of the war; perhaps, too, they did not generally object to learning in English in schools. Like the Protestant-Catholic clash, however, the cultural conflict between Germans and educational leaders also reached the Supreme Court, which provided an ultimate resolution to the teaching of foreign languages in the landmark *Meyer v. Nebraska* (262 U.S. 390) case in 1923. As part of legislation passed in 1918 forbidding instruction of any subject in a foreign language or any teaching of a foreign language, a teacher of German in the Zion Parochial School in Nebraska was convicted and fined for offering German instruction. The Court struck down the Nebraska statute, the majority arguing that the legislation violated the Fourteenth Amendment, the teacher's right to work in his profession, and the parents' rights to direct the upbringing of their children. With this decision, the Justices began to lay the legal groundwork for the modern use of bilingual instruction.

If the Court's holding brought to an end the legislative practice of forbidding foreign-language instruction, it could not erase the memory of deep discord between German Americans and public school officials nor undo the damage done to the German cultural community by the ban on foreign language and the laws specifically directed against Germans. In the wake of English-only and anti-German policies, Daniels reports that "in the public schools, the destruction was total: no German-language instruction program survived, . . . [which] hastened the death of most of the other cultural institutions of German America."[30] The extensive German-language press was foremost among these losses; it became a mere ghost of its former self after World War I.

Where once German immigrants had enjoyed some measure of success in maintaining their language through bilingual instruction, the increasing atmosphere of xenophobia and concomitant hatred of Germans led to efforts to acculturate and assimilate German students via compulsory attendance laws and mandatory English instruction. World War II only served to heighten fear of Germans again, and, as a combined result of the earlier xenophobia, the German language underwent a quick death as a native language spoken in homes. Fishman notes that "no other nationality group of equal numerical strength and living in one country [9 million in 1916] has ever been so well-nigh completely assimilated."[31]

Where religio-cultural conflict in the schools drove a deep wedge between Catholics and Protestants in the nineteenth century, cultural conflict around the use of the German language in schools, and foreign-language instruction in general, carved a deep chasm between immigrants and school leaders at the turn of the century. Though the Supreme Court ultimately vindicated foreign-language instruction, the German American community had by that time sustained devastating blows. Foreshadowing the contemporary debates over bilingual education, the desire to perpetuate ethnocultural membership through language maintenance in schools proved too threatening to political and educational leaders at the turn of the century.

AMERICANIZATION AND EDUCATION

It was not only Germans who were the targets of mandatory English and compulsory attendance laws. The xenophobia of the 1910s and 1920s encompassed all immigrant groups. The resulting hysteria led to an environment in which the assertion of ethnic pride and practice of ethnic rituals aroused great suspicion. The school became, in these years, the primary vehicle to Americanize or assimilate the continuing waves of immigrants and immigrant children who came to America. Americanization, however, often meant the desire to eliminate or, minimally, to subdue all previous ethnic ties. The schoolhouse during this period actively and purposefully oppressed cultural diversity.

A wide confluence of events in the early 1900s led to the Americanization campaigns. Around one million immigrants per annum flooded urban centers, many of them coming from southern and eastern Europe. By 1908, the U.S. Senate Immigration Commission reported that across the thirty-seven largest cities in the country, fully 58 percent of all students had foreign-born fathers. Many Americans deplored the perceived cultural characteristics of the new immigrants and found popular and scientific justification for their beliefs in the many racist tracts that were widely published. World War I created a heightened fear of foreigners living in America, waking Americans up to the reality that the country could be isolationist no longer. As John Higham writes, "Suddenly conscious of the presence of millions of unassimilated people in their midst, Americans quaked with fear of their potential disloyalty."[32] It was in this general environment that the sweeping Immigration Law of 1917 was passed by Congress, excluding any adults who could not read, delineating a prohibited Asiatic zone, and, for the first time, mandating the deportation of any alien who preached revolution. The rapid industrialization of the American workplace, particularly in cities, also had an effect. Paula Fass notes that as work became industrialized and routinized, it lost its socializing force. Progressive politicians thus turned toward the schools as the chief socializing agent. Describing the attitude of school reformers in the 1910s, Fass writes, "The school was the only institution that could hope to alter immigrant culture where it was environmentally most permeable—the care and instruction of children."[33] More than ever before, Americans demanded patriotic loyalty to the country and sought in myriad ways, but primarily through public schools, to Americanize the immigrants and their children.

A rising class of progressive administrators in schools led the charge to meet the challenge of Americanization. In 1918, the U.S. Bureau of Education established a Director of Americanization and sent out a monthly *Americanization Bulletin*, which had a circulation of over fifteen thousand.[34] According to Lawrence Cremin, Americanization programs in the schools "ordinarily involved a complex process of socialization that went far beyond instruction in English and civics to include training in personal cleanliness, middle-class values, and factory-like discipline, and, in many cases, the inculcation of disdain for the immigrant heritage."[35] History textbooks were rewritten to be more anglophilic and patriotic, and to diminish any critical treatment of traditional American heroes.[36] In many places, even such seemingly trivial matters as hygiene and penmanship were seen as further instruments of Americanization.[37]

Ellwood Cubberley, a Stanford University professor, was among the most prominent Americanizers. Cubberley sought through the schools to inculcate an American identity in the immigrants, erasing their previous ethnic allegiances and replacing them with American ones. He also draped his recommendations in the mantle of scientific knowledge, giving them an authority with the general populace and with legislators that extended beyond mere opinion. In a passage often cited to illustrate the dark side of prevailing sentiment among most educational progressives, Cubberley proclaimed in 1909,

> These southern and eastern Europeans are of a very different type from the north Europeans who preceded them. Illiterate, docile, lacking in self-reliance and initiative, and not possessing the Anglo-Teutonic conceptions of law, order, and government, their coming has served to dilute tremendously our national stock, and to corrupt our civic life. . . . Everywhere these people tend to settle in groups or settlements, and to set up here their national manners, customs, and observances. Our task is to break up these groups or settlements, to assimilate and amalgamate these people as a part of our American race, and implant in their children, so far as can be done, the Anglo-Saxon conception of righteousness, law and order, and popular government, and to awaken in them a reverence for our democratic institutions and for those things in our national life which we as a people hold to be abiding worth.[38]

Similarly, the New York superintendent of schools announced in 1918 that the duty of public schools was to teach "an absolute appreciation of the institutions of this country [and] absolute forgetfulness of all obligations or connections with other countries because of descent or birth."[39] In short, public schools were viewed as the crucible of the vaunted "melting pot" (the title of an Israel Zangwill play in 1908). Through compulsory education, immigrant children would enter the schoolroom as members of a foreign culture and exit a few years later as Americans.

But in some cases even draconian Americanization programs were considered incapable of producing good citizens, properly stripped of previous ethnic loyalties. The rise of psychology and IQ testing had led to sweeping proclamations of the alleged innate abilities of various ethnic groups. The predictable consequences of such studies followed easily. Clifford Kirkpatrick, for example, one of the more judicious investigators of the time, announced that "high germ plasm often leads to better results than high per capita school expenditures. Definite limits are set by heredity, and immigrants of low innate ability cannot by any amount of Americanization be made into intelligent American citizens capable of approximating and advancing a complex culture."[40] The immigrants Kirkpatrick had in mind of course, were the eastern and southern Europeans that Cubberley had earlier named as the main targets of Americanization in the schools. But by 1926, Kirkpatrick was merely providing scientific cover for what Congress had already legislated. Immigration was virtually shut off with the Immigration Act of 1924, which linked future immigration to a quota system based on the 1890 census, guaranteeing that the undesirable newcomers from eastern and southern Europe would be barred entry.

How did immigrants respond to the attempt to prevent them from passing on their culture to their children? It was never easy, for as Fass writes, "Success in school, as the children of immigrants would find again and again, required a serious modification, if not an outright rejection, of the cultural bases of their identity."[41] But immigrants, for the most part, had come to America in search of a better life, and the public school was the first step in teaching their children how to succeed in their new land. By and large, immigrants supported the public school and attended willingly.[42]

One persuasive explanation for this acquiescence can be found in histories of immigration. Revisionist historians have stressed the ways in which immigrants were successfully able to resist "100 percent Americanization" and preserve ethnic loyalty in their children.[43] Oscar Handlin's studies of immigrants, for example, rejected the idea of total assimilation and found instead that the result of the immigrant experience was alienation and heightened group consciousness.[44] More recently, Lawrence Fuchs has argued that immigrants were assimilated into a public, civic sphere, but preserved for themselves a private sphere in which ethnic culture flourished.[45] Schools, however, were not the places where immigrants carried on their ancestral identities; it was more likely the family, the neighborhood, the church, labor organizations, or ethnic newspapers that helped maintain and foster ethnic ties.[46] Though there were exceptions, such as Leonard Covello's school in New York City, the public schools of the 1910s and 1920s were not hospitable places for immigrants to cultivate ethnocultural bonds.[47] To the contrary, the schools were hostile to immigrants' identities, more often engaged in attempts to erase previous ethnocultural bonds. If immigrants could preserve their culture through other venues, the strict Americanization campaigns in the schools were an acceptable price to pay for the possibility of giving their children a better chance to succeed in the United States.

From today's vantage point, however, many look upon the period as an unjust and oppressive expression of a nervous, xenophobic, and jingoistic America. To be fair, xenophobia and jingoism were not representative of all policymakers or the entire populace. Some well-known intellectuals of the era inveighed against a narrow-minded conception of American citizenship as resting on a pedestal of Anglo-Saxon culture. Horace Kallen argued for cultural pluralism, in which America was best seen as a container or federation of ethnocultural groups; John Dewey promoted hyphenated Americanism, in which citizens possessed an ancestral *and* an American identity; and Randolph Bourne saw in the waves of immigration an opportunity for America to become a transnational country of cosmopolitan citizens.[48] Yet these sources of resistance to the Americanization efforts were mostly a matter of intellectual controversy. Kallen's, Dewey's, and Bourne's ideas about what it meant to be an American had no effect on actual immigration policy and, according to most commentators, were equally inconsequential for educational policy.[49] Thus, despite the more enlightened thinkers of the era, in its outright attempt to suppress or erase the cultural identities of newcomers, coupled with the racist and discriminatory thinking that often underwrote the programs, Americanization is rightly seen as an ugly blotch in American history.

Like the Protestant-Catholic clash and the question of German bilingual education, the Americanization period can be viewed as a crisis of multiculturalism. In response to the increasing cultural diversity resulting from mass immigration, the educational and political leaders of the day rejected the notion that multiple cultures could peacefully coexist in society, and they looked to schools as the place forcibly to assimilate the newcomers. The widespread acceptance of multicultural education today means that schools not only tolerate the expression of ethnic diversity, but in fact often cultivate and celebrate it. It was not always so.

Contemporary Multicultural Conflict

What, then, does history tell us about the current debates concerning multiculturalism and multicultural education? One simple answer to this question is that today's controversies about multicultural education are not unique. Similar dramas have played themselves out in America's past. The nineteenth-century clash, for example, between Protestants and Catholics is reminiscent of today's arguments between public school leaders and fundamentalist Christians. In several recent court cases, fundamentalists have challenged the alleged secular humanist bias of public school curricula. The best known of these cases is *Mozert v. Hawkins County Board of Education* (827 F.2d 1058 [1987]), where Tennessee fundamentalists claimed that exposure to diversity within a multicultural reader constituted an indoctrination in secular humanism and therefore violated the parents' rights to religious freedom of expression and to direct the upbringing of their children. Fundamentalists' general dissatisfaction with public schooling is also reflected in the fact that enrollment at Christian day schools grew at a greater rate in the 1980s and 1990s than enrollment in any other school system, public, private, or religious. Other fundamentalist parents have decided to abandon schools altogether, leading to the recent boom in homeschooling, a subject I discuss in greater detail in chapter 6. The conflict between fundamentalists and public school leaders has also partially fueled the recent movement for school vouchers. In this, the fundamentalists' desire either to have public schools accommodate their religious beliefs or to have the state fund their own private schools resembles the stance of the Catholics over a century ago.

Similarly, as I have already noted, the strife between German immigrants and educational and political leaders at the turn of the century presaged current debates about bilingual education. Contrary to popular belief, questions about the primacy of English within public schools are not new. The fierce controversy in California over the 1998 ballot referendum to restrict bilingual education to a one-year transition program calls to mind the similarly deep anxieties that many Americans felt at the turn of the century about German-language instruction. Education in a foreign language received constitutional standing, in fact, in the 1923 *Meyer* case that arose over whether classes could be offered in German. And finally, the bitter Americanization campaigns of the 1910s and 1920s anticipated current questions about the recognition of ethnic group identities in public schools. School leaders in the progressive era, as we have seen, largely believed that schools should not recognize ethnic groups, but attempt instead to delete ethnic loyalties, particularly those of immigrants from southern and eastern Europe. The progress of the multicultural ideal in America is reflected in the fact that current debates about multicultural education are not about *whether* schools should recognize ethnic identities, but about the *extent to which* the curriculum should expand to include authors representing minority groups. Americanization is a discredited movement, and though some schools certainly continue to marginalize minority students, they are today in their very mission or purpose not as *explicitly* oppressive of cultural diversity as they were in the past.

An examination of America's educational history thus uncovers the roots of contemporary debates about multicultural education. The roots are indeed deep and offer a usable history that can inform modern debates. A thorough analysis would yield a series of lessons about what has changed and what has remained the same since the founding of the common schools.[50] This is properly the subject of a much longer inquiry, but for my purposes I'd like to call attention to three important points.

First, it is immediately obvious that one significant discontinuity between multicultural debates of today and yesterday involves the status of African-Americans and Native Americans. Put simply, whereas questions about African-Americans, and to a lesser extent Native Americans, are currently central to multiculturalism and multicultural education in the United States, the inclusion of African-Americans and Native Americans in the educational system was not a topic of discussion prior to World War II. In the nineteenth and early twentieth centuries, blacks were either prevented from attending schools of any sort, forced to rely on the efforts of charitable northerners to organize schools, or legally shunted off into inferior, segregated schools.[51] That considerations of how to educate blacks rarely entered into the discourse of educational leaders—Dewey's hymn to hyphenated Americans conspicuously omitted African-Americans—reflects the consensus that blacks were unassimilable and, at bottom, perhaps uneducable. As for Native Americans, policymakers and educators did discuss how to educate them, yet their conclusions led them, in the words of historian David Wallace Adams, to see only two options: extinction or civilization. At the end of the nineteenth century, Native American children were sent, sometimes forcibly, to reservation and off-reservation boarding schools expressly designed to Christianize

and Americanize them.[52] The cultural conflicts that arose about the education of African-Americans and Native Americans in the past were rarely or
never about how public schools should respond; they were about creating
separate institutions that in practice almost always reinforced their second-
class status and citizenship.[53]

Second, there is a clear continuity between past and present. In both historical and contemporary multicultural conflicts, questions about U.S. identity and the meaning of citizenship occupy a central role. Each of the earlier
episodes reveals that religion, language, and ethnicity were intimately tied up
with popular conceptions of what it meant to be a proper or good American.
Current debates about multiculturalism reflect a similar concern, with some
of the most vocal critics blaming multiculturalism for the disuniting of
America or the erosion of citizenship.[54] Today, as in the past, debates about
how schools should respond to cultural diversity are also debates about national identity and citizenship and about whether certain religious beliefs,
linguistic practices, or ethnic identities ought, or ought not, to be recognized
and fostered in the schoolhouse. I return to the connection between multiculturalism and citizenship in later chapters.

Finally, I want to propose a controversial but plausible third lesson. A judicious consideration of the history of cultural conflicts in America suggests
that current multicultural conflicts pose milder, though certainly still vexing
and contentious, challenges than those in the past. Despite the fiery rhetoric
so often attached to debates about multiculturalism, I believe that today's
controversies today are less potentially divisive and threatening. We actually
have good reason to see progress in the way that schools have dealt with issues of cultural diversity. It is not, I should emphasize, a line of linear upward
progress. Progress has coexisted with frequent efforts at educational exclusion, discrimination, or coercion that served to constrict rather than broaden
the conception of U.S. identity and the multicultural ideal of a culturally diverse state, and these efforts continue in some ways today. The advancement
of multiculturalism is better seen, to borrow Desmond King's phrase, as a
"punctuated development path."[55] Conflict over cultural diversity, both inside and outside the schoolhouse, will surely never disappear entirely, yet in
comparison to previous eras, the terrain on which cultural clashes are fought
is less fraught with peril and the likelihood that ethnocultural groups will be
purposefully oppressed, marginalized, or excluded by the liberal democratic
state with respect to citizenship generally and educational opportunity
specifically.

I say this for two reasons. The first is that multicultural education, and acceptance of multiculturalism in general, is simply standard practice in most American schools. Though he admits it with ambivalence, Nathan Glazer has recently opined, "We are all multiculturalists now."[56] If my own experience as a public school teacher is any guide, multicultural education is a non-negotiable given. Debates about multicultural education today are about how best to accommodate cultural differences—about the expansion of the school curriculum, the questioning of the Western canon, the inclusion of new cultural perspectives in the classroom, and the adoption of diverse pedagogical strategies to reach children of different cultural backgrounds. To be sure, religio-cultural conflict is a potent force still, as reflected in debates over school prayer and the popularity of Christian day schools and homeschooling. But little in the contemporary scene would suggest that public schools are in danger of forcing an entire segment of the population to start an alternative school system, as happened with the Catholics. To be sure, questions about the educability of certain ethnic and racial groups remain today, as reflected in such books as *The Bell Curve*.[57] But little in the contemporary scene would suggest that educators might classify certain groups of students as genetically inferior or encourage "absolute forgetfulness" of students' cultural attachments, as happened in the Americanization campaigns. The question of bilingual education is perhaps something of an exception here. The 1998 debate over Proposition 227 in California, which restricted the duration of native-language instruction to no more than one year before transitioning to all-English classes, caused significant rancor and has provoked other states to initiate similar legislation or referenda. But even so, there is little reason to believe that the United States is on the verge of declaring English its official language. With large and rapidly growing percentages of Spanish-speakers in three of the most politically important states—California, Texas, and Florida—Spanish-speaking immigrants are unlikely to be as legislatively or judicially marginalized today as German-speakers were in the late nineteenth and early twentieth centuries. All things considered, educators accept cultural diversity today with a much greater willingness than in the past. Schools have been purged of any endorsement of religion; schools now routinely champion the ethnic diversity of their students rather than "Americanizing" newcomers.

A second reason is that, by some objective measures, ethnocultural minority groups are better off today, in and out of schools, than they were in the past. This includes the position, obviously, of Catholics and European immigrants but, what is more striking and important, it includes the status of the two most wronged U.S. minorities: African-Americans and Native Americans. Notable proximate causes for the improvement include the integration of the military, beginning in 1948, the rejection of separate but equal schooling in 1954, the passage of the Civil Rights Act in 1964, and the Immigration and Nationality Act in 1965 (which removed quotas based on national origin in immigration and struck the concept of race from the law), to name a few major legislative and judicial acts. Within schools, ethnocultural minorities, including African-Americans and Native Americans, have better access to schools and are far better educated than they were one hundred, or even fifty, years ago.[58] In 1971, 82 percent of whites, 59 percent of blacks, and 48 percent of Hispanics attained a high school degree or equivalency certificate; in 1998, the situation had improved, with the greatest gains being made by blacks and Hispanics: high school degrees were held by 93 percent of whites, 82 percent of blacks, and 63 percent of Hispanics.[59] More impressive, the 1970s and 1980s saw a significant narrowing of the achievement gap between blacks and whites.[60] Out of schools, Jennifer Hochschild documents "unambiguous improvements" over the last fifty years in African-Americans' occupational status and political involvement, and a massive growth in the black middle class.[61] Americans today are significantly more tolerant of diversity and racial integration than they used to be.[62] Moreover, surely one of the most reliable measures of acceptance of diversity, rates of intermarriage, are at all-time highs both between races and between religions.[63] This is an admittedly incomplete survey of different indices, and I hasten to add that the objective improvement in the condition of minorities in some respects does not mean that enough has been done, or that minorities are on an equal footing with white Americans. To the contrary, large and seemingly intractable problems still exist. The disproportionate rates of poverty and school dropout for minorities, the recent widening gap in academic achievement, and continuing discrimination in housing and work all put to a quick rest any hope that U.S. ideals of inclusion, tolerance, and equality have been fully realized. Nevertheless, the clear advance of inclusion, tolerance, and equality in schools across the country over the past one hundred years reflects in part the advance and greater acceptance of multicultural ideals.[64]

So what explains the enormous heat and anguish generated by multiculturalism today? This is a complex and difficult question, but let me suggest one possible answer offered by Orlando Patterson. Patterson writes of "the outrage of liberation" in which "a formerly oppressed group's sense of outrage at what has been done to them increases the more equal they become with their former oppressors."[65] This is a an untested hypothesis, yet it gains some empirical support in Jennifer Hochschild's finding that "poor blacks now believe more in the American dream than rich blacks do, which is a reversal from the 1960s."[66] Hochschild's analysis shows that blacks who have progressed the most feel the greatest sense of disillusionment, are more likely to perceive discrimination, and are more likely to believe that American society is racist. The surprising mechanism apparently at work here is that the more one succeeds, the more indignant and suspicious one becomes when faced with intolerance or discrimination. The result, if Patterson and Hochschild are correct, is that, real evidence of progress notwithstanding, feelings of anger, sorrow, alienation, and bitterness are more intense than in earlier eras. This paradox might explain the level of heat given off by the culture wars, despite objective improvement since earlier episodes of cultural conflict.

I suggest this paradox as a hypothesis, not a statement of fact. There are other possible explanations. But it is not my purpose to unravel the sociological issues of how cultural diversity is experienced by different groups. My interest resides in the normative implications of how multiculturalism is interpreted theoretically and implemented politically. Recognizing the ascendancy, or greater acceptance, of the multicultural ideal leads to a set of new and difficult questions. What, for example, is the current normative understanding of multiculturalism? Is multiculturalism about the securing of group identities or the blurring of group identities? Is multiculturalism about inclusion or self-chosen terms of exclusion? What are the philosophical implications of multiculturalism for U.S. identity, citizenship, and civic education? What is the relationship between multiculturalism and the classically liberal framework of government of the United States? Many people believe, for example, that multiculturalism is used to reject the idea that a common culture or set of values must bind all citizens together. As historian John Higham says, "Now any claim for centeredness, any affirmation of a unifying national culture, [has become] ipso facto oppressive."[67]

Having surveyed historical tensions around issues of multiculturalism in American schools, I want next to examine these questions, particularly those which point to some tensions between liberalism and multiculturalism in political theory. How do liberal political theorists and multicultural political theorists handle issues involving respect for cultural diversity and the cultivation of political virtues and civic unity? In chapters 2 and 3, I explore some tensions between liberalism and multiculturalism in political theory with regard to this question.

A Multicultural Critique
of Liberalism

In the first chapter we saw that the history of American education reveals a constant engagement of schools with the challenges of cultural diversity, or the descriptive fact of multiculturalism. Similarly, liberal political theory, and especially contemporary liberal theory, has always dealt with the challenges of diversity. In fact, liberalism has often been interpreted as a response to conditions of pluralism or multiculturalism.[1] Liberals, from John Stuart Mill to John Rawls, take for granted the existence of diverse and conflicting ways of life and attempt to articulate a political theory that enables the peaceful and just coexistence of persons and groups motivated by different ends.[2] Liberalism arose historically and, in its current formulations, begins theoretically with the descriptive fact of multiculturalism.[3]

In recent years, however, liberalism has been criticized by multicultural theorists. In this chapter I present a multicultural critique of liberalism that indicts the frequent claim that liberalism ought to be neutral to the various conceptions of the good life pursued by individuals. Multiculturalists like Will Kymlicka insist instead that the liberal state acknowledge its non-neutrality to cultural groups.[4] Motivated by this insight, multiculturalists promote policies that center on groups and group rights rather than on the traditional liberal concern with individuals and individual rights. Pursuing this critique serves the dual purpose of pointing to some legitimate problems with liberal theory and, in the process, bringing into clearer view the positive demands and claims of normative multiculturalism alluded to in the previous chapter.

To accomplish this task, I focus first on the most prominent statement of contemporary liberal theory, John Rawls's *A Theory of Justice* and its recent reformulation in *Political Liberalism*.[5] Rawls's theory of political liberalism claims to be neutral to diverse conceptions of the good, or more specifically, to

what he calls "reasonable comprehensive doctrines." But this sort of neutrality is impossible, for both practical and theoretical reasons. Rawls's theory demands that its citizens exercise political virtues underwritten by the bedrock
value of personal autonomy. Autonomy, however, is not a value desired or
promoted by all persons or cultural groups. I then examine the claims of
William Galston, who recognizes the non-neutrality of liberalism, notes the
conflict between autonomy and diversity, and ultimately argues that liberalism properly protects diversity rather than promoting personal autonomy. I
argue that Galston's argument also fails.

My thesis is that the problems of liberalism and multiculturalism are best
understood by considering the educational presuppositions and implications
of each theory. My consistent focus in the next chapters, therefore, is on educational institutions.

The Fallacy of Neutrality

Many influential contemporary liberal theorists argue that liberalism is best
understood as a political theory that emphasizes neutrality; some view neutrality as the defining feature of liberalism.[6] While interpretations of neutrality vary, the most common view is that the liberal state ought to refrain
from promoting or privileging particular conceptions of a good life. According to this view there inevitably exist under conditions of pluralism numerous and incompatible conceptions of the good life, and the liberal state acts
unjustly if it identifies one (or several) of these conceptions as appropriate or
best for its citizens. When it is neutral, the liberal state ought not to take any
position on the truth or falsity of different ways of life. It should not care, for
example, if its citizens choose to lead lives devoted to scholarship, snow-
boarding, Sufism, secular humanism, or solitude. So long as citizens act in accordance with principles of justice to which they have consented, decisions
about the good life are the proper province of individuals, not the state.

John Rawls encapsulates this idea with the claim that the idea of the right
assumes priority over the idea of the good. By this, Rawls means that a liberal
theory seeks not to embody some particular conception and make it possible
for citizens to achieve this "correct" or best way to live; instead, a liberal theory assumes diverse and incompatible views of the good life and establishes a
neutral framework of justice whose principles apply equally to all and
wherein citizens decide for themselves what conception of the good to pursue, understanding that every other citizen shall enjoy the same liberty.

For Rawls, liberalism is expressly designed to answer the question, "How
is it possible that there may exist over time a stable and just society of free

and equal citizens profoundly divided by reasonable though incompatible religious, philosophical, and moral doctrines" (*PL*, xx). Note here that the underlying assumption is Rawls's belief that any society will be characterized by a multiplicity of these so-called "comprehensive doctrines." This is the fact of pluralism, or, as I characterized it earlier, descriptive multiculturalism.[7] A theory of justice relying upon or rooted in some comprehensive doctrine would be unjust and indeed oppressive, for citizens who lead lives devoted to reasonable though incompatible conceptions of the good could never consent to the overarching political structure in good conscience.[8] Rawls therefore seeks a *political* conception of justice, one detached from any particular comprehensive doctrine.

Jürgen Habermas summarizes Rawls's aim with the remark, "Political liberalism, as a reasonable construction that does not raise a claim to truth, is neutral toward conflicting worldviews."[9] In response, Rawls affirms the core idea of neutrality: "The central idea is that political liberalism moves within the category of the political and leaves philosophy as it is. *It leaves untouched all kinds of doctrines—religious, metaphysical, and moral—with their long traditions of development and interpretation*" (*PL*, 375; my italics). For Rawls, as for many other liberals, the challenge of the liberal state is to secure political agreement about fundamental principles of justice while remaining neutral to the various and often incompatible worldviews professed and lived by citizens. This is the essence of liberal neutrality.

At this point, a simple and obvious objection to Rawlsian neutrality arises. Why should the liberal state assume a position of utter neutrality to the ways of life chosen and pursued by its citizens? Is it not the very job of the state to set boundaries and limits, through legislation, a judicial system, and civil society, to the ends that citizens, as well as groups and corporations, may pursue? To be sure, neither Rawls nor any other major liberal claims that liberalism can be completely neutral, with political institutions having zero effect on or promoting absolutely equally all ways of life. Even a neutral framework of justice will place at least *some* constraints on possible conceptions of the good. Liberals would have, for example, ample resources to discourage or prohibit people who wished to lead lives devoted to racial discrimination or terrorist activity. Rawls recognizes that the demands of justice place some limits on what may count as a legitimate conception of the good. Total or simple neutrality would be as undesirable as it is impossible.

Rawls goes beyond simple neutrality and claims instead that political liberalism is neutral only to *reasonable* comprehensive doctrines. By this Rawls indicates that while political power may justifiably be exercised against groups who profess unreasonable doctrines, it must remain silent and leave "untouched" all reasonable comprehensive doctrines. "It is unreasonable for us to use political power, should we possess it, or share it with others, to repress comprehensive views that are not unreasonable" (*PL*, 61). Elsewhere Rawls says that "Political liberalism abstains from assertions about the domain of comprehensive views except as necessary when these views are unreasonable and reject all variations of the basic essentials of a democratic regime" (*PL*, 375).

Clearly, much turns here for Rawls on what he means by "reasonable" and "unreasonable" and what differentiates a reasonable from an unreasonable doctrine. Rawls says on the one hand that his account of reasonable comprehensive doctrines is "deliberately loose" and that "the only comprehensive doctrines that run afoul of public reason are those that cannot support a reasonable balance of political values" (*PL*, 59, 243). Rawls seems to imply here that most doctrines will be able to support the requisite political values. He supposes, for example, "that, except for certain kinds of fundamentalism, all the main historical religions . . . may be seen as reasonable comprehensive doctrines" (*PL*, 170). On the other hand, "there are always many unreasonable views" and it is political liberalism's task to "contain them—like war and disease" (*PL*, 64; 64, n. 19). Rawls's imprecision about what doctrines count as reasonable will be important in later chapters, but for now it suffices to note that Rawls limits the neutrality of the liberal state to only reasonable pluralism.

So Rawlsian liberalism is neutral with respect to reasonable comprehensive doctrines and interventionist with respect to unreasonable comprehensive doctrines. But it is important to distinguish here between two understandings of neutrality, one of which Rawls and almost all other liberals reject, the other of which Rawls and many others endorse. The first and unattractive sort of neutrality is *neutrality of effect*. This is the idea that the liberal state must in its constitutional essentials and public policies refrain from having any effect, positive or negative, on the ability of persons or groups to pursue the reasonable ways of life open to them. It must not make it more likely that individuals will embrace some particular conception of the good or make it more difficult for individuals to pursue the reasonable way of life that they affirm. Though Rawls's language occasionally suggests that he is sympathetic to neutrality of effect—the claim, for example, that political liberalism should leave comprehensive doctrines "untouched" sounds suspiciously like an endorsement of neutrality of effect—he clearly rejects it as impracticable (*PL*, 193–94). As Stephen Macedo has written, "There is no educational regime—just as there is no government policy—that is perfectly neutral in its effects, and we should stop looking for it."[10] The only kind of government policy that can be neutral in effect, it seems, is a government policy that has no effect at all, and if this is the case, we might as well do away with the policy.

The second sort of neutrality is *neutrality of aim*, or *justificatory neutrality*. This is the idea that the liberal state ought not to justify its constitutional essentials or public policies by reference to a schedule of valuable or less valuable ways of life. The state recognizes that neutrally justified policies may have non-neutral consequences, for these are inevitable as a matter of "commonsense political sociology" (*PL*, 193). It nevertheless must attempt to ensure that all citizens have, in Rawls's words, "equal opportunity to advance any conception of the good they freely affirm" (*PL*, 192), excepting, of course, unreasonable conceptions. Neutrality of aim aspires to a public justification of institutions and public policy that relies on no particular comprehensive doctrine or doctrines and therefore favors or disfavors no particular doctrine or doctrines.[11]

But even this qualified liberal neutrality is impossible. Using the insights of multicultural theory, I want now to show that liberal neutrality, even understood as neutrality of aim, is a chimera. From the perspective of multicultural theory, the liberal state privileges certain ways of life over others in the demands it makes on citizens in the development of political virtues, skills, and behaviors. Moreover, these civic demands will likely, if not certainly, color the ways in which citizens live their nonpublic lives. They will, in other words, shape in different degrees the way in which persons and groups seek out the good life that is best for them, depending on the congruence of the content of a person's or group's comprehensive doctrine with the substantive values of liberal citizenship. The demands and effects of liberal citizenship are decidedly non-neutral, favoring some cultural groups over others. Liberalism consciously and purposefully urges upon citizens a certain kind of character that outlines at least minimally the kind of person we are to be, which in turn affects the way cultural groups are able to form the character of their adherents.[12] To use a familiar phrase, liberalism is about soulcraft as well as statecraft.

Liberal states evince partiality to certain cultural groups or reasonable comprehensive doctrines in several ways. Iris Marion Young, for example, argues simply that neutrality requires lawmakers to adopt a detached and universal point of view which is no more than a fiction that serves to deny or obliterate cultural difference.[13] Will Kymlicka argues that because states cannot be neutral with respect to such things as language policy and national holidays, all states promote a national culture (some thicker and some thinner) that circumscribes the reasonable ways of life cultural subgroups may follow.[14] Philip Selznick notes that liberalism's non-neutrality can be recognized in "any robust conception of public health, environmental protection, or civic education."[15] Or consider, finally, such basic things as tax structures and marriage laws, both of which purposefully set out to provide incentives for certain choices and discourage, or forbid, certain other choices.

While each claim has merit, I believe the impossibility of neutrality is most glaringly evident when considering education. Focusing on education reveals the manner in which liberal neutrality is impossible in two powerful ways: (1) *in practice*, the historical operation of schools in liberal states demonstrates the clear privileging of some cultural groups over others, both in aim and in effect; and (2) *in theory*, the presuppositions that liberal theorists make about citizenship point to the imperative for a sort of civic education whose aims are decidedly non-neutral for cultural groups. The blinkered vision of contemporary liberal theorists when considering education has led many to ignore the actual practice of educational institutions and, worse, to ignore or underestimate the theoretical demands that liberalism places on a certain kind of civic education. I turn now to examine both the practical and theoretical problems of liberal neutrality with regard to education.

Liberal Neutrality and Educational Practice

In chapter 1 we saw how the actual operation of public schools in America has been anything but neutral in aim or in effect, from the pan-Protestant common school movement in the mid-eighteenth century to the language-discrimination laws at the turn of the century and the virulent Americanization campaigns during the 1910s and 1920s. Even a casual glance at the history of education would bring to light scores of other ways public schools have been supportive of some cultural groups and terribly prejudiced against others. (The mistreatment of Native American children and the exclusion or segregation of African-American children are but two of the more obvious examples). In short, the cultural bias of American schools is a recurrent theme in educational history.

But beyond the many historical examples that demonstrate how liberal neutrality *has not* been a reality, there are several general reasons why educational institutions simply *cannot* be neutral to diverse ways of life. First, the very establishment of a system of publicly funded common schools can be seen as non-neutral. After all, public education combined with the passage of compulsory attendance laws, represents a significant intrusion of the state into the private lives of citizens.[16] In the modern age, there exists no social institution, save perhaps taxation, that intervenes more directly and deeply into the lives of citizens than schools. Schools in fact represent the greatest of all intrusions insofar as taxation merely deprives individuals of the fruits of their labor and material resources. Compelling parents to send their children to schools for twelve years requires them to cede some authority over the upbringing of their offspring. It is a fantasy that twelve years of education of any sort could possibly leave, as Rawls suggests, all reasonable comprehensive doctrines "untouched."[17]

Second, even if educators wish to refrain from promoting or discouraging any particular set of goods, the actual practice of education reveals the futility of attempted neutrality. Educational theorists have long noted that *all* teaching is a value-laden enterprise. Schools are ethically charged places, carrying powerful normative currents, both intended and unintended. Teachers cannot help transmitting certain values to students, the most obvious of which is an emphasis on learning. The range of these values may vary from teacher to teacher and school to school, but assuredly no teacher can remain neutral both in aim and in effect to conceptions of the good life. Another reason teaching cannot be neutral is that curriculum construction is a process of exclusion as well as inclusion. We can imagine teachers attempting to be neutral in aim either by including all conceptions of the good life and giving them equal treatment, or by excluding all and not mentioning them. Obviously, it is as impossible to include everything as it is to exclude everything, for teachers must be teaching about something. If schooling consists of the pedagogy of teachers and the content of the curriculum, which leaves still unmentioned the so-called hidden curriculum of the school culture and role modeling of the adults, then neutrality is unattainable on both counts.

Finally, three practical, though by no means inconsequential, considerations are language issues, the schedule of school holidays, and dress codes. On language issues, the liberal state may aim to remain neutral by teaching simple literacy, rather than the literature of a particular culture. But the very choice of a language of instruction confers privilege on some ways of life and makes others more difficult. As Kymlicka argues, language is not a neutral medium; we pursue our conceptions of the good and live within cultural groups through a particular language.[18] While the existence of bilingual programs may accommodate ways of life for which English is not the dominant means of communication, the fact that all schools (in the United States) aim at developing fluency in the English language unavoidably favors cultural groups that communicate in English. As for school holidays, how the state schedules holidays typically reflects the pride of place given to a particular religious tradition and makes difficult the religious celebrations of minority religious groups. Moreover, some children who miss school in order to participate in the religious customs of their families may lose the opportunity to participate in school events, academic or nonacademic.[19] Finally, dress code regulations of schools may impose burdens upon some children whose religious clothing may be forbidden. A recent case in France over Muslim girls wearing the traditional chador illustrates the rancor such a problem can cause.[20]

LIBERAL NEUTRALITY AND EDUCATIONAL THEORY

That liberal theorists do not recognize the practical impossibility of neutrality regarding questions of the good life when considering how schools operate may not surprise us. After all, theorists concern themselves most often with the abstraction and coherence of clean principles rather than the messy details of how such principles are implemented and lived. Moreover, it could be argued that many of the historical examples are clear injustices and that the technical problems of pedagogy, curriculum construction, and choice of language can be overcome. School leaders often failed to endorse neutrality of aim, compounding the inevitably unequal effect of school policy on different groups. Failure to implement rigorous liberal principles of neutrality merely demonstrates the vast gap between liberal theory and liberal practice. The remedy would be ever more vigilant and careful attention to the demands of the theory, and ever stronger insistence on justifying the structure of educational institutions and policies without appealing to the superiority of some ways of life over others.

On the contrary, however, the closer one attends to the demands of liberal theory, the plainer it becomes that the educational presuppositions and implications of liberalism make neutrality a theoretical as well as a practical impossibility. The blind spot of contemporary liberal theorists extends from the institutional realities of education, described in chapter 1 and above, to the logical demands of the theory itself. More significant, citing the practical obstacles to be overcome in implementing liberal theory is a moot point if the theory itself implies that neutrality is impossible.

As before, I focus on Rawls as the representative of contemporary liberal theorists and levy against him a multicultural critique. My basic claims are easily summarized. Rawls's political liberalism demands political virtues of its citizens. The liberal state must educate citizens in order to foster these political virtues. Underlying these political virtues is the notion that citizens are

41

autonomous; therefore the liberal state must educate for autonomy. Autonomy is culturally non-neutral, a trait that has transformative potential for the various allegiances and affiliations of individuals and that, moreover, is not desired or fostered in all cultures. Some people and some cultural groups in liberal societies wish not to be autonomous and wish to avoid the development of autonomy in their children. Even attempts to disengage autonomy from liberalism, such as that by William Galston, fail. Put otherwise, I argue simply that close attention to the demands Rawls makes of citizens leads unavoidably to the conclusion that political or civic education will not only be a necessity, but a necessity that has non-neutral effects on reasonable diversity. If we are to be honest, we must admit that these effects are not unfortunate consequences but the purposeful aim of the liberal state. The task of outlining this complementary theory of civic education is the subject of chapter 5. For the remainder of this chapter I flesh out the argument summarized above.

The Non-neutral Educational Demands of Rawlsian Liberalism

From the perspective of multicultural theory, the liberal state privileges certain ways of life over others in the demands it makes on citizens in the development of political virtues. Recall that the goal of Rawlsian political liberalism is to recast a theory of justice from a political standpoint rather than from a rooted position in any particular comprehensive doctrine. Rawls says this is possible when citizens justify the use of political power by reference not to comprehensive doctrines but to what other citizens, equally situated in the public sphere, may reasonably accept. Fulfilling this political role, Rawls writes, assumes that citizens possess two moral powers—the capacity for a sense of justice and the capacity to form an individual conception of the good. But a sense of justice and the pursuit of some conception of the good do not suffice to realize justice in the liberal state. Political liberalism also requires that citizens exercise, as Rawls says, "the political virtues necessary for them to cooperate in maintaining a just political society" (PL, xlvi). Rawls underscores the importance of these virtues at several points in the text, noting that they are "very great virtues" which "constitute a very great public good, part of society's political capital" (PL, 157; also 171).

What are these essential political virtues? Considering the central role they play in his theory, Rawls is oddly reticent about enumerating them and, more significant, about describing how they are developed and sustained.[21] No section of either A Theory of Justice or Political Liberalism is devoted exclusively to the political virtues. No passage explains or even concisely summarizes his thoughts about them. The reader is left to assemble the list of these virtues and how they are developed and sustained from a smattering of references throughout the books.

Two key virtues are reasonableness and a sense of fairness (*PL*, 122, 157, 163, 194, 224). At other times we learn that the catalogue includes civility and tolerance (*PL*, 194); a spirit of compromise and a willingness to meet others halfway (*PL*, 157, 163); mutual respect (*PL*, 122); and a reluctance to engage in overt rebellion unless social injustices have persisted over time and are remediable in no other manner (*PL*, 347). Rawls stresses that as *political* virtues, they characterize the ideal of the good citizen, not the good individual, and thus have no necessary bearing on our private ways of life deriving from our respective comprehensive doctrines. "The political virtues," Rawls writes, "must be distinguished from the virtues that characterize ways of life belonging to comprehensive religious and philosophical doctrines, as well as the virtues falling under various associational ideals . . . and of those appropriate to roles in family life and to the relations between individuals" (*PL*, 195). In this way Rawls continues to hold that his liberal theory remains in the realm of the political, neutral to reasonable diversity.

Though Rawls never says so directly, I and many others believe it is clear that the political virtues must be developed in schools.[22] Virtues of reasonableness, fairness, civility, tolerance, and so forth, are certainly not innate. We are not born with the political virtues—nor, for that matter, with any particular conception of the good. It is not even safe to assume that individuals always have the *capacity* for the political virtues, much less the *ability* to exercise them. As all liberals do, Rawls assumes that families and cultural groups will provide the socialization that inducts children into a particular way of life or comprehensive doctrine. Nothing guarantees that each way of life will support or even be favorable to the political virtues. Indeed, under conditions of multiculturalism, it is virtually inevitable that the large set of reasonable comprehensive doctrines will contain some doctrines that are opposed to at least some of the political virtues. With respect to abortion, for example, the religious doctrine of many Catholics does not lead to tolerance and civility toward those with pro-choice convictions. With respect to the status of women, the doctrines of many religious groups do not support gender equality and equal voice in political and private decision making. Since Rawls can rely neither on the natural development of the political virtues nor on the hope that all reasonable ways of life will support them, that leaves schools as the only major social institution with the capacity and reach to foster the political virtues. Indeed, education in the liberal democratic state has traditionally been conceived as the main vehicle for creating citizens. A public system of schooling has, theoretically and historically, first and foremost civic purposes.[23]

At this point, before examining in greater detail the serious implications of Rawls's list of political virtues, which must include an account of how citizens learn them, it is worth pausing to remark on Rawls's comments about education in general. If Rawls is oddly reticent about the political virtues, despite their crucial role in his theory, he is practically mute about education, despite the equally crucial role it must play. In the more than one thousand pages of the combined lengths of *A Theory of Justice* and *Political Liberalism*, references to or discussions about education in the form of schooling can be found on a scant five pages.[24] To be sure, Rawls writes at length, at least in *A Theory of Justice*, about the family as a "school of justice" and elaborates a detailed account of moral development (see *TJ*, 462–79). Yet never does Rawls articulate either the specific aims of education that accord with his political theory or the need for some institutionalized system of education to carry out those aims.

Rawls's silence notwithstanding, it is possible to reconstruct from a variety of passages a clear sense that he believes a system of education to be necessary for precisely the civic reasons given above. Rawls says, for example, that his theory of justice is to apply to the "basic structure of society," by which he means the "main political, social, and economic institutions" and how they fit together into "one unified system of social cooperation from one generation to the next" (*PL*, 11; see also 257 ff.). The provision of schools available to all, it slowly becomes apparent, is an essential part of these social institutions. On one occasion Rawls calls it a "constitutional essential" that "below a certain level of material and social well-being, and education and training, people simply cannot take part in society as citizens, much less as equal citizens" (*PL*, 166; see also lix). In the most extended passage on education—a two-page comment that I examine in more detail later—Rawls argues that "Society's concern with [children's] education lies in their role as future citizens, and so in such essential things as their acquiring the capacity to understand the public culture and to participate in its institutions, in their being economically independent and self-supporting members of society over a complete life, and in their developing the political virtues" (*PL*, 200; cf. 199). With these remarks, Rawls appears at least to recognize the value of and need for education, emphasizing its civic rationale, if never expanding upon it in even minimal detail.

Having established the need for a civic education that encourages the development of the political virtues, I return to examine the non-neutral impli-cations of these virtues. A plethora of theorists, with both multicultural and liberal affiliations, have written about the decidedly non-neutral aspects of liberal citizenship exemplified by the exercise of political virtues.[25] Stephen Macedo has vigorously defended the transformative aspirations of liberal civic education, writing, "Not every form of cultural and religious diversity is to be celebrated, and not all forms of what can be labeled 'marginalization' and 'exclusion' are to be regretted or apologized for. Profound forms of same-ness and convergence should not only be prayed for but planned for without embarrassment."[26] Similarly, Jeff Spinner argues that liberal citizenship often alters and transforms our private identities, be they ethnic, racial, reli-gious, or otherwise.[27] If one aim of education is to develop the political virtues that Rawls requires, such an education will have unavoidable effects on cultural groups, most particularly on those which reject or discourage the exercise of these virtues, even if only within their own comprehensive doc-trines.

It is important to see that these effects are not mere by-products of neu-trally justified policies. To the contrary, they are planned for, residing in the basic architecture of political liberalism. To see how Rawls's political virtues are culturally non-neutral in aim, one need only consider what the virtues entail in the way citizens deliberate about political ends and the justification of policies. The political virtues prescribe for citizens a specific type of charac-ter in the public sphere, a character marked by its free and equal status and defined by its capacity to make independent, reasoned, and informed judg-ments about political questions ranging from the very constitutional struc-ture to the most mundane electoral issues that appear on ballots. Indeed, the free and equal status of citizens who share political power provides in some sense the *raison d'être* of the liberal state. In fostering the capacity for this free and equal citizenship, the liberal state asks its citizens to draw upon the political virtues and exercise skills and habits in the public sphere that have consequences for the plurality of ways of life led by the very same citizens in their private lives.

Consider a specific example. Take the virtue of reasonableness (foremost among the political virtues mentioned earlier) and its connection to public reason. Persons who are reasonable wish "to propose principles and standards as fair terms of cooperation and to abide by them willingly, given the assur-ance that others will likewise do so," and they accept what Rawls calls the "burdens of judgment," which indicate that the exercise of human reason does not result in unanimity on basic questions. Instead the world is characterized by reasonable pluralism (*PL*, 49, 54 ff.).[28] Persons are reasonable when they desire a social world in which they cooperate with others on a free and equal basis. Reasonableness is central to the exercise of public reason, a capacity that stands at the very heart of political liberalism. According to Rawls, public reason presupposes autonomy and describes an ideal of each citizen making independent and informed political decisions consistent with agreed-upon principles of justice; it requires a willingness to bracket one's own comprehensive doctrine, appealing instead to reasons that others might find acceptable from the similar standpoint of free and equal citizens (*PL*, 212 ff.). Public reason, Rawls notes, is exemplified in paradigmatic form by the Supreme Court, but it must be exercised by all, not just by politicians and judges. Public reason thus invokes a standard of democratic citizenship in which all citizens "should be ready to explain the basis of their actions to one another in terms each could reasonably expect that others might endorse as consistent with their freedom and equality" (*PL*, 218).

The crucial point here is that both reasonableness and public reason presume the autonomy of each citizen, a trait that underlies the political virtues in general and, according to some, the very notion of liberalism itself. By *autonomy*, I mean a person's ability to reflect independently and critically upon basic commitments, desires, and beliefs, be they chosen or unchosen, and to enjoy a range of meaningful life options from which to choose, upon which to act, and around which to orient and pursue one's life projects.[29] To conceive of oneself and others as free and equal beings, capable of deliberating upon and assenting to principles of justice and questions of politics, is to acknowledge the importance of autonomy. As Rawls writes, "Acting autonomously is acting from principles that we would consent to as free and equal rational beings" (*TJ*, 516). In another formulation, Rawls says that autonomy is "expressed in certain political virtues of citizens in their thought and conduct—their discussions, deliberations, and decisions—in carrying out a constitutional regime" (*PL*, 400). While the political virtues probably imply much more, they at least imply that citizens are autonomous. And in order to encourage citizens to act autonomously, the liberal state must educate its citizens to be autonomous; for, like the political virtues, autonomy is not inborn and is not supported by all reasonable ways of life.

But to admit this is to concede the multiculturalist critique: developing autonomous citizens is not neutral to cultural groups because autonomy is not a neutral character trait. It is a substantive value not promoted by all cultures or found in all comprehensive doctrines. Kymlicka expresses the problem most forcefully, arguing that, "Accepting the value of autonomy for political purposes enables its exercise in private life, an implication that will only be favored by those who endorse autonomy as a general value."[30] Some cultural groups socialize their members to defer to authority or tradition on important questions about how they conceive of the good and how it informs their lives. They do not view their members as free and equal, or even rational, and they do not encourage them to examine their way of life, or other ways of life, with a critical eye. We need only think about how some cultural groups often try to insulate or shield their members, especially children, from contact with the diversity of the world, or how others contain hierarchies of gender justified by reference to the natural order or to aristocratic and religious traditions. Developing autonomous citizens is partial to those cultural groups that themselves emphasize or cultivate autonomy and potentially corrosive of those that do not.

Consider two real-world examples, much discussed in the philosophical literature.[31] The 1972 Supreme Court case *Wisconsin v. Yoder* (406 U.S. 205) revolved around the claims of Amish parents that compulsory school attendance laws were inimical to the Amish way of life because exposure to the modern world would interfere with the religious freedom of parents to raise their children as they saw fit and, more seriously, threaten the survival of the Amish culture itself. The parents wished to withdraw their children from schools by the end of eighth grade, believing that freedom of religion and an interest in the survival of their culture warranted this limitation on the education of their children. From the perspective of the Amish parents, teaching their children to be autonomous and to exercise political virtues, like reasonableness, was unconstitutional, because a violation of their free exercise of religion. Such an education would promote the capacity for critically examining their ends and values and, likely, corrode their children's attachment to their comprehensive doctrine. The Court agreed and, in good multicultural fashion, exempted the Amish from compulsory attendance laws beyond the eighth grade.

A similar case arose in 1986, though with a different outcome. In *Mozert v. Hawkins County Board of Education* (827 F. 2d 1058 [1987]), Christian Fundamentalist parents requested that their children be exempted from a reading program that included excerpts of such books as *The Wizard of Oz* and *The Diary of Anne Frank*. The Fundamentalist parents argued, in effect, that mere exposure to diverse ways of life constituted an education in tolerance that called into question the truth of their religious beliefs, undermined their ability to raise their children as obedient believers in the Christian Bible, and therefore violated their freedom of religious expression. Claiming that exposure to diversity did not interfere with freedom of religion and citing the fundamental interest of the state to teach children civic values, the Tennessee State Court ruled against the Fundamentalist parents.[32]

The divergent court opinions notwithstanding, both cases illustrate the way in which an education for autonomy and the political virtues runs counter to the very possibility of the Amish or Fundamentalist parents pursuing their own conception of the good. While the justification for teaching autonomy and the political virtues arises from a political standpoint, their exercise clearly cannot be assumed to be confined to the political domain. Liberals must plan for autonomy—it is an aim, not a mere side effect—and it is hard to see how autonomy could be neutrally justified. Autonomy and the political virtues do not leave comprehensive doctrines "untouched"; autonomy is not culturally neutral.

At times, Rawls himself recognizes this and attempts to give an account of autonomy that is strictly limited to the political domain. But his statements on the subject are confusing. Sometimes he seems to believe that the simple conceptual demarcation of political autonomy from moral autonomy takes care of the problem. At other times he appears to acknowledge that the endorsement of even political autonomy will have non-neutral consequences for private identities.

On the one hand, Rawls recognizes that if liberalism promotes autonomy as a general moral value, applicable to both the political and private realms, then liberalism becomes a comprehensive conception of justice, which he views as untenable in the light of reasonable pluralism. His worry is that Kantian liberals or Millian liberals, who view autonomy as a moral ideal central to all aspects of individual life, prescribe too specific a conception of the good, one which rules out other conceptions that do not prize autonomy. Thus, recognizing that some reasonable comprehensive doctrines will not prize autonomy, and indeed discourage it, Rawls says that political liberalism "stresses the difference between political autonomy and moral autonomy, and it is careful to emphasize that a political conception of justice covers only the former" (PL, xliii, n. 8).

The consequence of promoting only a limited political conception of autonomy is that citizens are supposedly free in their nonpublic identities or private lives to live non-autonomously. A basic part of freedom, Rawls claims, is that citizens conceive of themselves as having the moral power to form and pursue a conception of the good. Political liberalism allows for the fact that "many persons may not examine their acquired beliefs and ends but take them on faith, or be satisfied that they are matters of custom and tradition. They are not to be criticized for this, for in the liberal view there is no political or social evaluation of conceptions of the good within the limits permitted by justice" (*PL*, 314). Thus, while all citizens must in their public identity be autonomous, Rawls says that in their "personal affairs, or in the internal life of associations" citizens "may have . . . affections, devotions, and loyalties that they believe they would not, indeed could and should not, stand apart from and evaluate objectively. They may regard it as simply unthinkable to view themselves apart from certain religious, philosophical, and moral convictions, or from certain enduring attachments and loyalties" (*PL*, 31). In short, persons *qua* citizens must be autonomous and reasonable; persons *qua* individuals need not be. By containing autonomy within the political domain, Rawls's theory of justice remains a political conception rather than a comprehensive conception. In our nonpublic identities, autonomy and the political virtues are not binding. Ultimately, Rawls's distinction between political and moral autonomy fails, for autonomy, as I explain in chapter 4, is less a capacity that we switch on and off at will than a sort of character that colors our lives as a whole. Kymlicka too criticizes Rawls on this point.[33] But for my present purposes, I mean only to show that Rawls attempts to uphold the value of autonomy by limiting its reach to the political arena.

Yet Rawls also recognizes at a few points in the text that fostering the political virtues in citizens may have unavoidable consequences for the nonpublic identities of citizens. I quote the following passage at length because it is at once Rawls's most extended comment on education in general and his most candid admission that, despite attempts to contain autonomy within the political domain, the demands of educating for the political virtues may affect the manner in which citizens view their private ends and goods. Political liberalism, despite its restricted aspirations, edges toward comprehensive liberalism.

> The liberalisms of Kant and Mill may lead to requirements designed to foster the values of autonomy and individuality as ideals to govern much if not all of life. But political liberalism has a different aim and requires far less. It will ask that children's education include such things as knowledge of their constitutional and civic rights, so that, for example, they know that liberty of conscience exists in their society and that apostasy is not a legal crime. . . . Moreover, their education should also prepare them to be fully cooperating members of society and enable them to be self-supporting; it should also encourage the political virtues so that they want to honor the fair terms of cooperation in their relations with the rest of society.

Here it may be objected that requiring children to understand the political conception in these ways is in effect, though not in intention, to educate them to a comprehensive liberal conception. Doing the one may lead to the other, if only because once we know the one, we may of our own accord go on to the other. *It must be granted that this may indeed happen in the case of some. . . . The unavoidable consequences of reasonable requirements for children's education may have to be accepted, often with regret.* (PL, 199–200; my italics)

With this passage Rawls brings together the major themes of this chapter. He acknowledges, in perhaps the only place in all his work, the central importance of education in the service of developing the political virtues. He also recognizes that such a civic education will be partial to certain ways of life over others, though he expresses regret about it. When considering the educational requirements of political liberalism, Rawls accepts that the limited aspirations of political liberalism may be thwarted. Thus, Rawls concedes the multiculturalist objection: though political liberalism may be conceived so as to leave reasonable comprehensive doctrines untouched, liberal neutrality is impossible. Liberalism must aim to construct the content of the character of its citizens, which has the effect of shaping the content of the character of citizens in their nonpublic identities, even if it does not prescribe or promote particular ways of life for them. As Rawls says elsewhere, "The institutions of the basic structure [of a liberal society] have deep and long-term social effects and in fundamental ways shape citizens' character and aims, the kinds of persons they are and aspire to be" (PL, 68).

Beyond just "spilling over," as Amy Gutmann has put it, into the realm of citizens' private lives, there is another reason, it seems to me, that Rawls would wish for individuals and not merely citizens to be autonomous to some significant degree. I have in mind here Rawls's insistence that citizens be guaranteed not merely a slate of basic liberties but that they be guaranteed the actual worth of these liberties (PL, 326 ff). The basic liberties constitute the first principle of justice for Rawls—prior in importance to the second principle, which governs the distribution of primary goods—and they include freedom of thought, liberty of conscience, freedom of association, and political freedoms to vote and run for office. But, as Rawls recognizes, the availability of material goods will affect the ability of persons to make use of their liberties. Thus, "the basic structure of society is arranged so that it maximizes the primary goods available to the least advantaged to make use of the equal basic liberties enjoyed by everyone" (PL, 326). In addition to material goods, however, people also need certain internal capabilities in order to make use of their freedoms. I do not have freedom of thought if I am unaware of the larger marketplace of ideas; I do not have liberty of conscience if I cannot conceive of being an apostate; I do not have freedom of association if I cannot evaluate and compare the reasons for joining some groups rather than others. While these internal capabilities may not describe any robust ideal of autonomy, certainly some of its associated characteristics, such as critical thinking and self-reflection, will be necessary. Amartya Sen has criticized Rawls's second principle of justice because people have different capabilities to convert primary goods into their well-being; I suggest that a non-autonomous person is less likely to be able to take advantage and make use of the basic liberties. This is to argue that autonomy is a desirable ideal in the private as well as public lives of persons, a thesis I return to in chapter 5.

But leaving aside the private importance of autonomy for the moment, it should be clear that educating citizens to be politically autonomous and exercise the political virtues makes political liberalism much more comprehensive than Rawls wants to admit. Though his work is heavily indebted to Rawls, Eamonn Callan has criticized him on exactly this point: "The distinction between political and comprehensive liberalism is far more porous than its devotees suppose, and Rawls's political liberalism in particular is really a disguised instance of comprehensive liberalism."[34] Whether or not the divide between political liberalism and comprehensive liberalism collapses conceptually or merely as a matter of political sociology, the demand that citizens become politically autonomous fatally undercuts liberal aspirations to neutrality.

WILLIAM GALSTON AND LIBERAL DIVERSITY OR LIBERAL AUTONOMY?

Whereas Rawls admits the centrality of autonomy to his liberal theory, William Galston argues that autonomy should be trumped by liberalism's commitment to diversity. Galston identifies two separate strands of the liberal tradition, which he dubs "liberal diversity," arising out of the Reformation, and "liberal autonomy," arising out of the Enlightenment.[35] Galston agrees with the critique of liberalism I have just given: educating citizens to be autonomous is an unjust and non-neutral interference with the ability of those citizens to lead unreflective ways of life. He goes one step further, however, in arguing that "liberalism is about the protection of diversity, not the valorization of choice" (523). Liberal diversity is superior to liberal autonomy because, Galston writes, "To place an ideal of autonomous choice . . . at the core of liberalism is in fact to narrow the range of possibilities available within societies. In the guise of protecting the capacity for diversity, the autonomy principle in fact represents a kind of uniformity that exerts pressure on ways of life that do not embrace autonomy" (523). Galston is correct to note that liberalism's emphasis on autonomy renders it partial to some ways of life. His argument that concerns for diversity ought to be paramount fails, however. I wish to conclude by showing how the value of autonomy remains central even to Galston's project of the "Diversity State," for Galston packs into his account a concern for autonomy which evinces itself specifically in his discussion about civic education.

Echoing the multicultural criticism of liberal neutrality, Galston's overriding concern is the protection of social diversity. From Galston's perspective, the promotion of autonomy, whether for individual or political reasons, compromises the existence of groups that do not encourage autonomy. He writes that, "autonomy is one possible mode of existence in liberal societies—one among many others; its practice must be respected and safeguarded; but the devotees of autonomy must recognize the need for respectful coexistence with individuals and groups that do not give autonomy pride of place" (525). If the purpose of the liberal state is to allow for diverse ways of life, or what Galston tendentiously calls "deep diversity," it cannot insist upon autonomous behavior among its citizenry.

What, then, for Galston are the limits to possible diversity? As we saw earlier, Rawlsian liberalism intends to protect diversity within the limits of reasonable comprehensive doctrines, or reasonable pluralism. Yet because Rawls and other liberals require political autonomy, these limits are in Galston's view too restrictive. Galston instead argues for "maximum feasible accommodation" or "maximum feasible space for the enactment of individual and group differences, constrained only by the requirements of liberal social unity" (524).[36]

Everything turns here of course on Galston's interpretation of the requirements of liberal social unity, which he calls "more than minimal" (524). Galston indicates several different requirements. These requirements, however, lead Galston back to a position of requiring autonomy of all citizens, thereby undermining his project of the "Diversity State."

He first tells us that the liberal state has a variety of public purposes.[37] These purposes afford the state a warrant to intervene in the lives of individuals and groups under certain circumstances. Galston says, for example, that the liberal state's interest in protecting human life permits it to forbid religious worship involving human sacrifice. The interest in promoting normal development of basic capacities permits it to prevent communities from stunting physical growth through malnourishment or binding. These two purposes, it must be admitted, rule out very little in the way of diversity.

The third purpose, however, is more restrictive and more telling. Galston writes that the liberal state's interest in developing what he calls "social rationality" would allow the state to forbid forms of education that disable its practice (525). Significantly, beyond declaring that social rationality is "the kind of understanding needed to participate in the society, economy, and polity"—a rather empty definition—he never defines this crucial capacity (525). Put in a more positive sense, Galston's liberal state promotes a "vigorous system" of civic education (528). He informs the reader that "the scope of permissible diversity is constrained by the imperatives of citizenship" (528, n. 29). Unfortunately, Galston never gives a detailed account of what this civic education comprises, nor what the imperatives of citizenship are. In a brief aside about education, Galston puzzlingly says that while the state is justified in promoting tolerance and exposing children to the existence of diverse ways of life, what the state "may not do is to prescribe curricula or pedagogic practices that require or strongly invite students to become skeptical or critical of their own ways of life" (529). Clearly, Galston's worry here is that in asking students to be skeptical or critical of their ways of life, he edges closer toward supporting autonomy. But it is a mystery how a teacher could simultaneously expose children to diversity yet not "invite" them to use this knowledge of diverse values by turning an inquisitive, critical, or skeptical eye toward their own culture or set of values. In short, by failing to define the key terms of social rationality, civic education, and the imperatives of citizenship, Galston appears to rely on the rhetorical force of his say-so that none of these requirements will in fact lead toward an endorsement of autonomy. His brief remark about education hints, on the contrary, at just such an endorsement.

Elsewhere Galston's reliance on autonomy becomes still clearer. He goes beyond an enumeration of the purposes of the liberal state and concedes that there must exist certain limits to what goods groups may pursue and what regulations groups may place on their members. But Galston wishes to distinguish between "the practices internal to ways of life and the movement among ways of life" (522). Liberals, he argues, should defend the capacity for movement among ways of life but not attempt to reconstruct the internal practices of groups. In Galston's words, persons should possess a "right of exit," so that they will not be coerced into or trapped within ways of life. Liberals should not insist, however, on imposing liberal principles upon the practices of groups beyond those that insure a right of exit.

Galston wishes to construct a diversity model of association in which "groups may be illiberal in their internal structure and practices as long as freedom of entrance and exit is zealously safeguarded by the state" (533). But the mere conferral of the formal right of exit does not suffice to guarantee its actual exercise. As I argue again in the next chapter, forms of education that discourage the autonomy of children by shielding them from a diversity of ways of life and restricting the capacity to question and criticize their own effectively disable the ability to exit the group. Portals of exit are in effect sealed shut when there are no windows to the outside world.

To be meaningful, rights of exit, as Galston recognizes, must include several elements. Galston's own list pushes him back toward a position of valuing autonomy. He cites the following: "knowledge conditions—the awareness of alternatives to the life one is in fact living; capacity conditions—the ability to assess these alternatives if it comes to seem desirable to do so; psychological conditions—in particular, freedom from . . . brainwashing; . . . and finally, fitness conditions—the ability of exit-desiring individuals to participate effectively in at least some ways of life other than the ones they wish to leave" (533–34). How, for instance, would it "seem desirable" to assess alternatives unless a person was in fact exercising a certain degree of autonomy? How would Galston flesh out the psychological conditions when thinking about permissible forms of education? Galston believes that despite the burden of his own argument, diversity trumps autonomy. But the lack of specificity in his argument combined with a realistic assessment of what is entailed in a substantive right of exit yields, on even a generous reading, a conclusion that still gives special emphasis to autonomy.

BOTH GALSTON and the multiculturalists agree that liberal insistence on autonomous citizens has clearly non-neutral effects on the diversity of ways of life in any society. Contrary to Rawls's ambition, liberalism—even the circumscribed political variety—does not leave reasonable pluralism "untouched". But whereas Galston's conclusion that the liberal state is partial leads him to a project in which the value of autonomy is subordinated to the value of diversity, multiculturalists like Kymlicka typically extend a slate of group rights in addition to the usual individual rights guaranteed by the state. More strongly, Avishai Margalit and Moshe Halbertal argue, for example, that all people must have a "right to their own culture," which means that, rather than assisting all citizens to learn the political virtues, the state must "abandon its neutral position and actively assist needy cultures, even when those cultures preach their own view of the good life which conflicts with other views within the state."[38] This is a wholly different form of state non-neutrality. I have argued here that Galston's project fails. In the next chapter I examine, from a liberal perspective, the remedy proposed by multiculturalists.

T H R E E

A Liberal Critique of
Multiculturalism

Whereas educational theories specifically designed to address the issue of cultural diversity have existed since at least the mid-nineteenth century days of Horace Mann, and whereas the specific phrase "multicultural education" has existed since at least the 1960s, the idea of multiculturalism as a political theory is relatively new.[1] Multicultural political theory represents the most recent development in the extensive commentary on contemporary liberal theory. For almost two decades after the publication of John Rawls's *A Theory of Justice* in 1971, the debate focused largely on liberals and their communitarian critics.[2] Since the early 1990s, however, and the arrival of Will Kymlicka's *Liberalism, Community, and Culture* and Charles Taylor's *Multiculturalism and "The Politics of Recognition,"*[3] multicultural theorists have managed what communitarians never could. For the most part, communitarianism existed as a powerful critique of liberalism but not a positive political theory unto itself. In contrast, multiculturalists have forwarded multiculturalism as an alternative to or significant reinterpretation of liberalism.

What unites multicultural theorists is the conviction that the emphasis in liberalism on individual rights and responsibilities does not suffice for justice when considering the inevitable partiality of the liberal state to some of the cultural groups contained within it. For many, the remedy of liberalism's failure to account for the importance of cultures and cultural membership is to defend a slate of group rights. A significant literature has evolved on the appropriate kind and scope of group rights for a multicultural theory.[4]

Yet, as several theorists have argued, the extension of group rights and accommodations within a liberal state leads to a clear tension. When the state seeks through collective rights to improve the status of minority groups and their members with respect to the larger society, it can also undermine the status of the weaker members within the group. Susan Moller Okin criticizes multiculturalism for this reason, arguing that group rights often reinforce the subordination of women within groups.[5] And Ayelet Shachar, more sympathetic to the multicultural project, nevertheless finds that multicultural accommodations can reinforce power dynamics that render the most disadvantaged group members, especially women, even more vulnerable. She labels this the "paradox of multicultural vulnerability."[6] Neither, however, focuses on those who are the most vulnerable and the least powerful: children.

Among the most important collective rights defended by multiculturalists is the right of minorities to exert far greater control over the education of their children. Such control comes in two general forms, either via the right to separate schools or culture-centric curricula, sometimes at state expense, or via the right to exemptions from educational requirements, such as compulsory attendance laws.[7] Consistent with my focus on the educational presuppositions and implications of political theories in earlier chapters, I concentrate here on the nature of group rights as they relate to education. For just as the problems of liberal neutrality surface most clearly when considering educational presuppositions and implications, so too do the problems of multicultural theories.

It is easy to understand why in culturally diverse states control over education is so important. First, and most obvious, schools are a central vehicle of cultural transmission, perhaps the most important vehicle next to the family. Beyond socialization within the home, schools play a crucial role in initiating children into the norms, beliefs, and rites of the larger group, forming and deepening their cultural identities in the process. For this reason, historically as well as presently, many parents choose a school for their children not (only) on the basis of academic quality but (also) with regard to what the child in the seat next to their son or daughter looks like or believes in. Second, when children of ethnocultural, religio-cultural, or national minority groups attend common schools, they have often been discriminated against as a matter of state policy or marginalized within the curriculum. Schools in many parts of the world, and especially in the United States, as we have seen, have historically attempted to strip away cultural attachments and beliefs in an effort to assimilate children of the adult members of minority groups to the majority culture. More subtly, schools have often failed in their curricula to recognize the existence and history of many minority groups, leading minorities to feelings of invisibility, inferiority, and second-class citizenship. And third, control over schooling also means that those in charge can decide who gets an education at all. Schools often restrict attendance to certain children, rein-forcing particular norms about those who are considered educable or worthy of education. Consider the history in the United States of preventing African-Americans from attending schools, or forcing them to attend impoverished schools, or the current practice in many parts of the world of educating only boys.

In this chapter I examine the educational presuppositions and implica-tions of the work of several multicultural theorists who identify themselves as working within the liberal tradition: Avishai Margalit and Moshe Halber-tal, Chandran Kukathas, Will Kymlicka, and Joseph Raz. The primary prob-lem with these multicultural theories, I argue, is that despite their alleged adherence to liberal values, they are nevertheless seriously deficient from a liberal perspective. I contend that their defense of multicultural accommoda-tions in education tends to neglect the potential perils of accommodation. I do not wish to press the typical fear, however, that extending cultural rights threatens the value of common citizenship and leads to Balkanization. My sense is that, at least in the U.S. context, such fears are greatly exaggerated. My concern is that accommodation policies meant to promote or preserve cultural groups potentially place the integrity of the group above the free-dom and equality of the individuals within, especially children. In particular, multicultural accommodation policies in education that grant rights to sepa-rate schooling or wholesale exemptions from state regulations amount in some circumstances to sanctioning the oppression of children.

Margalit and Halbertal, as well as Kukathas, claim that their theories are liberal because they aim to guarantee a so-called "right of exit" from any group. Kymlicka, whose work is the most sophisticated, claims his theory is liberal because he defends the rights only of those cultural groups that are themselves liberal (except in rare circumstances), and he takes seriously the value of autonomy, linking the capacity and exercise of it in an interesting and systematic way to cultural membership. While the freedom to dissociate from a group, seeking happiness elsewhere, is indeed central to the liberal tradition, I argue that the group rights supported by Margalit and Halbertal and Kukathas may serve to disable or severely impoverish the ability of chil-dren to exit from groups. And while the importance of autonomy is also central to the liberal tradition, I contend that Kymlicka's conception of au-tonomy is unsatisfactory and that, moreover, his defense of rights to separate schooling for some cultural minorities leaves him open to the same critique about exit that I levy against Margalit and Halbertal and Kukathas.

A RIGHT TO CULTURE?

I begin by considering the strongly worded work of Margalit and Halbertal, who articulate very straightforwardly the most basic claim of almost all multicultural theories: individual freedom and flourishing depend crucially on a person's cultural attachments. This rather unobjectionable claim leads to what, at bottom, is a strikingly elementary argument: if culture matters to individual freedom and flourishing, then liberals, who seek to guarantee freedom and facilitate individual flourishing, should also concern themselves with culture. Margalit and Halbertal thus begin their argument with the simple but dramatic assertion, "Human beings have a right to culture—not just any culture but their own."[8]

Note here, however, that the key assertion is not that cultural attachments are important *per se*, but rather that attachments to *one's own* culture are important. Now it is probably trivially true that people need cultural attachments in order to lead satisfying lives, but it is another question entirely whether or not people need to be attached always to their own cultural groups in order to lead satisfying lives. And prior to this question, we must ask a host of others about the meaning of "one's own culture": how will one's own culture be identified? Who shall be the identifying agent(s)? Are multiple cultural attachments possible? Can people change cultural allegiances?

These familiar questions raise some initial problems for Margalit and Halbertal, but it is important first to ask what follows from their notion of a right to culture. Margalit and Halbertal believe that "the right to culture may involve giving groups a status that contradicts the status of the individual in a liberal state" and that "protecting cultures out of the human right to culture may take the form of an obligation to support cultures that flout the rights of the individual in a liberal society" (491). Moreover, they say that the liberal state must "abandon its neutral position and actively assist needy cultures," not because this is in the interest of the majority but because it is necessary "to make it possible for members of minority groups to retain their identity" (492). Thus the motivating force behind the right to culture is an interest in protecting the existence of minority cultural groups.

For Margalit and Halbertal, then, cultural identification, or more precisely, identification with one's own culture, is so important that it generates a right that overrides other traditional liberal beliefs in freedom of choice, association, and movement. Minority cultural groups may be allowed to impose certain restrictions on their members as well as certain regulations on outsiders. Margalit and Halbertal say, for example, that the right to culture will permit groups to recognize only arranged marriages, or to forbid outsiders from entering or living in a particular geographical area. Moreover, using as an example the Ultra-Orthodox Jews in Israel, they assert that defending a right to culture issues in a defense of the subordinate status of women within the group (491–92).

The most significant implications of a right to culture, I believe, concern schooling. Margalit and Halbertal, at least in their assessment of Ultra-Orthodox Jews, seem to agree, calling education "an issue of central importance" (493). The right to culture justifies for Margalit and Halbertal the right to publicly subsidized separate schooling. They argue that the right to culture and the privileges that follow from it are not meant merely to protect cultures in danger of disappearing, but also to aid a minority group that finds it difficult to "maintain specific aspects of its culture without these privileges" (506). Thus for those groups whose ability to transmit their cultural values and beliefs to children may be compromised or undermined by attendance in public schools, the state ought to provide public assistance for separate educational institutions. Margalit and Halbertal say that, within the Israeli context, both Ultra-Orthodox Jews and Arab Israelis should be permitted to establish and maintain separate schools at public expense (493, 507). Should the state continue to regulate or oversee the structure and content of the separate educational institutions desired by each particular cultural group? Referring to Ultra-Orthodox society, Margalit and Halbertal note that "the school curriculum is controlled exclusively by the community, and there is a clear discrimination between the education of girls and of boys" (493). Boys engage in life-long study of the Torah, learning almost no secular subjects; girls receive a different curriculum and complete their studies before age twenty. Summing up their position, Margalit and Halbertal contrast the *conditional* right to control access to a community's neighborhood, based on a balance of the community's interest and the burdens that restricted access place on outsiders, with the apparently *absolute* right to maintain separate educational institutions. A right to culture, for Margalit and Halbertal, means that cultural groups, without state oversight but with state financial support, ought to be permitted to direct and control the education of their youngest members.

Given this list of implications regarding marriage, geographical access, and education, it is not difficult to discern how establishing a right to culture leads to potential conflicts with basic liberal beliefs. If the liberal state takes the freedom and equality of individuals seriously, it cannot permit a cultural rights program of the sort suggested by Margalit and Halbertal. The reason is that in the interest of preserving the culture, the rights extended to groups may sanction illiberal treatment of group members, not to mention the potential neglect of the development and sustenance of civic or political virtues in children.

Permitting, as Margalit and Halbertal do, "judicial autonomy in marital and family matters" (507) might qualify as a *prima facie* case against the supposed liberalism of their theory.[9] But consider their stance on separate education and their own example of the Ultra-Orthodox. How on liberal grounds can one defend an educational system where girls are denied simple equal educational opportunity, by which I mean equal access to schools and curricula? Equally worrisome from a liberal perspective is the fact that boys are denied the opportunity to study anything secular.[10] Given, as Margalit and Halbertal admit, that "Ultra-Orthodox culture is essentially illiberal" and that "there is no aspect of its members' lives in which it does not actively interfere, sometimes to the extent of compulsion," schooling that perpetuates a second-class status for women and that shields boys from engagement with secular culture is inconsistent with a liberal's interest in freedom, equality, and participatory citizenship (492–93). Group rights of the sort described by Margalit and Halbertal allow for illiberal treatment of individuals within groups.

Margalit and Halbertal might reply in two ways. First, they say that cultural rights are valuable only insofar as they are in the interests of individuals. Or more precisely, they say that "the individual's right to culture stems from the fact that every person has an overriding interest in his personality identity—that is, in preserving his way of life and the traits that are central identity components for him and the other members of his cultural group" (505). But the notion of personality identity as the grounds for a right to culture seems to me controversial at best and incoherent at worst, considering what Jeremy Waldron has called the "cosmopolitan alternative."[11] Do all individual adherents of a culture have similar personality identities? Must personality identities derive from the cultural unit into which a person is born? Do they alter over time? Can a person construct a personality identity out of multiple cultural materials? I comment at greater length on the importance of this cosmopolitan alternative later in this chapter.

Second, reminding readers that "the right to culture is based on its contribution to the basic interests of individuals," Margalit and Halbertal argue that each individual must always retain the right to exit a culture if he or she wishes to do so (508).[12] The right to culture does not, they write, "justify coercing those who wish to leave the culture to remain within it on the pretext that if people begin to leave, the culture will be destroyed" (508). Consistent with the value of personal autonomy, they aim to honor the capacity of individuals to examine their lives and preserve freedom of association by denying cultural groups the right to forbid exit.

But are the group rights they endorse themselves consistent with a meaningful right of exit? Given the restrictions Margalit and Halbertal are willing to tolerate even among self-described illiberal groups, this hardly seems the case. It is one thing simply to announce that cultural groups may not forbid their members from exiting; it is an entirely different matter to create the capacity for individuals to exercise this right. The distinction here is a familiar one, namely, between formal liberties and the actual worth of liberties. Margalit and Halbertal seem to me all too willing to sacrifice basic conditions for exercising a right of exit in the name of ensuring the continued existence of the group, all in order to preserve an individual's personality identity.

Think about the (absolute) right of cultural groups to separate educational institutions that Margalit and Halbertal defend. The Ultra-Orthodox education they describe—in its effort to shield students from secular society, in its reinforcement of gender inequality—seems unlikely to play a role in creating the conditions where students might be capable of revising or rejecting their religious attachments. (It seems equally unlikely to teach children the civic skills and behavior they need to be informed and active citizens.) Indeed, the Ultra-Orthodox education is designed exactly to prevent that. But we can imagine far worse scenarios. If the norms of a cultural group continually reinforced a message that girls and women were sources of evil, sexual temptresses, or merely unequal in all respects to men, would Margalit and Halbertal defend schools that taught these lessons? If the norms of a cultural group aim systematically to disable the ability of boys to think critically except with relation to the Talmud, or teach them to accept unerringly the dictates of elders, would Margalit and Halbertal defend an educational system designed to further this end? If the answer is no, Margalit and Halbertal offer no criteria by which to distinguish acceptable from unacceptable aims and forms of separate education. On their own admission, the relative liberality or illiberality of group practices would *not* count as such a criterion. In fact, far from distinguishing between liberal versus illiberal educational practices, they suggest that the state must not only tolerate separate schools, but actively support them financially. Yet when cultural groups are illiberal in their educational practices, it is hard to believe that the right of exit that Margalit and Halbertal guarantee to individuals will have any real substance. Rights of exit are meaningless without the capacity to exercise them.

Margalit and Halbertal are not alone in their reliance on the right of exit strategy. Multicultural theorists often seem to condition the justice of proposed group rights or accommodations on the right of individuals to exit. Yet, as Cass Sunstein and Jon Elster have argued, a person's preferences often adapt to the environment in which they form, all the more so when the environment puts up barriers to exposure to diversity. As a result, people's preferences, Sunstein writes, "need not be respected when they are adaptive to unjust background conditions; in such circumstances it is not even clear whether the relevant preferences are authentically 'theirs.'"[13] We may wonder, therefore, about the expressed preferences *not to exit* of adults who have received exceptionally illiberal educations; we may wonder, essentially, whether they have been indoctrinated. It is hard to see how a liberal state could justify multicultural accommodations in education that permitted indoctrination. But unless an education is provided that does not indoctrinate, that does not systematically adapt one's preferences and, over time, one's very character to uphold cultural norms, the right-of-exit strategy inevitably fails. If the right-of-exit strategy is even to be coherent, individuals must acquire the capacity to question the value of continued allegiance to cultural norms and practices, and ultimately to the group itself. This is necessary simply to begin the process of deciding for oneself whether exiting the group is, all things considered, a desirable pursuit.

In fact, we might express another concern about the right-of-exit strategy precisely because, even if one is capable of it, exiting one's group is, in the real world, a momentous and highly consequential decision. Since children are still dependent on their families for care, it is highly unlikely that many children would ever avail themselves of the exit option, even were they able to consider it. The costs of exit for children—possibly forgoing the continued love of parents and family, of suffering shame and ostracism, and so on—are so great that even those with the wherewithal to leave will have powerful reasons to remain. As for adults, those who would consider exiting are likely to be those who are already subject to illiberal and unjust treatment—internal dissenters or women, for example. To the extent that group rights or accommodations come conditioned on the ability of persons to exit, the burden of such accommodations is often borne by minority-group members who are already most vulnerable. As Ayelet Shachar notes, if a state extends collective rights to a minority group and tensions then arise between an individual and the group, it is the individual who must resolve the tension by deciding whether or not to stay. "By turning a blind eye to differential power distributions within the group hierarchy and ignoring women's heightened symbolic role in relation to other group members, the right of exit rationale forces an individual member into a choice of penalties: either accept all group practices, including those that violate your fundamental citizenship rights, or (somehow) leave."[14] Thus, even if education were to provide children a substantive as well as formal ability to exit, we might worry about the overall justice of the right-of-exit strategy.[15]

Returning, then, to Margalit and Halbertal, I conclude that even if they can answer successfully the difficult questions about what it means to have a right to *one's own* culture with which I began this section, or assuming that the confusing matter of a personality identity can be made clear, their theory fails on liberal grounds. If the right of exit is what makes their theory liberal, the group rights they defend, especially the allowance for separate and publicly subsidized educational systems, potentially undermine the very possibility of exit from the start. At the very least, we can say without any controversy that, given separate schools, the capacity to exit a group will be distributed differentially among citizens. Certainly the capacity for exit will be distributed differentially even in societies in which all persons receive the same education, or even in the most liberal of societies. My point here is not that unequal capacity to exit is unjust, but that a theory of group rights that institutionalizes the discrepancy should be called into question.

From a liberal perspective, then, the multicultural theory of Margalit and Halbertal is deeply troublesome, for while it claims to have the flourishing of individuals in mind, it preserves the integrity of cultural groups at the potential cost of the freedom and equality of individuals within groups. We could put the problem more generally by asking whether a multicultural theory that protects the right of cultural groups to treat their members illiberally deserves to be called a liberal theory. Margalit and Halbertal have provided no reason to answer in the affirmative, but it is a question that Chandran Kukathas asks directly and answers affirmatively. To his theory I turn next.

Cultural Communities and Self-Governance

Chandran Kukathas undertakes to defend the right of cultural communities, with whatever degree of liberal or illiberal cultural practices, to govern themselves without interference from the state. This aim poses in particularly stark terms a key question for liberal societies that extend group rights:

When may the liberal state intervene in the internal affairs of a cultural community? Kukathas's answer to this question is, "almost never." Liberalism, for Kukathas, is a regime of almost boundless tolerance.

Like Margalit and Halbertal, Kukathas argues that the multicultural theory leading to this answer retains an impeccable liberal pedigree. But rather than defending a right to culture or cultural rights *per se*, Kukathas says that the interests of cultural communities may be protected by "reassert[ing] the fundamental importance of individual liberty or individual rights"; that there is "no need to look for alternatives to liberalism or to jettison the individualism that lies at its heart."[16] So insistent on the liberal architecture of his theory is Kukathas that he writes, "The primary thesis advanced here is not that groups do not matter but that there is no need to depart from the liberal language of *individual* rights to do justice to them" (230; emphasis in original).

How then does he generate a multicultural theory from liberal individualist premises? Echoing Margalit and Halbertal, Kukathas argues that cultural communities matter "only to the extent that they affect actual individuals" and that "groups or communities have no special moral primacy in virtue of some natural priority" (234). But while cultural communities enjoy no privileged status, individuals form themselves into such groups out of their interest in their well-being. Viewing cultural communities as "private associations" or "electoral majorities," Kukathas then arrives at the conclusion that cultures should be respected "not because the culture has the right to be preserved but because individuals should be free to associate: to form communities and to live by the terms of those associations" (236–37, 238). This position has strong implications for Kukathas, for it simultaneously legitimizes the authority that cultures exercise over their members and insulates the culture from the supervisory gaze of the liberal state. Viewing the right of the individual to associate with cultural communities as absolute, Kukathas remarks that his view "imposes no requirement on those communities to be communities of any particular kind" and "in no sense requires that they be liberal societies; they may indeed be quite illiberal" (238).

Just how illiberal might a cultural community be before the liberal state could justifiably intervene? Kukathas implies that cultural communities should be self-governing almost without limitation. If Margalit and Halbertal appear partially blind to the illiberal implications of their theory, Kukathas at least recognizes the drastic consequences of curtailing the power of the liberal state. Consider these two passages:

[I]t has to be admitted that by liberal standards there may be injustice within some cultural communities: Freedom of worship may not be respected; women may have opportunities closed off to them; and the rights of individuals to express themselves may be severely restricted. (251)

[T]here would in such a society be (the possibility of) communities which bring up children unschooled and illiterate; which enforce arranged marriages; which deny conventional medical care to their members (including children); and which inflict cruel and "unusual" punishment.[17]

Kukathas's intellectual consistency is admirable, even if it does call into question his entire project. What, it might be asked, does Kukathas rule out? The only things Kukathas mentions are slavery, physical coercion, and cruel, inhuman, and degrading treatment (249–50).[18]

Many would surely take these statements as establishing a *prima facie* case that Kukathas's argument would fail the test of any theory of justice (much less the test of a *liberal* theory that promotes the freedom and equality of individuals). Under what circumstances might promoting illiteracy and condoning cruel and unusual punishment be just? But the manner in which Kukathas attempts to justify his conclusions as resting solidly within the liberal tradition is instructive, for it points again to the fundamental importance of education and illustrates a frequent error made by multicultural theorists.

The key to understanding Kukathas's conclusion is his view of membership in cultural communities as voluntary. This is an odd view. Most people regard membership in a cultural community as in many significant respects involuntary. After all, no person grows up without cultural connections—we are born into families whose race, religion, nationality, or social class, to name a few of the usual markers, begin a socialization process that is not of our choosing. Nevertheless, Kukathas says that "cultural communities may be regarded as voluntary associations to the extent that members recognize as legitimate the terms of association and the authority that upholds them." But crucially, "*All that is necessary* as evidence of such recognition is the fact that members choose not to leave" (238; my emphasis). Freedom of association is an absolute right for Kukathas; freedom of dissociation is equally absolute. Indeed, for Kukathas, the individual's freedom to exit a group is supreme—it is "his only fundamental right, all other rights being derivative of this right, or rights granted by the community" (238).

As for Margalit and Halbertal, then, the right of exit is a linchpin for Kukathas in his entire argument. Building upon individual interests, the legitimacy of cultural communities to exert authority over their members exists only insofar as those members freely consent to remain affiliated with the group. But for Kukathas, *the mere fact of membership signals consent*, regardless of the manner in which membership came about. The person born into a cultural group (with any range of liberal or illiberal practices short of slavery and physical coercion) and the person who in adult life chooses membership in a group (again with any range of practices) are from the standpoint of free association exactly identical, the "decision" to associate morally equivalent.

It is no accident, then, that Kukathas firmly rejects the value of autonomy as important either to individual flourishing or the exercise of citizenship. His view "does not . . . suggest that human flourishing requires that the individual be capable of autonomy or have the capacity to choose his or her way of life on the basis of critical reflection on a range of options" (246). Instead, Kukathas uses language of "acquiescence," as in the following: "The basis of the community's authority is not any right of the culture to perpetuation, or even existence, but the acquiescence of its members" (239).[19]

Thus, despite the signal importance of the right of exit or freedom to dissociate, in Kukathas's view a person need not be autonomous in order to exercise this right. Autonomy is for Kukathas a moral value that the state has no right to impose because many cultural communities—Kukathas mentions the Pueblo Indians as an example—do not value autonomy and individual choice. Were the liberal state to insist upon the value of choice, says Kukathas, "the larger society would in effect be saying that the minority culture must become much more liberal" (243; cf. 246). Such a demand is in Kukathas's eyes an instance of oppression.

Strangely, though, Kukathas does say that it is "crucially important" that each individual "enjoy a *substantial* freedom to leave" (252; emphasis in original). But his idea of substantial freedom requires almost nothing. Kukathas mentions but two conditions: the existence of a wider society open to individuals who opt to desert a group and a wider society that values freedom of association. In other words, Kukathas's defense of cultural communities is parasitic on the existence of a larger *liberal* society. Paradoxically, illiberal groups may on Kukathas's theory thrive best in liberal societies (252).

To put it charitably, Kukathas has an extremely implausible view of what might count as a substantial right of exit.[20] It is as if the ability to exit a group were secured simply via conditions external to the group, with no concern for what capacities individuals might have to develop on their own in order to dissociate. Given the extent to which Kukathas is prepared to tolerate the il-liberal practices of cultural communities, are there no positive measures nec-essary in order to say with confidence that a person could choose to leave? Is nothing necessary in order to make this a meaningful right?

Here the significance of education reveals the fault line in Kukathas's the-ory, for surely a rudimentary education is a minimal necessity for a mean-ingful right of exit. But Kukathas rejects the idea that the liberal state can compel any cultural community to educate its children. According to Kukathas, "The wider society has no right to require particular standards or systems of education" (238). Indeed, he criticizes Rawls's liberal theory for requiring public education.[21] He defends the right of the Amish to withdraw their children from school; similarly, gypsies would not be compelled to send their children to school, nor even to provide them with any education at home whatsoever (247–48). But can we say, as Kukathas suggests, that a child whose cultural community deprives him or her of a basic education and en-gagement with the outside world possesses a meaningful right of exit?

Insofar as a "substantial right of exit" and the freedom to associate (even when association is construed as mere acquiescence) are central elements of Kukathas's multicultural theory, I contend that some basic educational mini-mum must be equally central. Kukathas's theory, in my opinion, fails the test of liberal justice the moment it permits cultural groups to inflict cruel pun-ishments upon its members. This seems obvious. But it also fails liberal jus-tice if it allows cultural communities to deny their children basic education, basic literacy, and some exposure to the outside world.

Though Kukathas claims that his theory is based strictly on liberal princi-ples of individualism, the restrictions he imposes on the liberal state from in-tervening in the affairs of cultural communities are too severe. Since, for Kukathas, the mere fact of membership indicates acquiescence, the liberal state has no basis for protecting the rights of individuals, short of preventing physical harm and slavery. When the failure to exit a group implies acquies-cence or free association with a group, the state under Kukathas's theory is al-most boundlessly tolerant; the sanctity of groups takes precedence over a real interest in the freedom and equality of the individuals within the group.

Let me be clear. It is not that Kukathas ignores the issue of education. In-deed, he addresses it directly, saying that it is conceivable and indeed justifi-able for cultural communities to decide not to provide children with an education. Should individuals as children, or later as adults, fail to leave the group, Kukathas will understand this to mean acquiescence or freely chosen association, which in turn legitimates the authority the group exercises over its members.

This illustrates nicely a common mistake made by multicultural theorists, namely, conflating completely the interests of the adult members of a cultural group with the interests of their children. Acquiescence of the adults is taken to imply acquiescence of the children. Take, for example, the following comment on gypsies: "Because gypsy custom does not value schooling, the parents believing they can educate a child satisfactorily through informal instruction in the ways of their culture, only a minority of children receive formal education. Their freedom to associate and live by their own ways, however, would, by my argument, make this permissible" (248). But if the concern here is for the *children's* education, we must speak not (or not only) of the *parents'* freedom of association but rather (or also) of the child's. As Kukathas himself states in a separate essay, consent of adults should not confer obligations upon descendants, who cannot be said to have entered into cultural arrangements voluntarily. "Children," Kukathas writes, "are clearly *involuntary* immigrants."[22] Yet if this is the case, Kukathas undermines his entire argument about the importance of freely chosen association and acquiescence. After all, children do not freely choose membership in any groups; they are born into them. Their voluntary attachment to a group will come only after a certain maturity, which, to give meaning to the word *voluntary*, will include an education that teaches children to be sympathetic but critical examiners of both their and others' ways of life.

Where Margalit and Halbertal defend the right of cultural groups to receive state assistance for separate educational institutions, Kukathas defends the right of groups to be left alone to educate their children as they see fit, even if that means no education whatsoever. As I have tried to show here, contrary to their protestations, the educational implications of their respective multicultural theories demonstrate the impossibility of calling either theory consistent with liberal values. Both theories self-consciously defend the legitimacy of illiberal practices by cultural groups within a liberal state. When those illiberal practices are directed against children, in, say, the form of an education that prevents engagement with the diverse beliefs of other groups or in the form of no education at all, the state at once undercuts a meaningful right of exit and disables the ability of children to become informed, politically active citizens. For this reason, the multicultural theories of Margalit and Halbertal and Kukathas are unjust from a liberal perspective.

Chapter Three

Kymlicka's Liberal Defense of Minority Rights

In contrast to the almost blanket endorsement for state support of cultural groups given by Margalit and Halbertal and Kukathas, Will Kymlicka offers a far more sophisticated "liberal theory of minority rights."[23] Unlike Margalit and Halbertal and Kukathas, Kymlicka emphasizes the value of personal autonomy and applies his theory only to groups whose internal practices are themselves liberal. In doing so, Kymlicka attempts to avoid the problem of placing cultural purity and integrity above individual freedom. I agree with much of what Kymlicka says. Indeed, in criticizing liberal neutrality in chapter 2 I drew heavily upon his argument, and I believe that his theory of multicultural citizenship provides a number of important insights about the problems of relying upon a set of universally applied individual rights in order to achieve justice in a multicultural society. Nevertheless, I argue here that his theory suffers from two problems that serve to undermine his argument and obscure the signal importance of education in a liberal society, especially with respect to who controls it and what its aims are. The first problem concerns his defense of rights to separate schooling as a form of protection for national minorities from the broader society; the second concerns his unsatisfactory conception of autonomy.

Before explicating these problems, a few comments on Kymlicka's overall project are in order. Like other multiculturalists, Kymlicka connects freedom with culture. Membership in a secure, rich, and stable culture is a precondition for freedom of choice and individual flourishing (80–83).[24] With this argument, Kymlicka provided the basic framework of multicultural theory which many others have since followed. Kymlicka's sophistication arises partly from the number of important distinctions he makes in the course of the argument. Three are worth mentioning here. First, Kymlicka distinguishes between political communities and cultural communities, arguing that people are owed respect both as citizens and as members of their cultural groups.[25] A political community (i.e., a state) is not necessarily coextensive with a cultural community (i.e., a nation or people), and in fact most political communities are composed of multiple cultural communities. Cultural diversity within countries is the norm. Yet not all countries are diverse in the same way. This leads to Kymlicka's second distinction, that between multinational states and polyethnic states. Multinational states are those composed of national minorities, peoples incorporated by conquest or agreement into a single political unit. Polyethnic states are those composed of various ethnic groups, peoples incorporated via voluntary immigration.[26] Switzerland is an example of a multinational state, a consociational arrangement among four different cultural groups. The United States is an example of a polyethnic state, a country of immigrants from across the globe who are permitted, even encouraged, to retain a sense of their ethnic identity. Of course, a country may be at once multinational and polyethnic. The United States fits this bill; Kymlicka cites American Indians, Puerto Ricans, descendants of Mexicans in the southwest, native Hawaiians, and the Chamorros of Guam as examples of national minorities in the United States (11). Kymlicka argues that both national minorities and ethnic groups should receive certain group rights, though national minorities lay claim to stronger and more substantial rights, possibly including territorial sovereignty, than do ethnic groups. Finally, Kymlicka distinguishes between two kinds of group rights that either kind of cultural group may receive. He supports what he calls external protections, which refer to the right of a group to limit the power of the larger society to regulate the group. He rejects what he calls internal restrictions, which refer to the right of a group to limit the liberty of its own members for the sake of cultural solidarity or purity (7, 35, 152). On the basis of these three distinctions, Kymlicka builds an impressive case for why liberals, without sacrificing a commitment to individual autonomy, can and should promote some group rights (those that are external protections) for cultural minorities.

When considering rights to separate education, however, the distinction between external protections and internal restrictions breaks down. Kymlicka says that "we should aim at ensuring that all national groups have the opportunity to maintain themselves as a distinct culture, if they so choose" (113). Control over education is central to this task; it is necessary, Kymlicka argues, in order to ensure that the assimilative pressures of larger society, and especially of public schools, do not undermine the ability of such groups to survive (38).[27] Only to the degree that the values of the cultural group conflict with or repudiate the values of larger society will exclusive and culture-centric forms of education be important. Cultural minorities whose survival is threatened by exposure to larger society often seek to educate their children in restrictive ways. But whereas separate schooling in these cases does indeed provide a form of external protection for the adult members of a cultural group, it also creates a definite internal restriction for the children of the group.

Kymlicka makes clear that he supports rights over schooling for national minorities. But he also supports exemption rights for isolationist religious groups, at least when they are rooted in historical agreements and when their numbers are not so large as to threaten liberal citizenship generally.[28] Adherents of religious groups who seek to shield their children from the modern secular world and do not participate in civil society, in Kymlicka's view, might best be considered as "partial citizens" and be permitted therefore to educate their children according to the norms and values of their particular religious culture.[29] Consider again the case of the Amish or fundamentalist Christians. Kymlicka's argument implies that minority religious groups should be permitted to educate their children according to the norms and values of their particular religious culture. As the testimony in each court case detailed, the purpose of separate education or exemption from parts of the public school curriculum was to protect children from the allegedly baleful influences of secular society. Engagement with diverse ways of life was said to threaten the existence of the Amish way of life and condemn fundamentalist children to eternal damnation. The stated educational aims of the Amish and fundamentalists were not to enhance the choice-making capacities of children, but rather to diminish them. Speaking generally, the more that separate schooling increases the likelihood that children will not come into contact with the broader environment, the less the chance that children will ever be able reasonably to assess their own way of life, much less other ways of life.[30] K. Anthony Appiah rightly warns that cultural rights designed to ensure the survival of minority groups may seem desirable and just insofar as they apply to adults who freely choose membership in a group or enjoy the capacity to examine critically the ends of that group. But children neither choose membership in a group nor naturally have the capacity to examine its ends critically. Respecting cultural groups, in short, may not respect the autonomy of future adults born into the group.[31] In this way, external protections slide into internal restrictions. In promoting multiculturalism at the level of society and extending group rights such as separate schooling, Kymlicka potentially sanctions a form of cultural compulsion at the level of individuals. The development and exercise of a person's autonomy, which Kymlicka says he cares about, may be sacrificed to the external protections afforded the minority group into which he or she is born.

To be fair, Kymlicka says often that all children must get a liberal education (92, 102, 204, n. 11). He writes, for example, that a liberal society "not only allows people to pursue their current way of life, but also gives them access to information about other ways of life (through freedom of expression), and indeed requires children to learn about other ways of life (through mandatory education)" (82). But if this is so, Kymlicka's defense of rights for national minorities and some isolationist religious groups stands in tension with his support of liberal education. Historically, one of the first desires of cultural minorities—national minorities more than polyethnic groups—is to exert at least significant, if not exclusive, control over the educational experiences of their children. And even among polyethnic groups the impulse to direct the education of the their own children is not uncommon.[32] The form of this education is often illiberal. As Amy Gutmann says, "To save their children from future pain, especially the pain of eternal damnation, parents have historically shielded their children from diverse associations, convinced them that all other ways of life are sinful, and implicitly fostered (if not explicitly taught them) disrespect for people who are different."[33]

Kymlicka asserts an "unrelenting commitment to individual autonomy," the consequence of which is a refusal to defend group rights for cultures that do not seek to develop the autonomy of their members (154). He also writes that "to learn public reasonableness, students must come to know and understand people who are reasonable and decent and humane, but do not share their religion."[34] But insofar as Kymlicka defends either special subsidies for culture-centric forms of education for cultural minorities (think of the demands of the Ultra-Orthodox) or broad exemptions from any form of education (think of the demands of the Amish or of gypsies), he falls into the same problem for which I criticized Margalit and Halbertal and Kukathas: a right to separate education potentially undermines the very conditions of autonomy or of a meaningful right of exit. Possibly one may interpret Kymlicka as rejecting any form of education that restricts social and intellectual interaction with other ways of life. (His main concern, in fact, often appears to be the right of minority groups to an education in their own language.) But Kymlicka defends the rights of at least some cultural groups to exercise control over the scope and content of education. Kymlicka must be clearer about whether his liberal theory of minority rights includes rights to separate education or broad exemptions from educational requirements that are otherwise binding on other citizens, and, if it does, the extent to which the theory can accommodate culture-centric, illiberal forms of education. At the very least, it seems to me, Kymlicka must grant that multicultural accommodations in education should be approached on a case-by-case basis, rather than deciding at the level of theory that national minorities should have rights to separate schooling or exemptions from schooling.

Perhaps Kymlicka's ambiguity about education is merely accidental; he might simply rule out illiberal forms of education and insist that all children, regardless of cultural affiliation, must be educated so as to develop their autonomy. But I suspect that the ambiguity is not simply accidental. It may be related to the second problem with Kymlicka's theory, namely, an unsatisfactory, and sometimes confusing, concept of autonomy.

Kymlicka offers an emphatic and unabashed endorsement of individual autonomy (94, 105, 164–65). For him it is an essential feature of liberalism: "Liberals are committed to supporting the right of individuals to decide for themselves which aspects of their cultural heritage are worth passing on. Liberalism is committed to (perhaps even defined by) the view that individuals should have the freedom and capacity to question and possibly revise the traditional practices of their community, should they come to see them as no longer worthy of their allegiance" (152). Kymlicka in fact criticizes Rawls's refusal to endorse anything beyond political autonomy (231, n. 8). Kymlicka believes, as I argued in chapter 2, that the exercise of political autonomy has important consequences for one's private commitments and beliefs. He believes, moreover, that autonomy is defensible on its own terms, regardless of its application to public or private identities (163). Simply put, "We must endorse the traditional belief in personal autonomy," writes Kymlicka (163).

Because of Kymlicka's commitment to autonomy and his rejection of minority rights for illiberal cultures, some people find his theory to be *insufficiently* multicultural and not respectful enough of cultural differences. Kukathas, for example, criticizes Kymlicka for his intolerance of groups that do not cherish the capacity for autonomy; for Kukathas, promoting autonomy limits diversity instead of protecting it (242 ff.). Similarly, William Galston says that Kymlicka's insistence on attempting to liberalize autonomy-retarding groups amounts to the "cultural equivalent of the Vietnam-era principle of 'destroying the village in order to save it.'"[35] For these theorists, Kymlicka's multicultural theory is not permissive enough.

I have criticized Kymlicka from the opposite direction. I share his commitment to autonomy, yet I believe that the provision of group rights for separate schooling potentially denies the educational conditions necessary for developing autonomy and exercising a meaningful right of exit. My question concerns not whether Kymlicka is too permissive, but his peculiar understanding of autonomy, an understanding that is intimately tied up with his entire theory of minority rights. The basic issue is this: Most often Kymlicka views autonomy in terms of its value in giving individuals the ability to choose among significant and diverse options *within* a cultural group. But it is questionable whether this is the sort of autonomy liberals should defend. Why must the autonomous choices of individuals be hemmed in by cultural boundaries? On some occasions, Kymlicka himself seems to uphold autonomy in terms of its value in giving individuals the ability to choose among significant and diverse options *among* cultural groups. The difference here is worth underlining, for the respective understanding of autonomy affects the scope of minority rights, especially concerning education, in absolutely critical ways.

Recall that Kymlicka justifies a concern for cultural rights precisely on the basis that membership in one's own culture is a precondition for intelligent choice-making. "Cultures are valuable, not in and of themselves, but because it is only through having access to a societal culture that people have access to a range of meaningful options" (83). To understand this fully, it is important to ask specifically what is meant by "societal culture."[36] Societal cultures, Kymlicka tells us, are equivalent to a nation or people, a culture "which provides its members with meaningful ways of life across the full range of human activities, including social, educational, religious, recreational, and economic life, encompassing both private and public spheres" (76; cf. 18). He emphasizes that societal cultures are usually "institutionally complete" (78, 98). This is an atypically broad definition of culture, and this is significant for at least two reasons. First, it excludes many groups we typically think of as defining a meaningful way of life, groups based on class, gender, disability, sexual orientation, religion, and so on (18). Second, and perhaps more important, it means that immigrant ethnic groups either do not have their own societal cultures or should not be permitted to recreate their societal culture in their adopted country (78, 101). In Kymlicka's theory, immigrants are expected to (or conceived of as expecting to) integrate into mainstream society; only national minorities and nations have societal cultures.[37]

The unusual capaciousness of Kymlicka's definition helps us to understand, however, what he means when he says that "freedom involves making choices amongst various options, and our societal culture not only provides these options, but it also makes them meaningful to us" (83). Kymlicka says that cultural membership is a precondition for autonomous decision making within cultures. Secure location in and identification with a societal culture is said to provide a horizon of choices, a menu of possible roles to assume. Most succinctly: "The freedom which liberals demand for individuals is not primarily the freedom to go beyond one's language and history, but rather the freedom to move around within one's societal culture, to distance oneself from particular cultural roles, to choose which features of the culture are most worth developing, and which are without value" (91–92). Freedom and autonomy for Kymlicka therefore refer to the capacity to examine and revise one's ends, *but first and foremost as these ends are contained within and made available by one's societal culture.*

It is instructive to contemplate the educational implications of this understanding of autonomy. I have already argued that a policy of supporting external protections in the form of separate schools may in practice result in internal restrictions. But now we are well placed to tease out of Kymlicka's theory its deeper educational implications. Paradoxically, Kymlicka's politically progressive multicultural theory seems to require a politically conservative educational theory. That is, insofar as Kymlicka values primarily the freedom to move around one's culture (and not among cultures), the corresponding education to facilitate such movement will be an education that teaches children the skills for intracultural navigation. Learning about the variety of roles and values within a societal culture, and acquiring the skills necessary to adopt one or some among these, will be a fundamental aim of education. The educational companion to Kymlicka's multicultural political theory, therefore, becomes something like E. D. Hirsch's program of cultural literacy. Hirsch's book by the same title makes the argument that for children to become free and equal adults they must receive an education that teaches them about their cultural traditions and symbols.[38] Cultural illiteracy is, in Hirsch's analysis, the cause of much social injustice, for it narrows the scope of options available within a culture, preventing social and economic mobility. Indeed, echoing my conclusions here with respect to Kymlicka's argument, Hirsch writes, "The goals of political liberalism require educational conservatism."[39]

Can educational conservatism be the necessary companion of a progressive multicultural political theory? Kymlicka's conception of autonomy as free choice-making within the scope of a societal culture leads in this direction. Yet is this the sort of autonomy that liberals should value? I want to suggest that it is not. The value and importance of autonomy lies in enabling not only choice within culture, but also choice beyond one's culture. Moreover, I wish to suggest that the exercise of autonomous choice-making within or outside of one's culture is promoted by, and may in fact require, learning about the values and practices of other cultures.

Kymlicka himself appears at times to waver on the conception of autonomy he upholds, and this is most evident when he discusses education. Kymlicka would resist the conclusion that the educational complement of his multicultural theory is a pedagogically conservative program of cultural literacy. When Kymlicka discusses the proper aims of education, he champions a more progressive theory of education. But in this more progressive theory, Kymlicka seems to suggest that autonomy is not merely the capacity to move within one's societal culture, but also among other societal cultures. In reaction to the objection, for example, that cultural rights may be invoked to prohibit cultural interaction, Kymlicka says that "liberals cannot endorse a notion of culture that sees the process of interacting with and learning from other cultures as a threat to 'purity' and 'integrity,' rather than an opportunity for enrichment" (102, 204, n. 11). Elsewhere, indicating his support for cultural change, he notes that "people should be able to decide what is best from within their own culture, and to integrate into their culture whatever they find admirable in other cultures" (105).[40] Finally, in his most direct comment on this matter, Kymlicka writes that though autonomy is dependent on membership in a culture, "Over time, individuals can put these cultural contexts themselves into question and choose which culture they wish to live in."[41]

Given these comments on education, Kymlicka evinces uneasiness with autonomy conceived as choice-making within culture. Of what value is mutual learning unless it is meant to contribute to an individual's freedom to question, revise, and even move beyond one's societal culture?[42] Kymlicka's uneasiness is warranted. There are several problems, from a liberal perspective, with understanding autonomy as choice-making only within culture.

First, Kymlicka notices only half of what it means for a societal culture to be a context of choice. Cultures do indeed provide a range of choices and a variety of roles to assume; they establish horizons of possibility for their members. But horizons also have limits; they indicate the boundaries of choice and circumscribe the roles that a person can adopt. Cultures constrain as well as enable. Note also that societal cultures are not all equivalent in their capaciousness. Despite the fact that societal culture is defined broadly, some societal cultures provide for much narrower ranges of options than others; some have more restricted menus of sanctioned roles than others.[43] If a culture sets the context of choice for individuals, beyond which it would be difficult if not impossible to choose, then horizons of opportunity are always delimited by the relative vastness or narrowness of one's culture. In emphasizing the way in which cultural membership enables choice, Kymlicka overlooks the way in which membership also constrains choice. Though it is plain that not all societal cultures are equal in the range of choices they make available, they are all of equal standing for Kymlicka. For Kymlicka focuses not on the particular range of choice offered, or the substance of the actual choices; instead his concern is simply that the societal culture *is* the context of choice. We need not argue against this claim, but why does it follow that this is the context of choice that matters? Put differently, Kymlicka argues that liberals should care about cultures because freedom is connected with culture. But from this premise it does not follow that liberals should concern themselves only with the cultural group into which one is born. With a broader conception of autonomy, liberals might wish to protect choice-making among cultures or allow a person to cobble together a life whose values derive from multiple cultures.

Second, to say that liberals should protect cultures because they provide a context of choice presumes in fact that cultural groups are easily identifiable. Given Kymlicka's broad definition of culture, is it true that societal cultures are so easily distinguished from one another? Are cultures unified? Part of what defines a culture, after all, in addition to a shared history and language, is a shared commitment to a particular conception of the good, or to a narrow range of these conceptions. Cultures are said to develop particular ways of life.[44] But the broader the range of roles and ends that cultures offer their members, the more difficult it becomes to mark cultures off from one another, and the more difficult it becomes to say what members share in common. Kymlicka notices this himself, saying that as various cultural communities have become more and more liberal, they have become more and more similar, blurring the boundaries where one culture begins and another ends (88).

Third, even presuming that cultures are readily distinguishable, is it true that each person belongs only to one? Some people, as Jeremy Waldron suggests, are "cosmopolitan" and grow up with multiple societal cultures providing the relevant context of choice.[45] Think too of a child born to parents who belong to different societal cultures, say of a Native American mother and a Euro-American father or of a French Canadian mother and a British Canadian father. What will be the relevant societal culture for this child? The increasing number of mixed-race and multinational children poses a de facto challenge to the relevance of societal cultures. In the next section on Joseph Raz, I take up this cosmopolitan alternative at greater length.

Kymlicka's response to these objections might be to reemphasize that although the context of individual choice is passed down by each person's culture, the right of each person to assess, criticize, and revise these choices remains absolute. Individuals may never transcend the societal culture of their birth, but they may engage in critical appraisal and revision of it. "It is of fundamental importance that we be able rationally to assess our conceptions of the good in light of new information or experiences, and to revise them if they are not worthy of our continued allegiance," Kymlicka writes

(81). But without exposure to and engagement with other cultural beliefs and practices, the scope of this new information and experience must already be contained within the structure of a societal culture. I submit that the kinds of information and experience most likely to be of value in assessing one's conception of the good (or the range of roles within one's societal culture) are precisely those to be found *outside* one's own culture.[46] To assess whether particular conceptions of the good or particular roles are worthy of our allegiance we require for comparison some other, rival, conceptions of the good. These rival conceptions may conceivably be found within one's societal culture, but for the purpose of rational assessment and comparison, we may need to look beyond the scope of the familiar. For the purpose of actual revision, wherein new elements are incorporated into the culture, interaction with other cultures is probably a necessity.

It would take a detailed psychological and sociological argument to substantiate this claim. But the basic idea is that only the superhuman self-generate cultural criticism; for the rest of us, it is encounters with foreignness and novelty (through literature, friendship, travel, and so on) that spur us to assess or revise what we take as given. Reflect quickly upon your own experience: do not the moments in which the limits of the possible are most thrown into question—the moments when novel possibilities of how to lead a life present themselves most vividly, the moments that inspire us to call into question the way we have led our lives—occur most often when we experience something utterly foreign? Kymlicka insists that individuals must "have the conditions necessary to acquire an awareness of different views of the good life, and an ability to examine these views intelligently" (81). One of these conditions, I suggest, is not only *intracultural* learning and comparison, but *intercultural* learning and comparison.

But if intercultural learning and comparison are valuable, then why should the context of choice or range of options of another societal culture remain closed off to an individual? Insofar as mutual learning between cultures is valued, so too should a conception of autonomy that permits choice among cultures be valuable. And as previously suggested, we need not conceive of intercultural choice as binary—either we belong wholly to one societal culture or we reject it and affiliate with another. Autonomous choice among cultures may mean simply the freedom to appropriate the values of other cultures for oneself, to assert shifting allegiances and affiliations, and above all, to create for oneself a context of choice that extends beyond the culture of one's birth.

From a liberal perspective, then, Kymlicka's theory of multiculturalism is deficient in two respects. First, though he firmly endorses autonomy, his support of rights to separate schooling for national minorities and some isolationist religious groups potentially undermines its development and exercise. Second, his conception of autonomy as choice-making within culture may be found too limited. Kymlicka is right to connect autonomy and freedom with cultural membership, but it should not (need not) follow from this that the scope of autonomy is properly limited by cultural membership. Nor should it follow that the liberal state should enforce this limitation through its institutions. Liberals typically wish to defend the widest possible freedom for individuals; this is consistent not with predetermined cultural horizons but with autonomous choice whose bounds range beyond one's own culture. Such autonomous choice does not imply encouraging individuals to revise or reject their cultural affiliations; it implies instead that education must not be culture-centric, if the possibility of assessment and revision is to be made real.

THE MYOPIA OF RAZ'S LIBERAL MULTICULTURALISM

The final theorist I wish to examine is Joseph Raz, who has argued that liberalism in a sense entails multiculturalism. Raz presents the most staunchly liberal version of multiculturalism, defending autonomy in terms more emphatic than even Kymlicka and supporting choice-making within and among cultures. Yet despite Raz's liberal multiculturalism, his theory suffers from two significant problems. First, Raz falsely presupposes that individuals possess an allegiance or affiliation to a single culture. Just as societies may be multicultural, so too may individuals. Second, Raz's theory, like those of many other political theorists, is too often blind to the existence of children. This lacuna leads him to give arguments about autonomy that ultimately are contradictory; Raz strongly supports autonomy for all individuals yet appears prepared to exempt autonomy-retarding cultural groups from any state effort to develop autonomy in their children. Taken together, these problems call into question the practical usefulness and ultimate coherence of Raz's liberal multiculturalism.

Raz builds his case for liberal multiculturalism from an interest, at heart classically liberal, in the freedom and well-being of individuals. In Raz's view, liberalism exalts autonomous choice, which in turn gives individuals freedom of self-definition and makes possible individual flourishing: "Liberalism upholds the value for people of being in charge of their life, charting its course by their successive choices."[47] Further, the freedom to make choices is not a capacity that naturally springs forth from within individuals. Radical self-creation is a utopian (or perhaps dystopian) fantasy; we do not create our-selves, or choose among life's options, untethered to the social world. On the contrary, choices make sense only within a social context. Autonomous choice presupposes shared meanings and common practices among individuals.

For Raz, however, the social context he has in mind is quite specific: it must be a *cultural group*.[48] "Only through being socialized in a culture can one tap the options which give life a meaning. By and large one's cultural member-ship determines the horizon of one's opportunities, of what one may become, or (if one is older) what one might have been" (177). Furthermore, Raz ar-gues, an individual's connection with a cultural group constitutes one's sense of identity.[49] With the honor and dignity of one's identity at stake, it follows that slighting or, worse, persecuting a cultural group insults or discriminates against members of that group.

If a liberal government is interested in the flourishing of its citizens, then, it must necessarily take an interest in the well-being of the variety of cultural groups living within its borders. This, according to Raz, is not because cultural groups have some independent and overriding moral importance, but be-cause integration within a cultural group is a "precondition for, and a factor which gives shape and content to, individual freedom" (178). This conclusion mirrors that of Kymlicka, for whom culture and freedom are connected. Be-cause liberals concern themselves with the freedom and prosperity of indi-viduals, they must also concern themselves with the vitality of cultural groups. An awareness and support of multicultural policies thus arises di-rectly from liberalism's basic emphasis on individual freedom and well-being.

Two additional features of Raz's liberal multiculturalism are worth noting here. First, Raz comments that autonomy—the ability to choose freely—is meaningless without a diversity of valuable options from which to choose. A liberal's interest in fostering autonomy means that an individual's connec-tion to a cultural group must be respected and secure, that the individual must enjoy some real measure of choice *within* that cultural group, and, more significantly, as Raz sometimes seems to say, *among* cultural groups. Auton-omy, Raz writes, "is valuable only if one steers a course for one's life through significant choices among diverse and valuable options." He stresses that, "The picture this pluralistic and autonomy-based liberalism suggests is one in which the community and its institutions foster and encourage a wide range of diverse forms of life among which individuals are left freely to choose."[50] Freedom and flourishing, for Raz, mean having the autonomy to make choices both within and among cultural groups. For this reason, Raz champions a "right to exit," by which he means "the right of each individual to abandon his cultural group" (181). In short, valuing autonomy *within* groups places limits on what the state can do to groups and individuals; valuing autonomy *among* groups places limits on what cultural groups can do to their members.

Second, Raz makes plain that liberal multiculturalism does not imply the museumlike preservation of cultural groups. Change is inevitable, cultures are dynamic. "[Liberal multiculturalism] is not a policy of conserving, fossilizing some cultures in their pristine state" (181). Cultural groups are valuable only insofar as they contribute to the well-being of their adherents. When cultural groups are repressive or stagnant, liberal multiculturalism counsels intervention, for "fossilized cultures cannot serve their members well in contemporary societies" (182). Some cultures, like slave cultures, racially discriminatory cultures, and homophobic cultures, can be supported only by "neutraliz[ing] their oppressive aspects" (184) and guaranteeing a right of exit from them. In all cases, however, Raz urges "restraint and consideration in thinking of the means" (185) of intervention.

Raz's Presumption of Individual Monoculturalism

Raz's liberal multiculturalism is a policy of fostering and encouraging the cultural and material prosperity of cultural groups within a society while also protecting the right of individuals to exit a cultural group. It means, for example, that the state should generously support independent cultural organizations and that public institutions and private companies should respect the traditions (clothing, holidays, etc.) of cultural groups. It also has important implications for education: while all should learn and respect "the history and traditions of all the cultures in the country," children should be educated "if their parents so desire, in the culture of their groups" (189).

Raz's language throughout his essay, particularly in the latter remark about education, betrays one of his fundamental assumptions: individuals belong to only one cultural group. Everywhere Raz emphasizes that individual freedom and well-being are possible only with "unimpeded membership in *a* respected and flourishing cultural group" (189; see also 174, 177–78); he notes that children should be educated in "*the* culture of their groups"; he thinks the right of exit is important as a safeguard "for members who cannot develop and find adequate avenues for self-expression within their *native* culture" (187; my emphasis). Nowhere does Raz countenance the possibility of multiple cultural allegiances and loyalties.[51] According to Raz, societies are multicultural, but individuals are monocultural.

Why does Raz assume this? Here it might be helpful to turn to his definition of "cultural group." He fails to offer a precise definition in the liberal multiculturalism essay. He offers, however, a careful and detailed definition of a very close relative (perhaps twin)—"encompassing groups"—in a separate essay.[52] Encompassing groups are "groups with pervasive cultures" and groups where membership "is important to one's self-identity."[53] This already sounds like a "cultural group." But more significant for the comparison is Raz's statement that "the key to the explanation is in the importance of these groups to the well-being of their members."[54] The argument of this second essay, moreover, parallels the argument of the multiculturalism essay. Raz discusses, for example, the importance of membership in an encompassing group for the ability to make choices; since identity is tied up in such groups, it is harmful when groups are not respected. In almost every respect, then, when Raz talks about cultural groups, it sounds very much like the encompassing groups he discusses elsewhere.[55]

Let's be more specific. Raz says that encompassing groups are usually nations or peoples, but that they could also be racial, religious, or social classes.[56] Given this definition, one might expect that membership in multiple encompassing or cultural groups would be a normal and common phenomenon. Many people are simultaneously members of a racial group with a pervasive culture, a religious group with a pervasive culture, and a nation. Each of these memberships, individually and collectively, may be important for the person's identity and well-being. Yet Raz does not recognize this possibility. He notes that though "people growing up among members of the group will acquire the group culture," they need not be "indelibly marked." He explains, "People may migrate to other environments, shed their previous culture, and acquire *a new one.*"[57] Cultural emigration is possible; cultural *mélange* is not. The obvious assumption about monocultural individuals remains. Raz's explicit definition of encompassing groups provides no help in understanding why he never considers the possibility of multicultural persons. To the contrary, it only reinforces the impression that he views individuals as possessing, at any given time, membership in one and only one culture.

What evidence or argument exists to support my contention that individuals can be multicultural? Two reasons come immediately to mind: the facts of demography and biology; and philosophical arguments for "cosmopolitanism."[58] By the "facts of demography and biology," I simply mean to call attention to the increasing prevalence of mixed race and mixed-cultured persons.[59] Take for example, Tiger Woods. Woods is by birth part Thai, part Caucasian, part Native American, and part black. If racial groups can constitute cultural groups, as Raz admits, then at least two of these—Native American and black—qualify under current American social understandings as clear cultural groups. Furthermore, Woods was raised religiously as a Buddhist, which again qualifies as a cultural group under Raz's standards. Woods would appear to have allegiances to at least three cultural groups, by birth and early socialization (not by later emigration or mixing). Is it possible, or necessary, to identify one of these as primary? If schools are charged with educating children in the culture of their group, which culture will the school choose when educating a Tiger Woods? Can Tiger Woods be said to have a single "native culture?"

Jeremy Waldron gives some philosophical underpinning to the idea of multicultural, or, in his phrase, cosmopolitan individuals.[60] While Woods is rapidly becoming a multiracial icon, Waldron identifies Salman Rushdie as the paradigmatic cosmopolitan, a person who embodies and takes pleasure in appropriating and mixing himself into multiple cultural traditions. As Rushdie writes,

> I was born an Indian, and not only an Indian, but a Bombayite—Bombay, most cosmopolitan, most hybrid, most hotchpotch of Indian cities. My writing and thought have therefore been as deeply influenced by Hindu myths and attitudes as Muslim ones. . . . Nor is the West absent from Bombay. I was already a mongrel self, history's bastard, before London aggravated the condition.[61]

If not the racial mixture of Tiger Woods, then the national and religious hybridization of Salman Rushdie certainly gives cause to see these individuals as multicultural.

Waldron goes on, however, to give a host of other reasons for seeing Rushdie's hotchpotch self as the norm rather than as a freakish occurrence. Waldron notes the economic, moral, and political interdependence of human beings, arguing that our interdependence causes us to mix and mingle so that the borderlines of cultures are never clearly drawn. His conclusion reads as a direct rebuke to Raz, though Raz was writing two years after Waldron: "The cosmopolitan strategy is not to deny the role of culture in the constitution of human life, but to question, first, the assumption that the social world divides up neatly into particular distinct cultures, one to every community, and, second, the assumption that what everyone needs is just *one* of these entities—a single, coherent culture—to give shape and meaning to his life."[62] Societies are sometimes a confederation of cultures; so too are individuals sometimes a confederation of selves.

The phenomenon of multicultural, hybrid individuals thus challenges Raz's liberal multiculturalism in three ways. First, and most directly, it undermines his assumption that individuals are monocultural. Second, the admixture of cultures, both within individuals and within societies, makes it increasingly difficult to identify cultures as having clear boundaries; they are no longer Herderian wholes. It may be the case that cultures are most like weather patterns, blurred at the edges, one area seeping into the next. And third, if the previous two are correct, Raz must revise his belief that secure location within only one cultural group "is a precondition" for individual freedom (178). On the contrary, individuals may construct their identity and exercise their autonomy within a multiplicity of cultural frameworks. Thus, cultural groups must still be respected and supported, for they provide the material from which individuals gain sustenance and meaning. But Raz must now admit that programs of cultural support should not be aimed at protecting the integrity and flourishing of cultural groups; rather, they should provide for the possibility of blurring and admixture.

Autonomy for Illiberal Cultures?

The previous objections call into question the practical utility of Raz's liberal multiculturalism. The existence of multicultural individuals poses, as it were, an empirical challenge to Raz; it does not necessarily call into question the internal coherence of his argument. Multicultural individuals, in other words, may still fit into Raz's theory, for the importance of culture for individual freedom and well-being has not been called into question.

It seems to me, however, that problems with Raz's views on autonomy threaten to undermine the very logic of his argument. Raz argues for autonomy as a key value, one which enables individuals to chart their own course through life by making successive choices about who they are and what they will become. Yet Raz is also prepared to exempt certain cultural groups, even those which are autonomy-retarding, from state intervention. Raz is able to do this, I suggest, because he fails to consider the position of the child and instead focuses his attention on the fully developed autonomy of adults. Ignoring the potentially precarious position of children, his liberal multiculturalism promotes policies that may leave children within illiberal and nonautonomous groups a life without choice.

This is a strange and counterintuitive objection with respect to Raz, for within the range of contemporary liberal theorists, Raz is perhaps the preeminent defender of autonomy. Indeed, throughout much of his writing Raz notes again and again the central importance of autonomy. To wit: "We regard the fact that a life was autonomous as adding value to it. We think of our own lives and the lives of others as better for having been developed autonomously."[63] Recalling William Galston's division of liberalism into autonomy and diversity strands, Raz certainly elevates the capacity to choose over the maintenance of diversity. Raz notes, "Autonomy is, to be sure, inconsistent with various alternative forms of valuable lives."[64] Hence, a liberal society that prizes autonomy may be less diverse than a liberal society that prizes diversity. Raz doesn't hesitate here: "For those who live in an autonomy-supporting environment, there is no choice but to be autonomous: there is no other way to prosper in such a society."[65]

To what extent is Raz prepared to promote autonomy among the various cultural groups in an autonomy-based liberal society? At times, Raz appears prepared to go to great lengths to ensure that all citizens are autonomous. "One particular problem concerns the treatment of communities whose culture does not support autonomy. These may be immigrant communities, or indigenous peoples, or they may be religious sects. . . . Since they insist on bringing up their children in their own ways, they are, in the eyes of liberals like myself, harming them."[66] Raz contemplates the coercive closure of separate schools for illiberal cultural groups. But he finally decides that the viability of a culture is what should decide the level of intervention. The less viable and more stagnant a culture may be, the greater justification for intervention. As Raz says, the claims of multiculturalism "should not be pursued regarding cultural groups which have lost their ability to perpetuate themselves" (173). One indication of a stagnant cultural group, Raz notes, is when "the allure of surrounding cultures means that the vast majority of their young people wish to assimilate" (173). Thus, one strain of Raz's thought appears unshakably committed to the development of autonomy, even at the price of assimilating youth into other cultural groups.

Within this strain, children seem to figure prominently in Raz's considerations—he worries about the education of youth in an autonomy-retarding environment; he looks to children's choices in perpetuating their communities as an index of the cultural group's vibrancy. How odd it is, then, when another strain of Raz's thought is blind to the existence of children and exempts clearly illiberal groups from state intervention.

For starters, there is the previously cited passage where Raz says that if the parents desire it, children should be schooled in the culture of their group (189). This stands in simple contradiction to his statement that groups unsupportive of autonomy actually harm their children by raising them in their own ways. But the problem is larger than this simple contradiction.

The heart of the problem lies in Raz's consideration of the limits of tolerance, namely, the limits of how tolerant the autonomy-based liberal state that Raz supports can be of illiberal, autonomy-disregarding cultural groups. Raz states outright, "The limits of toleration are in denying communities the right to repress their own members, in discouraging intolerant attitudes to outsiders, in insisting on making exit from the community a viable option" (190). Yet Raz understands "repress their own members" to refer to adults in whom the capacity to choose is already developed. Repression would not include, to his mind, teaching children in ways that were not supportive of, or disabled, autonomy; therefore schooling within one's own group is not only tolerated, but encouraged.

Elsewhere Raz justifies restraint in intervention on the grounds that it violates the very autonomy of the adults within the illiberal cultural groups. "Governments should not use repressive measures . . . to discourage victimless immoralities. For such measures interfere with people's general standing as autonomous human beings."[67] It is clear from the context that the "autonomous human beings" of whom Raz speaks are all adults. A victimless immorality includes, apparently, raising children in a non-autonomous environment. How do we know this? In a footnote, Raz states that his argument "does not apply to enclaves of traditional premodern communities within our societies."[68] The Amish, in other words, are exempt from the framework of liberal multiculturalism. In the name of respecting the autonomy of adults, then, Raz demotes the autonomy of children.

By making children subservient to their parents' interests, by encouraging an education enclosed within a cultural group, Raz, the paradigmatic autonomy liberal, thereby condemns children born into autonomy-disregarding groups to a life without autonomy. Only in cases when the cultural group is deemed to be stagnating (and who is to make this decision?) does Raz grant the state leverage to intervene. This is extremely difficult to reconcile with Raz's other arguments for the superior value of the autonomous life. If Raz truly believes that parents "harm" their children when they discourage the development of autonomy in them, if he truly believes that the autonomous life is indeed "better," why then is he willing to tolerate illiberal cultural groups, vibrant though they might be? Raz ought to support state intervention into illiberal and autonomy-retarding cultural groups. He ought not say that all children should be educated, if their parents so desire, in the culture of their groups. He ought to guarantee that children, regardless of their group membership, are exposed to a variety of ways of life in order to promote an awareness of other life options. Raz's own words make the case:

"Since we live in a society whose social forms are to a considerable extent based on individual choice, and since our options are limited by what is available in our society, we can prosper in it only if we can be successfully autonomous."[69] By tolerating autonomy-disregarding groups, Raz not only makes it possible that their children will lead non-autonomous lives, he also makes it *impossible*, by his own argument, for them to lead flourishing lives.

A LIBERAL critique of multicultural theories finds significant problems that can be classed into four main categories. First, liberalism is inconsistent with measures of both positive and negative freedoms that various multiculturalists wish to extend to cultural groups. Margalit and Halbertal argue that minority cultural groups deserve state support in order to sustain and promote the flourishing of their ways of life. Kukathas argues that minority cultural groups should be self-governing, without interference from the state in all but the most extreme circumstances. The educational implications of these positive and negative freedoms, for these theorists, range from publicly funded separate schools that shield children from broader society to the right not to educate children at all. Both of these educational aims are unacceptable from a liberal standpoint. Second, liberalism demands that children's interests not be conflated with those of their parents. Respecting the autonomy of adults to affiliate themselves with cultural communities should not issue in respect for adults to educate their children in any manner they see fit. Third, the very notion of multiculturalism appears to assume that individuals possess only one cultural attachment. Liberals countenance the possibility, even the likelihood, that individuals may have multiple cultural attachments. Finally, there is some tension between conceiving autonomy as choice-making within culture and conceiving autonomy as choice-making beyond or among cultures. Which is the sort of autonomy that liberals should defend? How is autonomy connected to the ubiquitous right of exit championed by almost all multicultural theorists? The considerations of this and the preceding chapter, as well as these latter questions, necessitate a closer examination of autonomy. What does it mean to be autonomous? What sort of autonomy is most defensible or desirable in a liberal society?

FOUR

Minimalist Autonomy

> *The purpose of education, finally, is to create in a person the ability to look at the world for himself, to make his own decisions, to say to himself this is black or this is white, to decide for himself whether there is a God in heaven or not. To ask questions of the universe, and then to live with those questions, is the way he achieves his identity.*
> James Baldwin

The concept of autonomy captures something central to both the liberal tradition and multicultural theory in that it serves to inspire a respect for the dignity of individuals and the choices they make about how to lead their lives. The promotion of and respect for the autonomy of persons helps to do justice to the importance of cultural affiliations and attachments in our lives. The idea of autonomy figures prominently in the theories of liberals and liberal multiculturalists examined in the preceding chapters. Rawls explains why autonomy is necessary as a political ideal—for our roles as citizens in generating and consenting to principles of justice that are to govern the basic institutions of society and in deliberating about questions of public policy in the forum of public reason. Kymlicka and Raz go further, defending autonomy as a personal ideal—for its signal importance in our lives as individuals in enabling us to affirm, evaluate, and potentially revise our conceptions of the good. Whereas Rawls defends only a circumscribed ideal of political autonomy, Kymlicka and Raz endorse autonomy as a fundamental and pervasive ideal, encompassing both public and private identities and interests. In some sense, then, the liberal multicultural projects of Kymlicka and Raz turn out to be more broadly liberal than Rawls's political liberalism.

We have also seen, however, that other theorists *reject* autonomy as an important liberal or multicultural ideal. They hold that it is too wrapped up in individualist notions of the self or in comprehensive and controversial ethical

89

visions of the good life. Galston and Kukathas, as we have seen, give far greater priority to tolerance than autonomy in the liberal state, wishing to protect ways of life that prize obedience to authority over Socratic self-examination. Yet it is not always clear that theorists are talking about the same thing when they describe autonomy, the meaning of which ranges considerably from theorist to theorist. Autonomy turns out to be an extremely slippery concept.

If, as I believe, much of the controversy over the demands of liberal civic education turns on what it means to educate a person to be autonomous, it is of crucial importance to specify the meaning of autonomy. Prior to the question of whether the liberal state should educate for autonomy is another, and more fundamental, question: *What does it mean to be autonomous?* Given the centrality of this concept to discussions of liberalism, multiculturalism, and education, we should not rely on a set of intuitions about the meaning of autonomy, that is, self-creation, self-rule, freedom, individuality, choice-making. These varying intuitions fail to cohere; indeed, on closer inspection, they come into conflict. For this reason, appeals to autonomy often trigger rival and sometimes misleading interpretations. In this chapter, I aim to define as carefully as possible what I mean by autonomy in order to make clear why a liberal state should educate people to be autonomous. I shall defend what I call "minimalist autonomy," a modest conception of this much-invoked but rarely specified ideal. Let us begin by considering the very concept of autonomy.

Introducing the Concept

The idea of autonomy, like so many philosophical concepts, dates back to ancient Greece. Its root meaning comes from the Greek *auto*, meaning "self," and *nomos*, meaning "rule." Autonomy, understood as self-rule, originally applied not to individuals but to Greek city-states. To say that a state is autonomous, in ancient Greece or still today, is to indicate that the state enjoys, or should enjoy, the right to self-governance. Proponents of a Palestinian state, for example, often invoke the notion of autonomy in arguing that the Palestinian people should possess rights to self-determination and territorial sovereignty. Indeed, when considering the frequent cries for respect for autonomy in all corners of the world, from Iraq's demand that others respect its autonomy to nationalistic demands for the establishment of autonomous states in the Balkans, it is clear that autonomy is a deeply entrenched notion in global politics.

Autonomy also has deep roots in modern philosophy and political theory, referring not to states but also to persons.[1] People as well as states are said to be autonomous, or to have interests in autonomy. There are obvious parallels between autonomous states and autonomous persons—both indicate something about the freedom of a state or person to rule itself in some general sense, to be free from the coercion of outsiders. Almost all the theorists I have examined invoke personal autonomy. Rawls argues, for example, that the autonomous decisions of persons are the legitimating conditions of the establishment of principles of justice by which all consent to be governed. Kymlicka's defense of group rights, to take another example, applies only to minority groups that respect the autonomy of their members. Several critics have commented, correctly in my opinion, that many political theorists simply assume autonomy to be a valuable condition and avoid either defending it or explaining what is meant by it.[2] But as I have tried to show here, autonomy cannot be viewed as uncontroversial. On the contrary, it is a much-contested ideal in terms of its definition as well as its worthiness. William Galston and Chandran Kukathas both argue, for instance, that a liberal preoccupation with autonomy opposes deep cultural diversity;[3] indeed, one of the central claims of chapter 2 was that Rawls's defense of political autonomy is what makes political liberalism non-neutral to cultural groups.

But the importance of the idea of autonomy extends far beyond political theory; it is a key concept in a staggering range of fields. In addition to political philosophy, the concept of autonomy is central to moral philosophy, bioethics, psychology, feminism, rational choice theory, and philosophy of education.[4] Debates in psychology echo philosophical debates in the way that autonomy is sometimes alleged to be a universally desirable ideal and sometimes alleged to be a cultural artifact of some societies and not others. Some psychologists see the absence of autonomy as predictive of psychopathology; others see its presence as a potentially pathological Western ideal of consumerist individualism.[5] For a concept so widely invoked across disciplinary fields, it is surprising that so little consensus exists concerning its meaning and importance. Or perhaps its plasticity is what accounts for its popularity.

In what follows I examine the idea of autonomy as it applies most specifically to work in political theory. My purpose in doing so is not to engage in conceptual analysis of the ordinary meaning of the word. I am not trying to capture the underlying architecture of how people use the term. I intend rather to provide and defend a particular but rigorous characterization of the concept, one that I hope will be compelling, especially for those who consider themselves committed to liberal values. In the interest of foreshadowing my conclusions and introducing some of the vocabulary I use, I define autonomy as a person's ability to reflect independently and critically upon basic commitments, values, desires, and beliefs, be they chosen or unchosen, and to enjoy a range of meaningful life options from which to choose, upon which to act, and around which to orient and pursue one's life projects. To say that a person is autonomous is to say something about the individual and about the broad social and institutional environment in which the individual lives. I will defend this definition as a modest or minimalist conception of autonomy, the capacity for and exercise of which is necessary for persons to participate actively in civic affairs and in order to lead a good life.[6] In the course of defending a minimalist conception of autonomy, I also highlight the way in which autonomy is notoriously susceptible to distortion or misinterpretation by its detractors. In spite of their criticism of autonomy, Galston's and Kukathas's arguments, on closer inspection, turn out to depend on the minimalist brand of autonomy I defend. It will be useful to begin this discussion by making three distinctions.

THREE DISTINCTIONS

First, when speaking about the autonomy of a person, we may refer variously to the autonomy of a specific action or the autonomy of a person's life or character. Gerald Dworkin characterizes this as local versus global conceptions of autonomy.[7] It is possible to discuss whether a person acted autonomously in a particular situation. To make such a determination, we might ask whether an individual felt free to act in the manner she chose or whether the act was in any way coerced. We would want to know whether an individual had weighed various alternatives or whether the act was undertaken unthinkingly or reflexively, whether an individual shaped the action herself or whether she acted merely by aping the actions of others. But autonomy is better understood globally, applying not to discrete acts but to a person's life as a whole. When we ask whether or not people are autonomous actors or agents, we normally mean to ask about the extent to which they are able to lead the life they desire for themselves, to act upon the commitments, values, wishes, and beliefs they deem worthy. We are asking whether they exhibit an autonomous *character*, a character that is exhibited in the way that a person adheres to his conception of the good life. Autonomous persons are discernible not on the basis of any particular act but on the basis of the overall shape they give to their lives, the freedom they have in making decisions for themselves that relate to fundamental aspects of their lives.

To bring out the importance of thinking about autonomy as a character ideal, consider the reasons one might want to respect another person's autonomy. When political theorists invoke the autonomy of individuals, they do not mean to refer to any singular act but rather to a person's overall life. If I respect your autonomy, I do not respect your right to make your own decisions in isolated instances but your right to chart the course of your own life, to affirm and pursue a conception of the good. A repressive government might allow its subjects the right to choose autonomously which supermarket to patronize or what car to drive but forbid religious freedom or restrict a certain class of persons from career opportunities. We would not say, however, that this government respects the autonomy of its citizens. Autonomy properly refers, then, not to discrete acts but to the general scope of a person's life, especially to those decisions of great significance for the quality of one's life as defined by each person. Political theorists talk about the autonomy of persons not because it is important that we act autonomously in every instance, but in order to indicate the importance of individual control of one's life and freedom from the control of others.

The second distinction to be made is whether autonomy should be conceived as a matter of degree or as an "on/off" capacity or condition. Are people autonomous in differing degrees, or are people simply autonomous or not autonomous? This appears to be an easy question: for obvious reasons, autonomy must be a matter of degree.[8] People are not born autonomous. Infants, as well as the very aged or very sick, are utterly incapable of directing their lives and are fully dependent on other human beings for their care. If autonomy implies the ability of people to make independent and meaningful decisions about the sort of life they wish to lead, then autonomy is something that must *develop* and that will be exercised in different degrees at different stages of life.[9] Furthermore, the exercise of autonomy will vary by degree not only within each person over a lifetime, but also by degree across persons. Individuals are variously capable of leading autonomous lives, some more so than others. Some people exhibit stronger autonomous characters than others do. A range of factors contribute to the degree to which any individual exercises autonomy, including physical and mental health, wealth, native talents, social conditions, and family attachments, to name just a few. Different biological and environmental endowments certainly affect, though they do not determine, the capacity of any individual to exercise autonomous choice. The capacity for and exercise of autonomy is not something equally distributed.

Yet this picture of autonomy as a matter of degree does not tell the whole story. While the extent to which people *exercise* autonomy may vary, *respecting* autonomy is a different matter. Here autonomy is not considered a matter of degree but an on/off condition. Governments (or people) either respect the autonomy of an individual or not; they do not respect autonomy variably, commensurate with the degree to which persons themselves are autonomous. If a government policy is justified on the basis of a respect for autonomy—such as prohibitions on paternalistic action—then all people who are autonomous are respected equally, without regard to the degree of autonomy they exhibit. Policy should not discriminate among those who are highly as opposed to moderately autonomous.[10] Government policies crafted on the basis of respecting autonomy commensurate with the degree to which individuals are autonomous would seem unfair and would almost certainly be impossible to implement. Consider, for example, how to justify policies concerning the age of consent. Rather than attempting to measure the extent to which different individuals exhibit the maturity necessary to make autonomous decisions about engaging in sexual relations, the state simply assumes that individuals of an agreed-upon age are autonomous. It would be disturbing if the state were to justify its paternalistic policies on the basis of an investigation into the autonomy of each individual; the means to do so would likely be highly intrusive. Instead, the state marks off some people as non-autonomous (e.g., severely mentally handicapped persons, psychopaths, etc.) and considers all others as autonomous.[11] A common way of explaining this distinction is to defend a "threshold" conception of autonomy, meaning that once a person surpasses a basic threshold capacity for autonomy, he must be respected as a completely autonomous person.[12] Above a certain threshold, autonomy may no longer be seen as a varying capacity, but rather a condition or feature of a human being that is "on."

I wish to highlight this circumstance, for it points to a very important aspect of autonomy—a distinction between exercising the *capacity* for autonomy and respecting the *condition* of autonomy—that often leads to confusion. In a liberal multicultural society, people are certainly free to forgo reflection on their lives for the sake of fidelity to tradition. In granting them this right, liberal societies express respect for autonomy. Thus, a theorist who argues that respect for autonomy is important may generate from this a host of rights that restrict others from intervening in the person's affairs. Indeed, autonomy is often connected to the very idea of rights, and is said by some to undergird the notion of human rights.[13] But a theorist who defends the importance of exercising autonomy may generate from this not (only) rights against interference but (also) certain policies to encourage its development. These policies may even be paternalistic, interventions that cut against the stated preferences of an individual. Even when children approach the threshold capacity for autonomy, it may be inappropriate for teachers or others to respect their autonomy. Instead, they might appropriately act to foster its fuller realization.

The final distinction to note is that between autonomy and the closely related ideas of freedom and liberty. In casual discussions, autonomy is often equated with freedom and liberty. To be sure, autonomy implies the ability and interest of a person to act freely. Conversely, restricting a person's freedom or liberty inhibits what a person wishes to do, which in turn can constrain the kind of life she wishes to lead, which therefore undermines her autonomy.[14] But being autonomous is not reducible to acting freely. Autonomy carries with it an implication of directing one's life through choices made independently and reflectively. To be free or to have liberty implies, on the other hand, an absence of constraints (negative liberty) or organization of character (positive liberty) that enables choice-making but says little about the overall course and character of a person's life. Gerald Dworkin gives an example of people who elect to restrict their lives in various ways—for example, by entering a monastery or joining the army. Their lack of liberty, however, does not indicate that they lead non-autonomous lives. Conversely, people may possess freedoms and liberties but still not be autonomous. Impressionable young adults are free to mimic in every possible way the lifestyle of their favorite movie stars; but to the extent that they slavishly follow suit, never making their lives their own, we would not say that they lead autonomous lives. Similarly, an average person may have the same freedoms and liberties as every other person, but, by dint of mental incapacities, poor health, or even bad luck that dictates the sort of life he leads, have drastically reduced autonomy. In general, then, we may say that freedom and liberty are conducive to autonomy but not dispositive of it. It is hard to imagine a person exercising autonomy without ever possessing any significant freedoms. But the mere presence or absence of freedom cannot determine whether or not a person is autonomous.

To summarize: Personal autonomy is best understood as referring to the overall life of an individual, not to specific acts. Further, insofar as we refer to the capacity for or exercise of autonomy, it is best conceived of as a matter of degree; but insofar as we refer to respect for the autonomy of persons, it is best conceived of as an on/off condition. In the first case, individuals display differing degrees of autonomy; in the second case, individuals either are autonomous or not. Finally, autonomy is related but not reducible to liberty or freedom. This discussion, I hope, has brought out many aspects of and under-lying intuitions about autonomy. I turn now to examine several definitions of this complex term.

A Range of Definitions

Autonomy has been given a wide range of definitions by numerous philoso-phers and political theorists over the years. These definitions invoke a variety of ideas, some familiar from the three distinctions I just made. Autonomy is said to involve, among other things, self-legislation of moral laws, self-creation, self-authorship, the Socratic examined life, self-determination, sover-eignty, authenticity, integrity, freedom from outside influence, freedom from obligations, independence, individuality, simple freedom, simple agency, or the basic capacity to make choices.[15] Quite obviously, complete self-legislation of moral laws is an exponentially more stringent conception of autonomy than simple freedom or capacity to make choices. In the former case, autonomy is defined so demandingly that few persons could be said ever to be auton-omous; in the latter case autonomy is defined so laxly that few could be said ever to be non-autonomous. The purpose of this brief section is not to review every possible definition but to illustrate the range of definitions of auton-omy, setting the stage for my own defense of minimalist autonomy in the next section.

The most demanding and perhaps most influential definition of auton-omy is that of Immanuel Kant.[16] Kant described what is often referred to to-day as moral autonomy. Autonomy for Kant is understood to be a property of the rational wills of all human beings. Humans display or exercise their au-tonomy by generating through their reason moral laws which are binding not only for themselves but for all humanity. Kant's famous "categorical im-perative" enjoins that a person act only according to those maxims that can be consistently willed as a universal law. In this way moral autonomy makes each person both author and subject of the moral law. But as Thomas Hill notes, Kantian autonomy implies not merely self-authorship and imposition of the moral law; it implies also that internalized moral principles must be recognized as "unconditional requirements of *reason*."[17] Moral autonomy, as Kant conceived it, severs autonomy from emotion and worldly passions and connects it deeply with rationality. Now the idea that each person gener-ates the moral law of the universe from within, binding both for oneself and others, is an extraordinary ideal but hardly something realized in practice by average human beings.[18] Moreover, Kant has been criticized for his exces-sively rationalistic view of autonomy, which seems to vitiate the possibility of acting autonomously if we choose to act out of loyalty or love rather than out of duty to the dictates of reason.

Slightly less stringent than Kantian moral autonomy is autonomy conceived as self-creation or authorship. To speak of an autonomous life as one that is self-created is to indicate that an autonomous person blazes her own path in life, generating for herself the moral ideals she follows (but not that others follow as well). Alexander Nehamas describes well what self-creation entails:

> To create a self is to succeed in becoming *someone*, in becoming a *character*, that is, someone unusual and distinctive. It is to become an individual, but again not in the strict sense in which an individual is anything we can point out and reidentify, anything that, like human beings and material things, exists independently in space and time. To become an individual is to acquire an uncommon and idiosyncratic character, a set of features and a mode of life that set one apart from the rest of the world and make one memorable not only for what one did or said but also for what one was.[19]

This is the image of the radical individualist or Nietzschean superman who overcomes the prevailing and common forms of life around himself and invents his own way of living. The self-creator, unlike Kant's morally autonomous person, need not answer to the unwavering voice of reason. On the contrary, our notion of the self-creator probably owes much to nineteenth-century romantic visions of the artist who follows inner passions, somehow alone in the world, crafting in the process a wholly unique life.[20]

Similarly, to speak of an autonomous life as authorship is to indicate that a person plays the singularly decisive role in making his life what it is, crafting an existence as a writer crafts a novel. Self-authors may not be the actual creators of the panoply of values their lives embody or the set of goals they pursue; in authoring their own existence they may borrow or appropriate values and goals from others. But they suffer from the existential equivalent of the anxiety of influence. They are burdened by the weight of historical influences. Self-authors seek to be original. Never does one slavishly follow tradition or custom; neither does one pattern oneself after idols or heroes; nor does one adhere to a pre-existing moral code, like a religion. Instead, the autonomous person as author composes a life from the variety of cultural values and goals around him or her.

But while we may at least recognize something potentially human about an autonomous life as self-creation or authorship, very few persons would qualify as autonomous by this definition. Few would, I believe, even desire to be autonomous by this definition. It is the rare individual who creates a new existence or form of life, the rare individual who wishes away the traditions and customs of familiar and time-honored communities. The problem is that self-creation and authorship cut against communal ties, often forged by birth and therefore unchosen, that play important parts in our lives. But our membership in communities is usually not taken to indicate a lack of autonomy but is seen instead as a necessary component of leading a worthy and fulfilling life. The autonomous person as self-creator or author registers very high on a scale of individualism or self-reliance, traits that often seem connected to the concept of autonomy. Yet this need not be so. Autonomy as self-creation or authorship seems unable to encompass many kinds of lives we would consider to be characterized by some appreciable degree of autonomy. Consider, for example, people who find freedom, peace, and happiness through faith in some deity and active participation in a religious community. Despite their religious devotion, we would likely say that they still may direct their lives, may still choose from among many options the kind of people they wish to be and become, and most important, may still decide in the future to revise or reject the commitments, religious and otherwise, that they have made. It must be possible to be autonomous yet not invent or script one's own existence. Autonomy ought not be equated with atomistic individualism.

A somewhat more modest, realizable and, I would suggest, desirable conception of autonomy is that of sovereignty or self-determination. The sovereign or self-determined life is one in which no outside person or force controls a person's destiny. Sovereign individuals are free to make significant choices about how they will lead their lives, capable of reflecting upon their current commitments, values, and goals, and potentially revising or rejecting them if they come to decide they are no longer worthy; they actively shape their lives through the cumulative decisions they make over the course of a life. To be a self-determining person is consistent with communal ties and obligations, provided the person is capable of reflecting upon, reassessing, and potentially changing such ties and obligations. Think of persons who choose to devote themselves to the received traditions of their family, who opt to forgo opportunities to live different kinds of professional and personal lives in order to remain closely attached to their children and relatives. An autonomous person as sovereign is neither coerced into particular commitments or decisions nor drifts aimlessly through life without asserting herself and pursuing the goals and projects she values and desires. The idea of autonomy as sovereignty or self-determination appears more resistant to the charge that more exacting definitions of autonomy exclude the majority of humans from its regular exercise. But sovereignty and self-determination stand in need of fuller description to count as full definitions of autonomy. In particular, the idea of reflection upon commitments, values, and goals seems to indicate a split-level view of the self, where a higher-order self reviews or reflects upon the lower-order motivations of the same self.

MINIMALIST AUTONOMY

The foregoing discussion indicates the breadth and variety in the way autonomy has been conceived by philosophers and political theorists. My discussion also hints at my conviction that the best, or most defensible, conception of autonomy is a minimalist one.

Moral autonomy in the Kantian sense, or as self-creation or authorship, describes an ideal of character that is at once beyond the grasp of most human beings and probably not desired by them anyway. Few of us are capable, or even wish, to govern our lives exclusively according to the universal dictates of reason.[21] I suspect that equally few wish to be self-creators or authors of their own existence. The loyalties and attachments that people have, either by birth or by choice, to various groups—family members, neighborhoods, peers, occupations, professional associations, ethnic groups, religious communities, and nations, to name but a few—function in most lives as crucially valuable compasses for living a good and flourishing life. People typically find no inconsistency between saying that they chart their own course in life and control their own destiny and knowing that others may be charting the same course or pursuing the same destiny. Indeed, it is the explicit desire of many people *not* to be self-creators or authors, but to lead lives conjointly with others, to be like other people. In short, conceptions such as Kantian moral autonomy and self-creation or authorship are too exacting to encompass the forms of life most people actually live or would wish to live.

Strong conceptions of autonomy are troublesome, then, because they are rarefied. They describe an ideal that only a few may achieve. Let me be clear, however. That strong conceptions of autonomy are rarely achieved by real people need *not* be a mark against such conceptions. It is when autonomy performs an important role in the foundational architecture of a political theory that we can begin to see how an exacting ideal can be problematic. As I mentioned earlier, people have an interest in exercising autonomy not only because of the putative goodness of an autonomous life but also because it grounds the notion of respect for autonomy. To respect a person's autonomy, in the liberal tradition, proscribes paternalistic actions and prescribes a discriminating toleration, even when people's actions affect others in less than beneficial ways; it delimits a sphere of inviolability around individuals, permitting them to pursue the kind of life they wish to lead. For some, autonomy is the very foundation of rights. But if strong conceptions of autonomy lead us to conclude that only a few people will in fact be autonomous, then respect for autonomy would appear to apply only to those rare few. Perhaps one might argue that states and persons should treat all individuals as if they were autonomous, except in a few egregious and agreed-upon cases. Such a claim obfuscates the simple fact that autonomy is not an inborn or developmentally inevitable condition. In order to generate good reasons for respecting the autonomy of persons, the state needs also to take careful steps to promote the development of autonomy. If a political theory grounds the notion of rights or respect for human beings in their autonomy, a strong conception of autonomy seems to undermine the theory.

For these reasons, and others discussed below, we should defend a minimalist conception of autonomy. Minimalist autonomy will not insist that an autonomous life be one that makes the person both author and subject of universal moral laws, nor will it insist that people create for themselves a life unlike any other. What is important for a minimalist conception of autonomy is that autonomous persons are self-determining, in charge of their own lives, able to make significant choices from a range of meaningful options about how their lives will unfold. Isaiah Berlin, describing positive liberty, captures the general idea well:

> I wish to be the instrument of my own, not other men's, acts of will. I wish to be a subject, not an object. . . . I wish to be a somebody, not nobody; a doer—deciding, not being decided for, self-directed and not acted on by external nature or by other men as if I were a thing, or an animal, or a slave incapable of playing a human role, that is, of conceiving goals and policies of my own and realizing them.[22]

Minimalist autonomy will describe a character ideal that is not utopian but realistically attainable by human beings who live in autonomy-promoting environments and who receive support for its development.

To begin to give the idea more shape, consider what happens when a person has a so-called mid-life crisis. Ann, let us say, has led a conventional middle-class life, attempting to balance the demands of her career and her family. She lives in the suburbs, participates occasionally in local community organizations, and maintains a small circle of friends much like herself. Ann's mid-life crisis, were she to have one, would involve an evaluation she makes about the worthiness of the life she leads and the person she has become. She steps outside herself, figuratively, and assesses the values her life embodies, the commitments she has made, and the goals and projects she pursues. Her sense of crisis arises when she concludes that her life is not as worthy as she once thought or that she once hoped it would be; she realizes that, on re-flection, she is dissatisfied with at least some of the central values, commit-ments, goals, and projects of her life. She decides that her life is not flourishing, according to her own lights, and she wishes to reorient it, chart a new direction, rejecting or revising some of her previous commitments. We can imagine innumerable scenarios here. Perhaps she wishes to quit the "rat race" and move to the country; perhaps she wishes to move to the city and pursue artistic talents that she had abandoned years ago; perhaps she realizes she has married poorly and has made compromises that she wishes she hadn't; or perhaps she decides that being closer to her aging parents is more important to her than she once thought. The details are unimportant. What I mean to highlight is the way in which a mid-life crisis reveals the sense in which people can evaluate important life commitments, desires, projects, be-liefs, and so on, and, on reflection, attempt to alter them *or* to reaffirm them on an autonomous basis.

I use a mid-life crisis as an illustration not because autonomy presupposes moments of radical disorientation or because the exercise of autonomy de-mands that we break with the course of our past lives. Far from it; au-tonomous persons exercise their autonomy, though less dramatically, in everyday life. The point of the example is sharply and vividly to illustrate the exercise of an autonomous character. It is also important to avoid drawing the conclusion that autonomy is unsettling or threatening. On the contrary, ex-ercising minimalist autonomy can be construed (and experienced) as empow-ering. The capacity to direct one's life, or potentially redirect it, is better seen as testimony of the strength rather than fragility of a person. It points up the manner in which persons who possesses an autonomous character are able to reflect upon the worthiness of their lives and act upon such reflection. That people in a mid-life crisis consider making important changes in their lives, even painful ones, calls attention not to their confusion but to their sense that they are in fact in control of their lives. It underscores the deeply-seated no-tion that acting as pilot of one's course in life is important.[23]

Organizing this basic idea into more philosophical language, we may say that minimalist autonomy refers to the ability of persons to examine and evaluate their underlying commitments, values, desires, motivations, and be-liefs. Humans are capable, that is, of forming second-order volitions about their first-order desires; they form preferences about their preferences.[24] For instance, I may desire to drink beer every evening yet also desire not to want to drink beer. I may be agnostic but desire to discover a deeper religious motivation. In short, the exercise of minimal autonomy reflects the capacity of humans for reflective self-examination.

Important to this second-order reflection is that it is independent, not controlled by others. It is possible, in other words, for my friends to inform me that my daily beer-drinking routine is problematic and force me to stop (or enroll me in a prevention program). It is possible for my proselytizing parents to compel me to devote myself to God. But we would not say that the person who unhesitatingly and unthinkingly followed the advice or exhortations of others was autonomous. The formation of second-order preferences must be uncoerced, the product of a person's own reflective and evaluative capacities. Independence of judgment is integral to minimalist autonomy.

An important qualification must be made here, however. It may appear that minimalist autonomy excludes certain forms of life—those committed, for example, to obedience to tradition, or to rules, or to a ruler. But this reflects a view of autonomy that associates the ideal with individualism. There is ample room for many different ways of life, including those that are rooted in faith, within the ambit of autonomy. The devout Catholic whose daily actions and life projects hew closely to a prescribed path may appear to lead a non-autonomous life. But this person may have decisively committed himself or herself to Catholicism after deep reflection, choosing quite consciously and purposefully to lead a religious life of careful and dutiful fidelity. What matters for minimalist autonomy is that the decision to lead a life of any sort—liberal or traditionalist, agnostic or devoted, cosmopolitan or parochial—be reached without compulsion from others and always be potentially subject to review, or critical scrutiny, should the person conclude that such a life is no longer worth living.

We might worry, however, that choosing autonomously to live a substantively dependent life is in tension with autonomy as a character ideal. As Eamonn Callan argues, the autonomous person needs actually to *use* the skills of autonomy—critical self-reflection, for example—to ward off non-autonomous preference formation and in order to sustain one's autonomous character.[25] The implication here is that an autonomous person who chooses to be, say, an obedient servant to a religious doctrine or leader, will slowly begin to acquire emotional dispositions and susceptibilities that, over time, make it unlikely that he will at some future date deploy the skills of critical self-reflection that would permit a reevaluation of his commitments, values, and beliefs. In short, though the devotee chose to live a substantively dependent life, absent other venues in which to exercise the skills of autonomy, the long-term effects of such a life will be to corrode his autonomous character. Callan is right to say that autonomy is not an automatically self-sustaining character ideal; in order to have the capacity for autonomy, one must at least occasionally exercise independent and critical self-reflection. A person ceases to be autonomous when she is no longer capable of summoning forth critical self-reflection. Yet while the corrosion of an autonomous character is possible, it is equally possible that the religious devotee frequently reaffirms his decision to lead an obedient life. We can imagine the religious devotee who is tempted and tested yet nevertheless remains steadfast in his belief and devotion. This person's autonomous character is more likely to be reinforced than corroded.

Contrary to popular conception, therefore, autonomous persons are not marked off by their individualism and self-reliance. Autonomous persons are distinguished from non-autonomous persons by the way in which they adhere to, and continue over time to endorse, their conceptions of the good. I agree with Joseph Raz when he writes, "The life of an autonomous person is distinctive not by what it is, but how it has come to be what it is."[26] A conception of minimalist autonomy places no *prima facie* restrictions on the kind of life a person may lead. According to this conception, a person may be a surfer or a scholar, devout or agnostic, recluse or socialite, rugged individualist or deeply committed to a community.[27] What matters is the extent to which people subject their commitments, values, and beliefs to critical scrutiny, the extent to which people consent to and view their motivations as authentically their own, not the imposition of others.

Gerald Dworkin comments that a person who always does whatever her mother tells her may still count as autonomous.[28] The quip is meant to reflect his view that procedural rather than substantive independence is what is important to autonomy. But when we acknowledge that autonomy is a character ideal and not merely a set of skills that is occasionally deployed by a person, we must distinguish between two forms of procedural independence: weak and strong.[29] Weak procedural independence is true, I contend, while strong procedural independence is false.

Weak procedural independence marks the fact that it is logically possible for a person autonomously to come to endorse any way of life, including a non-autonomous way of life. To the extent that a person is procedurally independent in the weak sense, autonomy is consistent with any conception of the good. That is to say, autonomous persons exhibit weak procedural inde-

pendence insofar as it is possible to endorse a way of life that eschews deep reflection on a regular basis. To the extent that we autonomously choose a life
marked by substantive dependence, we exhibit the (weak) procedural independence of an autonomous character.[30]

Strong procedural independence suggests, however, that in becoming capable of autonomous choice, a person will not be predisposed to favor any
particular species of conceptions of the good over alternative species. (By a
species of conceptions, I mean a subclass whose members bear a strong family resemblance, such as those that entail rigid hierarchical social relations.)
But this cannot be true. Minimally autonomous persons will not be indifferent or neutral to ways of life, endorsing them simply on the basis of their individual preferences or because they happened arbitrarily to find themselves
as a result of their birth a part of one way of life rather than another.
People who exhibit an autonomous character, precisely because they have an
autonomous character and not just a toolbox of skills they can deploy, will be
predisposed to endorse ways of life in which they can exercise their autonomy. The upshot is that while it is intelligible to say that a person can autonomously choose to lead a non-autonomous life, as a sociological matter it
is highly unlikely that autonomous persons will endorse such a life with
great frequency. Minimally autonomous persons will be procedurally independent in the weak but not in the strong sense.

I want to emphasize, again, however, that minimalist autonomy, even
when construed as a character ideal, accommodates the obvious fact that a
great majority of our initial commitments, values, beliefs, and so on are initially unchosen. Minimalist autonomy does not describe an ideal of persons
who create themselves out of whole cloth, individuals abstracted from the
sinews of everyday life. Much, after all, in a person's life is initially *unchosen;*
we are never unencumbered selves. People are born in a specific place, at a
specific time, to a specific family, and in specific communities each with specific histories. We do not choose our family, country, color of our skin, initial
religion or lack thereof, social milieu, language, or historical moment. Each of
these factors unquestionably colors our lives in involuntary ways. But that
these encompassing factors of life are unchosen does not obviate the possibility of exercising autonomy or of coming to possess an autonomous character.
While we do not begin life as agents capable of reflecting critically upon the
conditions of our birth, such a capacity may develop over time as we move
from childhood to adulthood. Insofar as this capacity for second-order critical
reflection does develop and is exercised free from coercion, a person can
achieve minimalist autonomy.

Yet critical and independent second-order reflection on first-order commitments, values, desires, and beliefs is not the entire story; it is a necessary but not sufficient condition of minimalist autonomy. We must add still one more element. In addition to scrutinizing one's own ends, the exercise of minimalist autonomy requires that in making decisions about how to shape and order one's life a person have real options from which to choose. Independent and critical reflection on first-order commitments would be of little value if, after deciding that one's commitments no longer commanded one's allegiance, there were no others to adopt or pursue. As Raz says, "A person is autonomous only if he has a variety of acceptable options available to him to choose from, and his life became as it is through his choice of some of these options."[31] For self-determination to have value, persons must be able to make choices from an array of real possibilities.

These possibilities, moreover, must be meaningful, not trivial. If the only options open to me are small variations on the same theme, the value of the menu from which I choose is nil. To say, for example, that I exercise autonomy in choosing a beverage, I must be able to choose from a variety of different drinks—that is, milk, juices, sodas, wines, beers—not just from an assortment of ten different kinds of bottled water. But this illustration is potentially misleading, for meaningful choices of minor things as what beverage to drink do not contribute mightily to a person's autonomy. Meaningful options in major areas of one's life—where one lives, one's job, one's friends, one's religious beliefs, with whom one associates, one's relation to cultural beliefs—are what contribute to the making of an autonomous life. To the degree that options in these areas are limited to an identical or similar set of choices, individuals will lack autonomy. Choice is implicit in autonomy; but it is *quality* and *variety* of choice that matters, not necessarily *quantity.*[32]

Summarizing, then, the conception of autonomy I defend refers to a person's ability to reflect independently and critically upon basic commitments, values, desires, and beliefs, be they chosen or unchosen, and to enjoy a range of meaningful life options from which to choose, upon which to act, and around which to orient and pursue one's life projects. Minimalist autonomy understood as self-determination encompasses both evaluative capacities and a real ability to act on one's evaluations, if necessary adopting new commitments, changing one's values, altering previous desires, or revising old beliefs from a spectrum of meaningful possibilities. Before moving on to consider the important distinction between exercising autonomy and respecting autonomy, I wish to touch on two final points.

First, the obstacles to (any conception of) autonomy can be either *internal* or *external*, or both. Typically people consider external impediments to be the main obstacles to autonomy. External impediments are constraints on action, potentially including coercion, indoctrination, legal restrictions, physical restraint. A prisoner locked in a cell is not autonomous, and neither is a slave. The prevention of external impediments results in a defense of negative liberty. But there are internal impediments to autonomy as well. These potentially include mental and physical handicaps or diseases, a lack of reason, anomie, or, perhaps most important, pervasive ignorance. A mentally deranged person, for example, is not autonomous because she is not self-determining, she lacks an ability to reflect critically upon the major commitments of his life, potentially changing them. Avoidance of relevant internal impediments is a defense of positive liberty. As Lawrence Haworth puts it, autonomy implies the absence of external obstacles through self-rule vis-à-vis others and the absence of internal obstacles through self-control vis-à-vis oneself.[33] The development and exercise of autonomy, then, implies conditions of both negative and positive liberty, a self that is both free from others and internally empowered in important ways.

Second, minimalist autonomy is fully compatible with relational views of the self, with social embeddedness. A familiar criticism of autonomy is that it posits an "atomistic" or excessively individualistic view of the self.[34] If human agency exists on a spectrum from complete transcendence of communal attachments and traditions to complete immanence within communal attachments and traditions, the frequent tendency is to associate autonomy with transcendence. It is easy to see how an exacting conception of autonomy lends itself to this attack: autonomy as reliance on the self in a process of self-creation appears to ignore the social nature of human lives. The notion that to be autonomous, people must isolate themselves from others or consider their own ends and goals in the abstract, whatever that may mean, is indeed a corrosive view of our communal lives. But nothing about minimalist autonomy implies that the self is isolated or abstract, or even completely self-reliant. As I have argued, minimalist autonomy is consistent with individuals whose lives are deeply shaped by the community or communities of which they find themselves a part. It is equally consistent with individuals who follow the life paths set out for them by their parents (or community, or ethnic group, or nation, etc.), provided they are capable of forming second-order preferences about their first-order preferences and have a range of meaningful options from which to choose.

In fact, according to psychologists with views of autonomy similar to my own, autonomy not only is compatible with communal attachments but may require them for its support. Shorn of intimate and enduring relationships to others, autonomous development is thwarted as people feel unmoored or without foundation.[35] Such conditions lead not to second-order reflection on first-order values, beliefs, and life projects but to disabling feelings of alienation or disorientation. Autonomous persons are not mere corks afloat in a turbulent sea, bobbing unpredictably from one moment to the next as they are presented with an endless series of choices.[36] Nor are autonomous persons so given over to independent and critical self-reflection that they become paralyzed with uncertainty about their values, life plans, and projects.[37] Autonomous persons are revocably connected to other persons, groups, values, and life projects. Having an autonomous character in no way militates against deep and enduring attachments. Minimalist autonomy demands not atomistic individualism but the capacity for independent and critical second-order reflection. The ultimate outcome of critical reflection may never result in revision or rejection of the commitments, values, and beliefs that accompanied the conditions of a person's birth. It may instead result in affirming their familiar commitments, values, desires, and beliefs. Minimalist autonomy is not an ultra-intellectual conception. It does not expect people to be like Socrates. It is true that minimalist autonomy must be achieved—that is to say, it is not a simple property or inheritance of human beings—but it is not so demanding a capacity that it either presumes a deeply individualistic self or remains unattainable for many people.

RESPECTING AUTONOMY VERSUS EXERCISING AUTONOMY

To this point, much of my discussion has focused on what it means to exercise autonomy. Yet as I mentioned earlier, the idea of autonomy plays an important role in political theory not merely for the character ideal it outlines but for what follows from its possession. When a person is autonomous, governments and persons must, it is argued, respect his autonomy. Respect for the autonomy of persons can be (and is often) understood as a right that protects people from external interference.[38] When medical ethicists argue, for example, that patients, not doctors, should be permitted to make crucial decisions about the use of life support, the argument rests most often on respect for the autonomy of the individual.[39] So important is respect for autonomy that it is simply assumed by many economists and political theorists to be the normal condition of persons, grounding their expressed preferences and desires.[40] Preferences and desires shouldn't be respected, after all, if they really don't belong to the person or if they are the products of some process that precluded independent reflection and meaningful choice.

But respect for autonomy is clearly not the same thing as the exercise of autonomy. Respecting autonomy involves treating autonomy as an "on/off" condition; exercising autonomy is a matter of degree. Problems arise when theorists fail to make the distinction and obfuscate the conflicting implications of each. Respect for autonomy presupposes the capacity for its exercise. It would make little sense to respect a person, with all the implications that follow from it, for a capacity which she did not possess. But a single-minded insistence on the importance of respect for autonomy results in an imposition of negative liberty and fails to treat autonomy as a value to be pursued and supported. By contrast, promoting the capacity of persons to exercise autonomy leads in the opposite direction, toward support for policies that encourage positive liberty. Put simply, insofar as we respect a person's autonomy, we must delimit a sphere of noninterference around the autonomous individual; respecting autonomy counsels *against* paternalism. Insofar as we promote the capacity for and exercise of autonomy, however, we must create an environment and policies and programs that encourage and foster its development; promoting autonomy potentially *favors* paternalism, especially with respect to fostering autonomy in children. The allure of negative freedom is that it respects a person's ability to act autonomously, carving out space for a person to direct the course of her life. But nurturing the capacity for and exercise of autonomy must come *before* we respect it. The state should violate respect for autonomy in efforts to foster its exercise.

Theorists could miss this conclusion, however, in at least three possible scenarios. First, a theorist could miss the distinction between respect for autonomy and the exercise of autonomy, focusing only on respect. Second, a theorist could miss the distinction and focus only on its exercise. Third, a theorist could acknowledge the distinction but respect only the autonomous decisions of adults (because they do in fact exercise autonomy), which in turn could potentially compromise the development of the capacity for autonomy in their children. Let us examine the problems in each scenario.

The problem in the first scenario is fairly obvious. In invoking autonomy understood only as respect for autonomy, a theorist indicates the extent to which the state or other people are required not to interfere with the decisions each individual makes about his life.[41] But, as I have just argued, if opportunities for individuals to develop the capacity for autonomy are not provided, the state undercuts the very reason given for respecting its exercise. This realization is part of the reason why juveniles are often not punished to the same degree as adults are for identical crimes: the state recognizes that the capacity for autonomy is undeveloped in children. It is in part the reason why the desires of young children not to attend school are not respected: limits on autonomy at one stage can contribute to the exercise of autonomy later. Exclusive focus on respect for autonomy in this way can lead very quickly to constraints on its exercise. None of the theorists I have examined in earlier chapters commits this error, but some commit the next two.

The problem in the second scenario is the mirror image of the first, though the way it is problematic is much different. Some theorists focus on autonomy understood only as its exercise. But because they view the exercise of autonomy as unnecessary for leading a good life, they reject autonomy as an essential liberal ideal. As we saw in chapter 2, William Galston says that tolerance and deep diversity properly lay at the heart of liberalism, not autonomy. The state, according to Galston, has no business asking its citizens to exercise autonomous thought: "Autonomy is one possible mode of existence in liberal societies. . . . The devotees of autonomy must recognize the need for respectful coexistence with individuals and groups that do not give autonomy pride of place."[42] Similarly, Margalit and Halbertal and Kukathas argue that the promotion of autonomy actually limits diversity in its corrosive effects on communities that do not encourage the development of autonomy. Exercising autonomy asks too much, say these theorists; rights of exit are sufficient protection for individuals.[43] Each of these theorists wishes to give greater latitude to individuals and communities to pursue forms of life that do not valorize the exercise of autonomy.

Unfortunately, none of the theorists offers a detailed definition of autonomy, equating it simply with an emphasis on choice-making. Now if autonomy is conceived in the stringent ways I described above—as moral autonomy or as connected to the substantively independent life of the rugged individualist or self-creator—I would be inclined to agree with their conclusions that the promotion of autonomy would be unjust. But given the definition of minimalist autonomy, I believe that the claims of each theorist in fact rest on respect for the autonomy of individuals. Galston, Margalit and Halbertal, and Kukathas all defend people or groups who lead lives that they call non-autonomous. Thus they defend, for example, the rights of the Amish or the Ultra-Orthodox. But they mistake a way of life as indicative of one's autonomy or non-autonomy, rather than focusing on the how one adheres to a conception of the good. As I argued earlier, no way of life is on its face non-autonomous. Procedural rather than substantive independence is necessary. It is possible, then, to describe Amish or Ultra-Orthodox adults as leading autonomous lives. I emphasize the word "possible" here, for what will determine the relative autonomy of their lives in my minimalist conception is the degree to which they possess a character that enables them to reflect critically and independently on their lives and, if they so decide, to change them. Minimalist autonomy, after all, underwrites the very idea of a right of exit, which each theorist defends. To exit a group, people must be able to reflect critically and independently on their commitments, values, desires, beliefs, and so forth, and to choose something new from a range of meaningful options. Thus, in defending a right of exit, Galston, Margalit and Halbertal, and Kukathas are actually supporting and respecting a conception of minimalist autonomy.[44]

Moreover, we can discern in their single-minded rejection of the exercise of autonomy an implicit respect for autonomy. In rejecting autonomy, they are defending the rights of individuals (and, in Margalit's and Halbertal's case, cultural groups) to be free from governmental interference. Each theorist wants greater leeway for people to lead lives that do not comport with the exercise of autonomy. In essence, they are arguing that governments should respect the autonomy of people (or cultural groups) to lead non-autonomous lives. In rejecting the exercise of autonomy they necessarily import a respect for it. The more vociferously they argue that the state should not interfere with autonomy-neglecting cultural groups, the more strongly they imply a respect for the autonomy of individuals in those groups. But as I have just argued, respecting a person's autonomy makes sense only insofar as there are conditions for its exercise. If I am right, then, it is incoherent to defend non-autonomous individuals or groups on the basis of a respect for autonomy. Before one can respect autonomy, one first needs to take steps to foster its development. Because, however, these theorists spurn the exercise of autonomy as necessary, they do not support conditions that encourage the development of autonomy for all. In defending educational policies of separate schooling or exemptions that serve potentially to retard or prevent the development of autonomy in children, Galston, Margalit and Halbertal, and Kukathas effectively undermine their own arguments against governmental interference in the lives of adults who lead lives that do not prize choice-making.

Galston, Margalit and Halbertal, and Kukathas might object that the conditions for the exercise of minimalist autonomy are so low that all can be assumed to achieve it. The mere fact of being human, they might argue, suffices to qualify a person as minimally autonomous and generates the restrictions on intervention they seek to defend. But this is clearly false. There are the obvious cases of infancy and old age, in which the capacity for critical and independent reflection is either nil or radically diminished. But leaving aside these easy cases, consider whether society should respect the autonomy of a depressed and suicidal man or the incessant cravings of a drug-addict. The person may insist that he in fact is committed to dying, or explicitly wishes to take drugs. But in such cases, we override respect for autonomy and intervene because we believe that the person is in the grip of something that over-whelms his rational sensibilities. In respecting the autonomy of the suicidal man, we allow him to demolish any future use of his autonomy; in the case of the drug addict, we say that the addiction is in control of his life, not him. Thus the mere fact of being human is not sufficient to establish a case for re-specting the autonomy of persons.[45]

The arguments of Galston, Margalit and Halbertal, and Kukathas there-fore founder with respect to their rejection of autonomy. Their claim that the exercise of autonomy is not necessary for leading a good life ultimately rests on a respect for minimalist autonomy. What, then, of the third scenario, in which a theorist recognizes the value of autonomy *and* distinguishes be-tween respect for autonomy and the exercise of autonomy, but neglects to take seriously the need to develop the capacity for autonomy in children. The problem, as should now be clear, is that such theorists fail to register the po-tential conflicts that arise in respecting the autonomy of adults in the deci-sions they make about the education of their children.

Will Kymlicka and Joseph Raz commit this mistake. As we saw in the pre-vious chapter, both are strong defenders of the ideal of autonomy. But they are strangely blind to the fact that children are not born autonomous and must be educated to develop their autonomy. Kymlicka defends group-based rights to education that, granted to parents who wish to socialize their chil-dren so as *not* to question their commitments and way of life, effectively un-dermine the development of minimalist autonomy. Moreover, his conception of autonomy as choice-making within societal cultures potentially places un-due constraints on the nurturing of minimalist autonomy. The educational conditions necessary to encouraging Kymlicka's conception of autonomy seem to me insufficient in some cases to encourage the development of mini-malist autonomy, which requires intercultural comparisons and contrasts, making real and vivid the options of other cultures as well as one's own.

Raz is even more insistent about the importance of autonomy than Kym-licka. In his argument for liberal multiculturalism, Raz acknowledges the necessity of a supportive environment for promoting the exercise of auton-omy, but willingly exempts autonomy-retarding cultural groups from state intervention aimed at developing the capacity for autonomy. As in Kym-licka's case, then, children born into these cultures are potentially short-

changed. Raz encourages the exercise of autonomy in adults but does not recognize that respecting the autonomy of adults may inhibit its development in
their children. Kymlicka and Raz must admit that promoting the development of autonomy in children will mean supporting policies that sometimes
go against the autonomous choices of parents and counsel intervention in
cultural groups that wish to prevent or discourage the exercise of autonomy
by children.[46]

The distinction between respecting autonomy and exercising autonomy
must be kept clear because without it we are easily led toward conclusions
supportive only of negative liberty. We are led to establish rights that restrict
the intervention of the state or other people in the affairs of autonomous
adults. By now, it should be obvious that I believe the development of autonomy, even minimalist autonomy, requires support of positive liberty. A great
variety of supports are necessary for enabling and maintaining the exercise
of minimalist autonomy, among them relationships with parents, friends,
loved ones, in addition to a social environment in which choice is possible and
meaningful options exist. As Richard Dagger argues, "autonomy is not something that one can achieve solely through individual effort."[47]

The liberal state is limited in what it can do to promote minimalist autonomy; it cannot, for example, change the contingencies of one's birth, decide
who one's friends should be, or prevent mental and physical handicaps that
might inhibit autonomy. But the state *can* provide an education for all children, and it *can* set as a fundamental aim of education the development of autonomy. An education that attempts to develop the critical and independent
reflective capacities of children is an extremely important vehicle for nurturing the capacity for autonomy.[48]

A Liberal Theory of
Multicultural Education

*It is the office of the school environment to balance the various elements in
the social environment, and to see to it that each individual gets an opportunity to escape from the limitations of the social group in which he or she is
born, and to come into living contact with a broader environment.*
John Dewey, *Democracy and Education*

*Today, education is perhaps the most important function of state and local
governments. Compulsory school attendance laws and the great expenditures for education both demonstrate our recognition of the importance of
education to our democratic society. . . . It is the very foundation of good citizenship.*
Brown v. Board of Education

In chapter 1 I sketched a history of multicultural education in the United
States, arguing that tensions between respecting the cultural pluralism of
Americans and attempting to create a unified citizenry have always been
present in efforts to teach schoolchildren. In chapters 2 and 3 I turned to debates in contemporary political theory for lessons about what education in a
culturally diverse liberal state ought to look like. Finding that autonomy was
a prominent but easily misinterpreted theme for both liberals and multiculturalists, I examined in chapter 4 the concept of autonomy and defended a
minimalist conception. I am now finally in a position to build upon this work.

On the one hand, multiculturalists are right that the liberal state cannot
be neutral to the culturally based ways of life pursued by its citizens. When it
engages in the liberal soulcraft of fostering the autonomy of its citizens, the
state privileges those groups which themselves value autonomy and disad-
vantages those groups which do not. Liberalism is not hospitable to all forms
of diversity, nor even to all forms of what Rawls would call reasonable diversity.[1] To the extent that the liberal state cultivates the autonomy of its citi-

zens, it creates in the process an environment in which autonomy-friendly ways of life are far likelier to flourish than autonomy-unfriendly ways of life. If we were to imagine the liberal state as a petri dish, we would find that some ways of life would thrive, others would survive, and still others would be unlikely to persist over time. Liberalism, like any political philosophy, itself constitutes a kind of culture, understood in the medical sense of the term. It provides a hospitable environment for some, but not all, human ends and ways of life. Liberals should own up to and offer an explicit defense of the particular transformative and partial aims of the liberal state.

On the other hand, liberals are right that multicultural theorists often elevate an interest in the sanctity of cultural groups above an interest in guaranteeing the freedom and equality of the children within groups. By defending policies intended to shore up the position of cultural minorities, especially through separate schooling or exemptions from education, multiculturalists potentially sacrifice the autonomy of children and threaten their exit capacities in order to support the integrity of cultures. I believe that the conception of minimalist autonomy I have described is the most defensible conception for a liberal theory, defining a capacity that the liberal state has a fundamental interest in helping all to develop and achieve to a significant degree. Thus, when Brian Barry writes that sooner or later every theorist "must take his stand on the proposition that some ways of life, some types of character are more admirable than others," my response is, in large part, to describe the life of the minimally autonomous person.[2]

The analysis of the previous chapters was generated to a large degree by asking first what the educational preconditions and implications of a theory are, and then whether these are consistent with the aims of the theory itself. All along I have argued and tried to show that contemporary political theorists pay insufficient attention to the educational preconditions and implications of their theories. Often a theorist simply leaves crucial educational questions undeveloped. Rawls's political liberalism, for example, demands that unreasonable doctrines in society be contained and asks that citizens exercise public reason and develop a range of political virtues in their public deliberations, yet says almost nothing about how schooling can or should contribute to these tasks. Political liberalism, I have argued, contains significant educational presuppositions about which Rawls is largely silent. At other times a theorist will describe educational implications that seem to conflict with the theory itself. Margalit and Halbertal, Kukathas, and Raz, for example, all indicate support of educational institutions that undermine a key element of their theories, namely, a right of exit.

Interest in questions about education has been growing of late among political theorists.[3] Yet some of the greatest political philosophers—Plato, Aristotle, Rousseau—saw political theory as almost indistinguishable from educational theory. The politically naïve reader who stumbled across the *Republic*, the *Politics*, or *Emile* might understandably describe these texts as educational handbooks. The most significant American philosopher of the twentieth century, John Dewey, found philosophy itself to be inseparable from educational theory. "If we are willing to conceive education as the process of forming fundamental dispositions, intellectual and emotional, toward nature and fellow men," Dewey wrote, "philosophy may even be defined *as the general theory of education.*"[4]

When compared with their forebears, contemporary theorists, especially the most significant among them, such as Rawls and Kymlicka, neglect to a distressing degree educational questions that are fundamental to the success of their projects. When we realize that bedrock questions of how to ensure the legitimacy and stability of a state implicate education directly, political theory needs to take philosophical work on education seriously. And when political theorists begin to take philosophical work on education seriously, we begin perforce to describe an educational theory, to posit the aim(s) of education.

Now I take it for granted that any educational theory for the modern world must aim at educating all students to high levels of academic achievement, so that they may succeed in finding meaningful and productive work. That a liberal society must, as the mantra goes, "educate youth for the twenty-first century," implying that the skills required in the increasingly international and technological workplace are changing, goes without saying. In a highly industrialized modern society, education must naturally serve vocational aims.

But it cannot serve vocational aims exclusively. As I discuss in chapter 7, politicians and educational policymakers in the United States have for the past twenty years focused their energies far too frequently on reforming schools in order to improve the ultimate productivity and competitiveness of workers and therefore of the national economy. Comparatively little attention has been paid to what the civic aims of education in a modern liberal democracy should be or how they should be met. These civic aims are the subject of my concern here.

A fundamental challenge for political theorists today—one which emerges from the previous chapters—is to articulate an educational theory that is at once properly respectful of cultural differences and mindful of the need to cultivate autonomy and common political values in the state's youngest citizens. The theory must avoid, at one extreme, the onerous and oppressive burdens that schools, and by extension the state, have placed on cultural groups in the past. In theory or in practice it cannot permit, for example, the instances of religious, ethnic, linguistic, or racial discrimination I surveyed in the first chapter. The theory must also avoid, at the other extreme, an uncritical promotion of diversity at the expense of a civic mission to develop in all persons minimalist autonomy and the relevant political virtues. In theory or in practice, it cannot permit, for example, a school system whose aim is simply to reproduce and reinforce the religio- and ethno-cultural groups in the society. The challenge of any educational theory, as many American commentators have put it, is to navigate successfully between protecting the *pluribus* while also promoting an *unum*.

In this chapter, I respond to this challenge by outlining a liberal theory of multicultural education that describes and defends the non-neutral aims of education in a liberal state, properly respects but nevertheless shapes the cultural diversity of people within it, and focuses squarely on developing the autonomy of children. I shall argue that liberal multicultural education has two main components: first, its aim is to develop minimalist autonomy, the exercise of and respect for which serve a variety of core public and private interests; second, the content of education must be to some extent multicultural, by which I mean that all students must learn about other ways of life and acquire some understanding of the history, practices, and values of diverse cultural groups. As I shall attempt to show, these two components are not independent, but are in fact connected in important ways. I also argue that such an education can be justified with respect to both the citizen and the individual. Liberal multicultural education is warranted, in other words, because it is in the civic and individual interests of all people in a liberal state. It serves the civic goal of helping to realize the legitimacy and stability of a liberal society over generations, where all people, as free and equal citizens, are capable of sharing in the exercise of political power. It serves the individual goal of developing a certain autonomous character that is a condition for living a good and flourishing life in a liberal society.

This chapter elaborates the two components of liberal multicultural education. The first component—educating for minimalist autonomy—has both a civic and individual justification. The second component—multicultural content—crucially facilitates the development of autonomy and also contributes to the development of political virtues, such as public reason and mutual respect. It also possesses an independent justification, namely, that multicultural history is true history. By the end of the chapter, I hope to have articulated the outlines of a liberal theory of multicultural education appropriate for a culturally diverse liberal society that will hold some appeal for, though probably not entirely please, both liberal and multicultural theorists.

LIBERAL MULTICULTURAL EDUCATION: EDUCATING FOR MINIMALIST AUTONOMY

A defense of educating for minimalist autonomy involves two steps: first, I explain why the exercise of minimalist autonomy is something that actually requires an education; second, I defend the value of minimalist autonomy.

Minimalist autonomy, as I defined it in chapter 4, refers to a person's ability to reflect independently and critically upon basic commitments, desires, and beliefs, be they chosen or unchosen, and to enjoy a range of meaningful life options from which to choose, upon which to act, and around which to orient and pursue one's life projects. It is a decidedly modest conception of autonomy. Compared with other familiar conceptions, minimalist autonomy does not describe, to use the language of John Rawls, a comprehensive doctrine or full conception of the good. That is to say, a life characterized by the exercise of minimalist autonomy does not specify what is valuable in human life, does not determine the kinds of projects a person should pursue, does not give strict guidance on regulating a person's conduct, and does not unify a person's life into a precisely articulated scheme of thought.[5] Other conceptions of autonomy, as Rawls notes, do qualify as comprehensive doctrines: Kantian or Millian autonomy, for example, strongly emphasize rationality and individuality as ideals to govern the entirety of a person's life.[6] But as I argued in the previous chapter, minimalist autonomy describes a character ideal that finds it realization in the manner in which individuals cleave to their conceptions of the good, in the way they endorse what is valuable in human life and the projects they pursue.

But while minimalist autonomy does not describe a comprehensive doctrine, neither is it so minimal that it easily encompasses all lives. A state that promotes minimalist autonomy will circumscribe and narrow the kinds of lives likely to flourish. Minimalist autonomy does specify *some* things as valuable for human lives, such as freedom from the coercive control of others and the capacity for independent and critical second-order reflection on first-order ends. Neither a slave, nor a brainwashed cult member, nor an incapacitated or senile adult, nor a young child is minimally autonomous. Minimalist autonomy shapes our character and therefore makes it far more difficult to lead lives marked by obedience to unquestioned authority. It encourages free thinking and imbues the choices of individuals, not groups, with moral weight. We could say, then, that if minimalist autonomy does not describe a full conception of the good, it describes an underdetermined conception of the good. Leading a life characterized by minimalist autonomy does not specify what substantive values and commitments are best or worthy, but insists that the ability to examine and to affirm or potentially revise these substantive values and commitments, chosen or unchosen, is a good. Because of the truth of weak procedural independence, we must say that, strictly speaking, people, not ways of life, are either autonomous or non-autonomous. As a logical matter, minimalist autonomy is indifferent to whether one leads the life of the most solitary philosophy professor, the most cosmopolitan diplomat, the most isolated monk, or the most fraternal member of a kibbutz. But because of the falsity of strong procedural independence, minimally autonomous persons will not occupy some neutral standpoint from which different ways of life can be surveyed. Forms of life that accept authority without question, or that rebel against authority without reason or understanding, will fail to gain many adherents in a society that promotes minimalist autonomy.

As an *underdetermined* as opposed to *comprehensive* good, the capacity for and exercise of minimalist autonomy is entirely consistent with broad cultural diversity. Indeed, autonomy appears to go hand-in-hand with descriptive multiculturalism, for it is precisely respect for autonomy that underwrites the freedom of individuals to pursue different cultural ends. It allows individuals to make themselves without state interference into cultural purists or cultural mongrels. The demographic fact of multiculturalism is protected, perhaps even partially produced, in this sense, when governments respect the autonomous life choices made by individuals. But even as an underdetermined good, minimalist autonomy is not indiscriminately supportive of all forms of cultural diversity. As I showed earlier, many theorists reject autonomy on the grounds that it unfairly constrains diversity.[7] At that point, however, it was unclear what exactly was meant by autonomy. If by autonomy a theorist meant to valorize the life of a rugged, self-reliant individualist, then clearly the promotion of autonomy would limit diversity, for there would be no room for the person to choose a collective life within a community of like-minded people. I have since rejected this overly stringent ideal of autonomy in favor of minimalist autonomy, which accommodates traditional as well as modern forms of life, affirmation of the encumbrances of one's birth as well as efforts to free oneself from them. When we resist the too-frequent temptation to associate autonomy with self-reliance, or self-creation, or separation from other people or groups, we can see that being autonomous does not preclude the sharing of one's life with others, the following of advice, the desire to be like other people, or the sacrifice of one's own interests for those of others. But let it be clear: even minimalist autonomy limits possible forms of diversity. Requiring independent and critical reflection is potentially corrosive of those cultural traditions that inscribe rigid hierarchies of domination, or that emphasize unquestioning obedience to authority, or that shield children from other ways of life, like the Amish in the *Yoder* case. Minimalist autonomy embraces a wider range of cultural diversity than, say, moral autonomy; but to claim that it is hospitable, or neutral, to all cultural groups would be a lie.[8]

Perhaps the most obvious reason minimalist autonomy is neither hospitable nor neutral to all cultural groups is that people are not born autonomous; they need to be educated to be so. Autonomy, as I argued previously, describes a character that must be cultivated. (We might say that while all people are born with the *capacity* to become autonomous, they are not born with the *ability* to exercise autonomy. Our capacity for autonomy must be developed, which implies further that the exercise of autonomy will be exhibited by different people in different degrees.) Not all cultural groups wish to cultivate even the conditions of minimalist autonomy in children; therefore, for those cultures, the liberal state's promotion of autonomy will be threatening.

The liberal state can promote or cultivate minimalist autonomy in a number of ways. It can seek, for example, to eliminate or minimize external and internal obstacles to autonomy of the sort I discussed in chapter 4. Thus, the state fosters autonomy when, among other things, it guarantees rights to free speech, provides quality medical care for all its citizens, and contributes to an environment that makes available meaningful options from which to choose.[9] Much of this support, however, assumes that the capacity for autonomy has already been developed; these measures do not educate the person to be autonomous, but sustain and enhance the already existing ability to be autonomous. They are the background conditions of minimalist autonomy.

If minimalist autonomy is a good, albeit underdetermined, then the state must not only support background conditions for its exercise, but provide an education for its development. The achievement of minimalist autonomy must be a central aim of education within the liberal and multicultural state. There are, I believe, two justifications for educating for minimalist autonomy—one rooted in the individual interests of the person, the other rooted in the civic interests of the state. As I now turn to these dual justifications, it is worth underlining that, whereas my argument in chapter 4 was to present a coherent conception of autonomy that matches, I hope, our basic intuitions about autonomy, the current argument constitutes an explanation of the value of autonomy to both individuals and citizens. To argue that a primary aim of liberal multicultural education is the cultivation of minimalist autonomy is to argue for the crucial value of autonomy in the liberal state.

Justification on the Basis of Individual Interests

Why might the exercise of minimalist autonomy be in the interest of every individual? The claim, after all, is a rather dramatic and far-reaching one, for it implies that, absent minimalist autonomy, a person cannot live a flourishing life. Indeed, just this sort of claim provokes objections on the ground that many lives do not exhibit the characteristics of minimalist autonomy and are nevertheless good and decent, even flourishing, lives. Is the child who is socialized by parents, cultural group, or country to be unquestioning and dutiful in all respects with regard to worthy, perhaps even objectively worthy, ends incapable of flourishing? Who is the theorist to pronounce, after all, that a person needs to be critically reflective in order to lead a flourishing life?

I can respond to this by tempering my claim, if only slightly. I do not wish to argue that the exercise of minimalist autonomy is an absolute condition of leading a good life, binding at all times and in every possible place. I do not wish to claim, in other words, that minimalist autonomy is a transcendental good, necessary in all and every social arrangement that human beings might find themselves living in. I contend that minimalist autonomy is a necessary good for persons living in a culturally diverse, liberal society. As Joseph Raz writes, "For those who live in an autonomy-supporting environment there is no choice but to be autonomous: there is no other way to prosper in such a society."[10] A society that supports autonomy—the ability to choose an occupation, religion, spouse, place to live, and so on—affects, as Raz says, the entire system of social values. The autonomous life in a liberal society is not, therefore, simply one among many valuable ways of life; it constitutes the backdrop (or underdetermined good) which permits those multiple ways of life themselves to thrive.

Minimalist autonomy is necessary to individual flourishing in a liberal society for two closely related reasons. First, the exercise of minimalist autonomy is deeply connected to self-respect, a fundamental or primary good in liberal societies. Second, the exercise of minimalist autonomy prevents in children the development of servility to the values of their parents or the traditions and norms of the cultural group(s) and state in which they are born. Let us examine each reason in turn.[11]

Autonomy and Self-Respect

According to Rawls, self-respect is "perhaps the most important primary good."[12] By this, Rawls means that all persons desire self-respect, believing their lives would be measurably worse off without it. Self-respect contributes to well-being by giving a person "a sense of his own value, his secure conviction that his conception of the good, his plan of life, is worth carrying out."[13] In other words, people with self-respect will regard their respective ends, their commitments and life projects, as important to pursue. Beyond this, people with self-respect will also believe that they are capable, so far as it is possible, of realizing their goals. As Rawls says, "Without [self-respect] nothing may seem worth doing, or if some things have value for us, we lack the will to strive for them."[14] If we do not have self-respect, it becomes extremely difficult to treat ourselves, and indeed others, as moral agents. Self-respect endows individuals with a sense of value, their own and others', and motivates them to pursue their determined conceptions of the good. Without self-respect, a person cannot lead a flourishing life, for they will be unable to attribute worth to their own life projects and will be disinclined, in any case, to pursue them.

Self-respect, so defined, requires minimalist autonomy. To regard one's ends as valuable and to see oneself as capable of carrying them out is to engage in a process of forming second-order beliefs about one's first-order preferences and values. The exercise of minimalist autonomy, in other words, consists to a large degree in the ability to make a meaningful assessment of the worth of one's values and to judge the degree to which their realization appears to be within one's power. My self-respect suffers to the extent that I am unable to examine the commitments, values, and beliefs I hold because, while I could acknowledge them as being *mine*, I cannot pronounce any judgment on their worth. Without the capacity to judge the worth of the substantive commitments of my life, to decide that the shape and direction of my life are actually valuable for me, I am merely the captive of my first-order motivations. I cannot respect myself, at least in any meaningful way, for ends or projects of whose value I am ignorant or to which I am indifferent. Reflecting critically and independently on one's way of life and acting on the result of this reflection thus give rise to an attribution of value to one's commitments and values, which itself contributes to one's self-respect. Insofar, then, as self-respect is a primary good necessary to leading a good life, minimalist autonomy makes self-respect possible.

Autonomy and Servility

Servility is a condition that implies a dutiful slavishness or submissiveness to others, an unwillingness or incapacity to make decisions or judgments for oneself. The obvious example of a servile person is a slave, though others are more familiar in contemporary society. Thomas Hill gives an example of a deferential wife, someone who is utterly devoted to serving her husband not because he compels her through mental and physical abuse, but because "she tends not to form her own interests, values, and ideals; and, when she does, she counts them as less important than her husband's."[15] A person could also be servile to one's parents, or cultural group, or even nation. In some important sense, people who are servile do not make decisions for themselves; they either allow or are forced to allow others to make decisions for them. Not only, then, do servile persons fail to form second-order evaluations about their first-order commitments, values, and desires, they also often fail to make their first-order commitments, values, and desires their own. Servile persons may be agents in the world, but they have renounced or are forbidden their *own* agency. As Hill says, to be servile is to lack a rightful place in a moral community.[16] It should be obvious, I hope, how servility is incompatible with flourishing, which implies at a bare minimum a position in the world as a moral agent.

Servility is not only incompatible with flourishing, it is also incompatible with self-respect. A person with self-respect, after all, values commitments in life that are his own and conceives of himself as capable of carrying them out; he assumes responsibility for his life. People who are servile cannot be self-respecting, because they do not pursue ends which are their own.

Connecting this with earlier remarks, if self-respecting people are not servile, and minimalist autonomy contributes to self-respect, then minimalist autonomy will also serve to avoid conditions of servility. A person who develops the capacity for and exercise of minimalist autonomy exhibits independent reflection on her own ends. Servile people lack both independence and ends that they reflectively endorse. Were the deferential woman to examine her life projects and values, she would recognize that they were in fact not hers but those of her husband. In this circumstance, she might seek to commit herself to new ends, and, provided her husband did not prevent her from doing so, her pursuit of new ends that were her own would mark her as a moral agent striving to realize her own conception of the good (which in turn might give rise to self-respect). However, she may also decide that, on reflection, she truly does desire to commit herself to the support of only her husband's projects and values. She, in effect, *chooses* to serve him. In this circumstance, her life may not appear very different from its previous state. She adheres to a set of ends that are not her own and that render her life one that, from an outsider's perspective, would appear to be non-autonomous. But, in fact, a crucial element has changed, for she has asserted her own independent agency, formed a second-order preference about her first-order motivations, and, provided the other conditions of minimalist autonomy hold (i.e., that her reflection is critical and that there are other possible and meaningful options around which to orient herself), made an autonomous decision about how she wishes to shape her life. She acts upon a will that is her own. She is no longer servile.[17] To the extent that she goes beyond the capacity to assert her own will and acquires a disposition to continue to direct attention and reflection to the reasons she endorses her husband's ends and values, the woman would also possess an autonomous character. She would be minimally autonomous.

We might say, then, that minimalist autonomy is a condition for, on the one hand, achieving self-respect and, on the other hand, avoiding servility. Because self-respect and the avoidance of servility are required to live a flourishing life for any individual, we can also say that the exercise of minimalist autonomy is required for flourishing. Achieving a minimally autonomous life is therefore in the interest of every person in a liberal society.

Justification on the Basis of Civic Interests

The idea that the state has a fundamental civic interest in assuring that all its citizens are minimally autonomous is easier to establish than the previous argument resting on individual interests. As I mentioned in chapter 4, a strong case can be made that the very idea of rights, in particular human rights, rests on viewing the individual as autonomous.[18] Respect for the autonomy of every individual gives rise to the notion that there must be significant restrictions on what the state or other people may do to a person; as these restrictions become codified into law, they become rights. A respect for autonomy is similarly behind much opposition to perfectionist political theories, that is, theories which claim to have identified the good for all citizens.[19] As Gerald Dworkin writes, "As a political ideal, autonomy is used as a basis to argue against the design and functioning of political institutions that attempt to impose a set of ends, values, and attitudes upon the citizens of a society."[20] Respect for autonomy requires that citizens be permitted to make their own decisions about the ends they will pursue, consistent with an equal liberty for others.

As this latter, antiperfectionist ideal implies, the exercise of minimalist autonomy also underlies some basic intuitions we have about the meaning of freedom in a liberal society. Rawls, for example, describes three respects in which citizens view themselves as free. First, they conceive of themselves and others as having the moral power to form, revise, and pursue a conception of the good; whatever particular conception of the good they pursue, they nevertheless retain their identity as free and equal citizens. Thus, the particular commitments of individuals do not compromise their status as citizens. Second, citizens view themselves as "self-authenticating," or entitled to enter into political deliberations and make arguments so as to protect or advance their conception of the good. Finally, citizens view themselves as responsible for the ends they pursue, viewing ends as revisable if, in their own estimation, the ends are no longer worthy or they are incapable of realizing them.[21] Minimalist autonomy, which involves independent and critical reflection on one's ends, contributes to and enlarges the freedom to form, potentially revise, and pursue ends, as well as underwriting the sense in which people are responsible for their ends.[22] Conversely, being free in these respects, as Rawls says, enables citizens to be autonomous.[23] Thus, autonomy and Rawls's tripartite understanding of freedom are deeply intertwined.

These considerations go a long way toward establishing a civic justification for educating for minimalist autonomy. But the most significant reason, by far, for the state to foster minimalist autonomy is that it is required to secure the legitimacy and stability of the principles of justice by which all will be governed. Problems of legitimacy and stability arise because, in a liberal state characterized by cultural diversity, a multitude of reasonable and sometimes conflicting conceptions of the good (or, to use Rawls's more recent terminology, "comprehensive doctrines") will exist. The main question that Rawls seeks to answer expresses the problem well: How can citizens share a common political conception of justice when their private conceptions of the good are diverse and possibly incompatible?[24] The problem is not merely that citizens will disagree about particular matters of policy that may be contentious (e.g., capital punishment, a just level of taxation, whom to elect, immigration policy, etc.). Any society will contain disagreements at this level. The problem Rawls confronts, rather, concerns what the theorist is to do when reasonable but irreconcilable disputes exist about the very framework of society, the principles of justice to which all will refer in attempting to resolve other disagreements. What, in this situation, is the basis of legitimacy for principles of justice? How can the stability of society be guaranteed over generations?

The answer Rawls gives to these questions, as I described in chapter 2, constitute the politically liberal society. Under Rawlsian liberalism, individuals first (hypothetically) generate political principles from behind a veil of ignorance in the original position, and then (in reality) affirm and apply these principles to a constitutional structure and other major political institutions through the exercise of public reason, or, the giving of reasons that abstracts in part from each person's comprehensive doctrine and appeals instead to what others could be reasonably be expected to endorse, as similarly situated free and equal citizens. In the original position, hypothetical individuals exercise autonomy by independently and critically examining possible principles of justice from among all conceivable options.[25] In the real world, citizens exercise autonomy by justifying the political decisions each makes, not on the basis of their respective comprehensive doctrines, but rather on the basis of what others as free and equal citizens might reasonably accept. As Rawls says, "Our exercise of political power is proper only when we sincerely believe that the reasons we offer for our political action may reasonably be accepted by other citizens as a justification of those actions."[26] Rawls concludes, "In affirming the political doctrine as a whole, we, as citizens, are ourselves autonomous, politically speaking."[27]

Let me put the point in less Rawlsian language. The civic justification of minimalist autonomy rests on the need for principles of justice and their application to political institutions and policies to be acceptable to citizens for reasons that all would recognize as valid, though not necessarily as congruent with their own personal ends and commitments. On the one hand, then, the state *respects* the autonomy of all citizens. For political principles and policies to be legitimate, the state cannot coerce or compel their acceptance. Taking the autonomy of its citizens seriously, the state needs to gain their consent on basic questions of justice and political policies, and it will need to facilitate and encourage their political participation on a free and equal basis. On the other hand, the state must cultivate the *exercise* of autonomy in its citizens. Because consenting to principles of justice and political policies in a diverse society will involve understanding that others are motivated by different ends, consent will involve reflecting critically and independently upon one's own conception of the good and upon others' as well. In order to formulate reasons that might be publicly acceptable, citizens must be capable of a critical appraisal of themselves and others. People who justify their political actions and decisions on the basis of reasons that others might reasonably accept have, in effect, recognized that a range of reasonable conceptions of the good exist and made an evaluation about how best to appeal to those who do not share their own life commitments and projects.

Putting these pieces together, we can conclude that for a liberal state to be legitimate, it must respect the autonomy of citizens in seeking their consent to principles of justice and their application to political institutions and policies. If the consent of citizens is to be uncoerced, citizens must have the capacity to reflect critically upon political principles, and upon their own and others' political arguments. As Harry Brighouse says, "It is empty to claim that a state is legitimate because its coercive actions would have been accepted by autonomous citizens unless that same state has ensured that each person has been able to become autonomous."[28] Legitimacy relies upon both respect for and the fostering of autonomy. Once legitimate consent to the political principles that will regulate society has been established, however, the question of stability arises. Given that principles of justice do not specify correct policies in detail, and given that citizens die and new ones are born, how will citizens with different and potentially incompatible conceptions of the good reach a stable consensus about determining the political institutions and policies that will govern them all? To achieve this stability, the liberal state must foster the exercise of autonomy so that citizens are capable of giving public reasons whose validity might be acknowledged by all; it must cultivate public reason, which in turn requires the exercise of minimalist autonomy.

Educating for Minimalist Autonomy by Degree

I have argued that an education for minimalist autonomy is justified with regard both to the private interests of the individual and to the civic interests of the state. Being minimally autonomous is necessary to live a good life in a liberal state and in order to help secure the legitimacy and stability of a liberal state. I wish now to push one step further and evaluate the respective educational implications of each justification. When we consider these implications, it seems to me that the degree of autonomy necessary to meet the individual's private interest and the state's interests is not identical. The civic justification for minimalist autonomy sets a higher standard than does the individual justification.

Consider that there are two ways to impede minimalist autonomy. On the one hand, autonomy would be subverted if someone or something prevented or outlawed its exercise. If, for example, the state forbids all but property-owning white men from voting, it effectively prevents the exercise of autonomy by many citizens, denying them the opportunity to participate in collective deliberations about the shape of the political society in which they have a crucial interest. Of course, such subversions of autonomy stain the history of the United States, as well as that of practically every other nation. The subversion of autonomy by preventing or forbidding its exercise in political contexts, I should also note, effectively compromises the legitimacy of the state. Note that this kind of subversion represents at once an *external obstacle* to autonomy and a failure of *respecting* autonomy. Such interference with autonomy is a common enough occurrence, but appeals to principles of justice, which in liberal democratic societies define all citizens as free and equal, are the appropriate remedy.

On the other hand, autonomy would also be subverted if someone or something failed to cultivate the capacity for its exercise. If, for example, parents or cultural groups seek to raise their children to be servile to certain elders, or to socialize them to assume a distinctly unequal status in the community, or, less dramatically, simply shield them from interacting physically or intellectually with the values of other ways of life, then the development of autonomy will be undermined. As before, such subversions of autonomy are not uncommon, occurring for instance when parents wish to inculcate values of unquestioning obedience and deference in their children. It can also occur when the norms of group life place enormous pressure on parents to educate their children in ways that conform to community expectations and that effectively limit the exit options for all involved. As Brian Barry argues, in such cases "the parents may be mere cyphers, putting a legal rubber stamp on a decision that they have no choice in making as long as they wish to remain in the group."[29] The subversion of autonomy in this way threatens the stability of a liberal state, insofar as children who are not autonomous will be unable to offer their free and uncoerced consent to the state and will be hampered in their abilities to engage in productive democratic deliberation with citizens of differing opinions. Unlike before, however, this kind of subversion represents at once the creation of an *internal obstacle* to autonomy and a failure to develop the capacity to *exercise* autonomy. Such interference with autonomy is also common enough, but it is not cured necessarily by recourse to principles of justice. For if people interpret principles of justice, as some of the theorists I've examined have, only to imply respecting autonomy, then efforts to foster the exercise of autonomy will be ignored. Instead, it is necessary to appeal to an educational theory that posits educating for autonomy as an elementary aim.

The question remains, of course, whether all citizens will consent to or uphold such an educational theory, thereby giving it legitimacy. The argument of this chapter has been that citizens can and should accept autonomy as an educational aim because it is in their interests as individuals and citizens to lead good and flourishing lives. For the individual, developing the exercise of autonomy helps prevent servility and contributes to self-respect. For the citizen, respect for autonomy grounds the inclusion of each person as an equal member of society, entitled to full participation in the construction of principles of justice and deliberation over their consequent application to political institutions and policies. Furthermore, a citizen's exercise of autonomy enables a critical and independent appraisal of her own and others' ends, which in turn contributes to the ability to offer reasons for political actions and decisions that might be accepted by all as consistent with public reason.[30]

Now recall that the exercise of minimalist autonomy is matter of degree. For obvious reasons, we are not all self-determining in the same degree; we do not all engage in critical and independent reflection on our life's values and projects with the same intensity or frequency. The question then arises, what degree of autonomy do we need to exercise in order to satisfy an individual's interest in being autonomous and a citizen's interest in being autonomous? While a precise answer may be impossible to establish, surely some precision would be desirable, at least insofar as it would contribute to understanding how far educating for autonomy should go.

It would simplify the educational task if the interests of the individual and the citizen in autonomy were equivalent in degree. But I doubt this is the case. It seems to me that, examining once again the reasons behind the individual and civic justifications for autonomy, the degree of autonomy necessary to avoid servility and achieve a rudimentary level of self-respect is less than the degree of autonomy necessary to participate as a citizen in society on a free and equal basis. For its contribution to individual flourishing, the degree of exercising autonomy is relatively low; for its contribution to civic life, much higher.

The reasons for this asymmetry are quite easy to see. The supercession of servility begins when individuals begin to form their own second-order evaluations about their first-order commitments and are free from external compulsion. In the same vein, once people have reflected upon their commitments, they have to some extent made them their own, even if they are the product of initially unchosen conditions. The uncoerced affirmation or ratification of one's ends, just as much as the reasoned attempt to revise or reject one's initially unchosen ends, signals the avoidance of servility. Just insofar as people's commitments and projects are their own and they adjudge that they are reasonably capable of realizing their commitments and projects, they have a rudimentary basis for self-respect.

Participating ably in civic affairs and offering public reasons for one's political actions and decisions require much more in the way of autonomy. As citizens, people will enter into public forums to deliberate about political issues with others who do not share their own particular commitments or way of life, who possess different and possibly conflicting ends, and who belong to cultural groups with different histories and values. As Rawls says, "This fact makes it rational for [citizens] to move out of the narrower circle of their own views and to develop political conceptions in terms of which they can explain and justify their preferred policies to a wider public as to put together a majority."[31] According to the component elements of minimalist autonomy, a high degree of its exercise would imply a highly developed ability to examine one's own and others' ends, as well as a broad awareness of a wide range of other meaningful options. In practical terms, this means that a person has been exposed to and engaged intellectually with a diverse palette of values, is able sympathetically to understand the commitments and ways of life of other people, and can imaginatively use all this information in crafting arguments designed to win the acceptance of others. This takes a person well beyond the avoidance of servility and the rudimentary requirements for some minimal amount of self-respect.

What, then, are the educational implications? Should recognition of the different levels of autonomy affect the way in which schools educate for autonomy? This brings us to questions of educational policy, which I take up in greater detail in chapter 7. But at this point it will be instructive to make two short comments.

First, I have often used examples of insular or orthodox religious groups to suggest that if they are given exclusive control over schooling, they may compromise the development of autonomy in their children. The implication might easily be drawn that children born into such religio-cultural groups would not be able to lead flourishing lives, for to the extent that they fail to exercise autonomy, they are to some degree servile and lacking in the conditions for self-respect. While I believe this conclusion to be true of extremely insular or very orthodox religious groups, a far greater danger comes in the form of communities that are extremely homogenous and severely isolated. The situation worsens for children when homogeneity and isolation are combined, as in the case of far too many urban areas in the United States, with socioeconomic marginalization, conditions of abject poverty, failed family structures, decrepit schools, few job opportunities, poor health, and little first-hand knowledge and experience of the world beyond their homes. The existence of any one or few of these conditions would not conduce to an insular socialization, but where they all hold, the negative effects on the development of a child's capacity to exercise autonomy or possess self-respect are pronounced.[32] The upshot is that, as a matter of actual fact, parents and cultural groups are hardly the only impediments to the development of autonomy. Social and economic obstacles that are at least in significant part the responsibility of the state are also to blame.

Second, to admit that the bar for educating for autonomy with respect to individual and civic interests rests at different levels is to acknowledge that educating for autonomy need not be a matter of maximizing options for children. Nor need it mean, as some theorists have claimed, that an education for autonomy must secure a "right to an open future."[33] On the contrary, the level of autonomy that a child should learn to exercise is, vis-à-vis her individual interests, enough to avoid servility and contribute to rudimentary self-respect, and, vis-à-vis her civic interests, enough to participate ably in political deliberations using public reason. While it is impossible to specify from a theoretical standpoint what these levels are, it *is* possible to say that maximizing options or requiring an "open future," implying that a person should be able to choose anything, is unnecessary as well as unfathomable. Minimalist autonomy requires that people enjoy a range of meaningful options from which to choose and potentially orient their lives, but it need not be the largest possible range, nor a range including all possible options that are open to others.

From the previous considerations, then, I conclude that educating for autonomy should be a fundamental aim of education, justified in relation to the individual and civic interests. I turn next to examine the second component of a liberal theory of multicultural education: the multicultural content.

Liberal Multicultural Education: Multicultural Content

Why should the education of children in a liberal democratic society be a multicultural education? I shall argue that the content of education must be to some appreciable extent multicultural for two reasons, one instrumental and one intrinsic. The instrumental reason is that multicultural education is a necessary condition of an education for minimalist autonomy and an important facilitator of the political virtues of mutual respect and public reason. In this respect, multicultural education and education for autonomy are inseparable; autonomy cannot be cultivated without it. The intrinsic reason is that multicultural education corrects the ethnocentric and chauvinist education so typical of years past, and as such is a truer representation of the history and current composition of the United States. In this section, I explore these dual justifications for multicultural education.

Invoking the need for multicultural education, however, begs for immediate clarification. It is hardly clear what is meant by multicultural education—the phrase has been used to refer to such a plethora of educational practices that it is more a slogan than a unified set of ideas about education. Among educational scholars, the leading theorist is James Banks, who defines five "dimensions" of multicultural education—content integration, a self-conscious knowledge-construction progress, prejudice reduction, equity pedagogy, and an empowering school culture.[34] In chapter 7 I examine some of the prevailing views of multicultural education, including Banks's, with a critical eye. But rather than enter into a definitional controversy about what precisely multicultural education should be, I mean to imply something fairly basic, and I hope, uncontroversial with the phrase. In endorsing multicultural education, I mean that at some point in their education, students should become aware of and engage intellectually with the history, traditions, and values of a diversity of cultures, especially but not limited to those encompassed by the population of their neighborhood, state, and country. A diversity of cultural histories, beliefs, and practices should be represented and taught in schools. A multicultural education is opposed, though it is rarely put this way, to a monocultural education, in which students study and learn about the history and values of only their own cultural group, where "own" refers most often to the cultural identity of their parents.

There are two basic delivery systems of a multicultural education. The first is curricular: students receive a multicultural education to the extent that they learn *about* the history and values of a multiplicity of cultural groups. Students can learn *about* the histories, traditions, and values of another culture through the usual pedagogical vehicles used in any classroom: by reading books, watching movies, listening to a lecture, and so forth. The second is more controversial, but almost certainly more powerful: students receive a multicultural education to the extent that they learn *with* other students who affiliate themselves with a multiplicity of cultural groups. That is to say, the efficacy of multicultural education likely increases to the degree that the school in which children learn is integrated, not segregated, by cultures.[35] Certainly both approaches to multicultural education are important, but school integration raises a number of very difficult problems. (For example, does the good of integrated schooling outweigh the state intervention in bussing in order to bring it about? What counts as an "integrated" school?) I leave aside questions about which approach a liberal theory of multicultural education requires. For present purposes, the aim of my argument is to establish first that multicultural education instrumentally facilitates the development of minimalist autonomy and important political virtues, and second that it is valuable on its own terms to redress narrow ethnocentric educational practices and texts of the past. Ultimately, questions about the most effective approach to multicultural education are empirical in nature.

Multicultural Education and the Cultivation of Minimalist Autonomy

Multicultural education fosters minimalist autonomy by (1) creating and enhancing the possibility of critical and independent reflection, and (2) making vivid to the student a diversity of cultural practices and values, which themselves may come to represent real and meaningful options that the student could choose and seek to adopt or pursue. Multicultural education contributes, that is, to both conditions of minimalist autonomy—the condition of critical and independent reflection on basic commitments, values, beliefs, and so forth, and the condition of there being a range of meaningful life options from which to choose, upon which to act, and around which to orient and pursue one's life projects. At its best, multicultural education is an education that engages students with value diversity, confronts them with a variety of social identities, enables but does not encourage the construction of a multicultural, or cosmopolitan, identity, and provides a forum for cross-cultural dialogue.

How does multicultural education foster critical and independent reflection? I suggested a provisional answer in my criticism in chapter 3 of Kymlicka's conception of autonomy conceived as enabling choice within culture. The information and experience most likely to be of value in assessing one's conception of the good, I argued, are those with some distance from what is already familiar. To be sure, no culture contains a rigid and unchanging set of values; the most plausible conceptions of culture view the inner dimensions and outer borders as dynamic and fluid. Cultural norms are historically contested and evolve over time. But cultures would not be distinguishable without some cohesive and enduring values and unity. In developing the capacity to reflect upon the values that are instilled into children as a result of the socialization of their earlier years, it will be of relatively little use to engage them only with those very same values, having the school replicate the socialization the child receives elsewhere. On the contrary, what facilitates the capacity for critical reflection is the introduction of and engagement with diverse and unfamiliar value orientations.

Exposure to and examination of other ways of life stimulates comparisons, illuminates contrasts, and encourages independence of thought. Without an awareness of cultural difference and an intellectual engagement with such difference, we risk concluding that our own way of doing things is the best simply because it is our own, or that our own norms and customs are universal rather than historical and mutable. The capacity to subject our own way of life to critical self-reflection and evaluation depends, after all, on our ability to compare one thing to another. The broader my knowledge and understanding of diverse ways of life, the deeper is my pool of contrasts, the broader are my categories of assessment, the richer my moral language and articulacy. If mine is the only way of life I know, how can I judge that it is in fact a worthy and valuable way of life? To make such a statement would be to say, in effect, I value my way of life because it is mine and not someone else's, my group's and not some other group's. But a world in which value rested simply on the fact of possession would be a very strange and subjectivist place, leading directly, it seems to me, into a pit of circular reasoning and relativism.[36] Every value that is espoused would be valuable simply because it is espoused. The ability to form a second-order evaluation about one's first-order desires cannot be achieved, then, without knowledge of a variety of other alternatives. A multicultural education teaches students about the ways in which diverse others lead their lives, the values around which they orient themselves, the standards by which they evaluate excellence. In the process, it makes students aware of other alternatives, giving them the tools they need to examine their own lives. Knowledge and understanding of the way other people live affords students the very leverage they need to understand and evaluate the way they live. In short, learning to exercise autonomy will mean in part learning to think otherwise. I cannot truly understand and autonomously affirm my own way of life, or wish for it to be otherwise, if I am never informed about alternative possibilities.

As Martha Nussbaum has shown, the claim that multicultural education is essential to facilitating an understanding of oneself and others, and to enabling critical reflection on oneself and others, is not a product of the modern world, but finds its origin in antiquity. "By the beginning of the so-called Hellenistic era in Greek philosophy," Nussbaum writes, "cross-cultural inquiry was firmly established . . . as a necessary part of good deliberation about citizenship and political order." Beyond its civic importance, a liberal multicultural education enables a "detachment from uncritical loyalty to one's own ways [that] promotes the kind of evaluation that is truly reason based." And she later concludes that "people who have never learned to use reason and imagination to enter a broader world of cultures, groups, and ideas are impoverished personally and politically."[37]

If multicultural education contributes to avoiding a problem of cultural self-immurement, it also acknowledges and provides an antidote to the fantasy that standards of evaluation might somehow be self-generated. The notion, for example, that persons are capable of being radically free, able to assess their ends from, in Thomas Nagel's famous phrase, "the view from nowhere," cannot be an important element of minimalist autonomy.[38] The development of minimalist autonomy does not assume that people reach some point at which they stand apart completely from their first-order commitments, desires, and beliefs; disembodied, as it were, from their own motivations.[39] It posits no contentious view of a ghostly metaphysical self who is detached from its ends, untethered to the real world, and suddenly capable of superhuman self-examination. On the contrary, minimalist autonomy recognizes that people never have a view from nowhere, that they are inescapably historical beings, inheriting traditions and values from the communities into which they are born. From the perspective of developing minimalist autonomy, then, what is important is not some sudden release from these traditions and values, but exposure to and engagement with other traditions and values. A multicultural education is designed to provide exactly this, thereby enabling critical reflection.

More than just enabling critical reflection, however, multicultural education also presents students with a diversity of values and traditions which may function, after self-examination, as real and meaningful options for the student to choose. Multicultural education can play a significant role in ensuring that people enjoy a meaningful variety of choice in life. Unless we learn about other ways of life, we risk finding that the only options available to us are those already familiar from the socialization our parents or cultural group have given us.

One can appreciate this dynamic most dramatically by thinking about creative or artistic production. Art is among the most obvious manifestations of culture—a possible source of pride for members and a material way of linking oneself to the roots of a cultural tradition. But clearly, artistic creativity is enhanced by exposure to and engagement with the traditions and values of other cultures. Artists continually seek new influences, new sources of inspiration, new ways of thinking. The imaginable options available to the artist who receives a culture-centric education are almost certainly more limited than those available to the artist who receives a multicultural education.

Thus, the musician, painter, choreographer, cook, director, writer, architect, or craftsman who learns about the music, artistic styles and media, dance, food, films, prose and poetry, buildings, and construction materials of other cultures widens the artistic options available to him. These other cultural traditions become real and meaningful options for the artist, either on their own terms or in amalgamation with what is already familiar. By expanding her palette, so to speak, the artist increases her creative autonomy.

We need not speak only about artistic creations, however. In expanding the cultural horizons of a person, the educator also expands the store of raw materials from which that person constructs or composes a life. Putting it crudely, multicultural education provides a toolbox for multicultural, or cosmopolitan, identity construction. It makes vivid to a person the cultural complexity of a multicultural state and a multicultural world, and provides the means for him to complicate his own self-understanding. People who exercise minimalist autonomy will have available to them a range of meaningful ends, projects to pursue, and values to guide them. As multicultural education teaches students about the diversity of ends in life, the multiplicity of life projects, and the plurality of values, it serves a critical role in opening up these options to students.[40]

This points, I think, to the oddity of Kymlicka's conception that the autonomy liberals should cherish is that which enables choice within cultures. On the contrary, it seems to me that while choice within a culture is no doubt important, the value of a multicultural education rests in fostering autonomy in such a way that capacities of critical reflection are enhanced and the range of meaningful options is expanded beyond one's culture. Moreover, we need not take what seems to me a primitive or simplistic view that the only value of critical reflection and multiple options is perhaps to decide one day to "exit" one's culture. That people face a choice between cultural immurement or wholesale rejection is preposterous. While "exiting" should remain an option, by far the more usual consequence of achieving an autonomous character will be an ongoing negotiation that results in the affirmation of some commitments, beliefs, and values, the contestation of others, and finally the rejection of some in favor of adopting new ones. Multicultural education contributes to autonomy not by encouraging defection from one's own way of life but by bringing examples of other cultural commitments, beliefs, and values to the fore; by making them real and vivid.

Multicultural Education and the Cultivation of Political Virtues

As important as multicultural education is as a means to develop minimalist autonomy, it is also plays an instrumental role in fostering important political virtues such as mutual respect and the capacity for public reason and democratic deliberation. This point has been amply developed elsewhere, so I do not provided an extended argument here.[41] I confine myself to a few supporting observations about the civic importance of multicultural education.

We can begin to grasp the civic importance of multicultural education when we consider that, historically, theorists like John Dewey have looked to the schoolhouse as an environment where children learn to see and understand diverse others and to appreciate the histories of the various groups that populate the country and have contributed to its development. Ideally, the school was to be a place in society where children might occupy a common space on equal terms. Students come to school, after all, already rooted to a large degree in a particular tradition—be it ethnic, religious, or otherwise. The school's role is not to strip students of their particularistic attachments, as was the goal of the nativist Americanization campaigns reviewed in the first chapter. The school's role is to get students thinking about political decisions that they will later make as citizens and that will affect people much different from themselves. So understood, a multicultural curriculum is not for cultural uplift but a political necessity.

Of all political virtues, perhaps the most frequently mentioned is mutual respect—the injunction that citizens must respect the values, ends, and beliefs of others on the basis that, just as they pursue a conception of the good, so are others equally entitled to the same liberty. Multicultural education makes mutual respect more than just an abstraction. For while it is one thing to proclaim that others have merited one's respect, without some minimal understanding and knowledge about other citizens, that respect rings quite hollow. In fact, without evincing a familiarity with the conceptions of the good which another pursues, claiming respect for him and his life projects is an act of condescension. I may tolerate other people without the least bit of knowledge about them; I may not, however, respect them.[42] Respect issues as well from the fact that when students understand the descriptive truth of multiculturalism, they will confront the reality that individuals of different cultural groups endorse different and incommensurate ends yet are all equal citizens, entitled to equal standing in the political arena. To the extent, therefore, that multicultural education helps to produce citizens who have mutual respect for one another, it encourages a proper respect for diversity. It helps to teach them why, and in what sense, they should respect views that they consider to be false. Citizens who respect one another will be motivated to engage neither in a form of moral or cultural dogmatism (i.e., my way of life is the best, and yours is wrong) nor in a form of approbation based on nothing more than an abstract awareness of diversity. Mutual respect will motivate citizens to engage each other in dialogue about their differences, holding out the promise that dialogue could alter their own self-understanding or the self-understanding of others.

The civic justification for multicultural education is strengthened still further by a moment's reflection on the skills required for exercising Rawls's public reason. If the legitimacy of political decisions rests on the extent to which citizens offer reasons for their political actions that abstract from their own conception of the good and appeal to what others, also abstracting from their own conceptions of the good, would accept as reasonable, then the work of formulating such "public reasons" will depend in part on what citizens know about the values of others. To give a public reason, in effect, a citizen needs some knowledge of what private reasons might motivate others.[43]

Robert Gooding-Williams argues that the very point of multicultural education is to open up the possibility of cross-cultural understanding and democratic deliberation. If deliberation in public forums requires an understanding of the differences that divide people, so that each person is able to produce arguments and reasons that the other will find reasonable, then an education that helps to foster such understanding will be a political good. "By disseminating the cultural capital of cross-cultural knowledge," Gooding-Williams comments, "multicultural education can cultivate citizens' abilities to 'reverse perspectives.' By facilitating mutual understanding, it can help them to shape shared vocabularies for understanding their moral and cultural identities and for finding common ground in their deliberations."[44] Similarly, Martha Nussbaum sees in literature an importance civic function. "It is the political promise of literature that it can transport us, while remaining ourselves, into the life of another, revealing similarities but also profound differences between the life and thought of that other and myself and making them comprehensible, or at least more nearly comprehensible."[45] In this sense, multicultural education is a hermeneutic endeavor in which the youngest citizens of a multicultural state enter into dialogue with that which is culturally different but of equivalent standing politically. The result is not only the possibility of self-transformation but an enhanced capacity for participating in civic deliberations through public reason. I return in the final chapter to explore in greater detail the pedagogy of multicultural education understood as facilitating hermeneutic dialogue.

The Intrinsic Good of Multicultural Education: A True History and Representation of the Polity

Finally, rather than seeing multicultural education only for its instrumental value in fostering minimal autonomy and a range of important political virtues, we must recognize that some form of it would be justified regardless of its instrumental use. Put simply, the right kind of multicultural education can be understood as a more accurate rendering of history and a truer representation of the diverse citizens who populate a nation and, ultimately, the world.

One of the basic motivations behind the movement in multicultural education in the United States has been to update school curricula to make them, on the one hand, less chauvinistic and exclusionary of the history and contributions of diverse groups to the evolution of the nation and, on the other hand, to be more reflective of the increasingly diverse student population currently in the classroom. Gary Nash and his coauthors of the recently completed National History standards document in painful detail the deeply ethnocentric and often racist underpinnings of history textbooks in the United States.[46] The purpose of the new history standards, Nash has argued, is to correct the predominant presentation of American history as a succession of triumphs and travails of great and usually white European-American men. A multicultural history chronicles the history of all Americans and all cultures which have contributed to the history of the country. Nash champions, therefore, ethnic studies, women's history, and social history, arguing that the work of historians in these areas over the past generation has led to a far more accurate and inclusive understanding of American history overall.[47] If multicultural education is the teaching of the roles played by different cultural groups and individuals who identified with cultural groups in the history of the country, then it is nothing more than good scholarship. Multicultural history is accurate history.

Moreover, a multicultural education that is inclusive will necessarily resist the urge to sanitize history, making the tale of America into a series of glorified fables about venerable leaders. Unlike many previous history textbooks, a multicultural education acknowledges straightforwardly and does not gloss over the country's history of sordid, oppressive, and discriminatory practices, frequent episodes of hate, and bitter struggles to achieve equality. But rather than drawing a skeptical lesson from the failures of America's past, Nash sees the fundamental narrative of American history as a tale of the increasingly successful attempt of America's practice to live up to its professed ideals, to close the gap between reality and theory.

In other school subjects, such as literature, multicultural education serves the salutary role of expanding the traditional canon to include the works of more than just white, European males. The reason for doing so does not depend on an argument that all cultures have produced works of excellence that must be read and appreciated, but the more mundane reason that African and Asian and Latino and Native American cultures, to name a few, constitute part of the national community. Learning about ourselves, our history, or our political system, where "our" is understood as referring to all those who are citizens, is a goal toward which multicultural education makes a mighty contribution.[48]

One final consideration in this regard is to acknowledge, as multicultural theorists have argued, that the omission or exclusion of sociocultural groups may constitute a clear harm. In their language, this is an error of "misrecognition" or "non-recognition." As Charles Taylor writes, the expansion of the traditional canon is important because those excluded "are given, either directly or by omission, a demeaning picture of themselves, as though all creativity and worth inhered in males of European provenance."[49] Insofar as the books read by students never portray, for example, cultural minorities, or only portray them in stereotypical or derogatory ways, all students suffer, and particularly those born into minority cultural groups. Similarly, the exclusion of African-American or Asian-American history from American history textbooks not only distorts history but makes it difficult for students of African-American or Asian-American parents to find lessons in the school about the history they may learn at home. As Amy Gutmann writes, "To teach United States history largely without reference to the experiences and contributions of Native Americans, African-Americans, Latino-Americans, and Asian-Americans, for example, constitutes an intellectual failure to recognize the contributions of many different cultures . . . to United States history. This intellectual failure morally damages democracy by conveying a false impression that members of these groups have not contributed significantly to making American politics what it is today."[50] Even if multicultural education did not instrumentally help to cultivate minimalist autonomy and certain political virtues, we should still defend it as a fundamental component of education for these various intrinsic reasons.

IMPLICATIONS OF A LIBERAL THEORY OF MULTICULTURAL EDUCATION

A liberal theory of multicultural education outlines the fundamental educational aims of a liberal state. For both civic and individual reasons, a liberal states owes children an education for minimalist autonomy. And in order to provide this education for minimalist autonomy, and for independent reasons as well, the state owes children a multicultural education. Putting the two components together and summing it all up in a phrase, we could say that the goal of liberal multicultural education is not to teach students who they already are, scripting for them a cultural identity; rather, the goal is to enable children to decide who they want to become and to be able to participate as informed citizens in a democratic and diverse state. Before moving on to examine the implications for authority over educational institutions, I want briefly to mention a few general implications of the liberal theory of multicultural education I have defended here.

First, note that one way of thinking about my conclusions is that I have upended the usual justification of multicultural education. Often, multicultural education is promoted in the interests of minority groups whose history and cultural achievements have been excluded from the mainstream curriculum. It is essentially a claim about identity politics: children of minority groups will see themselves reflected in the curriculum and therefore take pride in the accomplishments of their group; this will in turn increase their self-esteem. Critics like Arthur Schlesinger Jr. fault multiculturalism on the ground that it becomes ethnic cheerleading or education as therapy.[51] But in my analysis, the reason for a liberal theory of multicultural education is *civic*—it is in the interests of all citizens. A liberal theory of multicultural education is necessary for all students on grounds that they need it to develop minimalist autonomy (the exercise of and respect for which are themselves crucial to civic and individual interests), to foster political virtues, and finally to redress past and historically inaccurate ethnocentric curricula.

Second, a consequence of developing minimalist autonomy cuts against some common misunderstandings of self-identity. From the perspective of liberal multicultural education, individuals may have multiple cultural affiliations and loyalties to a diversity of cultural groups. Both liberal and multicultural theorists sometimes seem to assume that while societies are multicultural, individuals are not. Rawls, for example, presumes that all persons will espouse a single comprehensive doctrine; Margalit and Halbertal and Kymlicka argue for the right to one's own culture. But as cultural beliefs are not innate, it is quite possible to be socialized by the plurality of cultural groups around us. It is equally possible that, exercising one's autonomy, people may opt to cobble together a life embodying many different values, committed to several diverse ends, devoted to multiple cultural traditions. Seen this way, liberal multicultural education cherishes a freedom that secures for each individual the right to reinvent oneself, not only as a single self, but a self with multiple cultural loyalties and attachments. Let me be clear, however: it does not demand or even encourage that individuals become cultural mongrels, for autonomous individuals are free to affirm or endorse cultural purity as much as cultural hybridity. Liberal multicultural education simply makes a multicultural identity a real option for individuals.

Third, I do not believe that a liberal theory of multicultural education can prescribe, from the level of theory, any specific institutional arrangements of schooling. The theory does not imply, for example, closing down private and religious schools and forcing all children to attend integrated public schools. The theory does defend a vision of civic education that all students should receive. It suggests, therefore, greater suspicion of educational arrangements that tend to reproduce the home environment of the child in the school, shielding students from exposure to and engagement with diversity. But to endorse liberal multicultural education is emphatically not to endorse a unified, standard, secular education that all children receive in equal doses. Liberal multicultural education leaves much room for the exercise of parental and communal discretion.

Exactly how much authority parents and communities should have over the education of their children is another question. The articulation and pursuit of civic aims of education historically has conflicted with parents' interests or rights to direct the upbringing of their children. Can the liberal state permit parents to direct the education of their children entirely? This is the subject of the following chapter.

Testing the Boundaries of Parental Authority over Education: The Case of Homeschooling

This would be a very different case for me if respondents' claim were that their religion forbade their children from attending any school at any time and from complying in any way with the educational standards set by the State.

Justice White, commenting on the Amish in the *Yoder* case

The articulation and defense of educational aims provides an ideal of what the purpose of schooling should be. I have argued that a liberal and culturally diverse state ought to situate educational purposes within a liberal theory of multicultural education in which an education for minimalist autonomy and a multicultural curriculum are fundamental components. Children deserve as a matter of justice an education that cultivates their autonomy and that is multicultural. These aims, however, do not provide immediate guidance on how authority over educational institutions should be distributed. Certainly it is not only the state that has an interest in educating children. When conflicts between the parents and the state, or cultural groups and the state, over educational authority arise, how should these be decided?

When political theorists write about the boundaries of parental and state authority over education, they often write about two United States court cases—the Supreme Court's 1972 decision in *Wisconsin v. Yoder* and the Sixth Circuit Court's 1987 decision in *Mozert v. Hawkins County Board of Education*.[1] Such a staple of discussion are these two cases that it seems scarcely a book or an article on the topic of liberalism and civic education in the past decade has failed to address at least one of the cases in some detail.[2]

The unusual focus on these two cases is understandable, for they help to illustrate a number of central tensions in liberal theory generally, and a number of tensions in the demands of liberal civic education more specifically. The *Yoder* case, in which Amish parents were granted a partial exemption from compulsory attendance laws, raises a number of difficult questions about the scope of religious liberty, about the significance of claims that a cultural group's very existence may be threatened by state regulations, and about how much schooling is necessary to develop the bare essentials of citizenship. The *Mozert* case, in which Christian Fundamentalist parents were not granted an exemption from state regulations requiring public school children to read from textbooks exposing them to a diversity of value orientations, raises questions about how the clash between religious conviction and secular authority should be resolved within public schools, about whether exposure to value diversity constitutes an indoctrination in secular humanism, and about the limits of state authority in prescribing curricular materials for students. Both cases highlight questions about whether parents possess actual *rights* to direct the upbringing of their children and about how a liberal state should strike the proper balance among parents' interests, state's interests, and children's interests in education. These assorted questions are obviously of deep importance and warrant repeated analysis and scrutiny.

Though examinations of *Yoder* and *Mozert* continue to yield fresh insights and arguments, these cases attract the energy and attention of theorists to an unfortunate and disproportionately high degree. In my view, the gallons of ink spilled on *Yoder* and *Mozert* actually serve to sidetrack discussion of these more general questions to the extent that the best legal or moral resolution of neither case hinges on a widely applicable criterion of the limits of parental authority in education. Liberals, for example, may agree with conservatives that *Yoder* was correctly decided while disagreeing sharply about the appropriate scope of parental authority. Similarly, rival perspectives on *Mozert* depend crucially on how we interpret the educational demands of the plaintiffs.[3] If theorists really want a test case that compels us to focus on the limits of parents' authority over the education of their children, and to consider the proper balance of parents', state's, and children's interests in education, we should stop fixating on *Yoder* and *Mozert*. We should instead be looking at a burgeoning and, compared to the number of Amish defectors or Christian Fundamentalists challenging public school curricula, far more prevalent educational phenomenon: homeschooling.

Homeschooling is the education of children under the supervision of their parents within the home, apart from any campus-based school. As such, homeschooling represents the paradigmatic example of the realization of complete parental authority over the educational environment of their children. In no other setting are parents as able to direct in all aspects the education of their children, for in homeschools they are responsible not only for

143

determining what their children shall learn, but when, how and with whom they shall learn. If it is permissible for parents to homeschool their children, then we have gone a long way toward identifying the wide scope of parental authority over the education of their children, or put conversely, toward severely limiting the role of the state in educational supervision.

While *Yoder* and *Mozert* do raise questions about the extent of parental authority, homeschooling throws these questions into sharpest relief. At bottom, *Yoder* asks whether parents of a self-segregated religious order may exempt their children from compulsory attendance laws *after eight years of regular school attendance.* The Amish exemption applies only to the final two years of required attendance. At bottom, *Mozert* asks whether state authorities have the power to require students *in public schools* to read from specified texts that might expose a child to values other than or in opposition to those held by the child's parents. The *Mozert* parents were always free to withdraw their children from public schools and send them to a religious school in which the curriculum adhered more closely to their own beliefs.[4] Homeschooling raises the stakes over parental authority considerably: should parents have the authority to educate their children of any and all ages apart from any formal, institutional setting, public or private, where in current practice the regulations are minimal, often unenforced, and sometimes nonexistent? Homeschooling illustrates in its purest form parents' authority over the education of their children, and therefore it provides the ideal test case of the boundaries of this authority.

In this chapter, I take up the question of homeschooling. In the first section, I look at the recent history of homeschooling in the United States, showing that beyond its interest in purely theoretical terms, the actual practice of homeschooling also provides powerful reasons to focus attention on it. In section 2, I canvass a trilogy of interests in education—those of parents, state, and children—as a prelude to considering the justifiability of homeschooling. While each party shares an interest in educating a child to become an adult who is capable of independent functioning, the state has an independent interest in educating for citizenship, and the child has an independent interest in an education for autonomy, neither of which may be shared by parents. Building upon the liberal theory of multicultural education I defended in the previous chapter, I examine in section 3 the boundaries of parental authority over education by considering how to decide cases where interests conflict. I contend that at a bare minimum one function of any school environment must be to expose children to and engage students with values and beliefs other than those of their parents. Because homeschooling is structurally and in practice the least likely to meet this end, I argue that while the state should not ban homeschooling, it must nevertheless regulate its practice with vigilance. I then consider whether children's own voices deserve a place in legal decision making, and I conclude by briefly offering a few suggestions about the best means at the state's disposal to exercise regulatory authority and by considering some problems with regulation.

The History and Current Practice of Homeschooling

Schooling in the home is the oldest form of education. Traditionally, and across cultures, children have been taught at home by their parents or, sometimes, by tutors. This was also true in the United States in the late 1700s and early 1800s. But with the advent of publicly funded common schools in the mid-nineteenth century and the widespread passage of compulsory education laws in the early twentieth century, homeschooling practically disappeared.[5] In the early 1970s, the number of children schooled at home was estimated to be around ten thousand, and in 1983 around sixty thousand.[6] Parents who schooled their children at home were often prosecuted under compulsory attendance laws, and several states explicitly forbade homeschooling. Only since 1993 has homeschooling been legal in all fifty states.

During the 1990s, however, homeschooling exploded in popularity. Because many states do not collect data on homeschooling, and because parents sometimes resist the monitoring efforts of the state, accurate data do not exist.[7] Estimates of homeschooling pin the number of students at 350,000 in 1990, 750,000 in 1996, 1.3 million in 1998, and 1.9 million in 2000.[8] Growth has been exponential and, according to recent news reports, has accelerated due to fears of school safety following the shooting deaths of students at Columbine High School in April 1999.[9] Homeschooling is no longer a fringe phenomenon in American education.

To put these figures in perspective, it is helpful to compare the number of homeschooled students to the population of students enrolled in regular schools, public, private, or religious. If we take a conservative estimate of 1.3 million homeschooled students, we find that this figure is greater than the combined number of students enrolled in schools in Wyoming, Alaska, Delaware, North Dakota, Vermont, South Dakota, Montana, Rhode Island, New Hampshire, and Hawaii, the bottom ten states in school enrollment.[10] The 1.3 million figure is almost double the number of students enrolled in conservative Christian schools, which was 737,000 in 1998.[11] As if to symbolize the mainstream acceptance of homeschooling, the U.S. newsmagazine *Newsweek* devoted a cover story to the topic in 1998, giving explicit instructions to parents on how to begin homeschooling, and the United States Senate passed a resolution declaring 19 September 1999 "National Home Education Week."[12] When we consider the relative popularity of homeschooling, compared to the numbers of Amish children or Christian Fundamentalists, it seems all the more important for political theorists and educational policymakers to devote serious attention to the phenomenon.

Why do parents homeschool? Who is choosing to homeschool? And what explains the rapid growth of the past decade? The scattered studies of homeschooling reveal a host of motivations on the part of parents for removing their children from school in order to teach them at home, ranging from a desire for pedagogical innovation, a rejection of the secular ethos of public schools, a belief that the special needs of some physically or mentally handicapped children are better served at home, to a fear for the safety of children in schools. But researchers tend to agree that, as one historical survey concluded, whereas homeschools of the 1970s "reflected a liberal, humanistic, pedagogical orientation," the vast majority of homeschools in the 1980s and 1990s "became grounds of and for ideological, conservative, religious expressions of educational matters."[13] Today, it appears that the reason most, but not all, parents choose to educate their children at home is because they believe that their children's moral and spiritual needs will not be met in campus-based schools. Like the *Yoder* and *Mozert* parents, most homeschooling parents have religious objections to placing their children in a public, or even a private, school environment.[14]

Two factors are primarily responsible for fueling the expansion of homeschooling. First, the *Yoder* decision inspired many homeschool advocates to press their claims in state legislatures and courts, a strategy that has yielded significant victories.[15] Homeschooling is now legal in all fifty states, and at least thirty-seven states have explicit homeschooling statutes. Second, over the past few years the internet has provided the means to create homeschooling networks, distribute curricular materials, and offer legal advice.[16] Moreover, with its growing popularity has come mainstream acceptability; this in turn has made homeschooling yet more popular.

Though homeschooling is legal everywhere, states still have the authority to regulate its practice. Even in *Yoder*, the case granting parents the widest exemption from state regulations, the Court went to great lengths to indicate the singularity of the case, emphasizing that "[n]othing we hold is intended to undermine the general applicability of the state's compulsory school-attendance statutes or to limit the power of the state to promulgate reasonable standards."[17] But how states exercise their regulatory authority varies widely. Some states require homeschooling parents to register with their local school districts, others establish minimal academic qualifications for parents who will offer instruction, and still others mandate that parents submit portfolios of student work to school district administrators or that children take and score at acceptable levels on standardized tests. In many or even most states, however, it appears that regulations go utterly unenforced. In California for example, a state without any statute explicitly permitting homeschooling and whose laws make it among the most difficult places to school at home, parents must either qualify their homeschool as a private school, offer instruction by a certified private tutor, enroll in an independent study program at home using the public school curriculum, or enroll in a private school satellite program and take independent home study. Yet, according to a recent news report, "Most families do not report to the state at all, and many school districts turn a blind eye toward prosecuting parents for violating the compulsory public school attendance law."[18] At a more general level, James Dwyer has argued that despite having the authority, "states and the federal government have effectively relinquished all authority to oversee private schooling. . . . In contrast to the extensive regulatory scheme governing public schools in most states, there are virtually no constraints today on what religious schools teach or how they treat their students."[19] What Dwyer says of private and religious schooling applies with even greater force to homeschooling.

Even in states where regulations are enforced, the rules are often so minimal or full of loopholes that homeschools can be established and maintained with great ease and with barely any state monitoring. According to the Home School Legal Defense Association, forty-one states do not require homeschool parents to meet any specific qualifications, and only twenty-five states insist on standardized testing and evaluation.[20] In Virginia, for example, parents who intend to homeschool need only notify the local school superintendent, possess a baccalaureate degree, and submit a brief description of the curriculum they will use. And if the parents have sincere religious objections to these requirements, they are entitled to an exemption. In other words, parents with sincere religious beliefs in Virginia may legally remove their children from school and teach them at home without any state requirements or oversight of their homeschool whatsoever.[21] Similar religious exemptions exist in other states.

For both theoretical and practical reasons, then, homeschooling is an ideal test case for political theorists arguing about the boundaries of parental and state authority over children's education. From a strictly theoretical point of view, the very structure of homeschooling raises questions about whether the interests of the state in education can be met in a setting where parents control both the academic program and social interactions of children and can, if they so desire, effectively shield children from exposure to anything that offends the values and beliefs of the parents. From a strictly practical point of view, the actual practice of homeschooling reveals first that it is a widespread and growing phenomenon; second, that state regulations for establishing homeschools are often minimal and, even when in place, often go unenforced; and third, that the majority of parents who choose to home-school have conservative religious motivations, similar to the sort of parent in a case like *Yoder* or *Mozert*.

A TRILOGY OF INTERESTS: PARENTS, THE STATE, AND THE CHILD

As it currently stands in the United States, nearly two million children are homeschooled by their parents, learning in an educational environment that is more often than not wholly or nearly unregulated by any state or federal authority. These children receive an education over which their parents have exclusive or nearly exclusive control and authority. From the perspective of the liberal state, is this a problem? What are the boundaries of parental authority in educational provision?

To answer these questions, it is necessary to indicate who has an interest in education and to spell out what these interests are. And the first comment to be made here is that it is not only interests of parents and the state at stake. Children, who are subject to the education and thus most directly affected by educational decision making, also have an interest, which may conflict with those of their parents or the state. To decide what the boundaries of parental authority in educational provision may be, therefore, we must consider the interests of the parents, the state, and the child.

Let me emphasize that it is beyond the scope of this chapter to provide a complete account of the nature of parental authority over children generally. I aim more specifically to consider, given a general understanding of the interests at stake, the limits of parental control over educational provision. There are several reasons why a focus on parental authority is important and appropriate. One of these reasons, however, is *not* that I am suspicious of parental motivations to control the upbringing of their children. Much to the contrary, I focus on parental authority over education precisely because the liberal theory of multicultural education I defended in the previous chapter does not automatically yield the conclusion that the state should be the sole provider of schools, nor that the state should fund and control all varieties of schools. In a liberal state, there should be ample room for parental discretion over the education of their children. Another reason to focus on parental authority is that the current flow of educational trends and reforms, of which homeschooling is but one example, comprise powerful currents that place increasingly more responsibility and control in the hands of parents. I have in mind here the growing appetite for voucher programs and the popularity of charter schools, topics I shall return to discuss in greater detail in the final chapter. But again, these reforms give no reason to doubt the importance of parents in the provision of education for their children. They offer, however, a practical reason to examine the boundary of such discretion.

Parents' Interests in Education

Parents obviously have very strong interests in the education of their children.[22] In the abstract, these interests are twofold, grounded in the *self-regarding* interests of the parents themselves and grounded in the *other-regarding* claim that since children are dependent for their well-being on others, parents are best situated to promote their welfare. Let us consider each in turn.

Children are not mere extensions of their parents; they are not their parents' property. But we can acknowledge this truth while also giving due to the self-regarding interests of parents, or what Eamonn Callan calls the "expressive significance" of child-rearing. Parenting is for many people a central source of meaning in their lives. As Callan puts it, "Success or failure in the task [of parenting], as measured by whatever standards we take to be relevant, is likely to affect profoundly our overall sense of how well or badly our lives have gone."[23] Raising a child is never merely a service rendered unto another person but is the collective sharing of a life. If we think in common-sensical terms that adults often have children in order to fulfill their goal to have a family and to live life as part of a family, the sense in which child-rearing comes under the self-regarding interest of parents becomes clearer. It would be inconceivable for some people to lead what they would consider a good and flourishing life without having children with whom they had a close and abiding relationship, which is in part defined by the sharing not only of certain activities and rituals but also values and interests. Because schooling plays so important a role in cultivating the values and interests of children, parents cannot simply be indifferent to how their children are educated.

Of course, parents' interests in exerting authority over the provision of education for their children are also grounded in the interest of the children themselves. Children are dependent beings, not yet capable of meeting their own needs or acting in their own interest. Parents, it is generally believed, are best situated (better situated than the state and the children themselves) to act in the best interests of their children, or, in an alternative formulation, to promote their general welfare. In modern society, the welfare of a child depends in part on being educated. Therefore, as the guardians of their children's best interests or welfare, parents have an interest in the education that their children receive.

There is a problem with the "best interests" or "general welfare" standard, however. Despite the fact that the "best interest of the child" is the coin of the realm in legal decision making about children—judges routinely make rulings on the basis of the best interests of the child—it is not a logical necessity that a child's *parents* are the agents who will act on these best interests. Others—grandparents, siblings, aunts and uncles, family friends, or state officials—might be better able to promote the welfare of the child. And of course, when parents are clearly negligent or abusive to their children, whether intentionally or not, the state intervenes and awards guardianship to a relative or foster care family or, in the most dire situation, to the state itself (at a state orphanage, for example). Who is to say, then, that parents are best suited to pursue the best interests of children?

The best answer to this question is to consider the possible alternatives, all of which appear to be worse.[24] The more telling problem with the "best interests of the child standard" is that the best interests of a child do not admit of an objective answer. How does one define "best interests"? The answer depends very much, it seems, on a particular view of the good life. Secular parents (or state authorities), for example, may define the best interests of a child in a very different manner than deeply religious parents. This fact obviously cuts to the heart of the conflict in the *Yoder* and *Mozert* cases. But we need not view this only as an issue of religious difference to see it as a problem. People may differ drastically on their interpretation of best interests in nonreligious terms. Given plural conceptions of the good life, there will be no readily identifiable consensus about the best interests of the child in all cases.

In light of this, one response is to suggest that parents are ideally situated not to realize the best interests of their children, for that is an inevitably contestable standard, but rather to meet the basic developmental needs of their children, the content of which appears to admit of a more objective answer. The basic developmental needs of the child include shelter, food, protection, and, not least, nurture, affection, and love. These the parents are surely in the best position to provide, at least when compared to the state and the children themselves. The difficulty for parents, however, is that when the needs of children are reduced to such an elementary and unobjectionable level, they do not yield any corresponding interest in control over educational provision. Whereas the "best interest" standard clearly implicates some parental interest in having a say in or perhaps even directing the educational environment of children, the lesser "basic developmental need" standard has no such implication. Shelter, food, protection, and love are responsibilities of a child's primary caregivers; not, or at least not to a large degree, of a child's teacher. An interesting dynamic emerges. The greater substance one packs into the notion of a child's needs and interests, the greater claim one has to influence the education of the child but the less likely that there will be objective agreement about what these needs and interests are. Conversely, the less substance one packs into the notion of a child's needs and interests, the more likely one will be able to secure objective agreement about them, but only at the cost of failing to justify an interest in educational provision.[25]

Despite these difficulties, it remains clear that parents have substantial interests in the education of their children. To acknowledge that the best-interest standard is contestable is of course not to obviate parental interests. Even when there is violent disagreement about what constitutes the best interests of the child, the very fact of disagreement does not void the parental interest. To the contrary, we can conclude one of two things. Either the best-interest standard should not be used when making decisions about educational authority, in which case the parents' claims must rest heavily on the weight of their expressive, self-regarding interests.[26] Or, to the extent that the best-interest standard is employed, we cannot interpret "best interests" only from the perspective of the parents. When conflicts about the education of children arise, parents cannot wield a trump card based solely on their own understanding of their child's best interests. Thus, even before we have considered the state's interests and the child's interests, we can conclude that while parents clearly have substantial interests in the education of their children, it appears highly unlikely that they will be so weighty as to justify a claim that parents should command complete authority over the education of their children.

State's Interests in Education

Like parents, the state also has very strong interests in the education of children. In the abstract, these interests are twofold. First, the state has an interest in providing children a civic education such that they are familiar with and able to participate in the political structures of society. Second, the state has an interest in performing a backstop role to the parents in assuring that children receive a basic education sufficient to allow them to become adults capable of independent functioning. Both of these interests serve to justify a role for the state in exercising educational authority over its youngest citizens.

Historically, the civic interest of the state in providing and regulating education for children is familiar, and in American legal doctrine, well-established. Even in the *Yoder* case, for example, the Court acknowledged that the state possesses a fundamental interest in educating for citizenship: "There is no doubt as to the power of a State, having a high responsibility for education of its citizens, to impose reasonable regulations for the control and duration of basic education. Providing public schools ranks at the very apex of the function of a State."[27] In its landmark *Brown v. Board of Education* decision the Court opined, "Today, education is perhaps the most important function of state and local governments."[28]

I have argued that in a liberal theory of multicultural education the state has an interest in fostering minimalist autonomy in children and in assuring that they receive a multicultural education. Minimalist autonomy has a civic justification in that the respect for and the exercise of autonomy are connected to an understanding of freedom in a liberal society and are necessary to establish the legitimacy of principles of justice and their stability over generations. A multicultural education has a civic justification in that it plays an instrumental role in cultivation of minimalist autonomy and certain political virtues, including mutual respect and the capacity for public reason and democratic deliberation.

For some, the state's interest in education is much greater, and for others much less. The scope of civic education is a matter of intense debate, and in recent years, political theorists have interpreted the demands of civic education in very different ways. On the more demanding end of the spectrum, some argue that the state must teach children not only basic literacy but knowledge of public policy issues, the conclusions of contemporary science, a foundation in world and national history, the structure and operation of federal, state, and local government, and a broad palette of critical thinking and empathy skills necessary to facilitate democratic deliberation amid a multiplicity of competing interests and among diverse races, religions, and worldviews.[29] Others indicate that the state's civic interest in education lies more generally in assuring that children will have the opportunity and capacity to participate in public institutions and will come to possess a number of political virtues, such as tolerance, civility, and a sense of fairness.[30] On the less demanding side of the spectrum, some argue that civic requirements are more minimal, encompassing the teaching of tolerance and, as one theorist puts it, "social rationality."[31]

I say this to acknowledge that disagreement exists about how wide or narrow the scope of civic education should be and that some will reject the liberal theory of multicultural education I have defended. Yet even this acknowledgement underscores the simple point that on any reading the state does indeed have legitimate interests in educational authority based on providing children with the capacities to become able citizens, however citizenship and citizenship education are defined. While there is room for reasonable disagreement about the scope of civic education, no one seriously doubts that the state has an interest in some form of it. And, of course, seen historically, this has been the central and abiding rationale for the public provision of schooling.

Beyond providing a civic education, the state also has an interest in education because it must perform a backstop role to parents in ensuring that children receive some basic minimum of schooling such that they can develop into adults who are capable of independent functioning. By "independent functioning" I do not mean to imply anything about individualism or detachment from parental or communal relationships. I mean it in the innocuous sense that, because parents will die and no longer be able to provide for and support them, all children need to grow into adults who possess a baseline set of social, emotional, and intellectual competencies that enable them to navigate and participate in the familiar social and economic institutions of society. I have in mind here things like the need to acquire reading skills and basic mathematical literacy so that as adults they can do things as mundane as read street signs and as important as fill out a job application. In modern society, educational attainment and academic achievement have become increasingly important to independent functioning. We would rightly consider a child unfairly deprived who was denied the opportunity to be educated. While compulsory attendance laws arose in part to ensure that children received a civic education and to complement child labor restrictions, it is no exaggeration to claim that today educational attainment is essential simply in order to become an independent adult who is able to find a place in the workforce.[32] These educational outcomes, I should emphasize, are different from the exercise of citizenship, having to do not with the capacity for participation in political arenas and mechanisms but with the capacity to lead a life amid the main social and economic institutions of society.

Now while educational attainment may be necessary to acquiring the competencies conducive to independent functioning as an adult, we cannot conclude from this that the state must control and regulate all educational provision. On the contrary, since parents almost always share this interest in educational attainment and wish for their children to develop into independent adults in the sense indicated above, and since parents are better situated than the state to know their children's particular learning needs and capacities, the state properly exercises authority over the aspects of education necessary to becoming an independent adult in a backstop role. Pursuant to this task, the state provides and regulates publicly funded schools for those parents who wish to send their children to them. It also legislates that children shall attend schools until a specified age. But since the education necessary for developing into independent adulthood can be satisfied by a wide variety of curricula, pedagogies, and environments—any number of educational arrangements could lead to the desired outcome—parents should have on this matter wide discretion to choose or influence the form and content of the education which they believe best suits their children. When parents impede the development of these baseline competencies, through intentional or unintentional abuse or neglect, then the state should intervene.

The state thus possesses two distinct interests in the education of children: first, that children receive a civic education; and second, that children develop into adults capable of independent functioning. Parents and the state share the second interest but not necessarily the first. State interests most often clash with parents' interests where civic education is concerned.[33] Parents and the state may clash, for example, on their respective interpretation of what civic education requires, or in some cases parents may reject aspects of civic education altogether. As the *Yoder* and *Mozert* cases show, conflicts between parents and the state with respect to how children should be educated to become citizens are by no means uncommon.

Such conflicts lead to a set of very difficult questions. Should the state's interest in developing citizenship trump parents' interests in education when parents do not share the state's civic goals for their children? Can the state sometimes tolerate, if the stability of the state is not threatened, parents who will not provide an education that develops requisite citizenship capacities? Must children attend public schools in order for civic education to be most effective? What are the empirical findings on effective civic education?[34] At the very least, the clashing of parents' interests and state's interests leads to questions about how such interests might best be balanced, how such usually overlapping but occasionally competing interests may yield a just distribution of educational authority. But it is too early to seek an answer; we have yet to consider the independent interests of children.

Child's Interests in Education

I consider this much to be uncontroversial: both parents and the state have clear interests in education that lead to legitimate claims to exert authority over its provision. Typically, American social and legal institutions consider these to be the only interests at stake.[35] But as the subjects of the educational process, children have independent interests in education as well. They naturally have an interest in developing into adults capable of independent functioning, in the sense indicated above. And, as argued in the previous chapter, they have an interest in their prospective autonomy. This is because the exercise of minimalist autonomy in the political sphere is important in one's role as a citizen, and because becoming minimally autonomous is a necessary (though not sufficient) condition to living well in a liberal society.

Two prefatory comments: first, though the content of these interests may overlap with those of either the parents or the state, they are nevertheless *independent* interests. In certain circumstances, these independent interests may place children in conflict with their parents or with the state. Children's interests in education potentially conflict with their parents' interests when, for example, parents seek through the educational environment (and elsewhere) to satisfy an expressive interest in molding their children into certain persons without regard to the will of the children themselves. Think for example of the parents who wish to make a martyr of their child; or, in a less extreme example, of the parent who forces a child to quit, against her will, all forms of educational activity except those which promote the parents' expressive interest in raising, say, a virtuoso pianist. Children's interests in education may conflict with the state's interests in cases, for example, like *Tinker v. Des Moines Independent Community School District* (393 U.S. 503 [1969]), where the right of students to express themselves politically in schools clashed with the power of the state to control the educational environment of the school. Because of the possibility of conflict, it is important to identify children's interests as distinct and not subsume them under those of their parents or of the state.

Second, the fact that children are needy and dependent justifies a certain amount of parental and state paternalism with respect to educational provision, and also often necessitates that persons other than the child be able to represent his interests. Acknowledging the fact that children have independent interests in education does not mean that children are best suited to supervise the promotion of these interests; nor does it mean that they are able, especially at young ages, even to articulate them. But the problem of children's neediness and dependence, and the problem of who shall represent children's interests, does not invalidate the interests. It merely points to the need for debate about when paternalism over children is no longer justified and when, developmentally, children might capably represent themselves, especially in cases where interests conflict.

Turning then to delineating the child's interests in education, the first interest should seem obvious: a child has an interest in education because education is necessary to developing into an adult capable of independent functioning. Again, I do not mean to imply anything especially controversial about independent functioning. A child rightly expects to develop a set of competencies that make it possible for him or her to navigate and participate in the main social and economic institutions of society. The state and presumably the child's parents wish for this too. Except in the most unusual circumstances—where for example a child is severely disabled or mentally handicapped and cannot be expected to become capable of independent functioning, or when parents abuse or neglect their children in obvious and uncontroversial ways—all three parties, parent, state, and child, would seem to share this interest.

It is a child's prospective interest in autonomy that may be controversial and may not be shared. Minimalist autonomy, I argued in the previous chapter, is in the individual interest of all persons. And because autonomy describes a character ideal that is an achievement rather than an inheritance, it requires an education of a certain sort for its cultivation. Some parents or cultural groups may resist such an education because they do not wish for their children to become autonomous.

But to resist the cultivation of minimalist autonomy in children would be to undermine the conditions of legitimate consent and stability in a liberal society. One justification for educating for autonomy is rooted in the terrain of one's public or political life. As I just elaborated in the preceding section, for the exercise of state power to be legitimate and stable, citizens must autonomously consent to the principles of justice upon which the state is founded. If persons, as citizens, are to be able freely and without coercion or indoctrination to make decisions about the political structures that will govern them, if they are to be able to contest and perhaps resist the exercise of state power, and if they are to be able sympathetically to engage other citizens in democratic deliberation, they will need to acquire the skills and habits of minimalist autonomy.

Another, and perhaps more important justification for educating for autonomy is rooted in the terrain of one's private or personal life. Becoming autonomous is necessary, albeit not sufficient, to lead a good and flourishing life in a liberal society.[36] This is so, as I claimed in chapter 5, for two reasons. First, minimalist autonomy is necessary to establish the conditions of self-respect that enable a person to see her ends as valuable and worth pursuing. Without the capacity to subject our ends to critical reflection and thereby to come to cleave to them autonomously or to revise or reject them autonomously, we may fail to acquire the confidence that these ends deserve our approbation. It is hard to see how we could live flourishing lives without having the self-respect to believe that our own ends are worthy. Second, minimalist autonomy is necessary to avoid the inculcation of a servile disposition that would lead a child to subordinate his will to that of another person or persons. If we do not possess our own ends, in the sense that we have autonomously endorsed them, we risk becoming servile to those who would provide ends for us. But precisely because children are independent persons and the property neither of their parents nor of the state, their socialization should not be allowed to make them servile to their caretakers or educational providers. Neither parents nor the state can justly attempt to imprint upon a child an indelible set of values and beliefs, as if it were an inheritance one should never be able to question, as if the child must always defer and be unquestioningly obedient. In short, children must become minimally autonomous as a condition of achieving self-respect and in order to escape the condition of servility. And both self-respect and the supercession of servility are conditions of leading a good and flourishing life. Minimalist autonomy therefore, while of course not guaranteeing the living of a good life, is in the eudaemonistic interest of children, as of all persons.

Implications of the Trilogy of Interests

What can we conclude from this general survey of the interests of the parents, the state, and the child in education? In almost all cases, each party shares the goal of educating children to become adults capable of independent functioning. Indeed, many view the primary function of education to be the provision of capabilities, competencies, encouragement of talents, and fostering of scholastic achievement that enable children to develop into adults who can function on their own in society—who can secure work, care for themselves, and seek and develop their own interests. In fact, a harmony among parents, the state, and child frequently extends in practice across all interests. The parents' self-regarding interests may coincide with the state's interest in developing the child's capacity to exercise the rights of citizenship; the child's interest in becoming minimally autonomous may coincide with the parents' expressive interests and the state's interest in citizenship.

But this harmony of shared interests is not inevitable. As we have seen, the interest of the state in fostering citizenship may not be shared by the parents. Likewise, a child's interest in becoming minimally autonomous may not be shared by parents. At this point, some may object that while the state and the child do have these conflicting interests, only parents possess actual *rights* with respect to their children's education. This is a matter of some controversy.[37] I contend that, even assuming that parental interests rise to the level of rights, in addition to whatever rights parents have over their children's education, the respective interests of the state and the child remain. The state may take steps to promote certain civic virtues in children, and children should develop the capacities of minimal autonomy that entitle them, especially as adolescents, to a proto-right to self-governance. These two claims hold if parental rights are vindicated. They also hold, *a fortiori*, if there are no parental rights.

Put simply, no one set of parents', state's, or child's interests can trump the others and justify sole authority for any party over educational provision. Neither parents, nor the state, nor children themselves should unilaterally and without a countervailing balance direct and control the educational environment of children. Given the triad of interest-holders and the significance of their respective interests, a theory of educational authority that claimed only the interests of one party mattered could potentially establish a kind of parental despotism, state authoritarianism, or child despotism. Any defensible theory of educational authority will strike some balance among the three parties.

How should the balance of educational authority be struck? This seems to me a question that is impossible to answer theoretically.[38] There is ample room for democratic decision making about the proper distribution of educational authority, and a variety of institutional arrangements and governance structures are capable of meeting the interests of all three parties while remaining consistent with the requirements of justice. What we can do from the level of theory is examine the limits of such authority. And as promised, I want now to redirect our attention to the phenomenon of homeschooling in order to consider in the next section whether homeschooling—the educational arrangement which in both theory and practice tilts most heavily in the direction of parental interests and authority—permits the realization of both the state's and the child's interests in education. If under a scheme of complete parental authority the interests of the state and the child in education can be met, then homeschooling should be a legitimate educational practice, and we will have justified parental control of significant weight and scope. But if not, then not.

HOMESCHOOLING AND INTERESTS IN EDUCATION

The question, therefore, under consideration is, *When parental authority over the educational environment of their children is complete, as in homeschooling, can the state's and the child's interests in education be met?*

The answer to the question is clearly yes. Parents who homeschool their children, apart from any state regulation or authority, can realize the state's and the child's interests in education. In fact, some evidence suggests that in some circumstances, parents who homeschool their children may be better at achieving the state's and the child's educational interests than public or private schools. In a news article on homeschooling in California, for example, one child appears to suggest that the reason she wishes to be homeschooled is because the development of her autonomy is threatened in campus-based school settings. Speaking of her former school, she reported, "I didn't want to be there. All the kids are just like sheep, and they don't have any independence."[39] Indeed, some and perhaps many schools do a poor job of countering the peer pressure to which teenagers are so likely to succumb. Moreover, recent studies of homeschooled children show that they often outperform their public and private school counterparts in scholastic achievement.[40] It appears possible, therefore, that with respect to the child's interest in developing autonomy and the shared interest in academic achievement, homeschools can sometimes be more effective than traditional campus-based schools.

There is also a very practical reason that homeschooling should be a legitimate and important educational alternative. Some children, in particular those with severe or rare physical or mental disabilities, may have such specific learning needs or require such a tailored learning environment that public or private schools simply cannot accommodate them.[41] In this circumstance, justice and practicality require that the state permit parents to teach such children at home. Beyond the problem of severely disabled or impaired students, some families live in such rural or sparsely populated regions that the nearest school, public or private, may be many miles away. It may be cost-ineffective to build a public school for a small number of families living a great distance from other public schools or to provide public transportation to far-off schools. Instead, the state may find that permitting, or indeed facilitating, the homeschooling of such children is simply the only option available.

Because homeschools can feasibly realize the state's and the child's interests in education, and because homeschooling may in some circumstances be the only practical educational option, it would be unjust for the state to ban homeschooling. Educating children at home under the direction and authority of their parents must be a permissible form of schooling.

However, homeschools can also fail to realize the state's and the child's interests in education. Because some homeschools promote the autonomy of children and some conduce to high academic achievement does not imply that all do so. That they sometimes succeed or are sometimes practically necessary does not imply that the state should grant educational authority to parents whenever they express a desire to homeschool. By my account, parental authority must end when its exercise compromises the development of their children into adults capable of independent functioning or when it disables or retards the development of minimalist autonomy in children. This marks the outer boundary of parental authority over education.

Parents compromise the development of their children into adulthood when they are negligent or abusive, preventing children from becoming independent beings who can participate in the main social and economic institutions of society. One imagines cases of malnourishment, physical or mental abuse, or sheer neglect. In such circumstances, the intervention of the state on behalf of children is not controversial. The state acts in its backstop role. If parental authority over education does not foster the self-sufficiency and independence of children, the state must step in and ensure such outcomes.

The problem with homeschooling and parental authority over education arises not out of conflicts over whether children should become independent adults. Few people wish to defend the authority of parents who plainly care too little. The problem arises with parents who, as it were, care too much in seeking to prevent the development of autonomy in their children. I mean to suggest that parents who wish to control the socialization of their children so completely as to instill inerrant beliefs in their own worldview or unquestioning obedience to their own or others' authority are motivated often by a fervent care for, not neglect of, their children. Some parents may object to the idea that their children should receive an education that promotes their critical thinking and capacities for reflection on their own and others' ends, even when these are minimally defined. Being minimally autonomous, I have claimed, is in the interest of the child for personal and civic reasons. The fact that autonomy is necessary for liberal legitimacy and stability makes education for autonomy an interest of the state as well. Thus, parents who reject the facilitation of autonomy in their children find themselves in conflict with both the interests of the child and of the state.

We must therefore ask the question, What does it take, educationally, to become autonomous? Under what circumstances might homeschooling environments disable or retard the development of autonomy? We might imagine that the question admits of an empirical answer. Given a definition of minimal autonomy, some test or evaluation might be concocted to measure its development. The test could then be administered to homeschooled children. If they did not achieve at some determined level, state intervention would be justified.

The creation of such a test may be desirable, but it seems highly unlikely. The empirical measurement of autonomy, especially in children, seems to me an exceptionally difficult and probably quixotic quest. I wish to approach the question somewhat more abstractly. What structural aspects of the educational environment might promote or retard autonomy? What features of schooling are essential to fostering autonomy?

Meira Levinson suggests a bold answer: "It is difficult for children to achieve autonomy solely within the bounds of their families and home communities—or even within the bounds of schools whose norms are constituted by those from the child's home community. If we take the requirements of autonomy seriously, we see the need for a place separate from the environment in which children are raised."[42] Levinson argues, in other words, that children must attend institutional schools in order to achieve autonomy. In her view, "even the most well-intentioned and resource-laden parents" cannot accomplish what a school can with respect to fostering the development of autonomy.[43] On these grounds, Levinson would presumably rule out homeschooling as an educational alternative. But, as I have argued, banning homeschooling would be wrong. Levinson underestimates the capacities and indeed intentions of some parents to provide an education for autonomy within a homeschool setting.

If education for autonomy does not require the banning of homeschooling in all cases, what then does it require? According to the liberal theory of multicultural education I advanced in chapter 5, the cultivation of autonomy requires a multicultural education that exposes children to and engages them with cultural values and beliefs other than those of their parents.[44] To achieve minimalist autonomy, a child must know about ways of life other than that into which he has been born. It requires more than mere knowledge about the existence of alternative ways of life however. If mere knowledge sufficed, then even a casual glance at television, a drive down a city street, or a look at the newspaper would conduce to autonomy. But this is silly. To cultivate the capacity for critical reflection, students need sustained intellectual engagement with diverse values and beliefs. For its civic importance, minimalist autonomy requires that a child be able to examine his own political values and beliefs, and those of others, with a critical and sympathetic eye. And for its personal importance, it requires that a child be able to think independently and subject his ends to critical scrutiny, enabling autonomous affirmation or autonomous revision of these ends. If this is all true, then at a bare minimum, the structure of schooling cannot simply replicate in every particularity the values and beliefs of a child's home.

Clearly, not all homeschooling arrangements are troublesome in this regard. As an empirical matter, it is more likely that *some* approaches to teaching only the Bible will better engage students intellectually with diverse values and different ways of life than the banquetlike presentation of cultural ornamentation that currently passes for multicultural education in some public schools. But if there is any educational environment that might potentially be able to replicate the values and beliefs of a child's home, homeschooling is it. In homeschools, parents are able, after all, to control not only the curriculum and pedagogy but also the social environment of their child. Parents can severely limit social interaction and thereby curtail their child's opportunities to encounter other children from different backgrounds.[45] These informal opportunities to engage with difference are likely just as effective in facilitating the development of autonomy as the formal curriculum. Moreover, empirical evidence strongly suggests that the majority of homeschooling parents are motivated by a desire to control the moral and spiritual upbringing of their children. Indeed, some parents are eager to prevent their children from being exposed to anything contrary to the moral and spiritual values they wish their children to learn.

To be sure, exposing children to and engaging children with diverse values and beliefs is potentially threatening to some parents. As bell hooks has written of her own childhood, "School was the place of ecstasy—pleasure and danger. To be changed by ideas was pure pleasure. But to learn ideas that ran counter to values and beliefs learned at home was to place oneself at risk, to enter the danger zone. Home was the place where I was forced to conform to someone else's image of who and what I should be. School was the place where I could forget that self and, through ideas, reinvent myself."[46] But in the interest of children, these are risks that must be accepted, for parents cannot be entitled as a matter of justice to ensure that their child grows up to become exactly the kind of person they want her to be. To prevent the risk is to ask that the child become ethically servile to the parent.

The state must therefore ensure that all children, regardless of the environment in which they are schooled—private and religious schools as well as public schools—receive a liberal multicultural education that exposes them to and engages them with values and beliefs other than those they find at home. It does not require that children engage *always* with values and beliefs that conflict with those of the home, nor does it require that children receive maximal exposure and engagement in order to provide them with maximal options in life. A helpful illustration of this difference is provided by Justice White in his concurring opinion in *Yoder*. Noting that, while many Amish children may desire to continue living a rural existence within the Amish order, White wrote memorably that "others, however, may wish to become nuclear physicists, ballet dancers, computer programmers, or historians, and for these occupations formal training will be necessary. . . . A State has a legitimate interest not only in seeking to develop the latent talents of its children but also in seeking to prepare them for the life style that they may later choose, or at least to provide them with an option other than the life they have led in the past."[47]

The achievement of minimal autonomy does not demand that a child be capable of pursuing any life path imaginable. No one can be guaranteed the right to a future so open that she may choose any occupation or endorse any possible value or belief; neither the state nor parents owe it to children as a matter of justice to make it possible for them to choose lives of absolutely any sort. It is instead Justice White's final clause that I wish to highlight: children must achieve the minimal degree of autonomy necessary to provide them with options other than that into which they have been born; they must have an effective right of exit. Children are owed as a matter of justice the capacity to choose to lead lives—to adopt values and beliefs, pursue an occupation, endorse new traditions—that are different from those of their parents. Because the child cannot ensure for herself the acquisition of such capacities and the parents may be opposed to such acquisition, the state must ensure it for the child. The state must guarantee that children are educated for minimal autonomy. Thus, the state must not forbid homeschooling but regulate it, and strictly enforce such regulations, so as to ensure that the interests of the state and the child are met. It must also guarantee, of course, that children in public, private, and religious schools are educated for minimalist autonomy.

CHILDREN'S VOICES IN LEGAL CONTEXTS

Where in this analysis, one might ask, can or should children themselves exercise authority over their own education? Do their independent interests in education yield a claim to controlling their own education? More specifically, should children have a say in whether or not they are homeschooled? This is a difficult question, for while very young children clearly are incapable of exercising educational authority, it is nevertheless true that older children are capable of making informed and reasonable choices about their education, and about many other things as well.[48] If children were to decide unilaterally, a six-year-old might elect to attend a private school or homeschool (or no school at all), rather than a public school. But the preference of such a young child cannot be decisive, else children would not need guardians at all. But if a fifteen-year-old were to decide that he wanted to attend a public school rather than be homeschooled, or attend a public school rather than a private school, or be homeschooled rather than attend public or private school, should this preference carry moral or legal weight? And if so, how much?

A recent case in Virginia raises the question of what the state should do when older children wish to attend public school and their parents wish to homeschool them.[49] Jennifer Sengpiehl had been homeschooled for many years when, in her teenage years, she began to ask her parents to permit her to attend the local public school. Her parents refused and continued to educate her at home, at which point Jennifer's behavior began to deteriorate. In an attempt to teach her a lesson about obedience, her parents called the police after she had vandalized her bedroom and brandished a knife at her father. The involvement of the police led to a juvenile court date, where unexpectedly the judge ruled that Jennifer should attend a public school. Because the court records of juveniles are sealed, it is impossible to know the details of the case in order to assess the rationale of the judge's ruling or to make an informed judgment in Jennifer's case about how continued homeschooling or public schooling would or would not meet the parents', the state's, and the child's interests in education. Traditional jurisprudence has viewed questions about educational authority over children as a contest or balancing act between the interests of parents and the state. Should the court have presumed to weigh Jennifer's own preferences about how her interests in education could best be met?

In my view, if conflicts about education reach the court, judges should not presume an identity of interests between children and their parents. They should act with discretion in soliciting the voice of the child when there is reason to believe that a child may be autonomous and that the expression of a child's preferences in a legal context will not cause more harm than good. Because the ultimate resolution of any case will concern the child most directly, there are often reasonable grounds to inquire about children's preferences. This was the reasoning behind Justice Douglas's dissent in *Yoder.*[50] And there are a wide range of U.S. cases where ample legal precedent exists not only to solicit the opinions of children but to accord them significant weight. In cases concerning custody disputes, for example, courts routinely ask children for their preferences.[51] In disputes over the medical and mental health treatment of children, courts often evaluate the child's capacity to consent to or refuse the treatment in question.[52] In cases when juvenile delinquents assert or waive their rights, courts must attempt to ascertain whether they have done so voluntarily and knowingly.[53] And though it is controversial, many courts allow teenage girls who demonstrate maturity to seek and obtain abortions without the consent or even notification of their parents.[54] Though American jurisprudence demonstrates an inconsistent treatment of the position of children in legal proceedings, the presence of children's voices in courtrooms is far from unprecedented.

A key factor in deciding whether or not to solicit the views of a child in cases concerning conflicts over educational authority should be the expectation that a child has approached or achieved autonomy. Obviously, a child's age is crucial here. As a general rule, the older the child, the greater the likelihood that the child will have approached the threshold level of autonomy such that her preferences deserve respect and therefore should be accorded significant weight. The younger the child, the less likely it is that her preferences issue from an autonomous source. Walter Mlyniec has suggested, for example, that on the basis of available scientific evidence of child development, courts should presume that, absent evidence to the contrary, children above the age of fourteen have the ability to make decisions as well as adults.[55] Thus, courts might rightly presume to hear the voice of Jennifer Sengpiehl, a sixteen-year old, but not to solicit the views of Sundee and Travis Mozert, the middle-school-aged children in the *Mozert* case.

Even when judges have reason to expect that a child may be autonomous, they must still consider the possible harm to a child who is put into a potentially adversarial relationship with his parents and cultural group leaders, such as religious authorities. Should courts ask children to articulate views that, if opposed to those of their parents, will almost surely strain the relationship they have with some of the most important people in their lives? According an independent status to children, and assigning weight to children's views, may potentially disrupt familial and communal bonds. Jennifer Sengpiehl was already at odds with her parents before her case reached the courtroom, but I seriously doubt that the situation improved after the court ruled that, contrary to her parents' preferences, she should attend a public school. Since children, and perhaps especially teenagers, have a clear interest in the ongoing love and support of those people with whom they have the closest ties, courts should be wary about the possible consequences of introducing open conflict between children and their family and community. When judges have good reason to believe that soliciting the views of a child will lead to real psychological trauma or physical harm, they should proceed with real caution. And if they anticipate that the incorporation of a child's preferences will not play a significant role in the final outcome of the case, they should perhaps reconsider, or forgo, the solicitation of the child's opinion.[56]

It must be said, however, that the charge that attributing legal standing to children and listening for their independent views will harm them by producing conflict within familial and communal relationships is itself a dangerous position. As Martha Minow has noted, such objections have been used to justify domination and hierarchy in cases concerning criminalizing rape within marriage and assigning rights to employees in companies.[57] Moreover, in some instances, such as Jennifer Sengpiehl's case, familial or communal strife is already likely, and what the child is often seeking is protection of her considered interests, not a muzzle because it is believed the continued expression of her beliefs will introduce still more conflict. Courts should be wary not to compromise the position of the most vulnerable and least powerful, the children, in an ostensible attempt to forestall potential harm to them. And they should be especially wary, as I argued in chapter 3, not to discount or ignore the position of children, and their interest in becoming autonomous, because the preferences of their parents are couched in claims about the importance of cultural maintenance or stability.

The upshot is that judges must make a judgment call about when to solicit the views of children within a courtroom, taking into account the likelihood of a child's autonomy and an assessment about the possible negative consequences to the child. The interests of children should never be subsumed under those of their parents, but there need not be an automatic expectation that if a case reaches the courtroom, children should be called upon to express their preferences.

Of course, a judge's decision to solicit the expression of children's preferences says nothing about how much weight these preferences should be accorded. It may be that a judge solicits the view of an older teenager only to determine that the view was not expressed autonomously. Perhaps the child was under extreme pressure from his parents to articulate a particular position or preference, or perhaps the child aimed merely to please, or displease, his parents. When children do not appear to be autonomous, their views should not carry significant weight, and the state must defend its own interpretation of the child's interests in education. When children do appear to be autonomous, however, their preferences should become a factor in the decision calculus of the court. And when there is firm evidence that children have achieved minimalist autonomy, they acquire in my view a proto-right to self-governance. Their considered views about educational authority should weigh heavily in the mind of a judge who must consider how to balance the interests of the parent, state, and child in education. Autonomous sixteen- or seventeen-year-olds who wish to cease homeschooling, or to attend private rather than public school (at their own expense), or perhaps even to cease schooling altogether, have a strong case to have their autonomy respected. Whichever the circumstance, once a judge makes the decision to incorporate the voice of a child into legal proceedings, a further assessment must be made about the relative autonomy of the child.

It is, of course, extremely difficult to assess the autonomy of children.[58] As I mentioned earlier, it is unlikely that any simple test might be developed that would provide reliable information about the degree of autonomy exhibited by a child, or any person for that matter. However, judges are not wholly impotent in evaluating a child's autonomy. One way to attempt such an assessment is to initiate a conversation with the child about the matter being decided.[59] Children who are minimally autonomous will be able to provide reasons for their preferences, will be able to describe the sources of information for their preferences, and will evince an understanding of the possibility of other avenues of action or belief. Of course, judges need not conduct these conversations with children; they can also appoint a third party to do so. After such dialogues take place, courts would have a better vantage point from which to evaluate whether children display the critical reflection and thoughtful deliberation characteristic of autonomy or whether they are rebelling against or parroting their parents' beliefs without reasons, or are pressured by their parents to express a particular view that may not coincide with their own. The difficulties in making such assessments are real. But the fact of the matter is that courts are called upon routinely to do so in non-educational contexts such as medical and mental health treatment, custody, juvenile delinquency, and abortions without the consent of parents, even (and especially) when there are assertions of the free religious exercise rights of parents. There is no reason that educational conflicts like those in *Yoder* and the Sengpiehl case should be treated any differently.

A final concern is that unmanageable administrative burdens might befall courts if they were frequently to incorporate a child's voice and preferences into legal proceedings involving conflicts between the state and parents over educational authority. But the implication here is not that courts should hear every case in which a child's educational interests potentially conflict with the interests of his parents, or hear the cases of all parents who claim that state regulations undermine their attempt to direct the upbringing, religious or otherwise, of their children. To the contrary, courts should prefer extra-legal mechanisms for the negotiation and resolution of disputes, and they should encourage the establishment of such mechanisms. Perhaps more often than not, conflicts about educational authority can be resolved before they reach a court. A concurring judge in the *Mozert* case, for example, noted his "profound sense of sadness" at the decision, for "at the classroom level, the pupils and teachers . . . had in most cases reached a working accommodation."[60] The state can certainly set up, and indeed often has set up, procedures and venues for the negotiation of conflicts over homeschooling, as well as other educational disputes (e.g., conflicts over the provision of special education, opting out of sexual education curricula, and so on). Surely some cases will still need to be heard by courts. But the possibility of an administrative burden in these cases should not outweigh the justice due to litigants, especially when children, and their futures, are involved.

Regulating Homeschooling

It is worth exploring briefly the kinds of homeschooling regulations the state might promulgate and some likely problems with such regulations. Over the past decade the regulations on homeschooling have eased dramatically and, where they exist, are often unenforced. Whereas some states once forbade homeschooling, its practice is now legal everywhere, with actual regulations varying significantly from state to state. Such regulations have included requirements that parents be certified teachers or have a college degree, that they submit a curricular plan to local educational authorities for review and administer standardized tests to their children in order to gauge their academic progress, that school officials make periodic visits to homeschools to evaluate the educational progress of children, that parents keep attendance records and meet a minimum number of days in school or hours spent learning, and that parents submit regular reports to local educational authorities.

The fact that regulations have diminished and in some cases disappeared and the increasing prevalence of wholly unregulated homeschools are causes for concern. The state must indeed regulate homeschools in order to assure that its own and the child's interests in education are met.

What regulations are most appropriate to this task? Regulations are properly a matter of democratic politics, not deduction from theory, but at a bare minimum, I imagine the following will be necessary. First, the state must require that any homeschooling parents register their homeschools with local educational authorities, who in turn should be required to collect this information and report it to the state. Such action will allow states to collect more accurate data on homeschooling, help make decisions about how to distribute resources for homeschoolers, and enable simplified communication between school leaders and homeschooling parents. At the moment, since many parents have never notified districts of their homeschooling intentions and arrangements, states have few means to track homeschooling and compile aggregate data. By requiring registration with local officials, the state can more effectively distinguish between truants and homeschooled children.

Second, the burden of proof that homeschools will satisfy the state's and the child's interest in education must rest with the parents who express the desire to homeschool. Parents must demonstrate to relevant education officials that their particular homeschooling arrangements are up to determined educational standards, and there ought to be clear procedures, including avenues of appeal, for resolving disputes about whether such standards have been met. Aligning the burden with parents is important, because if the homeschooling arrangements were presumed to be satisfactory unless the state were to show otherwise, the state would have to resort to difficult and intrusive means to make such a case. Especially in light of the number of homeschooled students today, school officials cannot be expected personally or closely to monitor the activities of all homeschools.

Third, because the state must ensure that the school environment provides exposure to and engagement with values and beliefs other than those of a child's parents, the state should require parents to use multicultural curricula that provide such exposure and engagement. They must, in other words, convince relevant public officials that the educational environment of the home fits somewhere within the ambit of the liberal multicultural education I defended in the previous chapter. I imagine that parents could satisfy such a regulation in a variety of ways: they could submit their curriculum for review to local school officials, they could choose curricular materials from a state-approved list, or they could allow their children to enroll in some public school activities or classes, or community-college courses, in which intellectual engagement with cultural diversity is a central task. Surely other methods are possible.

And fourth, the state should require homeschooled children to take annual standardized tests to measure academic progress. If children repeatedly fail to make academic progress relative to their peers in public or private schools, the state should intervene and compel school attendance.

This short list of regulations is tentative and provisional, for I am unsure about the most effective way to craft regulations pursuant to meeting both the state's and the child's interest. It is far easier to point out the problems with regulating homeschooling. Foremost among these is that religiously motivated homeschooling parents may simply reject the very notion of submitting to a secular authority over matters concerning the upbringing of their children. It is not that deeply religious parents refuse to acknowledge the power of the state generally, for such a position in a liberal democracy would be clearly untenable. Rather, the problem arises when secular state authority is exercised over the rearing of children. Conflict between the state and religious parents on this score may be endemic and inevitable. In my view, even given the deep importance of religious freedom, the state cannot relinquish its regulatory role in education in cases where parents invoke their religious beliefs as a bulwark against secular authority. Children themselves are entitled to free religious exercise, and are anyway due as a matter of justice an education that fosters their autonomy.

Another problem with regulation is that the supposed beneficiaries of educational regulation—children—are not politically organized and are therefore incapable of advocating for their own interests in the policy and legislative arenas. In contrast, homeschooling parents in recent years have been exceptionally powerful lobbyists for their interests at the grassroots, state, and federal level.[61] Following the lead of the Christian Coalition, homeschool parents have banded together into networks of advocacy organizations, and they are able to flood representatives' offices with phone calls and mail on short notice in order to urge or kill the passage of specific bills. In the face of such organized advocacy, the lack of any comparable lobbying effort on behalf of children's interests means that homeschool groups representing parental interests will likely continue to lessen and erase regulations. The problem, it must be stressed, goes beyond the recent political efficacy of homeschool parent groups; it appears to be inherent in the political process of enacting regulations. Because children are a politically inert group, regulations in their interest must be defended by other organizations, such as the

Children's Defense Fund, which typically have less at stake in homeschooling, or by state officials, who are of course responsible for a much broader children's agenda than guarding against homeschooling abuses. Thus, successful regulatory action is likely to be stimulated only when the homeschool parent lobby loses its power and/or comparably powerful children's advocacy groups decide to press specifically for homeschooling oversight.

A third problem with regulating homeschooling is what Cass Sunstein labels the overregulation-underregulation paradox.[62] The idea is that aggressive statutory controls designed to maintain strict compliance often result in practice in under-enforcement or minimal regulations. When regulations are many and elaborate, they often require significant spending, time, and human resources in order to enforce them. I can imagine this paradox at work in homeschooling regulations quite easily. Given the numbers of homeschoolers, local school authorities would need to devote considerable time and energy to tracking parents and children who have opted out of the public school system. To the already harried educators, spending significant time or devoting significant resources to tracking homeschools may seem wasteful. After all, by removing their children from public schools, parents reduce the public system's funding. Moreover, the very idea of making periodic home visits or meeting with parents to assess curricular materials and monitor educational progress can be unappealing. Being a truant officer or homeschool monitor is surely among the more thankless jobs in society.

The overregulation-underregulation paradox can be mitigated by placing the burden of proof on parents to demonstrate that homeschools will meet the educational interests of the state and the child. But it does not remove it entirely. It appears, therefore, sensible to keep regulations strict but minimal and as nonintrusive as possible.

In the past few years, another and very different regulatory problem has arisen. Some parents who homeschool their children wish to avail themselves and their children of the resources of the local public school—extracurricular activities and sports teams, the library, computers, and internet facilities, guidance from schoolteachers on curricular matters, and in some cases certain academic offerings.[63] Most state laws currently make it difficult for parents to claim such resources as a right; homeschoolers are assumed to have exited the public school system and thereby to have forgone the resources it has to offer. As the number of homeschooled children continues to grow, this is likely to become a new frontier in homeschool legal battles. Some school districts have adopted a conciliatory approach and have set up offices to provide curricular and pedagogical resources for homeschooling families, and to facilitate connections with school activities. But the administrative burdens placed on public school teachers and administrators to allow homeschool parents selectively to choose the resources that the public school has to offer are undoubtedly large, and they distract needed attention from the regular students in the classroom. Technological advances may mitigate these burdens by permitting wholly new ways of providing and distributing information. At least one district has set up what it calls a "virtual charter school," where it offers homeschooling families via the internet the guidance of public school teachers, standardized testing, career counseling, real-time chats with teachers and students, and the purchasing power of the district.[64] The avowed purpose of the virtual charter school is to lure families that had deserted public schools to reconnect with public education.

Though some might worry that continued development on this front heralds an era of education where the public school is essentially a provider of a menu of services and activities from which parents choose what they want, the new technology can also serve to reconnect people to the campus-based school in different ways.[65] There are a host of open questions about the consequences of homeschool-public school partnerships, but to the extent that bringing children back within a campus-based school environment conduces to meeting the interests of the state and the child in education—especially to the extent that it brings children into social and intellectual contact with other children of diverse backgrounds—such partnerships should not be summarily dismissed or discouraged. In fact, finding ways to draw homeschooling families back to the public school system seems to me a necessary complement to the passage of effective regulations.

Pedagogical and Policy Implications

In the previous chapter I argued that a liberal theory of multicultural education, which takes as a fundamental aim the development of minimalist autonomy via a multicultural education, counsels a stricter regulatory role for the liberal state concerning the practice of homeschooling. My claim was that parental authority over the education of their children should end when the preferred educational environment of parents threatens to thwart the cultivation of minimalist autonomy, and that children have independent educational interests that, at least in some contexts and at certain ages, can be represented and articulated by children themselves. This suggests a new architecture for evaluating the merits of cases in which parents wish to exempt their children from educational requirements, whether in homeschools, or in public, private, or religious schools. Such an analysis represents an initial step in demonstrating the application of the theoretical work detailed in earlier chapters of this book. In this final chapter, I take a few more steps toward this end by considering the pedagogical and policy implications of liberal multicultural education.

Important limitations, however, qualify my discussion. For reasons I suggested in the introduction, no theory, at whatever level of detail, can provide a complete blueprint for how educational institutions should be structured or for how the specifics of educational practice within classrooms shall proceed. This is so, I believe, for two reasons. First, since schooling is above all else a relational activity between teachers and students, the potential rectitude of theoretical principles is no substitute for the wisdom and expertise of local actors. No matter what the theory demands, actual teaching must begin, as John Dewey recognized, at least in large part with the interests and experience of the students. For this reason, many of the fine-grained particularities of teaching and learning are best left to those at local levels. Second, the his-

tory of education, in the United States at least, reveals a long tradition of local decision making and of the limited impact of state or federal policymaking
on educational practice.[1] Were it even possible to translate educational theory
into educational policy, and educational policy into educational practice with
seamless ease, theorists would still need to overcome the historical tradition
of decision making at local levels. For these reasons, a political theory about
education is best understood as providing a broad framework that serves to
guide and shape educational policy and practice, within which specific issues
of pedagogy and educational policy can profitably be discussed.[2]

Another limitation is that a single chapter on implications can no more
than illuminate the range of pedagogical and policy issues that arise out of or
are affected by theoretical considerations. A full treatment of the implications
of the liberal theory of multicultural education I have defended would require a book itself. Rather than delve deeply into any particular pedagogical or policy issue, I have opted instead to treat several issues with relative
brevity. While my approach sacrifices specificity, it nevertheless has the advantage, I hope, of engaging a broad range of teachers and policymakers in debate.

With these qualifications out of the way, I undertake in the following
pages to do two things. First, I review the mainstream literature on multicultural education, written by education scholars, and contrast with it the
pedagogical approach that flows from the liberal theory of multicultural education I have advanced. I cast doubt on the frequent incantation in multicultural education literature that encourages teachers to engage in so-called
"culturally congruent" pedagogy and instead argue that educating for minimalist autonomy counsels teachers to pursue a dual pedagogical agenda: promoting hermeneutic dialogue in the classroom through which students
acquire a greater capacity for cultural interpretation, understanding, and
evaluation, and promoting a cosmopolitan outlook, encouraging students to
look beyond the borders of their own country and to focus on potential similarities rather than differences among all human beings, regardless of their
particular cultural affiliations. Second, I consider the policy implications of
liberal multicultural education and examine three of the most prominent
trends in U.S. school reform—vouchers, charter schools, and the small-
school movement. Liberal multicultural education would require that educational policy reflect the public purposes of education, and would call attention
to the state's legitimate authority to regulate all forms of schooling—public,
private, religious, and homeschooling—in light of these purposes.

PEDAGOGY AND LIBERAL MULTICULTURAL EDUCATION

It is a curiosity that the literature on multicultural political theory and the literature on multicultural education, despite their common adjectival descriptor and common motivational source—cultural minorities—so rarely intersect. Multicultural theorists often point to the central importance of educational reforms, and multicultural educators often assume the value of cultural pluralism, yet the multicultural theorists are highly unlikely to cite multicultural education scholars, and vice versa. To the extent, however, that political theorists must be concerned with the educational presuppositions and implications of any theory, and to the extent that any articulation of educational aims and ends must locate itself within a civic or political framework that extends well beyond the classroom and schoolhouse, one would expect a richer engagement between the two fields. Both fields suffer from their mutual absence of awareness.

The liberal theory of multicultural education I have defended has pedagogical implications, and I wish to sharpen the force of my overall argument by contrasting my own conclusions about pedagogical implications with what currently counts as "best practice" within the multicultural education literature. What I shall call "mainstream" multicultural education literature promotes a number of important and helpful claims about education reform and is motivated at bottom by a pressing concern that is shared by political theorists of any stripe: to do educational justice to children in schools, regardless of their skin color, ethnicity, class, or creed. However, from the perspective of liberal multicultural education, the unfortunate penchant of multicultural education scholars to categorize students by culturally determined learning styles leads to the deeply problematic pedagogical recommendation that teaching be "culturally congruent," a practice that in its worst manifestations results in a pernicious form of ethnoracial stereotyping.

Multicultural Education Literature

It is dangerous to talk about the field of multicultural education in general. The literature is vast, and reflects a wide variety of approaches. To simplify my task in characterizing it, I focus on its central and most influential figures in the United States. Foremost among these is James Banks, whose career in the field spans back to the early 1970s and whose many books and articles are standard texts within teacher education programs. He has also participated in the preparation of widely noted curricular guidelines issued by the National

Council for the Social Studies, and is the editor of the *Handbook of Research of Multicultural Education*, the definitive text in the field.[3] Banks and his many collaborators and followers constitute what is mainstream multicultural education—the views and research most likely to be known and taught in schools of education and professional development programs.

It is important to note that mainstream multicultural education is not consumed with ethnic cheerleading or oblivious to the dangers of Balkanization, as popular opinion and many of its critics, such as Arthur Schlesinger Jr. and Dinesh D'Souza, would have it.[4] Molefi Asante's promotion of Afrocentrism and his notorious ideas about Sun people and Ice people are almost uniformly rejected by mainstream multicultural education.[5] To the contrary, the predominant motivation behind mainstream multicultural education is not ethnocentrism but that educators and educational policy should cease to disparage, or worse, destroy, the cultural differences that students bring with them into schools. In light of the frequent efforts at coercive, unidirectional cultural assimilation that so often went hand-in-hand with a decidedly negative evaluation of the intellectual abilities or civic status of immigrants, African-Americans, and Native Americans, some of which I described in the first chapter, there is good reason for the multiculturalists' emphasis on honoring cultural difference and resisting the history of privileging Anglo-Saxon definitions of citizenship. Multicultural education is set against cultural assimilation and racism and in favor of, as Banks writes, a democratic pluralist society "whose diverse racial, ethnic, cultural, social-class, and gender groups . . . are participating fully in its construction and reconstruction and are helping to determine its aim, goals, and beliefs."[6] From the standpoint of liberal justice and liberal multicultural education, this is an uncontroversial and shared aim.

In rejecting coercive cultural assimilation, mainstream multicultural educators point to the need to assure that all children learn and are not treated as deficient or deviant because of their skin color, ethnicity, class, creed, or disability. In a fully representative comment, Sonia Nieto writes that "rather than maladies to be cured or problems to be confronted, differences are an important and necessary starting point for learning and teaching and can enrich the experiences of students and teachers."[7] Teachers, in other words, should make no assumptions about the intelligence of students if their native language is not English, and should not have higher academic expectations for Asian-American and European-American students than for African-American or Mexican-American or Native American students. This too is an uncontroversial and shared aim.[8]

Pedagogical and Policy Implications

Mainstream multicultural educators insist upon reconstructing the curriculum in a more culturally inclusive manner. This is driven by two related concerns. First, a curriculum that does not acknowledge the presence and contributions of diverse cultural groups to the history of the country, or illustrates the existence of different groups in grossly stereotypical or demeaning ways (e.g., the warrior Indian tribes, the happy slaves), perpetrates the harm of nonrecognition or misrecognition on students. Second, the expansion of the curriculum to include the history of different cultural groups in the United States reflects a truer, more accurate history, not the concoction of a fiction in order for students to recognize cultural kin in their schoolbooks as a means to boost their ethnic pride. I provided an argument for multicultural education on just these grounds in chapter 5. In my view, the arguments of mainstream multicultural educators for, in Banks's words, curricular "content integration" are not only historically sound but also educationally essential. To be sure, the danger always exists that the actual implementation of a multicultural curriculum will trivialize culture through a culture-of-the-week serialization or a reduction of diversified history to sidebars about Harriet Tubman, Pocahontas, and Cesar Chavez.[9] But this represents poor practice, not any principled argument against the goal of creating a multicultural curriculum.

In terms of the curriculum, then, the recommendations of mainstream multicultural educators coincide with the implications of the liberal theory of multicultural education I have defended. What seem to me wrong-headed are the *pedagogical* recommendations of multicultural educators. James Banks's and especially Geneva Gay's work forward the claim that students of different cultural groups are likely to possess differing cultural learning styles and that for effective learning to occur, teachers must teach in a way that is variously labeled culturally congruent, responsive, consistent, mediated, or synchronized. Now cultural identity and differences are not irrelevant to whether students learn, but the implications drawn by many multicultural educators about culturally tailored pedagogical approaches are disturbing. Multicultural educators are on solid ground when they advocate teaching about cultural pluralism and diversity, where the emphasis is on reforming the curriculum, but they falter when they advocate teaching that is delivered through assumed cultural paradigms, where the emphasis is on reforming pedagogy and teacher training programs.

The focus on cultural pedagogies, it is important to realize, is for multicultural educators no secondary or tertiary concern. As Banks comments in an introduction to a chapter on pedagogy, "One of the most prevalent misconceptions about multicultural education is that the integration of content about diverse cultural, ethnic, and racial groups into the mainstream curriculum is both its essence and its totality."[10] Along with curricular reform, an emphasis on pedagogical reform is a central theme across the multicultural education literature.

So what is meant by culturally responsive teaching? Geneva Gay, its leading exponent, defines it as "using the cultural knowledge, prior experiences, frames of reference, and performance styles of ethnically diverse students to make learning encounters more relevant and effective for them."[11] The idea is that the cultural identities of students affect the learning process and that therefore teachers should align their instructional strategies with the cultural learning styles of different students in order to be successful and properly respectful. Thus effective pedagogical approaches are likely to vary across populations of culturally different students, and Gay urges teachers to practice "cultural communication" and "culturally congruent instruction" that will foster students' "cultural integrity, individual abilities, and academic success."[12] Culturally responsive teaching is primarily conceived not as an effort to recognize and foster the cultural identities of students; it is seen, by contrast, as integral to ensuring effective teaching and learning in general.[13]

In one basic and nontrivial sense, it is true that culture affects the teaching and learning process and therefore is important to pedagogy. For example, the customs of some cultural groups, such as southeast Asians, to resist eye contact with figures of authority may lead some teachers to attempt to "correct" or undo the practice in a way that is profoundly unsettling and that undermines the ability of such students to learn.[14] Similarly, African-American children who speak black English or "Ebonics" are often assumed by teachers to be exhibiting a deficient and lower-class slang in need of fixing rather than a linguistic difference that is no way deviant; there is good reason to consider it a dialect of its own in light of its complex grammatical structure and pronunciation patterns.[15] Finally, teachers often make assumptions about the intellectual talents or capacities of students based on their ethnocultural identities that lead them to have higher expectations for some students (e.g., Asians in math classes) and lower expectations for others (e.g., native Spanish speakers in English classes). In all of these instances, culture and cultural identities figure into the process of teaching and learning, and if teachers are to be successful, they must take into account the cultural or linguistic habits of students without attributing to them a deviant value or linking to them assumptions about intellectual ability.

It is also true, of course, that the greater sociocultural and political context can profoundly affect teaching and learning in the schoolhouse. The status of minorities in the broader society and the weight that ascriptive identities carry into the classroom combine sometimes to exert a powerful force on students' learning. This is obvious, for example, to any teacher in an ethnically and racially diverse school where academic success is often equated with "acting white." The sociologist John Ogbu attributes this phenomenon to a process of "cultural inversion," where involuntary minorities (i.e., those who have not voluntarily immigrated, such as Native Americans and many African-Americans) develop "oppositional identities" and are inclined to regard certain behaviors, talents, and symbols as representative of the majority white culture and broader society, and therefore inappropriate for them.[16] In a detailed ethnography of an urban high school, Signithia Fordham has shown this very process at work, also suggesting that some students will purposefully camouflage or sabotage their own academic abilities in order to maintain bonds with their fellow minority students who associate academic success with acting white.[17] A final example of how the sociopolitical context invades the classroom can be found in psychologist Claude Steele's research on what he calls "stereotype bias" or "stereotype threat."[18] Steele has found compelling evidence that the poor test performance, especially on standardized tests, of minority students can sometimes be explained by a debilitating concern about confirming prevailing negative stereotypes of their respective ethnoracial group in society at large. Consumed with disproving a negative stereotype, minority students are more self-conscious about their performance, tend to exercise undue caution, divert their attention to task-irrelevant concerns, and ultimately, disengage from academic efforts. If teachers want to be effective in any of these situations, they must be aware of and confront the fact that learning does not take place in a pristine educational vacuum, sealed off from the outside world.

Culturally Congruent Pedagogy

Mainstream multicultural education scholars are right to insist on the intersection of culture and learning to the extent that teachers should be aware of how culturally influenced customs may affect classroom behavior and dynamics and of how the sociocultural and political context of the greater society inevitably contaminates the classroom. Nevertheless, their main conclusions about the intersection of culture and learning, and the pedagogical recommendations that follow, rest on the dubious claim that there are ethnically and racially distinct learning styles, which in their most pernicious formulations represent the educational equivalent of ethnoracial profiling, asking teachers to reconstruct their pedagogy in insidious ways.

Consider the arguments of Geneva Gay. Gay claims that "compelling research demonstrates that school achievement improves when protocols and procedures of teaching are synchronized with the mental schemata, participation styles, work habits, thinking styles, and experiential frames of reference of diverse ethnic groups." This is so because "even without our consciously being aware of it, culture determines how we think, believe, and behave, and these, in turn, affect how we teach and learn." Gay acknowledges that culture is dynamic and that the shared features of any cultural group may vary widely among individual members. Nevertheless, there are, in her view, "modal personalities" of different ethnoracial groups and she asserts that "members of ethnic groups, whether consciously or not, share some core cultural characteristics."[19] Those who are highly ethnically affiliated, she claims, are most likely to exhibit the core cultural characteristics.[20]

If Gay, and the others who follow this line, were only interested in cataloguing the cultural habits and customs of different racial groups, this could possibly be seen as a benign exercise in describing cultural diversity. However, Gay and others assert that these cultural differences affect *cognition*, and that distinct ethnoracial learning styles emerge. The most common claim is that minority students tend to be so-called field-dependent or field-sensitive learners (favoring highly social and contextualized settings), and white students tend to be field-independent learners (favoring analytic matter devoid of social context).[21] But it is also common to find more specific ethnoracial distinctions. Thus, Gay argues that "highly ethnically affiliated African-Americans will exhibit strong preferences for 'group-ness' . . . because of the values their culture places on communalism, working collaboratively to accomplish tasks, affective emotionalism, and informal social interactions." By contrast, "Independence and self-initiation will permeate the various learning style dimensions for middle-class European-Americans, since their culture values competition, individualism, and upward mobility." Finally, while Asian-Americans tend to be "communal and group-focused," they are "quite individualistic and deductive in actual performance delivery."[22] Others propose the existence of actual biological differences between races that affect learning. One hypothesis is that blacks are right-brain governed, and therefore are "intuitive, nonverbal, creative, spontaneous, and expressive," while whites are left-brain dominated, and therefore "logical, mathematical, and sequential."[23]

By far the worst consequences of such assertions are the frequently accompanying bullet-point lists that give pedagogical guidance to teachers. The following list is drawn verbatim from the literature review entry on learning styles and culturally diverse students in Banks's definitive *Handbook of Research on Multicultural Education*.

African-American learners tend to:
- Respond to things in terms of the whole instead of isolated parts
- Prefer inferential reasoning as opposed to deductive or inductive
- Approximate space and numbers rather than adhere to exactness or accuracy
- Focus on people rather than things
- Be more proficient in nonverbal than verbal communications
- Prefer learning characterized by variation and freedom of movement
- Prefer kinesthetic/active instructional activities
- Prefer evening rather than morning learning

Hispanic students tend to:
- Prefer group learning situations
- Be sensitive to the opinions of others
- Remember faces and social words
- Be extrinsically motivated
- Learn by doing
- Prefer concrete representations to abstract ones
- Prefer people to ideas

Native American children:
- Prefer visual, spatial, and perceptual information rather than verbal
- Learn privately rather than in public
- Use mental images to remember and understand words and concepts rather than word associations
- Watch and do rather than employ trial and error
- Have well-formed spatial ability
- Learn best from nonverbal mechanisms rather than verbal
- Have a generalist orientation, interested in people and things[24]

This list is far from unrepresentative, and similarly astonishing stereotyping can be found in the work of Geneva Gay and Christine Bennett.[25] To be fair, these lists are almost always accompanied by cautions that ethnic learning styles should not be applied willy-nilly to every individual and that variations will occur across ethnoracial groups. And some question whether or not ethnic learning styles are even a helpful or scientifically sound concept.

Nieto, for instance, worries that "categorizing students' learning styles based on race or ethnicity can veer dangerously close to the racist implications drawn from distinctions on IQ tests."[26] Nevertheless, even Nieto, perhaps the most skeptical in the mainstream literature, approvingly cites Wade Boykin's claims that African-Americans in the United States generally practice a cultural style that emphasizes "spirituality, harmony, verve, communalism, oral tradition, and expressive individualism."[27]

This approach quickly leads down a destructive dead-end. When individual students are taken to be literal embodiments of culture, when cultural differences are taken to create ethnoracial learning styles, and when culturally tailored pedagogies are inscribed into classroom practice, multicultural educators find themselves promoting a form of cultural or racial or ethnic essentialism that leads to a system of differential classroom practices and expectations which seriously damages the interests of the very students multicultural educators hope to serve. These practices perpetuate in my view the harms visited upon minority students by earlier generations of educators.

The problems are legion. One might begin by pointing to the unsavory implications of culturally congruent teaching that flow from its underlying logic. Does the idea of ethnoracial learning styles imply that there are religious or socioeconomic or geographic learning styles? Should students be pressured to learn in their appropriate ethnic learning style? If ethnoracial learning styles exist, ought we to segregate students within classrooms in order to provide them with culturally congruent teaching?[28] Should we practice cultural matching between teachers and students?

One might raise basic empirical objections to the alleged academic benefits of culturally congruent teaching. As Sonia Nieto herself asks, how can the success of urban Catholic schools at educating African-American youth be explained when, as she puts it, "generally the pedagogy and curriculum of Catholic schools can be characterized as traditional and Eurocentric"?[29] Or how might one explain away the volumes of research indicating that group-based and cooperative learning, which one would assume to be inappropriate for the learning style of whites, nevertheless yield significant benefits for all students, not just for minority students?[30] Or one might wonder about the fact that several of the scholars cited by multicultural educators as evidence of the connection between culture and cognition forthrightly reject the idea that teachers should tailor their teaching to the ethnicity or race of students. Shirley Brice Heath's work, for example, on the different questioning rituals of working-class blacks and middle-class whites is widely cited by multicultural educators, and yet she argues vigorously against ethnoracial stereotyping and would find the notion of core cultural characteristics, even if a person is not aware of them, abhorrent. "No group of students," she writes, "no matter how they are categorized within the United States today, will reflect a single unified coherent set of specifiable behaviors—linguistic or cultural—exclusive to a single sociocultural unit."[31]

Finally, one might question the entire idea of ethnoracial learning styles and cultural congruity because it assumes that students are pervasively defined by only one cultural group. Like certain of the multicultural theorists I examined in chapter 3, multicultural educators tend to presume a fixity of cultural identity, the existence of, in James Banks's words, a "primordial" identity.[32] The pedagogical recommendations that come packaged within ethnoracial categorizations seem unable to accommodate the possibility that students may identify themselves with, and be products of, multiple cultural communities; the recommendations resist cultural hybridity or mélange. If there is a multiethnic or multiracial learning style, it is absent from the mainstream literature. Sonia Nieto concludes two of her books by arguing that *teachers* need to become "multicultural persons" in order to succeed in teaching ethnically diverse classrooms but notes only in an aside that students themselves are increasingly likely to be multicultural rather than monocultural. She writes that "the identities of young people of many diverse ethnic and racial backgrounds defy easy categorization" and that "the multiple identities of youths have important and far-reaching implications for the development and implementation of multicultural education: it is evident that simplistic and bounded conceptions that focus just on special racial or ethnic groupings fail to capture the realities of many urban youths who live with complicated and heterogeneous realities."[33] Indeed, the very idea of ethnoracial learning styles founders, in my view, when confronted with these complicated and heterogeneous realities.

For these reasons, mainstream multicultural education scholarship mistakenly endorses culturally congruent teaching, as if the cultural identities of students were not only already given but define a single cultural register that creates a cognitive learning style through which they must be taught. As Shirley Brice Heath comments, "Perpetuated in current approaches to multicultural education is the view that ethnic or 'cultural' communities are homogenous across classes, regions, and histories of imaginations, when, in fact, they are constantly realigning themselves into different 'communities.'" Heath believes that the within the daily lives of many young people, "racial and ethnic identities are always situated and multiple."[34] If we take seriously the likelihood that students will move within multiple social, linguistic, behavioral, and even ethnic and racial identities, culturally congruent teaching must be rejected as a pedagogical straitjacket. And even if it *were* true that ethnoracial identity was singularly pervasive and defined a range of specific learning styles, we should still reject the practice of culturally congruent teaching on the ground that it would thwart the development of minimalist autonomy. For minimalist autonomy requires exposure to and engagement with cultural difference, not a careful sheltering of students within assumed cultural paradigms.

I therefore reject the pedagogical dimension of mainstream multicultural education scholarship. Instead, multicultural education, as I argued in chapter 5, is best understood as a form of liberal education for all students. Liberal multicultural education, and the pedagogy recommended by it, endeavors not to reify the cultural identities of students, taking them as already given, but to understand children as developing human beings who are in the midst of learning to negotiate the terms of their identities and as developing citizens who need to respect and learn to engage in dialogue with their fellow students and future citizens, whatever their cultural affiliations.

The Hermeneutical Pedagogy of Liberal Multicultural Education

The liberal theory of multicultural education I defend counsels a pedagogical approach that differs greatly from the recommendations embraced by mainstream multicultural education scholarship. In my view, the pedagogy of liberal multicultural education is at heart hermeneutical and seeks to expand the interpretive and experiential horizons of individuals, aiming in the end to cultivate a cosmopolitan outlook in each student. I explain this hermeneutical pedagogy in the following section and defend it from the frequent charge that a pedagogy seeking to expose children to and engage students with cultural diversity results in a thoroughgoing cultural relativism.

The pedagogy of liberal multicultural education aims at a hermeneutical process of reciprocal interpretation and understanding in which students attempt to understand different cultural values and take up the position of culturally different others. It is often thought that doing so implicitly, or even explicitly, sanctions cultural relativism. Richard Bernstein, for example, calls multiculturalism "a code word for an expanded concept of moral and cultural relativism."[35] The ubiquitous injunction to respect different cultures all too often becomes a reason for teachers to avoid engaging in moral discourse, especially if disagreement seems likely.[36] It is not uncommon to walk into an average high school history classroom and see posters that admonish students: "Do not judge other cultures." But the hermeneutical pedagogy consistent with liberal multicultural education rejects nonjudgmental relativism and fosters, ideally, a "fusion of horizons" through cross-cultural dialogue.

What is a "fusion of horizons?" The phrase comes from Hans-Georg Gadamer, the foremost twentieth-century theorist of hermeneutics, or the general study of interpretation and understanding.[37] Within debates about multiculturalism, it was Charles Taylor who first appropriated Gadamer's language of fusing horizons.[38] The idea, at root, is quite simple. We cannot fully understand cultural values or practices that are different from our own without opening ourselves to the potential truth of other points of view, without trying to grasp meaning from the point of view of the other. Such openness requires two things. First, it assumes that students do not view themselves or their cultural worldview as an impenetrable cocoon, as if no effort at understanding could ever succeed. In Michael James's words, students "must assume that their worldviews are more like distant but open horizons, understandable through vigorous interpretive effort."[39] Second, it requires a slowness to judge or an interpretive generosity that precludes a knee-jerk assessment of other cultures, cultural practices, or cultural products from one's own point of view. I cannot be a competent or sympathetic interpreter or judge of, say, Chinese art from the Ming dynasty when I possess a familiarity only with the assumptions and standards of the Western art tradition since the Renaissance. What must happen, instead, is an attempt to inhabit a position within the cultural horizon of the other, which permits not only increased understanding of cultural difference but opens the possibility of expanding one's own evaluative horizons.

Fusing horizons involves the development of common vocabularies of comparison that allow each person to perceive the other in as undistorted a manner as possible. Such perceptions lead to an understanding that *transforms the interior standards* of each person engaged in inquiry. Taylor explains, "We learn to move in a broader horizon, within which what we have formerly taken for granted as the background to valuation can be situated as one possibility alongside the different background of the formerly unfamiliar culture."[40] Thus, after studying and attempting to understand cultural values or practices that are different from their own, students will find that their interpretative capacity and tools of evaluation have expanded. Referring not simply to cross-cultural inquiry but to any effort at understanding, Gadamer says, "To reach an understanding in dialogue is not merely a matter of putting oneself forward and successfully asserting one's own point of view, but being transformed into a communion in which we do not remain what we were."[41] Hermeneutical inquiry endeavors, thus, to generate a common or shared horizon of intelligibility.

Teachers of liberal multicultural education need not, indeed should not, introduce the study of other cultures simply to hold them up as museum exhibitions of the wonderful blossoming of cultural diversity, or to suggest that all cultures and practices are equally valuable. Neither cultures nor specific cultural values and practices are to be studied as interesting specimens, the classroom equivalent of a trip to the botanical garden to see the colorful flowers. To suggest that all cultures must be rated as equal in worth undermines the very possibility of evaluation itself, be that evaluation positive or negative. Moreover, to tolerate on principle all cultural practices is itself disrespectful to individuals of other cultures, for it suggests that people's self-worth is so fragile that moral disagreement and dialogue would be harmful to them. This is insult rather than respect. A multicultural education that engages students intellectually with cultural diversity leads not to mindless tolerance or appreciation, but to the possibility of making evaluations that are less ethnocentric because the standard of making any evaluation has expanded in a dialogic broadening of horizons. Moral arrogance is replaced by moral understanding and humility; any temptation to rush to judgment about cultural difference is replaced by an impulse toward cross-cultural dialogue.

But beyond the possibility of making less ethnocentric judgments, the special value in the hermeneutical process of fusing horizons is that students may come to understand *themselves* in a new light. Acquiring new vocabularies of comparison opens up novel ways of interpreting and understanding oneself, of reflecting upon that which animates one's own way of life. As Thomas Hill puts it, learning about cultural diversity "challenge[s] one's customary ways of thinking, feeling, and perceiving so that one becomes more open to the possibility of values that one could never imagine when bound within a single cultural experience."[42] Writing on cross-cultural hermeneutics, Jay Lampert notes that to interpret and understand others, we implicitly enter into a dialogue in which self-critique is possible.[43] When students (or adults) attempt to understand the position of others, they by necessity contrast and place in dialogue (internally or in actuality) their own cultural standpoint. In the process of cross-cultural inquiry, students unavoidably end up reflecting on their own values and practices, viewing them from the perspective of a broader horizon of evaluation. In the language of hermeneutics, a sincere attempt to interpret and understand others results in the foregrounding of one's own interpretive biases and prejudices. A liberal multicultural education pedagogy of fusing horizons thus insists on the necessity of making assessments and judgments, not only of others but also of oneself.

What this begins to sound like, then, is a pedagogy of fostering minimalist autonomy. If a multicultural education initiates a hermeneutical process of understanding that culminates in a fusion of horizons, the end result is not merely greater knowledge of cultural diversity and an ability to recognize, as public reason demands, that others are motivated by values and goods different from and potentially incompatible with one's own. The result is also an increased capacity to subject one's own cultural values and goods to critical scrutiny with an expanded evaluative repertoire. Individuals learn to reflect independently and critically upon basic commitments, desires, and beliefs, be they chosen or unchosen. And this ability, contrary to the implications of culturally congruous teaching, makes possible the cosmopolitization of one's identity as much as an autonomous adherence to cultural purity.[44]

If a hermeneutical pedagogy tied to a multicultural curriculum seems likely to foster minimalist autonomy, the purpose of such a pedagogical approach, like that of liberal multicultural education itself, is civic in nature. In chapter 5 I explained why cultivating the autonomy of children was necessary for developing in them the political virtues such as public reason and mutual respect. In a classroom inquiry whose subject matter is the potential conflict of cultural beliefs and values, and in which students abstract from their own conceptions of the good and are able to consider political issues from the perspective of others, students will have taken a large step toward recognizing the difficulty of finding a common standpoint from which to make political decisions. When students take a further step and forge common evaluative ground through a fusion of horizons, the classroom experience may become, to some extent, the enactment and exercise of public reason.

Finally, what is especially compelling about adopting the pedagogical goal of fusing horizons is that the process of hermeneutic interpretation and understanding of cultural differences is particularly well-suited to the classroom. Establishing common ground between those who perceive themselves as culturally different is undoubtedly a difficult task. But if teachers of liberal multicultural education insist on interpretive generosity, intercultural understanding, and ultimately push students toward making evaluations based on a fusion of horizons, the common ground to be established may very well be the *consequence*, not an assumed ingredient, of the classroom inquiry. In other words, where, prior to classroom inquiry, students might regard cultural diversity as a reflection of how others are different from them, after an inquiry in which students reconstruct their evaluative perspective, they may find that they now *share* significant beliefs or values with others. Returning to the example of interpreting Chinese art, I may come to find, for example, that there are important similarities in the techniques of artists from the Ming dynasty and the Western Renaissance that allow me to judge instances of both based on identical criteria; what was formerly considered foreign now becomes shared. The optimism about discovering common ground among culturally diverse people arises therefore not simply from telling students what is true about all people, regardless of cultural identification, but from discovering that in attempting to interpret, learn, and understand cultural differences, students find that they, as well as others, have come to share something as a result of inquiry. They will have expanded their horizon of evaluation to the point where each student's perspective has incorporated something from the other. Fusing horizons, then, bears the promise of creating common ground among children from different cultural traditions, even if that commonality is conceived as a future possibility. As Lampert says, "situating commonality in the future means that cross-cultural interpreters need not share an identical set of texts from the past [where texts are understood to mean more than just books, but also beliefs, values, and practices], as long as they are willing to produce a space within which their children can speak together, a highly uncertain space within which neither side can control the interpretation of its traditions."[45] In a controlled classroom space where children are engaged in the common activity of working through a multicultural curriculum, the possibility of achieving a hermeneutical fusion of horizons seems more likely than elsewhere.

At this point, a practical illustration is in order. I draw this example from a book by Melinda Fine, in which she explores how teachers deal with values within classrooms.[46] Fine shows both the pedagogical difficulty in managing value diversity in the classroom and the enormous potential for significant learning to occur when it exists. One classroom she depicts is led by a teacher who uses a curriculum called Facing History and Ourselves, in which students learn about historical incidents that raise difficult issues of moral conflict. The teacher, Marysa, seeks to engage her class in dialogues, pushing students to learn from both the history lessons and each other. In a week-long inquiry inspired by lessons about anti-Semitism in Germany, Fine describes how the class of religiously diverse students dealt with deep questions of religious difference—Why do some people believe in one deity and others in many? Is one religion truer than another? Was Jesus Christ the Son of God?

Marysa encourages her students to voice their perspectives and listen to those of others. Due in part to her pedagogical approach, Fine concludes that religious relativism was not the result of discussion. Rather, the classroom experience made possible a broadened opportunity at evaluation. Fine comments, "No matter what their religious perspective, students remained more or less open to each other and themselves throughout the class. By 'open' I do not mean to suggest that students willingly *ceded* their own individual beliefs, but rather that they willingly *tested* them through listening to each other and dialoguing together."[47]

Fine also describes one student, Abby, who has been struggling with how to combat anti-Semitism. Fine says that after learning about the perspective of Palestinians, Abby's hard-line position on silencing those against the Jews has changed some. But in the end, Abby has a new understanding of how to engage in political debate. Fine quotes Abby's new conviction:

> I *really* believe that there needs to be some change in the world today! And I think that a *really* important part of *change* is understanding what someone else is *thinking*. . . . If you just *come* out and *say* what you think, and give *no* regard to what the *other* person is thinking, then that will create anger. And *resentment*. And they really won't be open to change. . . . I'm usually one of the only ones speaking up, and I *really* want to know what other people think about what I am saying . . . so maybe I could either argue it out, and *really* try to tell them what my point of view was, or just hear what other people are thinking about. . . . Because if they don't *speak*, I'm totally, totally closed off from anything that they're thinking about.[48]

Abby here gives vivid testimony, in the vocabulary of a thirteen-year-old rather than that of a philosopher, of the power of adopting a hermeneutical pedagogy within a liberal multicultural education. Through learning about the cultural differences of others, Abby yearns simultaneously to understand others better and to subject her own views to new criticisms. Though neither would use the phrase, what Fine describes repeatedly in her book, and what Abby hopes for at the end of her inquiry, is a fusion of horizons. What results, though neither Fine nor Abby may say so, is the cultivation of autonomy in students.

I could adduce numerous other examples of what a hermeneutical pedagogy might look like in practice. It's important to see, for example, that hermeneutical dialogue does not require an actual conversation between individuals, but can take place as an *internal* dialogue provoked by an encounter with a text, picture, or film. By reading novels set in distant places, or that depict different cultural settings, or that present unfamiliar people and beliefs, any student, indeed any person, can experience the broadening of horizons I have described above. The illustrations from Fine's book suffice to show, however, that a classroom which deals with cultural differences may produce a greater capacity for evaluation, both of oneself and of others. Far from teaching cultural relativism, and far from endorsing cultural congruity in teaching, the aim of making judgments and assessments about cultural values and practices through a broadening and fusing of interpretive and evaluative horizons is the appropriate pedagogical accompaniment to a liberal theory of multicultural education.

Cosmopolitan Outlook

Liberal multicultural education is incomplete without a consideration of the vast cultural diversity beyond the borders of one's own country. Teachers of liberal multicultural education should incorporate a thoroughly cosmopolitan outlook, encouraging students to study an array of cultural diversity that is both *intra*national and *inter*national in scope. Moreover, in the light of ever-increasing global interdependence and common global threats to all forms of humanity, teachers of liberal multicultural education should encourage students to focus on potential similarities among various peoples and, perhaps, in the final analysis, to consider themselves "citizens of the world," or in Martin Luther King's phrase, members of "one global village."[49]

One reason that liberal multicultural education insists upon a cosmopolitan outlook is connected to its evaluative aims, and a second reason is connected to its civic justification. On the one hand, through studying and attempting to understand cultures completely foreign to Americans, students learn about different ways of living a life, new beliefs and practices with which to compare their own. As Martha Nussbaum notes, "If we do not undertake a [cosmopolitan] educational project, we risk assuming that the options familiar to us are the only ones there are, and that they are somehow 'normal' or 'natural' for the human species as such."[50] In a country such as the United States, where most are already terribly ignorant of the rest of humanity, cosmopolitan education teaches that the United States, though diverse, is nonetheless limited in cultural scope; that the efflorescence of cultural diversity that has animated all of humanity is significantly wider than that which is found in our political home.[51]

On the other hand, a cosmopolitan outlook is connected to the civic justification in that the liberal principles enshrined in American political documents make consistent reference to all human beings, not just American citizens. Using Nussbaum's words once again, "If we really do believe that all human beings are created equal and endowed with certain inalienable rights, we are morally required to think about what that conception requires us to do with and for the rest of the world."[52] If multicultural education encourages every student to take seriously the rights and responsibilities accorded to each citizen, it ought also to encourage the same students to think about these rights and responsibilities beyond national borders. A cosmopolitan approach consistent with liberal multicultural education projects students' attention and concern out into the world, rather than focusing exclusively on national issues and problems.

We can appreciate the necessity of such global concern when we take into consideration the increasing economic and political interdependence of world cultures and the imposing global threats that ignore cultural as well as national distinctions. If for no other reason, teachers of liberal multicultural education should insist finally on a cosmopolitan outlook because of the changing relationship among nations and peoples in the modern era. It is a commonplace today that national economies are not self-contained but deeply interdependent. International markets, money flows, and divisions of labor have global effects. The rapid advance of technological innovation has forged connections among distant parts of the world that only a generation ago were unthinkable. Perhaps most important, however, are global threats such as the growing ozone hole, global warming trends, atomic and chemical weapons, and widespread ecological deterioration that force us to consider wider notions of solidarity than those offered up by individual cultures or states. Radioactive clouds, acid rain, and rising ocean levels do not abide by cultural or national lines of division. As Czech President Václav Havel says, "The planetary civilization to which we all belong confronts us with global challenges."[53] That these international forces and threats affect people of all cultures mandates that an education mindful of cultural difference adopt a cosmopolitan perspective.

Thus, the cosmopolitan outlook of liberal multicultural education urges students to study and absorb varied cultural experiences, domestic as well as foreign. It exhorts students to consider the implications of the liberal values that help identify them politically. And it teaches that global forces affect all, that there is some truth in the slogan "One earth, one humanity, one destiny."[54] Global citizenship is not defined necessarily by a mythic past or robust set of shared values and traditions; we are global citizens to the extent that we share a common fate on the planet.[55] A cosmopolitan outlook therefore invites students to cast their vision beyond themselves, their culture(s), and their nation, beyond the particular to the global; in the process, it encourages students to discover how all humans are united, what we all share in common, however meager or small. It seeks to construct solidarity along the lines of what Richard Rorty calls an expanding circle of "we," that is to say, learning to see others as beings like we are—all equally susceptible to pain and cruelty.[56]

Finally, I want to emphasize that though a cosmopolitan outlook recommends a consideration of cultures far from one's homeland, it does not imply that we ought to devote the *majority* of time and attention to what is foreign. Teachers of liberal multicultural education still should concentrate firmly on the cultures, peoples, and problems within our own country. Following an argument outlined by Amy Gutmann, multicultural education should focus mainly on domestic cultures for three reasons.[57] First, just as it is a practical impossibility to include the *entire* panoply of, for example, American cultural diversity in the curriculum, so it is impossible to include and study *all* world cultures in the curriculum. Second, it is important that children come to understand and respect that which is closest to them, both culturally and geographically. And third, learning the civic rights and responsibilities of one's own country is meant primarily to enable the exercise of those rights and responsibilities within that country, for it is in this national venue that citizens will be most empowered and most able to engage in the social, connected criticism that seeks to match liberal ideals with actual practice.[58]

Policymaking and Liberal Multicultural Education

Meira Levinson argues that the policy consequences of finding that children deserve an education for autonomy are nothing less than closing religious schools, at least in the U.S. context, and regulating private schools so heavily that they become virtually indistinguishable from public schools.[59] James Dwyer argues that the policy consequences of defending the independent interests of children will be a regulatory structure designed to reconstitute completely the present condition of Catholic and Fundamentalist schools in the United States.[60] Levinson's and Dwyer's proposed regulations cut sharply against the long history of private and religious schooling in the United States, both of which enjoy Constitutional protection. Like Levinson, I have defended autonomy-promoting education, and like Dwyer, I have argued for the incorporation of children's interests within any decision-making calculus about who shall wield educational authority over schooling. Does then the liberal theory of multicultural education I have advanced require closing or utterly reconstituting religious schools and regulating private schools so stringently that they become mere copies of public schools? The answer is no, on both counts.

Policy Boundaries

Liberal multicultural education sets boundaries to permissible educational structures and limits to the distribution of educational authority, but it does not impose specific institutional arrangements. Indeed, a variety of institutional arrangements are consistent with liberal multicultural education. As the analysis in the previous chapter showed, even some forms of home-schooling, though they should be strictly regulated, potentially comply. There is no one best system, nor should there be. The ambit of liberal multicultural education allows ample room for parental choice and for collective and democratic deliberation about particular matters of policy. This is so because a culturally diverse, liberal state houses a pluralism of reasonable ways of life, whose adult adherents will wish to influence the kind of education their children receive in different ways. The state cannot prescribe strict educational uniformity, in institutional design or curricular content, lest it threaten to stamp out the reasonable pluralism that, as Rawls suggests, arises naturally as the result of the exercise of human reason under political structures that are free and long-standing.[61] At the same time, the liberal state cannot give unlimited deference to cultural diversity. It justly provides publicly funded schools and regulates all other schools to achieve certain civic purposes of education that are necessary to its legitimacy and stability, and to guarantee that the individual interests of children in becoming autonomous and capable of independent functioning are met. As we have seen, such schooling is non-neutral and in fact actively engages in a form of soulcraft, which inescapably shapes the cultural diversity that is likely to thrive in the liberal state.

I contend that the liberal theory of multicultural education I have developed is the proper framework for doing justice both to the diverse educational aspirations that attend cultural pluralism in the liberal state and to the legitimate civic purposes of education in the liberal state. On the one side is a refusal to enforce strict educational uniformity and on the other an insistence that regulations exist to satisfy the state's and the child's interests in education. In between lies a space that certainly accommodates a variety of institutional structures, including some that are not run by the state, such as private schools, religious schools, or homeschools. The need for public regulation of any form of schooling does not mean that all schools must be publicly provided or controlled.

Though it accommodates a variety of institutional structures, the general terrain of liberal multicultural education is not endlessly expansive. What, then, are the outer limits of the general terrain of liberal multicultural education, beyond which schools must be disallowed? These boundaries flow out of the analysis in the previous chapter.

The parental limit, as I argued, is reached when parents wish to thwart the development of autonomy in their children or prevent their children from becoming capable of independent functioning. An education for autonomy is necessary for the civic reason of establishing the conditions for the legitimacy and stability of the liberal state, and is necessary for the moral reasons of both avoiding servility (to the state, the parents, or a cultural group) and establishing a necessary condition of self-respect. Thus homeschools and religious schools that seek to inculcate a servility to parents or a particular worldview, and public schools that consistently fail to provide an education that cultivates the critical reasoning skills necessary for autonomous character development would be disallowed, reconstituted, or closed by public authorities.

The limit of the state is found, as I just suggested, in any attempt unilaterally to provide and control all forms of schooling. The liberal state is restrained from monopolizing the provision and control of schooling for two reasons. First, to assume complete control over education would potentially disable the legitimate self-regarding (or expressive) and other-regarding interests of parents in the education of their children. Since in a pluralist society, the self-regarding interests of parents will take many forms (some will wish for a religious upbringing, some will want their children to have a sustained education in the arts or music, and so forth), a state which provided and controlled schooling for all children would be at best unfairly indifferent to the interests of some parents, and act at worst in inimical and unjust ways to the interests of others. Second, were the state to be the sole provider of and authority over a system of schools that was standardized down to fine-grained details of curriculum and pedagogy, children and parents might rightly worry about the specter of state-imposed uniformity, a consequent homogenization of individuals, and the ultimate erosion of social diversity. This, of course, was John Stuart Mill's concern about state provision of schools.[62] Within a modern setting, Mill's concern is in my view wildly exaggerated, for even state-controlled public schools exhibit enormous diversity and are in any case far from the only socializing influence on children. Nevertheless, a state that insisted on monopolizing provision of and authority over schooling could attempt to standardize its citizenry in tyrannical ways, as the United States, for example, once attempted in forcibly removing Native American children from their communities and sending them to state-run boarding schools, where the purpose of schooling was cultural eradication and coercive Americanization. Thus, though the state may impose regulations concerning mandatory attendance, it cannot require attendance only at schools that are operated by the state. The state must be willing to share educational authority with parents.

Finally, the interests of the child also set a boundary. Children cannot be permitted to exercise authority over their education in such a way that they threaten the future development of their autonomy. Parents and the state justly act paternalistically in striving to foster autonomy, even if a child would resist those efforts. Once a child has achieved a threshold level of autonomy, however, she acquires, as I suggested in the previous chapter, a proto-right to self-governance. This proto-right might permit in certain circumstances the decision of an autonomous child, likely to be an older teenager, to make decisions about her education that run counter to those of the parents, or even to opt out of schooling altogether. But a six- or a ten-year-old would be forbidden from refusing to be schooled.

The range of permissible institutional arrangements of schooling is limited by these three boundaries. Within this terrain there is wide, though not unconstrained, room for the flourishing of cultural diversity, for the expression of diverse parental interests, for the pursuit and realization of state interests in education, for the possible incorporation of children's voices into decision making when conflicts arise over educational provision, and for democratic deliberation among citizens about particularities of teaching and learning. In practical terms, the upshot is that while a diversity of institutional arrangements, public and nonpublic, for the delivery of education fit comfortably within the framework of liberal multicultural education, the liberal state must always retain a regulatory role. No school can be exempt from state regulations, monitoring, and inspection.[63] And of course, the state must be as vigilant in regulating public schools as it does private and religious schools.

Policy Guidelines

Having defined the boundaries, what can be said about the schools that inhabit the space within these boundaries? A liberal theory of multicultural education not only sets limits to possible institutional arrangements of schools, but also provides some general guidelines about what schools that exist within these boundaries will look like. Let me mention five here.

First, I assume that regulations must exist to assure that all schools provide an education in the fundamental skills and knowledge necessary to independent functioning and the ability to exercise the rights of citizenship. All schools must teach children to read, to write, to achieve basic mathematical literacy, and so on. They must also provide an education that conveys to students the organizational structure of their federal, state, and local governments, a rudimentary outline of the history of the country, and an explanation of how to navigate the political domain (i.e., the process of voting, of lobbying for legislation, and so on), and some understanding of their rights and the laws of the country. Without these basic literacies and civic knowledge, no child could successfully find employment or make use, if desired, of his rights of citizenship. Insisting upon providing a set of minimum skills and a basic understanding of political organization, processes, and history is of course not inconsistent with realizing that there will almost certainly be pressure on schools to do much more, such as giving all students an education that affords them the opportunity to attend college.

Second, all schools—public, private, religious, and home-based—must be autonomy-promoting environments. I have already discussed in detail the kind of educational environment that promotes the development of autonomy: a vigorous and rigorous multicultural curriculum that exposes children to and engages them with cultural beliefs, values, and traditions different from those they are taught at home; and a hermeneutical pedagogy that aims at broadening and fusing the interpretive horizons of students. Other conditions, far more mundane but no less important, are also necessary to establish an autonomy-promoting environment. The state must ensure that all schools strive to provide a safe atmosphere in which children can interact both inside and outside the classroom without fear for their physical safety; a school culture that prizes intellectual inquiry and achievement, and offers opportunities for artistic expression; and a peer culture that neither crushes individuality nor exiles and ridicules those who are perceived to be different. Different schools may create autonomy-promoting environments in different ways. A multicultural education need not be standardized so far as to specify what cultures to study. The talents and personalities of different teachers will infuse their pedagogy in different ways, and school and peer cultures will inevitably vary and take on local coloration, depending on the institutional arrangement of the school (e.g., schools with religious affiliations will have a different ethos than schools without them) and on the kind of community where the school is located (e.g., large, comprehensive urban high schools will have a different ethos than small rural schools). But whatever the curricular, pedagogical, and building culture variations, the liberal state must regulate for autonomy by ensuring that the school, through its curriculum and pedagogy, does not aim solely to replicate and reinforce the worldview of the parents or cultural groups of the children who attend the school.

Third, the regulations that accompany a liberal theory of multicultural education can and should reflect what educators call "developmental- and age-appropriate practice." Regulations should take into account the varying needs and capacities displayed by children of different ages and developmental stages. For example, teachers charged with educating for autonomy will wonder whether hermeneutical inquiry is a real possibility for elementary school children. Young children have not yet developed the systematic higher-level reasoning skills required to articulate comparison and contrasts, and can have little grasp of interpretive generosity. Cultural interpretation, understanding, comparison, and evaluation demand patience, empathy, tolerance, a finely tuned sensibility, and the capacity for critical thinking—all things that younger students do not yet possess to a large degree. In fact, as Eamonn Callan points out, the cultivation of autonomy may depend upon developmental antecedents that a premature exposure to robust cultural diversity may inhibit.[64] Were elementary school to be the stage at which educators attempted a full-blown intellectual engagement with a diversity of cultural beliefs, values, and traditions, the result could well be utter confusion or debilitating fear. On this basis Callan concludes that parents who consent to enroll their children in common, integrated schools at later ages may have a claim for separate schooling (where all children are immersed in a singular worldview) at early ages.[65] This seems reasonable to me, though it is also important to point out that while young children are not yet capable of mature intellectual engagement with cultural diversity, this need not imply that a multicultural education or understanding of diverse value orientations should be foresworn in elementary school. Even at this young age, perhaps *best* at this age, children can become *aware of* and *appreciate* cultural diversity without yet being asked to engage in critical reflection upon their own and others' beliefs and values. This is actually common practice in many elementary schools, where children read fairy tales of many different cultures, learn about the customary dress, cuisine, or artistic products of different cultural groups, and hear different languages for the first time. Older students would build on this awareness and appreciation, and on their developing skills of respectful dialogue, toward a broader understanding, and ultimately, toward hermeneutical inquiry.

Differentiating among age-appropriate practices indicates that educators must not view every element of liberal multicultural education as happening at once, within the same classroom. It opens up the possibility that we might plausibly view educational authority as resting most heavily with parents when children are young, with the balance gradually shifting to the state as children grow older, and finally coming to rest fully with children themselves once they have achieved autonomy. Such a view helps to accommodate the varying educational aspirations of different cultural groups within a diverse liberal state while ensuring that the educational interests of the state and the child are met. The plurality of institutional arrangements and governance structures that are likely to arise as a result do not constitute a contradiction or problem for the liberal theory of multicultural education I defend, but re-flect an entirely appropriate acknowledgement of the developmental and age-appropriate capacities of students.

Fourth, the regulations governing all schools should strongly encourage the teaching of foreign languages and urge not the teaching *of* religion but teaching *about* religion. Each of these practices, while not absolutely neces-sary to an education for autonomy, do much to foster the ability of students to consider and inhabit different traditions that illuminate and provide sig-nificant sources of meaning for diverse persons and groups. They increase a person's interpretive horizons and capacity for expression and understand-ing. Take the learning of a foreign language, for example. Beyond the obvious fact that learning a foreign language improves a person's capacity for cross-cultural dialogue, it also conveys the simple truth that one's native tongue is not the only medium for communication and understanding, but the accident of one's birth. In Martha Nussbaum's words, "It is very important for stu-dents to understand what it is like to see the world through the perspective of another language, an experience that quickly shows that human complexity and rationality are not the monopoly of a single linguistic community."[66] Learning a second language also helps students to appreciate the importance of their native tongue for the sense of home and belonging it so often creates, and for this reason potentially encourages students to understand better the position of linguistic minorities in liberal societies.

For similar reasons, the study of religious traditions can help students to see how other people have found diverse sources of spiritual inspiration and how deep-seated religious traditions have evolved over time. The goal here is not to insist that students consider their own religious views from the per-spective of others, or to suggest that all religious beliefs must be subject to ra-tional scrutiny and evaluation. This is itself a form of secular ethnocentrism, the idea that even faith-based worldviews must come under the scalpel of rational dissection to warrant continued adherence or assent. The goal rather is to ensure that students recognize that their own religious convictions, if they or their family have any, are not the only ones that have animated other people, and that, more important, other people may possess diverse religious beliefs (including agnosticism and atheism) but still be equal citizens, entitled to the same rights and freedoms as any other person. When religion is left out of a multicultural education, the danger is twofold. First, students may erroneously come to think that religious communities are not deep sources of identity for some people; in this case, religion is trivialized. Second, students may falsely come to assume that their own religious views are the only sources of spiritual meaning; in this case, the fact of reasonable pluralism is occluded. Teaching about religion rather than teaching religion directly is no doubt a difficult pedagogical and curricular undertaking. But it is better to confront the risks—from the stereotyping of certain religions as suspicious to the reduction of religion to a list of holidays and texts—than to omit teaching about religious traditions altogether, as has often been the practice in public schools in the United States.[67]

Fifth, and finally, the regulations pursuant to ensuring that the institutional structures and governance of all schools stay within the bounds of liberal multicultural education will have an impact on school funding. The funding of schools in the United States is largely driven by local and state tax revenues, and this leads to enormous disparities not only between public and private schools (which can charge any tuition they wish), but also among public schools themselves, even when they are in the same geographical area. These funding disparities lead to a landscape where wealthy parents can buy a prep school education for their children and poorer families cannot, where tax-revenue-rich towns can provide better schools than tax-revenue-poor towns, and where wealthy parents can donate enormous sums to their local public schools and poorer families cannot.[68] The fact that a quality education depends for many children in the United States on the luck of their birth into a poor or well-off town or family is clearly objectionable on egalitarian grounds.[69] But the current level of disparities is equally objectionable on grounds that appeal not to equity but to the minimum threshold provision of schooling necessary for the cultivation of autonomy. Schools such as those depicted in Jonathon Kozol's *Savage Inequalities,*[70] in which the physical plant is crumbling, teachers go without supplies, and students go without books, and in which arts, sports, and extracurricular activities are considered expendable, inevitably threaten and likely defeat the cultivation of autonomy. Woefully funded schools can hardly be expected to provide an autonomy-promoting environment for students.

The exact consequence of regulations on school funding is too complex a subject to address in any depth here. Financial expenditures, for example, need not be identical for every student; those with disabilities, for instance, may require greater resources. Neither must financial expenditures be identical across districts or states; differences in labor costs, facilities maintenance, transportation costs, and so on will force differential expenditures. And of course there are major debates about the effect of increased spending on educational outcomes.[71] Nevertheless, it seems to me undeniable that the policy framework of liberal multicultural education cannot permit disparities where some schools cannot afford to repair decaying buildings, purchase textbooks for students, or hire qualified teachers, while others have every amenity imaginable. The savage inequalities readily apparent to any regular visitor to urban schools clearly disadvantage the minority children who predominantly attend these schools, are a clear affront to equality of educational opportunity, and, most important for the view I have advanced, impede the creation of a school environment that fosters the autonomy of students.[72] I propose no solution here, but stress that the regulations of liberal multicultural education would address the current funding disparities.

THE PRACTICAL consequences of the sum of these regulations would be significant if applied to the current landscape of U.S. schooling, but would clearly leave wide latitude for parental influence and local decision making about the precise institutional arrangement, governance structure, and curriculum of schools. Certain kinds of homeschools and fundamentalist religious schools that consciously insulate children from the value diversity of a culturally plural state would be disallowed. And chronically failing public schools where the campus is unsafe or where large proportions of students never learn the fundamental skills and competencies that are the foundation for independent functioning, vocational success, and (not least) the development of autonomy would be overhauled or closed. In addition, state regulations would force schools to adopt some kind of multicultural curriculum in order to ensure that no school simply reinforced or mirrored the values of a particular cultural community. Therefore, religiously affiliated schools could continue to provide an education steeped in one particular tradition but would be required to teach children about the religious and cultural diversity of the larger society, and indeed, of the entire world. And they would be required to teach about this diversity not merely as a descriptive enterprise, but with the intent of promoting the autonomy of students and fostering the civic virtues of mutual respect and public reason. No school would be permitted to consider the identity of children attending it as permanently defined by the cultural community of their parents.

The end result, I imagine, would be a landscape of differentiated schools that would each pass regulatory muster, with variety not only in religious affiliation and source of funding but in general ethos. Some schools, for example, might pursue the back-to-basics Core Knowledge program endorsed by E. D. Hirsch, and others would adopt the principles of progressive pedagogy endorsed by Ted Sizer and his Coalition of Essential Schools; some elementary schools might be Montessori and some Waldorf; some schools would emphasize experiential learning and others a more traditional, teacher-centered pedagogy; some high schools might be large and offer a comprehensive curriculum and a wide array of extracurricular activities, and other high schools might be small and offer a relatively specialized curriculum geared around, say, drama and the arts or math and science; some schools would aim to serve children with special needs (those with learning disabilities, for example), and others would strive to "mainstream" all students within their classrooms. Catholic and other religiously affiliated schools would exist alongside public schools; college-preparatory high schools would exist alongside vocationally oriented high schools. It would be impossible to specify the variety of schools from a theoretical standpoint. The main conclusion is that the state would approve, regulate, and monitor every school, and parents and children would choose where to attend.

LIBERAL MULTICULTURAL EDUCATION AND CONTEMPORARY SCHOOL REFORM

This educational landscape and my suggestion that parents and children be able to choose from among an array of different kinds of schools call to mind trends in contemporary school reform. Having indicated the general nature of the policies and regulations recommended by a liberal theory of multicultural education, I conclude by addressing the implications of this theory for three prominent reform efforts: vouchers, charter schools, and the small-school movement. Each of these reforms has been touted as a potential redeemer of schooling and has been subject to widespread debate. I cannot hope to provide a comprehensive review of even one of these reforms, which would require a far longer analysis. Instead, in the space remaining, I briefly examine how each might be shaped to fit within the broad civic educational project of the liberal theory of multicultural education. They all have the potential to contribute to the civic purposes of schooling, but they also pose certain dangers to liberal multicultural education. Vouchers pose a danger of excessive privatization, where market mechanisms erode state regulatory controls. The small-school movement risks creating schools that are excessively tight and insular communities. Charter schools pose both risks. The challenge of liberal multicultural education would be to shape these reforms in such a way as to harness the benefits of each without succumbing to these dangers.

Vouchers

First proposed by the economist Milton Friedman in 1955, the general idea behind vouchers is that, rather than funding public schools directly, the state should provide parents with a voucher equivalent to the amount of money spent per pupil in the local public school.[73] Parents then decide where to send their children. Most voucher plans are designed so that the vouchers may be used at private and religious schools, as well as public schools. All schools would therefore receive public funds, and parents would have complete discretion in choosing where to send their children to school. Of course, voucher plans can be designed in any number of ways: to include or exclude religious schools, to permit or forbid the introduction of for-profit schools, to give differential voucher sums to different parents, to be limited only to poor parents, and so on. The underlying mechanism, however, of transferring public monies to parents in the form of a voucher to be used at a school of their choosing is the same in every scheme, and it is upon this core idea that I shall focus my comments.

Vouchers have gained enormously in popularity in the 1990s. Numerous states have placed voucher referendums on their ballots, including Oregon, Colorado, California (twice, in 1993 and 2000), Washington, and Michigan, though no referendum has ever been passed. Debates over federal and state legislation to introduce vouchers are now commonplace. National polls show growing support for vouchers in the 1990s, though always accompanied by larger numbers showing support for the public schools.[74] Voucher experiments of different sorts have been tried or are underway in Milwaukee, Cleveland, Dayton, Washington, DC, Florida, and New York City, and are increasingly popular in other parts of the world as well.

The ongoing debate about vouchers is marked by rhetorical excesses on both sides, with some claiming that vouchers will be the panacea that revolutionizes the education system all by itself and others foreseeing nothing less than educational doomsday. In my view, it is far too early to make an empirical judgment about the effects of vouchers, either on the academic achievement of the children who use them or on the surrounding public schools whose students have withdrawn and enrolled elsewhere. Numerous studies are underway, and in general the evidence is mixed.[75] What can be said, however, is that contrary to popular perception vouchers are not inherently antidemocratic or antiliberal. Voucher schemes have been advanced by radical liberals as well as libertarian conservatives.[76] Everything hinges on their design. The introduction of choice and marketplace mechanisms into the educational system, given appropriate regulations, is not inimical to securing the civic purposes of education. Moreover, we can reject opposition to vouchers resting on the claim that vesting parents and children with choices unjustly turns education into a commodity rather than a public good. As Harry Brighouse rightly points out, choice already exists in a state-run system of schools insofar as parents make choices about schools by deciding where to live.[77]

From the perspective of liberal multicultural education, what matters about vouchers is how any plan would be constructed so as to ensure that the educational interests of children and the state are met. That is to say, an acceptable voucher plan would condition the use of a voucher on a school's willingness to provide a basic education in an autonomy-promoting environment where students learned also core civic knowledge and the virtues of mutual respect and public reason. A voucher plan, by contrast, that left the educational marketplace unregulated and allowed the matrix of parental decisions to be the sole arbiters of the educational environment of children would threaten and corrode the public authority necessary to guarantee a child's basic interest in autonomy and the state's basic interest in teaching certain civic knowledge and cultivating certain civic virtues. A voucher plan of the latter sort effectively privatizes education by endowing parents with complete educational authority. As I have argued, parents are for a variety of reasons not infallible guarantors of the child's and the state's interest in education; therefore, relying on parental choices as the demand lever to stimulate educational supply, without an adequate system of controls over the supply, risks undermining or occluding the public purposes of education. Thus a liberal theory of multicultural education could not permit, for example, the unsuccessful California ballot proposition in 2000 offering all parents in the state a $4,000 voucher to use at the schools of their choosing without restriction. This proposition provided no regulatory mechanisms for the state to hold private and religious schools accountable to the state.

The danger of vouchers, therefore, is that they will privatize educational decision making, vesting authority only in parents, and in the process eviscerate the regulatory authority of the state necessary to ensure that the child's and the state's interests in education are met. Properly designed, however, I can imagine at least two kinds of voucher plans that would fit within the ambit of liberal multicultural education. One would be a limited or targeted voucher plan designed to give new choices to parents and children who are stuck in failing public schools. Ideally, of course, the state would exert its regulatory power and reform failing schools so that they would consistently provide a quality education. Unfortunately, the chronic failure of some urban schools, despite reform efforts, is plain. When reform efforts have failed at schools that are unable to teach children the educational basics of reading, writing, and math, and cannot even provide a physically safe learning environment, there is a strong social justice argument to provide parents with new options. The voucher plan recently enacted in Florida appears to have this underlying rationale. The state grades schools based on standardized test results, attendance, and graduation rates, and the families of students attending schools that receive the very worst ratings are eligible for a voucher that they may use at a private or religious school, or neighboring public school.[78] Though the Florida plan does not condition the acceptance of a voucher at a private or religious school on accepting greater state oversight, when compared to the current alternative of leaving children in chronically failing schools, the voucher appears likely to improve the educational outcomes of students on a wide range of basic skills, a prerequisite for an education for autonomy. In this scenario, vouchers serve as a means to escape from a public school that does not promote even the state's own interests in education and has shown itself impervious to the state's efforts to improve it. Seen in this light, it is helpful to remind ourselves that the relevant comparison of the likely effects of a voucher program is not to the ideal public school system, but to the existing school system, which is without doubt severely dysfunctional in some urban districts in the United States. The responsibility of the state to improve these schools is clear, and when the state cannot, and the failure endures over years, a voucher plan targeted at the children in such schools is justifiable.[79]

A second acceptable voucher plan would be universal rather than targeted in scope. Its design would allow all parents and children to choose from an array of diverse schools that were publicly accountable to the state.[80] The point of public accountability would be to ensure that the purpose of schooling was not only to respond to the preferences of parents about how their children should be educated but to safeguard the independent interest of children in becoming autonomous and the civic interest of the state in educating its citizens for autonomy—a necessary condition of liberal legitimacy and stability—along with cultivating the political virtues of mutual respect and public reason. In a landscape of publicly accountable schools that all successfully met the child's and the state's interests in education, the only reason, so far as I can see, that a state would have to withhold public funding from any school would be to comply with the First Amendment separation between church and state. This might require exempting religiously affiliated schools from a voucher program.[81] Outside the United States, of course, there is no such obstacle, and even within the United States, there is great debate about whether a voucher program including religious schools would be constitutional.[82] But regardless of whether or not religious schools are included, the underlying voucher mechanism of granting control to parents to choose from among a diverse set of regulated schools remains unimpugned.

There are many other difficult issues that any worthy voucher proposal would have to address. I mention just a few here to indicate the range of potential problems: how to prevent schools from unfairly "creaming" students, or refusing to accept (or easing out) the most difficult to educate; whether to provide transportation costs for parents who would have their children attend a school beyond their immediate neighborhood; how to provide rich information about schools to parents so that they can make informed choices; what to do about parents who are bad choosers or are indifferent to the education of their children; and how to stimulate sufficient supply-side action to create new schools in rural areas.

From the perspective of liberal multicultural education, the goal would be to design the voucher plan in a way as to regulate the supply of schools strictly enough to guarantee that the child's and the state's educational interests were met, and to address the above issues, but not in the process create a regulatory apparatus so unwieldy or overbearing as to discourage or choke-off the supply-side creation of diverse schools. The more strings attached to public dollars, the less likely, perhaps, that private and religious schools will want to accept vouchers, or that educational entrepreneurs will wish to start new schools. This is a fundamental tension that may be ineradicable. And perhaps it is impossible in practice to create a voucher system that culls the benefits of competitive market energies without eroding the regulatory authority of the state. I do not know, and only actual experiments with vouchers will yield an answer. But my point here has not been to endorse vouchers, but only to show that they are not necessarily inconsistent with the liberal theory of multicultural education I have defended. We should resist voucher proposals that privatize education by putting educational decision making wholly into the hands of parents and dismiss state authority over schools. Instead, we should remain open to the possibility that limited or universal voucher proposals might yet be shaped with the guiding public purposes of education in a culturally diverse liberal state in mind.

Charter Schools

Charter schools are a recent innovation in American education. Started in 1991 in Minnesota, the general idea behind charter schools is to allow the creation of publicly funded schools that are freed from a variety of local, state, and federal educational regulations but remain accountable to some public jurisdiction. Charter school legislation differs in the thirty-seven states that now permit them, but the typical scenario finds some group of people, usually parents, teachers, or community activists, applying for a "charter" from a state or local agency, which, if approved, is granted for a specified period of time, usually five years, on the condition that the schools meet their stated goals and agree to some basic accountability about academic achievement, curricula, attendance, and so on. Charter schools are public schools, in that they receive public funds and are open to any child, but they often resemble private schools in that they are smaller, have a distinctive mission, and have far more control over finances, curriculum, and staffing decisions. They are also attended by children whose parents have chosen the school. In the 1999– 2000 school year, about 1,600 charter schools were in operation around the country, educating approximately 250,000 students.[83] (It is worth noting that the sum total of homeschoolers exceeds the number of students in charter schools by a factor of at least six. Despite this, charter schools have received far more media coverage and policy attention than homeschooling.)

Unlike vouchers, charter schools enjoy wide popularity and bipartisan political support. Their very appellation derives from a speech given by Albert Shanker, the former head of the largest teacher's union, the American Federation of Teachers, whose backing of the reform one might not necessarily expect. They reflect a widespread dissatisfaction with the public schools and their resistance to reform, and represent an attempt to inject entrepreneurial energy into the system without privatizing it through vouchers. Their main exponents laud them for their promise to reinvigorate public education by creating a large number of autonomous schools that, freed from many burdensome state regulations, may create powerful, innovative, mission-driven learning communities. When several charter schools exist in any given area, parents would have multiple educational options and, it is hoped, the traditional public schools would be forced to improve in order to compete. It is a good sign that charter schools, thus far at least, have often been designed to offer children in urban areas additional options, have not exacerbated racial segregation in schools, and show little signs of creaming the best students from surrounding schools.[84] Skeptics, however, worry that charter schools, because they are small, will not be able to provide adequate services for disabled and special education youth, and, more generally, worry about the enormous start-up work involved, which often necessitates massive fundraising efforts, and about the growing pains and long-run prospects of charter schools, especially as they appear highly dependent on charismatic leaders.[85] With respect to the most sought-after outcome, student achievement and shaking up surrounding public schools, it is, as with vouchers, far too early to make a decisive empirical judgment.[86]

From the perspective of liberal multicultural education, the simultaneous promise and peril of charter schools lies in the drive to create distinctive, mission-driven learning communities. On the one hand, the creation of charter schools promises not only to provide new educational options for parents and children who are stuck in unsuccessful public schools but also represents the formation of a voluntary association by the concerted efforts of local citizens. As such, charters have the potential to animate educational activity within civil society, an area of American life that social scientists such as Robert Putnam have warned has severely atrophied over the past generation.[87] Thus some charter school enthusiasts find charter schools to be an instrument of civil society and community rejuvenation in the tradition of Tocqueville. "[Tocqueville] would surely regard charter schools as vibrant contemporary examples of Americans' enduring zest to form new organizations to meet human needs. As a middle path between the impersonal agencies of government and the private affairs of individuals and families, charter schools are precisely the sort of mediating institution that forges healthy communities."[88] Indeed, charter schools stimulate the involvement of the local community in education, for in order to be approved, they often require the support of parents and sometimes the participation of various community organizations. By involving the broader community in education, charter schools provide natural opportunities for students to learn about and connect to the world beyond the classroom, and they also serve as the seedbed for the creation of social capital not only in students but in the community at large. In its final report, the 1998 National Commission on Civic Renewal praised charter schools for just this reason, urging the passage of charter school legislation in every state and federal support for charter schools.[89] In this view, charter schools further the aims of liberal multicultural education by offering op-

tions to parents with children in failing schools and contributing to the revival of civic associational life.

On the other hand, the creation of charter schools holds peril in potentially encouraging and sanctioning the formation of narrowly defined learning communities that serve the private purposes of distinct groups. Charter
schools are characterized by a particular mission or ethos, as outlined in their
charter document. Depending on the particular mission or the community
involved in launching the school, the charter school may turn out to be an ex-
traordinarily homogenous place. Though charter schools, as public schools,
must remain open to any applicant and cannot discriminate based on race,
ethnicity, creed, or academic ability, the school's charter may be defined in
such a way as to attract applicants along a particular social cleavage, be that
racial, ethnic, religious, or socioeconomic. One critic of charter schools notes,
for example, that "charters usually invite just certain types of families to participate, be they classified by race, religious affiliation, or philosophical commitment to strict discipline or innovative pedagogy. Charter schools, almost
by their special-mission definition, are rarely inclusive institutions."[90] Looking at the range of charter schools in existence, one finds evidence of such
narrowness. Charter schools exist that have been constructed to cater to loose
bands of homeschoolers, a group of Iraqi Muslim farmers, employees at the
Houston Medical Center, and rural Amish in Kansas. At the latter Yoder
Charter School, the majority of the students are Amish, and the school's explicit mission is to "reinforce the values taught at home, including responsibility, compassion, honesty, and strong work ethics."[91] In this view, charter
schools will diversify the kinds of schools available to parents in different
communities by creating a multitude of small schools wholly lacking in *internal* diversity. This outcome is made more likely because charter schools
are almost always small schools.[92] The unhappy result is the creation of
school communities that are far more likely to be committed to reinforcing
only the particular beliefs and values of children's families, rather than engaging them with cultural diversity.

Depending on how they are regulated, therefore, charter schools can either promote or undermine the aims of liberal multicultural education. If the
distinctive missions of individual charter schools are designed and marketed
to accommodate the parental preferences of specific social groups, charter
schools represent voluntary associations designed to further not the public
interest but the parochial interest of each particular group. The resulting
school culture is hardly likely to be an autonomy-promoting environment
where students encounter children and ideas of different backgrounds. In-

deed, to the extent that parents choose to send their children to narrowly defined charter schools, there may be pressure on teachers not to present children with ideas that run counter to what they learn at home. All told, charter
schools would therefore elevate the weight of parental authority over education while attenuating state authority. Rather than giving due regard to the
civic purposes of education and strengthening civil society, charter schools
could become insular learning communities and exacerbate already existing
social cleavages. For this reason, Bruce Fuller writes, "Charter school founders—
leading their human-scale institutions and, in the aggregate, the charge to
decentralize government—may paradoxically erode the strength of public
authority and the very agencies on which their livelihood depends. For if
charter schools are to essentially serve the tribal agendas of well-off white
parents, faithful homeschoolers, la Raza devotees, even Mormons and Muslims, then why should society continue to support the public purposes that
hold together public education?"[93]

Yet this is not an inevitable outcome. In order to assure the promotion of
the state's and the child's interests in education, liberal multicultural education would insist that charter schools not distinguish themselves on the basis
of ethnoracial, religious, or other cultural divisions in society. Schools can create distinctive missions that give parents choices without serving or reinforcing tribal agendas. Because, as publicly funded entities, charter schools are
accountable to public authority, the power of the state to set conditions for
their creation, and for the renewal of each charter, is uncontested. The policies
recommended by liberal multicultural education would set rules about the ap-
proval of charter applications that insist upon an autonomy-promoting learning environment, the adoption of a multicultural curriculum, and the teaching
of relevant civic knowledge and virtues. In addition, in order to foster the creation of a diversity of schools that are also characterized by internal diversity,
charter applications that strive for inclusive and diverse student populations
should receive preference over those that seem likely to appeal to exclusive
and homogenous populations. Finn, Manno, and Vanourek advocate the adoption of several "boundary conditions" that seem helpful in this regard:

- Charter schools must not discriminate against students (or others) on
  the basis of race, ethnicity, gender, age, or disability.
- Charter applications that portend racial, religious, or ethnic conflict or
  division shall not be approved.
- Charter schools must not teach or practice religion.[94]

The result of such guidelines would be to stimulate the creation of schools
that do not correspond to social divisions, but that give parents choices from a

diversity of publicly regulated and accountable educational environments. As I described earlier, schools might distinguish themselves by general curricular approach (back-to-basics, progressive pedagogy), sponsoring body (group of teachers, group of parents, community organizations, etc.), educational philosophy (Montessori or Waldorf school), and so on. In this way, the liberal theory of multicultural education would shape charter school policy to protect the various interests at stake in education and prevent the erosion of public authority while simultaneously accruing its potential benefits without straitjacketing groups who wished to start schools.

Small-School Movement

Like charter schools, the small-school movement is a recent phenomenon in American education. Its emergence represents a reversal of policy direction from past generations of reforms, where the push was to consolidate districts and create larger and more comprehensive schools, especially at the high school level.[95] In addition to increasing efficiency, large schools were thought better able to offer coherent instruction to students differentiated by age, talents, and interests, and to provide more and better academic and extracurricular opportunities. Many current educational policymakers argue, however, that the large size of schools, especially in urban areas, creates impersonal learning environments that cannot pay sufficient attention to the academic, social, and emotional needs of individual students, that stress control of students over intellectual development, and where a sense of community and shared educational purpose is lost.[96] Efforts to create small schools, usually fewer than 350 students, have sprung up across the United States, most prominently in New York City, Chicago, Philadelphia, and Oakland, and continue to garner much attention.[97]

The impersonal nature of many large, comprehensive schools is undeniable, especially in the elephantine urban high schools forced by the population growth in cities to admit students far beyond their intended capacity. A colleague of mine during my public school teaching days in Houston, Texas, taught in a comprehensive high school enrolling more than four thousand students, where she presided over a homeroom class of more than thirty-five students, all with the last name Perez. While her homeroom experience may have been atypical, it symbolizes the difficulty that many teachers in large schools have in getting to know their students as individuals. In 1998–99, the average size of a high school in the United States was 786 students, of an elementary school, 478 students, though in cities and large suburbs the numbers are much higher.[98] Small schools, by contrast, are designed to enroll half as many. As schools grow, class size usually grows, making it more difficult for teachers to form relationships with students. One study famously dubbed the comprehensive American high school the "shopping mall high school," a place where students choose from an enormous assortment of courses and extracurricular options and where teachers strike unspoken "treaties" with students specifying the "common understanding . . . that passing, and hence graduation, is contingent on orderly attendance rather than on mastery of anything."[99]

The research conducted thus far on small schools is overwhelmingly positive. Examining the small-school reform effort in Chicago, where more than 150 small schools of fewer than 350 students at the elementary, middle, and high school level were created between 1990 and 1997 (some freestanding schools, some so-called "schools within a school"), researchers found that graduation rates rose, student achievement rose, violence and fighting declined, student retention rates dropped, and teacher satisfaction with the professional environment increased.[100] Most impressive, small schools reduced the achievement gap between poor and minority students and wealthier and white students. Studies elsewhere have documented similar effects.[101] Questions have been raised about the extent to which creating small schools is a viable systemic reform strategy, for large districts educate tens and often hundreds of thousands of children. Dividing these students into schools of 400, even in a "school within a school" format, seems impossible. Nevertheless, the effects of small-school reform, especially on children from poor families, are impressive.

This is all welcome news from the perspective of liberal multicultural education. There are, however, two areas of concern. First, like the perils of charters, small schools may be too small and become in effect "boutique schools" that attract distinct communities of students and have insular learning environments. Second, one might wonder whether the size of large schools permits greater opportunity for students to interact, both in and out of class, with students of diverse backgrounds, and whether the expanded academic and extracurricular offerings in a large school provide an important arena of choice for students. In short, perhaps large schools, with their greater educational options and potentially more diverse student body, are better autonomy-promoting environments than small schools.

The first concern is legitimate. To the extent that small schools are designed with a distinct mission to serve and reinforce the values of some particular community, they risk becoming a boutique line of schools within a larger district. As with charter schools, the problem arises that promoting a diversity of distinct small schools comes at the price of internal diversity and inclusivity. Unlike charter schools, however, there are few signs that small schools are being created to cater to the tribal interests of particular groups. The intentional creation of small schools exists primarily in urban areas and aims to alleviate the impersonalization and alienation experienced by many students in large schools. Small schools do sometimes target specific populations of students, such as economically disadvantaged students or at-risk students. But they do so not in order to appeal to the cultural values and beliefs of their parents, but with an eye toward improving the educational achievement of students in an environment where each student has an ongoing and caring relationship with a network of teachers and other students, and where there is less violence and isolation. By increasing the possibility of personalized learning, small schools can avoid stigmatizing generalizations and combat the possibility of stereotype bias that may be prevalent in larger schools. In a commentary on small schools and race, Linda Powell observes that in small schools, "Any student is far more likely and able to be known as an individual—with a collection of skills, needs, dreams and talents—rather than just another 'at-risk minority' youth."[102] Moreover, the small-schools literature often emphasizes, rather than sanctions or encourages, the importance of a heterogeneous student and faculty body.[103] In their current form, then, small schools seem unlikely to become excessively tight and insular learning environments. Liberal multicultural education would strive to ensure that it remains so.

The concern that large schools are better autonomy-promoting environments than small schools is less persuasive. It is true, on the one hand, that larger schools provide more opportunities for students to encounter children who come from different backgrounds, and that they provide more academic and extracurricular options. Large schools are better able to offer a rich array of elective courses, including foreign language instruction and comparative religion, that may be fertile intellectual ground for the development of critical thinking and multicultural engagement. These must be counted as features that promote autonomy and, equally important, as a context in which children can exercise it. Stephen Macedo also praises big urban schools and districts because they foster a "broad social mixing," a tolerance of differences, and ideally, racial harmony.[104] Large schools, on his account, are superior to small schools in their ability to cultivate important civic virtues.

On the other hand, the very largeness of schools tends to erode crucial features of an autonomy-promoting environment and to make civic virtues beyond tolerance, such as mutual respect, more difficult to achieve. I suggested earlier that autonomy-promoting environments would be places that prize intellectual inquiry and achievement and where students are not alienated or isolated by the prevailing school or peer culture. Large schools typically fail on both counts. As the authors of *Shopping Mall High School* argue, the size of large schools forces an acceptance of tolerance, or a live and let live attitude, as the only glue that binds schools together. Thus, they claim, "Tolerance . . . precludes schools' celebrating more focused notions of education or of character. 'Community' has come to mean differences co-existing rather than people working together toward some serious end."[105] The importance of muting conflict and enforcing tolerance, they argue, is what leads teachers and students to strike the "treaties" that emphasize control and orderliness over intellectual inquiry and achievement. The stress on control and orderliness is often heightened by the frequency of violence on large campuses, which many claim is due in part to the alienation and isolation that students feel when lost amid a sea of pupils and harried educators who have little time to establish ongoing, caring relationships with more than a handful of children.

An unsafe and alienating learning environment, no matter the number of curricular and extracurricular options, ultimately inhibits the development of autonomy. Moreover, educating for autonomy, as well as fostering mutual respect, requires an intellectual engagement that small, personalized learning environments are clearly superior in providing. When students have strong relationships with teachers and each other, and when they are known by all members of the school community, a greater sense of connectedness may develop that provides support for the social and emotional growth of students, establishes the groundwork for high academic achievement, and fosters the baseline conditions of trust and openness that allow hermeneutic dialogue and inquiry to proceed. Successful and ongoing intellectual engagement with cultural and value diversity, as any teacher knows, is a riper possibility in a small seminar setting than in a large lecture class. By opting to consolidate and increase the size of schools for the sake of augmented curricular and extracurricular options, when urban schools already overflow with students, educational policymakers may have sacrificed the personalization and focus on academic achievement necessary not only for a basic education but also for an education for autonomy.

Obviously, schools should strike an appropriate balance. Both very small and very large schools undermine the conditions necessary to cultivate autonomy. Ideally, a school culture encourages personalization without "boutique-ization." Ideally, schools should be large enough to provide some curricular and extracurricular choices to students without being so large as to create conditions that alienate and isolate students. Here, too, policymakers should be aware of the social, emotional, and academic needs of students on a scale appropriate to their age and development. In elementary schools, children most need a caring, warm, nurturing, and preferably small learning environment as they begin to learn and master basic academic skills. Later, when they have begun to acquire some of the capacities associated with autonomy, such as critical thinking skills, empathetic engagement, and self-reflection on their own values and beliefs, it is more important for them to be able to exercise their developing autonomy by making choices about elective classes, their extracurricular interests, and their social lives. A larger school with a more diverse array of opportunities seems appropriate at older ages. A liberal theory of multicultural education would seek to reap the clear benefits of a small school environment without forgoing some of the opportunities and greater diversity of larger schools. Clearly, however, under current circumstances, the overabundance of terribly large and impersonal schools represents a greater threat to liberal multicultural education than the small-school movement. Small, personalized learning environments that prize intellectual engagement and achievement are essential to the aims of liberal multicultural education.

A LIBERAL theory of multicultural education sets boundary conditions to permissible forms of schooling, ruling out those that reject education for autonomy or that refuse to acknowledge the legitimate interests of parents, the state, and the child. It also aims to shape pedagogy and educational policy within these boundary conditions. I have described how, pedagogically, it counsels against culturally congruent teaching and in favor of classrooms that aspire to hermeneutical, inquiry-based learning. And I have shown how educational policies, including those of vouchers, charter schools, and the small-school movement, might be crafted in order to promote the goals of liberal multicultural education.

The overriding point of this chapter is that, no matter the school reform under consideration, pedagogy and educational policymaking should be guided by the purposes of education. The unalloyed appeal to improving test scores at any cost, often accompanied by calls to farm the delivery of schooling out to private providers who may be more successful at driving test scores up, tends to highlight the economic purposes of education and promote the view of education as the sole and proper province of parents. This obscures the public purposes of education, and the role of state authority in advancing them. These public purposes should be understood not only in civic terms—that is, to educate for citizenship, and all it entails—but so as to ensure that schools succeed in meeting the independent interests of children in an education for autonomy. A liberal theory of multicultural education is flexible enough to permit institutional diversity in schooling and support a wide array of different kinds of schools. It leaves space for the legitimate interests of parents to exercise discretion in choosing an educational environment for their children. Yet it resolutely insists on the importance of state authority in shaping educational policy for public purposes. Reforms or school policies that resist or undermine the legitimate role of the state in acting to provide an education for autonomy must for this reason be rejected.

CONCLUSION

Human history is becoming more and more a race between education and catastrophe.

H. G. Wells

Few things in life concern the everyday lives of people more than schools. The average American spends over sixteen thousand hours going to school as a child—the equivalent of attending class, twenty-four hours a day, seven days a week for almost two years. Add to this any time spent at college or university, and the total exceeds twenty thousand hours. A few years after finishing school, most people start worrying about school yet again, this time about the schools that their children attend, starting the cycle afresh. Put very simply, no social institution touches the lives of more people, for longer periods of time, than the schoolhouse.

The fundamental importance of schools was recognized well before they were a common fixture in society. Thomas Jefferson, for example, drafted bills in Virginia for the general diffusion of knowledge even before the U.S. Constitution was adopted. Over the course of the nineteenth century, the system of public schooling now familiar to us took root, expanding rapidly. As states passed compulsory education laws, schools enrolled more and more children through the early years of the twentieth century. In its landmark *Brown v. Board of Education* case in 1954, a unanimous Supreme Court declared what had become obvious to all: "Today, education is perhaps the most important function of state and local governments." So important has school become at the beginning of the twenty-first century that a high school diploma is considered an absolute prerequisite for entry into the job market and postsecondary education necessary for securing a well-paying job.

Questions about educational policy occupy a prominent place in political discourse today. From a historical perspective, we can attribute this fact to the increasing importance of education for vocational success and to the rapid expansion in educational attainment over the past fifty years. Though it is routinely unappreciated or overlooked, the change in educational attainment of the general populace since World War II is nothing short of astonishing. As recently as 1960, less than half of Americans (41 percent) had completed high school. In 1998, by comparison, 82 percent had obtained a high school degree.[1] As levels of access and attainment have increased, anxieties have risen about the quality of education that students receive as compared to students in other countries, and about the consequences of a substandard education for the nation's position as a global power and its economic vitality. The 1957 Sputnik launch, for example, spurred a spate of reforms in science, math, and foreign languages in order to compete with the Soviets. Similarly, the 1983 Nation at Risk report struck an alarmist tone and pilloried the educational system of the United States, saying that if it had been imposed upon Americans by a foreign power they would have considered it an act of war.[2] With ever more Americans going to and graduating from school, and heightened concern about the quality of education in every school, politicians and the public have assigned an importance to education heretofore unmatched.

Despite the prominence of education in political debate, many have noted how the civic purposes of schooling have been obscured, and even forgotten, by a narrowing focus on economic and vocational aims. Benjamin Barber remarks that "today, while education is widely discussed, the focus on performance, standards, global competition, and outcomes has largely eclipsed the linkage to citizenship."[3] Educational historians David Tyack and Larry Cuban similarly find that "in the last generation, discourse about public schooling has become radically narrowed. It has focused on international economic competition, test scores, and individual 'choice' of schools. But it has largely neglected the type of choice most vital to civic welfare: collective choices about a common future, choices made through the democratic process about the values and knowledge that citizens want to pass on to the next generation."[4] By construing schooling in an instrumental fashion, connected to the acquisition of skills to enable individual success in the economic marketplace and national success in the global economy, the prevailing view of education becomes one of a private or consumer good. Indeed, the rising emphasis on homeschooling, vouchers, and charter schools reflects a profound discontent with the existing public schools but also, and perhaps more significantly, a move toward privatization and market idolatry, where parents and children operate as consumers within a relatively unregulated marketplace of educational products.

Conclusion

It has been the argument of this book that education has inescapable civic, not merely private, purposes, and I have sought to articulate a particular view of these purposes suited to a culturally diverse citizenry in a liberal democratic society. The liberal theory of multicultural education I have defended incorporates insights from both liberal political theory and multicultural political theory, rejecting the notions of liberal neutrality and the fixity of cultural identity. I have endeavored to show how the liberal state relies for its legitimacy and stability on the autonomy of its citizens and on their exercise of certain political virtues like public reason and mutual respect. I have also endeavored to show how a multicultural education contributes to the development of autonomy and these political virtues. And I have described how liberal multicultural education would strive to shape pedagogy and educational policy while refraining from providing too detailed a blueprint of educational practice.

Though the tide of public concern with education has never been higher, it is tempting to despair over the ebbing of attention to the public purposes of schools. We are awash in school reform proposals but enfeebled by an impoverished civic vocabulary when it comes to education. It is true that political theorists are largely and strangely silent about how education necessarily connects up with, and promotes or undermines, social justice and the ethos of the entire polity. It is true that educational policymakers pay far greater heed to boosting test scores than to fostering citizenship. And it is true that trends in education to privatize schooling tend to erode the regulatory role of the state and exalt the unregulated market. But there are nevertheless some promising signs that the public purposes of education, however defined, have not been forgotten.

I wish to conclude by calling attention to current trends in scholarship and educational policy that give reason for optimism rather than pessimism concerning the future prospects of articulating, defending, and promoting the public purposes of education. I have already discussed in these pages some of the recent work in political theory that questions the idea that a liberal state can or should aspire to neutrality. With the increasing acknowledgement that the liberal state actively shapes the character of its citizenry, scholars such as Stephen Macedo, Eamonn Callan, and Meira Levinson are turning toward describing and justifying the relevant sort of character formation each deems necessary or desirable. Scholars disagree about the importance of different political virtues and the extent to which a state should seek to inculcate them, but there is a growing agreement, I believe, that any particular political theory depends for its successful realization on some educational prerequisites, which implicate the need for the state's involvement in schooling. A growing awareness of the intersection of political theory and educational theory is dawning, and with it a reinvigorated debate about the public purposes of education and the relationship of schooling to the state.

This much, I hope, is clear already from the foregoing chapters. What may be less clear, but no less important, are two quiet but unmistakable trends in educational policy. The first trend is a loosely coordinated series of efforts to rejuvenate civics and government classes. Its primary manifestation is found in the publication in 1994 of the National Standards for Civics and Government.[5] These standards were developed with federal funds, along with other disciplinary standards in English, history, and math, for example. They are *voluntary* standards, meaning that they are not binding in any way on states or local districts but instead serve as detailed organizing frameworks around which schools and teachers may choose to structure their curricula. The civics and government standards seek to cultivate civic competencies in three inter-related areas—civic knowledge, intellectual and participatory skills, and civic dispositions—and they are broken down by three grade levels (kindergarten–4th grade, 5th–8th grade, and 9th–12th grade), in order to account for age-appropriate learning. The standards have met with widespread support since their issuance, and they have been adopted as the baseline framework for the periodic civics assessment portion of the National Assessment of Educational Progress (NAEP) administered by the U.S. Department of Education.[6] Endorsed by and incorporated into the NAEP test, the standards promise to have a longer shelf-life and greater influence than garden-variety curricular guidelines issued by educational organizations.

It is important to point out in this respect that recent work by Richard Niemi and Jane Junn in analyzing the results of previous NAEP civics assessments has overturned decades-old research about the ineffectiveness of civics and government courses in cultivating political knowledge and able citizenship. Despite wide agreement that formal schooling is the most consistent correlate of political knowledge, much research from the 1960s had found that while level of schooling attained made a difference, classes in government and civics did not. Using a much larger and richer set of data, Niemi and Junn conclude just the opposite: independent of all other factors, schools' civics curricula, especially in later grades, make a significant difference in acquisition of political knowledge.[7] Their finding may give new impetus to the revival of explicit courses in civics and the bolstering of the civics content of American government classes.

The Center for Civic Education, which coordinated the development of the National Standards in Civics and Government, has also created a successful civics program, We the People, that has garnered Congressional support and has begun to find wider adoption in schools across the country.[8] We the People is aimed primarily at engaging middle school students in problem-based activities designed to promote understanding of and responsible participation in state and local political processes; and at engaging elementary and high school students in activities, culminating in a simulated legislative hearing, designed to promote an understanding of the U.S. Constitution and the Bill of Rights. Independent evaluations have demonstrated the effectiveness of the programs, and their success has spawned the development of still other civic education materials by other organizations, including the American Bar Association and the Constitutional Rights Foundation.[9]

The second trend is the rapid growth of community service and service learning in K-12 schooling. Many schools now encourage or even require students to engage in community service activities. Other schools have adopted service learning initiatives, which combine service with classroom learning and academic instruction in order to promote critical, reflective thinking and a sense of civic responsibility.[10] According to a 1999 study by the U.S. Department of Education, 32 percent of all public schools and over half of all high schools offer service learning components in their curricula.[11] The Corporation for National Service, created in 1993, supports and conducts evaluations of such efforts.

The growth in community service and service learning offers hope that students will learn to become involved in their local communities and come to understand how such participation supports a vibrant civil society. Some service experiences are better than others, of course, and I would endorse Rogers Smith's recommendation that service programs be seen as opportunities for students to explore the lives of people different from themselves in order "to get a richer understanding of the variety of conditions, histories, opportunities, and constraints that constitute the lives of the hugely diverse American citizenry of today."[12] In so doing, service programs may play an integrative role in fostering the possibility of mutual understanding and dialogue between people who otherwise would not meet, and could help students of all backgrounds to learn ways of participating in and affecting their neighborhoods and the broader communities of which they are a part.

The voluntary civics standards, associated assessments and programs, and community service and service learning initiatives reveal that the civic ends of education have not been completely overcome by economic aims. Though they fly beneath the radar and escape the notice of most people, these efforts are strong enough to be familiar to most teachers and policymakers. And these efforts connect up well with the liberal theory of multicultural education I have defended. The civics standards make plain the importance of political knowledge and the promotion of civic attitudes, behaviors, and dispositions, such as critical reflection on self and others, that are fully consonant with and seem likely to forward minimalist autonomy. Community service and service learning, when thoughtfully designed, provide ongoing opportunities for students to experience and come to understand the lives of diverse others, and offer students a forum for practicing able citizenship as well as learning about it within the traditional classroom. Taken together with the new spate of scholarly work on political theory and education, the civics standards and service initiatives emphasize the broad and historical civic purposes of education in which schools play a crucial role not merely in preparing students for later life but represent a core social institution in the realization of the legitimacy and stability of the state. We would do well to encourage and pay greater attention to scholarship and policy efforts on the civic purposes of education, including the efforts just described.

IN THE FINAL analysis, education is always and ineluctably about the next generation, and as such it expresses our collective hope in the future. This is why we turn so readily to schools as a vehicle for progress. The United States in particular has always invested hope in the promise of education. It was the first country to institute a publicly supported and locally controlled system of schools, and it sought through these schools to inculcate civic virtue as well as to prepare students for the workplace. In 1897, John Dewey published an educational manifesto that concluded with the uncharacteristic fervor of a preacher: "I believe that the teacher is engaged, not simply in the training of individuals, but in the formation of the proper social life. . . . I believe that in this way the teacher always is the prophet of the true God and the usherer in of the true kingdom of God."[13] It is no understatement to think of schooling as a sort of secular religion, a grand canvas upon which we project our individual and collective hopes and anxieties about the future.

Schools serve to help realize the deepest aspirations of parents, cultural communities, the state, and children themselves. In a liberal democracy characterized by wide cultural diversity, these aspirations will sometimes overlap and sometimes come into conflict. The liberal theory of multicultural education I have defended represents my attempt to provide a framework for sorting out these conflicts that is rooted in the distinctive civic purposes of education in a multicultural democracy. I hardly expect mine to be the final word. But I hope that, whatever the merits of my case, I have offered con-vincing reasons for scholars, policymakers, and practitioners to see education in a way that gives due regard to its deep civic importance. Schools are almost certainly the best institution over which the state has influence for shaping the public identities of its youngest citizens and for educating children so that they may be better able to lead flourishing lives, by their own lights.

NOTES

INTRODUCTION

1. Alexis de Tocqueville, quoted in Werner Sollors, *Beyond Ethnicity: Consent and Descent in American Culture* (Oxford: Oxford University Press, 1986), 3.

2. See, for example, Ronald Takaki, *A Different Mirror: A History of Multicultural America* (Boston: Little, Brown, 1993); Edward Countryman, *A Collision of Histories* (New York: Hill & Wang, 1996).

3. See, for example, Iris Marion Young, *Justice and the Politics of Difference* (Princeton, NJ: Princeton University Press, 1990).

4. See, for example, Charles Taylor, *Multiculturalism: Examining the Politics of Recognition*, ed. Amy Gutmann (Princeton, NJ: Princeton University Press, 1994).

5. See, for example, Anthony Appiah's "Culture, Subculture, Multiculturalism," in Robert Fullinwider, ed., *Public Education in a Multicultural Society* (Cambridge: Cambridge University Press, 1996).

6. See Will Kymlicka, *Multicultural Citizenship* (Oxford: Oxford University Press, 1995), 50ff.

7. See John Higham, *Send These to Me: Immigrants in Urban America* (Baltimore: Johns Hopkins University Press, 1975); and Lawrence Fuchs, *The American Kaleidoscope: Race, Ethnicity, and the Civic Culture* (Hanover, NH: Wesleyan University Press, 1990).

8. See, for example, Robert Fullinwider, ed., *Public Education in a Multicultural Society* (Cambridge: Cambridge University Press, 1996); Yael Tamir, ed., *Democratic Education in a Multicultural State* (London: Blackwell, 1996). Other important contributions include Michael Walzer, *On Toleration* (New Haven, CT: Yale University Press, 1997); Martha Nussbaum, *Cultivating Humanity: A Classical Defense of Reform in Liberal Education* (Cambridge, MA: Harvard University Press, 1997); Joseph Raz, *Ethics in the Public Domain* (Oxford: Clarendon Press, 1995); and Michael Walzer, *What It Means to Be an American* (New York: Marsilio Books, 1992).

9. An astounding number of books locate the dispute in education and cast it in militaristic terms. See, for example, Todd Gitlin, *The Twilight of Common Dreams: Why the Culture Wars Have Wracked America* (New York: Hyperion Books, 1996); and Richard Bernstein, *Dictatorship of Virtue: How the Battle over Multiculturalism Is Reshaping Our Schools, Our Country, and Our Lives* (New York: Knopf, 1995).

10. John Dewey, *Democracy and Education* (New York: Free Press, [1916] 1966), 328, emphasis in original.

11. See Lorraine Smith Pangle and Thomas Pangle, *Learning of Liberty: The Educational Thought of the Founding Fathers* (Lawrence: University of Kansas Press, 1993).

12. Eamonn Callan, *Creating Citizens: Political Education and Liberal Democracy* (Oxford: Oxford University Press, 1997).

13. Stephen Macedo, *Diversity and Distrust: Civic Education in a Multicultural Democracy* (Cambridge, MA: Harvard University Press, 2000).

14. National Commission on Civic Renewal, *A Nation of Spectators: How Civic Disengagement Weakens America and What We Can Do about It* (College Park, MD: University of Maryland, 1998).

15. Robert Putnam, "The Strange Disappearance of Civic America," *American Prospect* 7, no. 24 (December 1996).

16. Raz, *Ethics in the Public Domain*, 174. See also James Bohman, who equates Rawls's "fact of pluralism" with cultural pluralism in "Public Reason and Cultural Pluralism," *Political Theory* 23, no. 2 (May 1995): 253–79. See also Isaiah Berlin, *The Crooked Timber of Humanity* (New York: Vintage Books, 1992).

17. See Will Kymlicka, *Liberalism, Community, and Culture* (Oxford: Clarendon Press, 1991), and *Multicultural Citizenship*; Raz, *Ethics in the Public Domain*; and Chicago Cultural Studies Group, "Critical Multiculturalism," *Critical Inquiry* 18 (spring 1992): 530–55.

18. See Molefi Kete Asante, *The Afrocentric Idea* (Philadelphia: Temple University Press, 1987); Diane Ravitch, "Multiculturalism," *American Scholar* 59 (summer 1990): 337–54.

19. See Nash, "Multiculturalism and History: Historical Perspectives and Present Prospects," in Fullinwider 1996, 183–202; and Anthony Appiah, "Culture, Subculture, Multiculturalism," in Fullinwider 1996, 65–89.

20. Raymond Williams, *Keywords: A Vocabulary of Culture and Society*, rev. ed. (Oxford: Oxford University Press, 1983), 87.

21. Roger Just, "Who Are We?" *Times Literary Supplement*, 8 May 1998, 11.

22. Samuel Huntington, *Clash of Civilizations* (New York: Simon and Schuster, 1996).

23. Finally, I must also acknowledge that the popular notion of culture as a way of life shared by some particular group, so commonly used by political theorists, is not shared unambiguously among anthropologists, in whose discipline the concept first received sustained academic attention. Clifford Geertz notes that anthropologists themselves are more divided than ever about the meaning and proper study of cultures—so divided, in fact, that in his judgment the very coherence of the discipline is threatened: "The division [of anthropology] into sharply opposed schools of thought—into overall approaches conceived not as methodological alternatives but as dug-in world views, moralities, and political positionings—has grown to the point where clashes are more common than conclusions, and the possibility of a general consensus on anything fundamental seems remote" (Geertz, "Culture War," *New York Review of Books* 42, no. 19: 4).

Geertz himself favors a view of culture at odds with my usage. For Geertz, "Culture is best seen not as complexes of concrete behavioral patterns—customs, usages, traditions, habit clusters—as has, by large been the case up to now, but as a set of control mechanisms—plans, recipes, rules, instructions (what computer engineers call 'programs')—for the governing of behavior" (Geertz, *The Interpretation of Cultures* [New York: Basic Books, 1973], 44). According to this view, humans are not so much participants in cultures, interacting in and among cultural diversity, but are determined or made by culture. Born into the world with some natural predispositions, we become fully human through culture. Thus Geertz writes that "we are, in sum, incomplete or unfinished animals who complete or finish ourselves through culture—and not through culture in general but through highly particular forms of it: Dobuan and Javanese, Hopi and Italian, upper class and lower class, academic and commercial" (49). In a comment more relevant for my purposes, Geertz says, "our ideas, our values, our acts, even our emotions, are, like our nervous system itself, cultural products" (50). On this view, the notion that people could ever critically evaluate the worth of their culture is thrown into doubt, and the idea that people could ever choose to exit their cultural group and elect to affiliate with another seems impossible. One can no more shed one's culture than one can shed one's intestines or brain.

But the capacity to evaluate and potentially reject one's cultural bonds in favor of others is something I wish to argue for in this work. Following common usage among political theorists, I believe that culture does indeed play a significant role in determining who we are, but it is not the sole determinant. Conceived of as a set of values and traditions that constitute the framework of a particular way of life, it is entirely possible, under certain conditions, for people to reflect upon, criticize, and even exit their cultural groups. Their ideas, values, acts, and emotions may be influenced by growing up within a particular cultural group; but they will not necessarily be wholly determined by that group. I say this not to suggest that Geertz is wrong in his definition of culture, but merely to acknowledge that the meaning I employ is not universally held.

CHAPTER ONE

1. John Dewey, "Nationalizing Education," in *John Dewey: The Middle Works*, vol. 10, ed. Jo Ann Boydston (Carbondale: Southern Illinois University Press, 1988).

2. Ismael Reed, ed., *MultiAmerica: Essays on Cultural Wars and Cultural Peace* (New York: Viking Books, 1997); Todd Gitlin, *The Twilight of Common Dreams: Why America Is Wracked by the Culture Wars* (New York: Metropolitan Books, 1996); Philip Devine, *Human Diversity and the Culture Wars: A Philosophical Perspective on Contemporary Cultural Conflict* (Westport, CT: Praeger, 1996); John Green, *Religion and the Culture Wars: Dispatches from the Front* (Lanham, MD: Rowman & Littlefield, 1996); Richard Bernstein, *Dictatorship of Virtue: How the Battle over Multiculturalism Is Reshaping Our Schools, Our Country, and Our Lives* (New York: Knopf, 1995); Russell Jacoby, *Dogmatic Wisdom: How the Culture Wars Divert Education and Distract America* (New York: Free Press, 1994); Henry Louis Gates, *Loose Canons: Notes on the Culture Wars* (Oxford: Oxford University Press, 1992); Gerald Graff, *Beyond the Culture Wars* (New York: W. W. Norton, 1992); Richard Bolton, ed., *Culture Wars* (New York: New Press, 1992); James Davison Hunter, *Culture Wars: The Struggle to Define America* (New York: Basic Books, 1991).

3. Data taken from Nathan Glazer, *We Are All Multiculturalists Now* (Cambridge, MA: Harvard University Press, 1997), ch. 1.

4. Many others argue that multiculturalism is myopic in its narrow focus on racial and ethnic culture to the exclusion of religious and class differences; see David Hollinger, *Postethnic America: Beyond Multiculturalism* (New York: Basic Books, 1995); and John Higham, "Multiculturalism and Universalism: A History and Critique," *American Quarterly* 45, no. 2 (1993): 195–219.

5. David Tyack and Elisabeth Hansot, *Managers of Virtue: Public School Leadership in America, 1820–1980* (New York: Basic Books, 1982), 5.

6. For a concise history of the link between Protestantism, republicanism, and good citizenship, see Rogers Smith, *Civic Ideals: Conflicting Visions of Citizenship in U.S. History* (New Haven, CT: Yale University Press, 1997), 209–20. For a longer reading with an emphasis on the civic aspirations of the common school founders, see Stephen Macedo, *Diversity and Distrust: Civic Education in a Multicultural Democracy* (Cambridge, MA: Harvard University Press, 2000), 45–87.

7. See David Tyack, *The One Best System: A History of American Urban Education* (Cambridge, MA: Harvard University Press, 1974); and Carl Kaestle, *Pillars of the Republic: Common Schools and American Society, 1780–1860* (New York: Hill & Wang, 1983).

8. Quoted in Thomas James, "Rights of Conscience and State School Systems in Nineteenth-Century America," in *Toward a Usable Past: Liberty under State Constitutions*, ed. Stephen Paul and Gottlieb Finkelman (Athens: University of Georgia Press, 1991), 127. Ironically, then, in glossing over sectarian differences within Protestantism, the Protestant crusaders could claim to the general public that they were accommodating diversity. In fact, of course, they failed to recognize that the "non-sectarianism" of the King James Bible was hardly accommodating to Roman Catholics.

9. For immigration statistics, see Lawrence Fuchs, *The American Kaleidoscope: Race, Ethnicity, and the Civic Culture* (Hanover, NH: University Press of New England, 1990), 36–8; on the size of the Catholic Church in 1850, see John Higham, *Send These to Me: Immigrants in Urban America,* rev. ed. (Baltimore: Johns Hopkins University Press, 1984), 21.

10. Fuchs, *American Kaleidoscope,* 36–37.

11. See Diane Ravitch, *The Great School Wars: A History of the New York City Public Schools* (New York: Basic Books, 1974), 34.

12. Ravitch, *Great School Wars,* 45.

13. Tyack, *One Best System,* 86. Substitute "minorities" for Catholics and "Eurocentric books" for Protestant Bible, and you have a fair description of multicultural conflict in education today.

14. Kaestle, *Pillars of the Republic,* 170–71.

15. James, "Rights of Conscience," 128.

16. For the previous two examples, see Kaestle, *Pillars of the Republic,* 171.

17. Fuchs, *American Kaleidoscope,* 41.

18. Quoted in Tyack and Hansot, *Managers of Virtue,* 74–75.

19. See Tyack, *One Best System,* 105.

20. See Diane Ravitch's rich account of the Hughes story in Ravitch, *Great School Wars,* part 1.

21. Cremin says that this decree, "for all intents and purposes established a Catholic school system in the United States." Lawrence Cremin, *American Education: The Metropolitan Experience, 1876–1980* (New York: Harper & Row, 1988), 128.

22. Tyack, *One Best System,* 78.

23. Tyack, *One Best System,* 106.

24. For statistics on German immigration levels, see Fuchs, *American Kaleidoscope,* 21.

25. Quoted in Steven Schlossman, "Is There an American Tradition of Bilingual Education? German in the Public Elementary Schools, 1840–1919," *American Journal of Education* 91, no. 2 (1983): 151. Schlossman argues that the practice of German-language instruction in the nineteenth century provides an imperfect precedent for understanding the contemporary practice of bilingual education. According to Schlossman, the kind of German-language instruction offered in most places was very different in character from the kind of bilingual education desired and offered today. But Schlossman's main point, that German-language instruction was a deeply politicized issue, connected to evolving notions of American identity, reflects a striking similarity, I believe, to current debates about bilingual education.

26. For the previous examples, see Tyack, *One Best System,* 107–8; and Tyack and Hansot, *Managers of Virtue,* 79.

27. See Tyack, *One Best System,* 109.

28. See Nancy Faires Conklin and Margaret Lourie, *A Host of Tongues: Language Communities in the United States* (New York: Free Press, 1983), 229.

29. Joshua Fishman, *Language Loyalty in the United States* (The Hague: Mouton, 1966), 238.

30. Roger Daniels, *Coming to America: A History of Immigration and Ethnicity in American Life* (New York: Harper Collins, 1990), 161.

31. Fishman, *Language Loyalty,* 249.

32. Higham, *Send These to Me,* 53.

33. Paula Fass, *Outside In: Minorities and the Transformation of American Education* (Oxford: Oxford University Press, 1989), 24.

34. For a description of the energetic and extensive efforts of the Americanization division, see Desmond King, *Making Americans: Immigration, Race, and the Origins of the Diverse Democracy* (Cambridge, MA: Harvard University Press, 2000), 91 ff.

35. Lawrence Cremin, *American Education: The Metropolitan Experience, 1876–1980* (New York: Harper & Row, 1988), 237.

36. Jonathan Zimmerman, "Each 'Race' Could Have Its Heroes Sung: Ethnicity and the History Wars in the 1920s," *Journal of American History* 87, no. 1 (2000): 92–111.

37. See Tamara Plakins Thornton, *Handwriting in America: A Cultural History* (New Haven, CT: Yale University Press, 1996), 161–64.

38. Ellwood Cubberley, *Changing Conception of Education* (Boston: Houghton Mifflin, 1909), 15–16.

39. Quoted in David Tyack, "Constructing Difference: Historical Reflections on Schooling and Social Practice," *Teachers College Record* 95, no. 1 (1993): 13.

40. Quoted in Fass, *Outside In*, 264, n. 26.

41. Fass, *Outside In*, 61.

42. Tyack helpfully warns, however, that speaking of the generic "immigrant" can be misleading. Retardation rates among immigrant children were disproportionately higher among southern Italians and the Polish. Likewise, other studies document higher rates of truancy and dropouts for Italians and Polish immigrants. The public school, evidently, did not Americanize evenly. It favored those groups which were deemed most assimilable (i.e., northern Europeans). See Tyack, *One Best System*, 243 ff.

43. See, for example, Nathan Glazer and Daniel Patrick Moynihan, *Beyond the Melting Pot* (Cambridge, MA: Harvard University Press, 1963); and John Bodnar, *The Transplanted* (Bloomington: University of Indiana Press, 1985).

44. For this reading of Handlin, see Gary Gerstle, "Liberty, Coercion, and the Making of Americans," *Journal of American History* 84, no. 2 (1997): 532 ff.

45. See Fuchs, *American Kaleidoscope*.

46. See Gerstle, "Liberty, Coercion, and the Making of Americans," 537.

47. For more on Covello's belief in the health of maintaining previous cultural ties, see Tyack, *One Best System*, 239 ff.

48. See Horace Kallen, *Culture and Democracy in the United States* (New York: 1924); John Dewey, "Nationalizing Education," in *John Dewey: The Middle Works*, vol. 10, ed. Jo Ann Boydston (Carbondale: Southern Illinois University Press, 1988); and Randolph Bourne, "Trans-National America," in *War and the Intellectuals: Collected Essays, 1915–1919* (New York: Harper & Row, 1964).

49. On the impotence of intellectual opposition to Americanization, see Lawrence Cremin, *The Transformation of the School: Progressivism in American Education, 1876–1957* (New York: Vintage Books, 1964), 69.

50. Several scholars have recently attempted to unearth the roots of modern debates about multiculturalism. Desmond King's excellent new book argues that the immigration and Americanization debates of the 1910s and 1920s "illuminate how different groups' values have always been present in the United States, a significant precursor to the recent multicultural and group rights politics" (King, *Making Americans*, 1). See also Nathan Glazer's *We Are All Multiculturalists Now*, ch. 5; and R. Laurence Moore, "Bible Reading and Nonsectarian Schooling: The Failure of Religious Instruction in Nineteenth-Century Public Education," *Journal of American History* 86, no. 4 (2000): 1581–99.

51. See, for example, James Anderson, *The Education of Blacks in the South, 1860–1935* (Chapel Hill: University of North Carolina Press, 1988). Summing up the predominant sentiment of the Reconstruction Era, Rogers Smith writes, "Like other postwar intellectuals, educators increasingly stressed doctrines of social evolution which suggested that it was unwise to extend opportunities beyond vocational training to blacks" (Smith, *Civic Ideals*, 324).

52. David Wallace Adams, *Education for Extinction: American Indians and the Boarding School Experience, 1875–1928* (Lawrence: University Press of Kansas, 1995). After the devasta-

tion visited upon Indians by the U.S. Army in the early and middle nineteenth century, they then suffered an unjust educational invasion in the late nineteenth and early twentieth centuries. As the president of the Lake Mohonk Conference, an annual meeting on the so-called Indian question that began in 1883 and lasted over thirty years, announced in 1891, "We are going to conquer the Indians by a standing army of school-teachers, armed with ideas, winning victories by industrial training, and by the gospel of love and the gospel of work" (27).

53. The absence of African-Americans and Native Americans from the main educational policy debates of the day does not mean, of course, that the debates about religion, language, and ethnicity had no effect on them. To the contrary, the absence probably served in many cases to stoke already existing suspicions about the impossibility of their assimilation or education. As King writes, for example, of debates over immigration policy: "[They were] conceived in terms of desirable and undesirable immigrants, . . . which not only cemented judgments about particular types of Europeans but also fed and reinforced prevailing views of groups already present in the United States" (King, *Making Americans,* 2).

54. See, for example, Arthur Schlesinger Jr., *The Disuniting of America: Reflections on a Multicultural Society,* 2d ed. (New York: W. W. Norton, 1998); and Peter Salins, *Assimilation, American Style* (New York: Basic Books, 1997).

55. King, *Making Americans,* 3. Rather than talking about any single course of development, positive or negative, Rogers Smith sees in U.S. history "multiple traditions" of liberalism, republicanism, and ascriptive inegalitarianism with respect to citizenship (Smith, *Civic Ideals*).

56. This is the title of Glazer's 1997 book, in which he says that multiculturalism has won an unheralded and undebatable victory in public schools (Glazer, *We Are All Multiculturalists Now,* 4 ff).

57. Richard Herrnstein and Charles Murray, *The Bell Curve: Intelligence and Class Structure in American Life* (New York: Free Press, 1994).

58. Citing Department of Education statistics, Orlando Patterson writes that "in 1940 there was a four-year gap in median years of schooling between Euro-Americans and Afro-Americans; by 1995 this gap had been reduced to a few months"; see *The Ordeal of Integration: Progress and Resentment in America's "Racial" Crisis* (Washington, DC: Civitas/Counterpoint, 1997), 20. Patterson also remarks, "Afro-Americans, from a condition of mass illiteracy fifty years ago, are now among the most educated groups of people in the world, with median years of schooling and college completion rates higher than those of most European nations" (21). With respect to improvements in the education of Native Americans, one can point to the Indian Reorganization Act of 1934, which suspended the official U.S. policy of eradicating Indian culture and introduced the teaching of Indian history in Bureau of Indian Affairs schools, and the Indian Self-Determination and Education Act of 1978, which gave tribes the authority to negotiate with the Bureau to structure the operation of schools. For a general overview, see Jon Reyhner, "Changes in American Indian Education: A Historical Retrospective for Educators in the United States," ERIC Document Reproduction Service, no. ED 314228 (Charleston, WV: ERIC Clearinghouse on Rural Education and Small Schools, 1989). See also K. Tsianina Lomawaima, "Educating Native Americans," in *Handbook of Research on Multicultural Education,* ed. James Banks (New York: Simon & Schuster, 1995), 331–47.

59. U.S. Department of Commerce, Bureau of the Census, *Current Population Survey* (March 1998).

60. For extensive discussion, see Christopher Jencks and Meredith Phillips, eds., *The Black-White Test Score Gap* (Washington, DC: Brookings Institution Press, 1998). See especially the chapter by Larry Hedges and Amy Nowell, "Black-White Test Score Convergence Since 1965," 149–81.

61. Jennifer Hochschild, *Facing Up to the American Dream Race, Class, and the Soul of the Nation* (Princeton, NJ: Princeton University Press, 1995), 39–41. She also documents a lack of

improvement in residential segregation across races and ethnicity and a polarization of the black community into middle class and poor (42 ff).

62. For a review of the literature on expanding tolerance, see Robert Putnam, *Bowling Alone* (New York: Simon & Schuster, 2000), 352 ff. See also Alan Wolfe, *One Nation after All* (New York: Viking Press, 1998).

63. See U.S. Bureau of the Census, 1960, 1970, and 1980 Subject Reports on Marital Status and 1991 and 1992 Current Population Reports, P20, nos. 461 and 468. For tables comparing intermarriage rates from 1960 to 1992, see the following web site: http://www.census.gov/population/socdemo/race/interractab1.txt. Americans are also far more tolerant of intermarriage today. Robert Putnam reports that in 1963, 61 percent of Americans supported legislation outlawing intermarriage, but that in 1998 only 11 percent did (Putnam, *Bowling Alone,* 352).

64. Speaking of Afro-Americans (his preferred term), Orlando Patterson concludes, "There is undoubtedly much to complain about. But on balance, there can be no doubt that the record of the past half century, especially the past thirty years, has been one of progress, in some cases considerable progress. The positive progress made toward social, political, and cultural inclusion has been phenomenal, reflected in the impressive growth of the middle class and the not insignificant penetration of the nation's upper class by Afro-Americans. Even in those areas where major problems remain, the long-term trends are in the direction of significant improvements" (*Ordeal of Integration,* 48).

65. Patterson, *Ordeal of Integration,* 64.

66. Hochschild, *Facing Up to the American Dream,* 72.

67. See Higham, "Multiculturalism and Universalism," 206.

Chapter Two

1. Liberalism arose in part, according to many, as a response to religious pluralism. See John Rawls, *Political Liberalism* (New York: Columbia University Press, 1993), xxv ff.

2. Rawls, for example, writes that "a crucial assumption of liberalism is that equal citizens have different and indeed incommensurable and irreconcilable conceptions of the good" (*Political Liberalism,* 303).

3. Will Kymlicka notes further that almost all countries of the world are culturally diverse, meaning that no nation-state can escape the problems that attend a multicultural citizenry; see his *Multicultural Citizenship* (Oxford: Oxford University Press, 1995), 1.

4. Other multicultural theorists echo Kymlicka's criticism. See Charles Taylor, *Multiculturalism: Examining the Politics of Recognition,* ed. Amy Gutmann (Princeton, NJ: Princeton University Press, 1994); Iris Marion Young, *Justice and the Politics of Difference* (Princeton, NJ: Princeton University Press, 1990), ch. 4; Avishai Margalit and Moshe Halbertal, "The Right to Culture," *Social Research* 61, no. 3 (fall 1994): 491–510.

5. John Rawls, *Political Liberalism* (New York: Columbia University Press, 1993). This book represents Rawls's response to two decades of criticism and assumes detailed familiarity with *A Theory of Justice* (Cambridge, MA: Harvard University Press, 1971). I abbreviate further references to Rawls's books in this chapter, in both the body and footnotes, with *PL* and *TJ,* respectively. I base my reading of Rawls largely on *PL,* though I refer back to *TJ* where necessary.

6. In addition to Rawls, see also Ronald Dworkin, *A Matter of Principle* (Cambridge, MA: Harvard University Press, 1985); Bruce Ackerman, *Social Justice in the Liberal State* (New Haven, CT: Yale University Press, 1980); and Charles Larmore, *Patterns of Moral Complexity* (Cambridge: Cambridge University Press, 1987). For critical discussion of liberal neutrality and a sampling of those who see neutrality as the central feature of liberalism, see Robert Goodin and Andrew Reeve, eds., *Liberal Neutrality* (London: Routledge, 1989).

7. I do not mean to imply here, however, that Rawls believes that various comprehensive doctrines correspond neatly with various cultural groups. Ethno-cultural and religio-cultural

groups are often the bearers of distinct ways of life, or comprehensive doctrines, but they need not be. Utilitarians and Kantians, for example, espouse different comprehensive doctrines but do not necessarily belong to separate cultural groups. Christians and Muslims espouse different comprehensive doctrines, however, which do serve as the framework for distinct cultural groups. The existence of plural conceptions of the good life and the legitimacy of having different people pursue different conceptions of the good are fundamental assumptions of a liberal society. Since cultural groups, in my understanding, are often demarcated by their devotion to and practice of distinct ways of life (or conceptions of the good), liberalism would appear to allow for, or even protect, cultural pluralism. In its effort to accommodate multiple comprehensive doctrines, liberalism can be interpreted as contributing to the rise of multicultural claims. Value pluralism and descriptive multiculturalism are therefore linked. As Joseph Raz says, "Multiculturalism arises out of a belief in value pluralism, and in particular in the validity of the diverse values embodied in the practices which constitute the diverse and in many ways incompatible values of diverse societies"; see Joseph Raz, *Ethics in the Public Domain* (Oxford: Clarendon Press, 1995), 174; see also 11, n. 13.

8. Paralleling the fact of pluralism, Rawls calls this the "fact of oppression" (*PL*, 37).

9. Jürgen Habermas, "Commentary on Rawls," *Journal of Philosophy* 92, no. 3 (March 1995): 110.

10. Stephen Macedo, *Diversity and Distrust* (Cambridge, MA: Harvard University Press, 2000), 121.

11. One must wonder, however, why persons and groups that are negatively influenced by policies should feel any different about their situation simply because the policy was intended to be neutral in aim and not neutral in effect. Such considerations have led some to the conclusion that, to the extent that neutrality of aim is a goal, the liberal state must take steps to minimize the effects, even if unintended, or to compensate those persons and groups adversely affected by state institutions and policies. See, for example, John Tomasi, *Liberalism Beyond Justice: Citizens, Society, and the Boundaries of Political Theory* (Princeton, NJ: Princeton University Press, 2001).

12. For similar arguments and observations, see Eamonn Callan, *Creating Citizens: Political Education and Liberal Democracy* (Oxford: Oxford University Press, 1997); Stephen Macedo, *Liberal Virtues* (Cambridge: Cambridge University Press, 1990); Jeff Spinner, *The Boundaries of Citizenship: Race, Ethnicity, and Nationality in the Liberal State* (Baltimore: Johns Hopkins University Press, 1994); and Philip Selznick, *The Moral Commonwealth* (Berkeley: University of California Press, 1992).

13. Young, *Justice and the Politics of Difference*, ch. 4.

14. See Will Kymlicka, *Multicultural Citizenship* (Oxford: Oxford University Press, 1995); and, for a more concise statement, "Misunderstanding Nationalism," *Dissent* (winter 1995): 130–37.

15. Selznick, *Moral Commonwealth*, 303–4.

16. Compulsory attendance laws, it bears noting, were passed largely in the early twentieth century in order to combat the perceived lack of values among children of some groups, in particular immigrant groups; see David Tyack, *The One Best System* (Cambridge, MA: Harvard University Press, 1974), 66–71.

17. For a specific example, note that Rawls would consider libertarianism a reasonable philosophical doctrine. Yet libertarians of all stripes have long complained that government intervention in the form of compulsory school attendance is unjust. They see schooling as inevitably transmitting substantive values that may contradict those that parents want their children to receive. From the libertarian perspective, compulsory attendance laws are non-neutral; schools intrude into the private lives of citizens and violate the rights of parents to raise their children as they see fit; see Stephen Arons, *Compelling Belief* (New York: McGraw-Hill, 1983); and Sheldon

Richman, *Separating School and State: How to Liberate America's Families* (Fairfax, VA: Future of Freedom Foundation, 1994).

18. See Kymlicka, *Multicultural Citizenship*, especially chap. 5: "The view of language as a 'culturally neutral medium' has been thoroughly discredited in the literature. In any event, it is simply not true that teaching in the English language in public schools is totally divorced from the teaching of the history and customs of the anglophone society" (221, n. 6).

19. See, for example, Michael Walzer's story of his childhood rebellion against high school basketball games being scheduled on Friday evenings, the day on which his family observed the Jewish Sabbath. Walzer, in "Minority Rites," *Dissent* (summer 1996): 53–55.

20. For a full discussion of the French case, see Amy Gutmann, "The Challenges of Multiculturalism in Democratic Education," in *Public Education in a Multicultural Society,* ed. Robert Fullinwider (Cambridge: Cambridge University Press, 1996); Anna Elisabetta Galeotti, "Citizenship and Equality: The Place for Toleration," *Political Theory* 21, no. 4 (1993): 585–605.

21. By contrast, Stephen Macedo, who builds on a platform of Rawlsian liberalism, is far more forthcoming about the requisite civic virtues, their implications for both public and private life, and the institutions necessary to foster and sustain them. "For a liberal democracy to thrive and not only survive," he writes, "many of its citizens should develop a shared commitment to a range of political values and virtues: tolerance, mutual respect, and active cooperation among fellow citizens of various races, creeds, and styles of life; a willingness to think critically about public affairs and participate actively in the democratic process and in civil society; and a willingness to affirm the supreme political authority of principles that we can publicly justify along with all our reasonable fellow citizens" (*Diversity and Distrust*, 10–11).

22. See Macedo, *Diversity and Distrust;* Gutmann, *Democratic Education;* Callan, *Creating Citizens.*

23. The historic civic mission of the public school is reflected in many standard histories as well as countless Supreme Court decisions. In *Ambach v. Norwick* (1979), for example, the Justices wrote, "The importance of public schools in the preparation of individuals for participation as citizens, and in the preservation of values on which society rests, long has been recognized by our decisions" (441 U.S. 68, 76).

24. This according to the indexes of the books, which are exceptionally detailed and lengthy.

25. Kymlicka, *Multicultural Citizenship;* Young, *Justice and the Politics of Difference;* Spinner, *Boundaries of Citizenship;* Stephen Macedo, *Liberal Virtues* (Oxford: Clarendon Press, 1990); Stephen Macedo, "Liberal Civic Education and Religious Fundamentalism: The Case of God v. John Rawls?" *Ethics* 105, no. 3 (April 1995): 468–96; Margalit and Halbertal, "Right to Culture."

26. Macedo, *Diversity and Distrust*, 2. I am generally in broad agreement with Macedo's argument that liberal citizenship entails transformative goals. But he fails in my view to appreciate the cardinal significance of autonomy. Macedo defends what he calls "civic autonomy," a circumscribed ideal that falls short, in his account, of a comprehensive commitment to critical thinking. Given what he writes elsewhere—"All citizens should be capable of thinking critically about their private beliefs for the sake of honoring the demands of liberal justice" and "promoting (in public schools and elsewhere) core liberal virtues, such as the importance of a critical attitude toward contending political claims, will probably have the effect of encouraging critical thinking in general"—he seems to me to be making a distinction without a difference (*Diversity and Distrust*, 240, 179).

27. Spinner, *Boundaries of Citizenship,* 3.

28. Rawls invokes the term "reasonable" in order to distinguish it from "rational," and while he straightforwardly declines to define "reasonableness" directly (*PL*, 48), his comments indicate that the most important difference is the public-directed nature of the reasonable and the private-directed nature of the rational. The reasonable is connected, Rawls says, to the capacity for a

sense of justice; the rational to the capacity for a conception of the good (*PL*, 52). "Insofar as we are reasonable, we are ready to work out the framework for the public social world, a framework it is reasonable to expect everyone to endorse and act on" (*PL*, 53–54). Persons who are rational are motivated by self-interest and effective or efficient means-ends reasoning. (Rawls qualifies the rational by acknowledging that rational agents need not be concerned exclusively with self-benefit; self-interested individuals may still be motivated by interests, like attachments to communities and places, that extend beyond the boundary of the self (*PL*, 51).

29. I examine and defend this conception of autonomy in chapter 4.

30. Kymlicka, *Multicultural Citizenship*, 162.

31. I discuss these two cases in greater detail in "Opting Out of Education: *Yoder, Mozert*, and the Autonomy of Children," forthcoming in *Educational Theory*.

32. Judge Cornelia Kennedy noted in her concurring opinion, "Even if I were to conclude that requiring the use of the [reading series] or another similar series constituted a burden on appellees' free exercise rights, I would find the burden justified by a compelling state interest"; see *Mozert v. Hawkins County Board of Education*, 827 F.2d 1058, 1070 (1987).

33. Kymlicka, *Multicultural Citizenship*, 232, n. 9.

34. Callan, *Creating Citizens*, 13.

35. William Galston, "Two Concepts of Liberalism," *Ethics* 105, no. 3 (April 1995): 521. Further citations are given in parenthesis in the text.

36. The phrase "maximum feasible accommodation" appears in a short article of Galston's, "Value Pluralism and Political Liberalism," found in the newsletter for the Institute for Philosophy and Public Policy, at http://www.puaf.edu/ippp/galston.htm.

37. These purposes are elaborated in much greater detail in his book, *Liberal Purposes* (Cambridge: Cambridge University Press, 1991).

38. Margalit and Halbertal, "Right to Culture," 492.

CHAPTER THREE

1. See Nathan Glazer for a brief genealogy of "multicultural education," which began in Australia and Canada, and, as noted in the introduction, exploded into everyday usage in the early 1990s (*We Are All Multiculturalists Now* [Cambridge, MA: Harvard University Press, 1997], 8 ff.).

2. Michael Sandel and Amitai Etzioni are among the foremost communitarian critics of Rawls. See Michael Sandel, *Liberalism and the Limits of Justice* (Cambridge: Cambridge University Press, 1982), and *Democracy's Discontent* (Cambridge, MA: Harvard University Press, 1996); Amitai Etzioni, *New Communitarian Thinking* (Charlottesville: University Press of Virginia, 1995).

3. Will Kymlicka, *Liberalism, Community, and Culture* (Oxford: Clarendon Press, 1989); Charles Taylor, *Multiculturalism and "The Politics of Recognition": An Essay* (Princeton, NJ: Princeton University Press, 1992).

4. For a descriptive overview, see Jacob Levy, "Classifying Cultural Rights," in *NOMOS 39: Ethnicity and Group Rights*, ed. Ian Shapiro and Will Kymlicka (New York: New York University Press, 1997).

5. Susan Moller Okin, *Is Multiculturalism Bad for Women?* (Princeton, NJ: Princeton University Press, 1999); see also Susan Moller Okin, "Feminism and Multiculturalism: Some Tensions," *Ethics* 108, no. 4 (1998): 661–84.

6. Ayelet Shachar, "On Citizenship and Multicultural Vulnerability," *Political Theory* 28, no. 1 (2000): 64–89. See also Shachar, "The Paradox of Multicultural Vulnerability," in *Multicultural Questions*, ed. Christian Joppke and Steven Lukes (Oxford: Oxford University Press, 1999), 87–111.

7. Avishai Margalit and Moshe Halbertal, "Liberalism and the Right to Culture," in *Social Research* 61, no. 3 (fall 1994): 491 ff.; Chandran Kukathas, "Cultural Toleration," in *NOMOS 39*,

ed. Shapiro and Kymlicka (New York: New York University Press, 1997), 87; Iris Marion Young, *Justice and the Politics of Difference* (Princeton, NJ: Princeton University Press, 1990), 181.

8. Margalit and Halbertal, "Right to Culture," 491; further citations appear in parentheses in the text.

9. Ayelet Shachar's criticism of multicultural accommodations is aimed directly at issues of family law. See Shachar, "Paradox of Multicultural Vulnerability," 95–99.

10. For a similar complaint, see Okin, "Feminism and Multiculturalism, 661–84.

11. The cosmopolitan alternative suggests that individuals craft, or if one prefers language conveying less agent-directed activity, develop identities from diverse cultural materials. See Jeremy Waldron, "Minority Cultures and the Cosmopolitan Alternative," *University of Michigan Journal of Law Reform* 25, nos. 3 and 4 (spring and summer 1992): 751–94. See also Samuel Scheffler, "Conceptions of Cosmopolitanism," *Utilitas* 11, no. 3 (1999): 255–76.

12. Presumably this would imply the conscious rejection of one's personality identity and subsequent adoption of a new one, although Margalit and Halbertal never make this clear.

13. Cass Sunstein, "Should Sex Equality Law Apply to Religious Institutions?" in Okin, *Is Multiculturalism Bad For Women?* 88. See also Jon Elster, *Sour Grapes* (Cambridge: Cambridge University Press, 1983).

14. Shachar, "Citizenship and Multicultural Vulnerability," 80.

15. For a detailed discussion and criticism of the right-of-exit strategy, see Brian Barry, Culture and Equality (Cambridge, MA Harvard University Press, 2001), 149 ff.

16. Chandran Kukathas, "Are There Any Cultural Rights?" in *The Rights of Minority Cultures*, ed. Will Kymlicka (Oxford: Oxford University Press, 1995), 230. Subsequent citations of this work appear in parentheses in the text.

17. Chandran Kukathas, "Cultural Toleration," in *NOMOS 39*, ed. Shapiro and Kymlicka, 87. Michael Walzer, in a response to Kukathas in the same volume, comments on this passage with ironic understatement: "He is not interested in trivia" (109).

18. Forbidding cruel treatment would seem to rule out cruel and unusual punishment, but Kukathas does not explain this contradiction.

19. Or, "[W]hat matters most when assessing whether a way of life is legitimate is whether the individuals taking part in it are prepared to acquiesce in it" (246).

20. Will Kymlicka calls it "a bizarre view"; see "The Rights of Minority Cultures: Reply to Kukathas," *Political Theory* 20, no. 1 (1992): 143.

21. Kukathas's criticism echoes, to some extent, the multicultural critique of Rawls in chapter 2, in which Rawls's description of the requirements of civic education suggests a comprehensive (not merely political) liberalism. See Kukathas, "Cultural Toleration," 74 ff.

22. Kukathas, "Cultural Toleration," 96 (emphasis in original).

23. Kymlicka's argument has evolved over the past decade, beginning with *Liberalism, Community, and Culture* and culminating in *Multicultural Citizenship* (Oxford: Clarendon Press, 1995). Among multicultural theorists, he is exceptional both for the impressive scope of his theoretical contributions (in addition to provoking the debate between liberals and multiculturalists, Kymlicka has offered a passionate defense of liberalism against communitarian critics), and the globe-spanning range of practical examples upon which he draws. The phrase "liberal theory of minority rights" is the subtitle of Kymlicka's *Multicultural Citizenship*. Subsequent citations appear in parentheses in the text.

24. Kymlicka offers a lengthier argument for the connection of freedom and culture in his earlier book; see *Liberalism, Community, and Culture*, chs. 7–9. The form of his argument there would be followed by many others, including Margalit and Halbertal and Kukathas. Note the familiar ring to this passage: "Liberals should be concerned with the fate of cultural structures, not because they have some moral status of their own, but because it's only through having a rich and secure cultural structure that people can become aware, in a vivid way, of the options avail-

able to them, and intelligently examine their value" (165). However, as I shall show in the next section, Kymlicka takes more care to protect people's options than do Margalit and Halbertal or Kukathas.

25. Kymlicka, *Liberalism, Community, and Culture,* 151.

26. The sociologist John Ogbu made a similar distinction years earlier, calling attention to voluntary versus involuntary immigrants. The situation of African-Americans and Native Americans can be better understood, he argued, once theorists and social scientists view them apart from an immigrant model. See, for example, Ogbu's *Minority Education and Caste: The American System in Cross-Cultural Perspective* (New York: Academic Press, 1978).

27. Thus Kymlicka discusses separate schooling for Native Americans and French Canadians (12, 28, 38, 78). He also writes, "If a national group has full language rights and control over immigration, education, and resource development policy, then its long-term viability is secured" (Kymlicka, "Misunderstanding Nationalism," *Dissent* [winter 1995]: 137). It is less clear whether such rights would apply to ethnic minorities, though Kymlicka certainly indicates support for rights to public schooling in the language of any minority group (111). Whether he means by this entirely separate public schools or bilingual education programs within common schools is left unclear.

28. See Will Kymlicka, *Politics in the Vernacular* (Oxford: Oxford University Press, 2001), 306; see also Will Kymlicka, "Comments on Shachar and Spinner-Halev: An Update from the Multiculturalism Wars," in *Multicultural Questions,* ed. Christian Joppke and Steven Lukes (Oxford: Oxford University Press, 1999), 125.

29. Kymlicka is here following an argument made by Jeff Spinner-Halev. See Spinner-Halev, *The Boundaries of Citizenship,* and "Cultural Pluralism and Partial Citizenship," in *Multicultural Questions,* ed. Joppke and Lukes.

30. For an argument in this vein concerning Catholic schools, see Jim Dwyer, *Religious Schools v. Children's Rights* (Ithaca, NY: Cornell University Press, 1998).

31. See K. Anthony Appiah, "Identity, Authenticity, Survival: Multicultural Societies and Social Reproduction," in Charles Taylor, *Multiculturalism: Examining the Politics of Recognition,* ed. Amy Gutmann (Princeton, NJ: Princeton University Press, 1994), 157.

32. Consider, in a U.S. context, the connection between the 1960s ethnic revivalism and the community schools movement.

33. Amy Gutmann, *Democratic Education* (Princeton, NJ: Princeton University Press, 1987), 31.

34. Kymlicka, *Politics in the Vernacular,* 304.

35. William Galston, "Two Concepts of Liberalism," *Ethics* 61, no. 3 (1995): 523.

36. Kymlicka's use of societal culture is a new element to his argument, not present in his *Liberalism, Community, and Culture.* There Kymlicka talked about culture generally, but emphasized that he cared about cultural structures as opposed to the character or specific norms of cultures (166 ff.). His interest, he said, was in "the cultural community as a context of choice, not the character of the community or its traditional ways of life, which people are free to endorse or reject (172). But Kymlicka was criticized for alternating between talk of cultural structures as a context of choice and cultural structures as a *secure and stable* context of choice; see for example, John Tomasi, "Kymlicka, Liberalism, and Respect for Cultural Minorities," *Ethics* 105, no. 3 (1995): 580–603. Insofar as his argument rested on the security and stability of cultural structures, he could not avoid also endorsing the security and stability of the culture's character. Cultural rights then became a conservative argument for the preservation of the status quo. Accepting this criticism, Kymlicka no longer talks about security and stability of cultural structures, but about the importance of membership in societal cultures.

37. Kymlicka emphasizes throughout the book that, despite recurrent revivals in ethnic identity, immigrants should not be viewed as rejecting the notion of assimilation. On the con-

trary, immigrants seek full inclusion, claims Kymlicka. For a vigorous, occasionally strident, defense of this view, see Kymlicka, "Ethnic Associations and Democratic Citizenship," in *Freedom of Association*, ed. Amy Gutmann (Princeton, NJ: Princeton University Press, 1998), 177–213. He offers scant evidence for the claim and, in my opinion, it is a contestable one as applied to the United States. By explaining away assertions of ethnic particularity among immigrants, and by avoiding the allegedly anomalous situation of African-Americans, Kymlicka winds up in a position where the Chamorros of Guam generate more theoretical interest and attention than do immigrants and blacks. Within the context of the United States, this is an odd source of multicultural concern. Nathan Glazer, in fact, sees the energy behind multiculturalism in the United States as driven by the frustrations of the African-American community over the failed promise of the Civil Rights era. After many years of fighting for full equality and inclusion, assimilation and integration have been called into question (See Glazer, *All Multiculturalists Now*, 93 ff.). Indeed, many versions of multiculturalism, as I argued in chapter 1, can be seen as rejecting assimilation into one mainstream society and instead embracing some form of cultural pluralism. For more on this view of multiculturalism in the American context, see John Higham, "Multiculturalism and Universalism: History and Critique," *American Quarterly* 45, no. 2, esp. 206 ff.; Todd Gitlin, *The Twilight of Common Dreams* (New York: Metropolitan Books, 1995); and Arthur Schlesinger's critique, recently reissued in an updated version, *The Disuniting of America* (New York: W. W. Norton, 1998).

38. E. D. Hirsch, *Cultural Literacy* (New York: Vintage Books, 1988).

39. Hirsch, *Cultural Literacy*, xii. See also Hirsch, *The Schools We Need and Why We Don't Have Them* (New York: Doubleday, 1996). He writes there that "the only practical way to achieve liberalism's aim of greater social justice is to pursue conservative educational policies" (6).

40. Still elsewhere Kymlicka endorses a very Rawlsian view of public reason that implies an education beyond one's own cultural horizon: "Because reasonable people disagree about the merits of different religions and conceptions of the good life, children must learn to distinguish reasons based on private faith from reasons that can be publicly accepted in a diverse society. To develop this capacity, children must not only learn how to distance themselves from beliefs that are taken for granted in their private life, but they must also learn how to put themselves in other people's shoes" (*Politics in the Vernacular*, 309).

41. Kymlicka, "Misunderstanding Nationalism," *Dissent* (winter 1995): 134. It is somewhat unclear whether or not Kymlicka is speaking for himself here or summarizing the view of another writer. I have interpreted him as speaking for himself.

42. Seyla Benhabib criticizes Kymlicka on similar grounds, rejecting first the very coherence of the notion of societal cultures, and complaining second that "the goal of any policy for the preservation of cultures must be the empowerment of the members of cultural groups to appropriate, enrich, continue, as well as subvert the terms of their own cultures. The right to cultural membership entails the right to say 'no' to the various cultural offers made to one by one's upbringing, one's nation, one's religious or familial community. The exercise of autonomy is inconceivable if it does not only entail cultural reproduction but also cultural struggle and rejection, through which the old is transformed and new cultural horizons are articulated" (Benhabib, "The Liberal Imagination and the Four Dogmas of Multiculturalism," *Yale Journal of Criticism* 12, no. 2 [1999]: 406–7).

43. Even the most capacious societal cultures also constrain. This is true not just as a hermeneutical insight, but also as a reflection of the history of intolerance and discrimination in even egalitarian and liberal societies. Take, for example, the position of homosexuals or disabled persons in the United States. The point is that promoting liberal forms of education is not something that liberal states should do just for cultural minorities; it is something the liberal state needs to promote for all citizens.

44. Another way of describing the normative space in which members of cultural groups live

is to say that cultural groups provide for their members a *nomos.* See Shachar, "Citizenship and Multicultural Vulnerability," citing Robert Cover and Abner Greene, 65.

45. Waldron, "Minority Cultures."

46. Martha Nussbaum provides a host of examples about how this might happen. She writes, for instance, of the importance of studying human sexuality in ancient Greece, where gender norms were very different from those common today. When we do so, "we begin to see our own norms and practices as ours rather than as universal and necessary. In that way we learn something about ourselves and the choices our history and culture have made. We also begin to ask questions that we didn't ask before, such as whether we have good reasons for the distinctions and judgments we make. . . . Cross-cultural history, by showing us the variety of norms that have been endorsed by a species sharing a common biological heritage, prepares us to inquire further into the morality of our own sexual choices"; see *Cultivating Humanity: A Classical Defense of Reform in Liberal Education* (Cambridge, MA: Harvard University Press, 1997), 237.

47. Joseph Raz, "Multiculturalism: A Liberal Perspective," in *Ethics in the Public Domain,* by Joseph Raz (Oxford: Clarendon Press, 1994), 175. Subsequent references to this essay appear in parentheses in the text.

48. Raz has an interesting definition of a cultural group, which I discuss later.

49. I have chosen the strong formulation of Raz's argument here. What Raz actually writes is rather revealing. Perhaps anticipating the problems associated with cultures constituting identity, Raz writes, "In this way one's culture constitutes (contributes to) one's identity" ("Multiculturalism: A Liberal Perspective," 178).

50. Raz, "Liberalism, Skepticism, and Democracy," in *Ethics in the Public Domain,* 119, 123.

51. To be fair, Raz does argue that liberal multiculturalism "requires the existence of a common culture in which the different co-existing cultures are embedded" ("Multiculturalism: A Liberal Perspective," 187). This, however, is not the kind of multiple membership I have in mind. By multiple cultural allegiances and loyalties, I mean to indicate attachments to the distinct cultural groups that are embedded within this larger, but vaguely defined, "common culture." Raz never raises the possibility of these multiple memberships.

52. Raz offers this careful definition in an article coauthored with Avishai Margalit that originally appeared in the *Journal of Philosophy.* See Raz and Margalit, "National Self-Determination," in *Ethics in the Public Domain,* 125–45.

53. Raz and Margalit, "National Self-Determination," 133.

54. Ibid.

55. This leads to a puzzle. In general, Raz equates encompassing groups with nations or people, and he argues for their right to self-rule. Cultural groups, however, do not enjoy the same measure of self-rule, though they resemble in almost every possible way encompassing groups.

56. Raz and Margalit, "National Self-Determination," 132.

57. Ibid., 129; my emphasis.

58. A third possible reason could also be cited: the voluminous psychological literature on biculturalism and multiculturalism. See the excellent survey by Teresa LaFramboise, in LaFramboise, Coleman, and Gerton, "Psychological Impact of Biculturalism: Evidence and Theory," *Psychological Bulletin* 114, no. 3 (1993): 395–412. LaFramboise et al. conclude that the most powerful theory is that of "alternation," where it is assumed that "an individual can have a sense of belonging in two cultures without compromising his or her sense of cultural identity" (246).

59. Census data indicate that the number of multiracial children has quadrupled since 1970 (to 2 million). More significantly, a recent Department of Education study found that 41 percent of all public schools report that the racial categories used by the government are not accurately descriptive of their school populations; see "Racial and Ethnic Classifications used by Public Schools," National Center for Education Statistics (NCES 96–092), March 1996.

60. Waldron, "Minority Cultures."

61. Waldron, "Minority Cultures," quoting Rushdie's *Imaginary Homelands*, 404.

62. Waldron, "Minority Cultures," 782–83.

63. Raz, "Liberalism, Skepticism, and Democracy," 120.

64. Joseph Raz, *The Morality of Freedom* (Oxford: Clarendon Press, 1986), 395.

65. Ibid., 391.

66. Ibid., 423.

67. Raz, "Liberalism, Skepticism, and Democracy," 124.

68. Ibid., n. 30.

69. Raz, *Morality of Freedom*, 394.

Chapter Four

1. For an intellectual history of the development of autonomy in early modern philosophy, see J. B. Schneewind's *The Invention of Autonomy* (Cambridge: Cambridge University Press, 1998).

2. This charge is not true of either Rawls or Kymlicka, who both discuss and defend their understanding of autonomy. After surveying the work of Rawls, Ronald Dworkin, Thomas Scanlon, Robert Paul Wolff, and others, Gerald Dworkin comments that "about the only features held constant from one author to another are that autonomy is a feature of persons and that it is a desirable quality to have"; see Dworkin, *The Theory and Practice of Autonomy* (Cambridge: Cambridge University Press, 1988), 6.

3. Both Galston and Kukathas place the ideal of tolerance above autonomy. See Galston, "Two Concepts of Liberalism," *Ethics* 105, no. 3 (1995): 516–34; and Kukathas, "Cultural Toleration" in *NOMOS 39: Ethnicity and Group Rights*, ed. Ian Shapiro and Will Kymlicka (New York: New York University Press, 1997), 69–104.

4. In moral philosophy, the concept of autonomy was first invoked and developed by Immanuel Kant, who made autonomy the fount of morality itself; see his *The Groundwork of the Metaphysics of Morals* (New York: Harper & Row, 1964); see also Thomas Hill, Jr., "The Kantian Conception of Autonomy," in *The Inner Citadel: Essays on Individual Autonomy*, ed. John Christman (Oxford: Oxford University Press, 1989). In recent years, a great debate has emerged on the connection between autonomy and moral responsibility; see especially Harry Frankfurt, "Freedom of the Will and the Concept of a Person," included in the helpful volume *Moral Responsibility*, ed. John Martin Fischer (Ithaca, NY: Cornell University Press, 1986). For a standard treatment of the place of autonomy in bioethics, see Tom Beauchamp and James Childress, *Principles of Biomedical Ethics* (Oxford: Oxford University Press, 1994); Gerald Dworkin also takes up the problems of autonomous consent to medical procedures in his *The Theory and Practice of Autonomy* (Cambridge: Cambridge University Press, 1988). In psychology, the usual claim is that autonomy is the desired outcome of psychotherapy. In other psychological work, both Jean Piaget and Lawrence Kohlberg make autonomy central to their conceptions of moral development; see Piaget, *The Origins of Intelligence in Children* (New York; International University Press, 1952); and Kohlberg, *The Philosophy of Moral Development* (San Francisco: Harper & Row, 1981). Feminist theorists have been divided about the desirability of autonomy as an ideal. Some claim it is excessively individualistic and corrosive of a more particular "ethic of care" that is said to be common to most women. See Carol Gilligan, *In a Different Voice* (Cambridge, MA: Harvard University Press, 1982). Others believe autonomy, appropriately developed, is a crucial tool in fighting for women's rights. See Sharon Hill, "Self-Determination and Autonomy," in *Today's Moral Problems*, ed. Richard Wasserstrom (New York: Macmillan, 1975); and Jennifer Nedelsky, "Reconceiving Autonomy: Sources, Thoughts, Possibilities," *Yale Journal of Law and Medicine* 1, no. 7 (1989): 7–36. For debates about subversions of autonomy and its consequences for rational choice theory, see especially Meir Dan-Cohen, "Conceptions of Choice and Conceptions of Autonomy," *Ethics* 102, no. 2 (1992): 221–43; and Jon Elster, *Ulysses and the Sirens*

(Cambridge: Cambridge University Press, 1979), and *Sour Grapes* (Cambridge: Cambridge University Press, 1983). Finally, several philosophers of education have analyzed the concept of autonomy, and the meaning of educating for autonomy, in the 1970s. See especially, R. F. Dearden, "Autonomy and Education" in *Education and the Development of Reason,* ed. Dearden et al. (London: Routledge & Kegan Paul, 1972); and Denis Phillips, "The Anatomy of Autonomy," *Educational Philosophy and Theory* 7, no. 2 (1975): 1–12.

5. For the view that lack of autonomy in adolescents leads to pyschopathologies, see Richard Ryan, Edward Deci, and Wendy Grolnick, "Autonomy, Relatedness, and the Self: Their Relation to Development and Psychopathology," in *Developmental Psychopathology,* vol. 1, *Theory and Methods* (New York: Wiley & Sons, 1995), 618–55; and Richard Ryan, Julius Kuhl, and Edward Deci, "Nature and Autonomy: An Organizational View of Social and Neurobiological Aspects of Self-Regulation in Behavior and Development," *Development and Psychopathology,* vol. 9 (1997), 701–28. For the view that autonomy is a cultural construct especially salient in North America and Western Europe, see Hazel Markus, Patricia Mullally, and Shinobu Kitayama, "Selfways: Diversity in Modes of Cultural Participation," in *The Conceptual Self in Context: Culture, Experience, Self-understanding,* ed. Ulric Neisser and David Jopling (Cambridge: Cambridge University Press, 1997); and Hazel Markus and Shinobu Kitayama, "Culture and Self: Implications for Cognition, Emotion, and Motivation," *Psychological Review* 28, no. 2 (1991): 224–53.

6. As will become clear, I have been influenced in this definition of autonomy by Dworkin, *Theory and Practice of Autonomy,* and Joseph Raz, *The Morality of Freedom* (Oxford: Clarendon Press, 1986).

7. Dworkin, *Theory and Practice of Autonomy,* 14 ff.

8. Numerous philosophers describe the capacity for and exercise of autonomy as a matter of degree. See Dworkin, *Theory and Practice of Autonomy,* 32; Raz, *Morality of Freedom,* 154; Lawrence Haworth, *Autonomy: An Essay in Philosophical Psychology and Ethics* (New Haven, CT: Yale University Press, 1986), 45; Richard Lindley, *Autonomy* (London: Macmillan, 1986), 51.

9. I do not mean to suggest that the ways in which people are non-autonomous at the beginning of life and (sometimes) at the end of life are equivalent. In fact, there is good reason to see important asymmetries between the non-autonomy of a child and the non-autonomy of an ill or aging adult. The autonomy of an adult who has Alzheimer's, for example, will be in a degenerating condition. A young child, by contrast, may be non-autonomous but possess a future prospect of autonomy. The lack of autonomy possessed by the Alzheimer's-afflicted adult, therefore, has different implications than the lack of autonomy possessed by the young child. Paternalism in the case of the child, in order to foster her autonomy, will be far more justifiable than in the case of the adult, who may possess no realistic prospect of re-gaining the autonomous character she once had. Agnieszka Jaworska argues, for example, that so long as an Alzheimer's patient retains a "capacity to value," there are grounds to respect his current (as opposed to previous and perhaps fully autonomous) preferences about his life. In my view, however, this argument would not apply to children. Many young children clearly have a capacity to value in the sense indicated by Jaworska, yet because of their future prospect of autonomy, we have good reason not to respect their preferences and instead act paternalistically in order to foster the development of autonomy. See Jaworska, "Respecting the Margins of Agency: Alzheimer's Patients and the Capacity to Value," *Philosophy and Public Affairs* 28, no. 2 (1999): 105–38.

10. Brian Barry articulates the practical necessity of the on/off switch I describe here: "Every society has rules specifying the age at which people acquire different rights, such as the right to sign contracts, the right to drive, the right to vote, the right to marry, the right to buy cigarettes or alcohol, and so on. Although these ages are different in different societies, the age at which any given right is acquired is normally the same for anyone within one legal system. . . . It could be argued that this uniformity is absurd, because it is apparent that individuals mature at different

rates. But the obvious response to that is that making case-by-case determinations about the readiness of each individual to assume each right would be impossibly burdensome"; see *Culture and Equality* (Cambridge, MA: Harvard University Press, 2001), 200.

11. Within the mental health field, a good deal of controversy exists over whether mentally impaired adults should be considered sexually autonomous. Sometimes the state has acted paternalistically toward handicapped persons, forcibly sterilizing them.

12. For theorists who defend such a threshold conception, see Dworkin, *Theory and Practice of Autonomy*, 31–2; and Joel Feinberg, "Autonomy," in Christman, ed., *The Inner Citadel*, 29–30.

13. See David A. J. Richards, "Rights and Autonomy," in Christman, ed., *Inner Citadel*, 205. Even more strongly, John Christman comments that many moral theorists "see the relation between autonomy and the possibility of human agency as the foundation of morality in general, and of human rights in particular" (Christman, "Constructing the Inner Citadel: Recent Work on the Concept of Autonomy," *Ethics* 99, no. 1 [1988]: 119).

14. See Dworkin, Theory and Practice of Autonomy, 18.

15. In generating this list, I relied in part on Feinberg, "Autonomy," and Dworkin, *Theory and Practice of Autonomy*.

16. The key text here is Kant's *Metaphysics of Morals*. I also profited greatly from Hill's "Kantian Conception of Autonomy," 90–104.

17. Hill, "Kantian Conception of Autonomy," 93, emphasis in original.

18. As unrealizable as Kant's ideal may be, it served as the constructivist basis for Rawls's *A Theory of Justice* (Cambridge, MA: Harvard University Press, 1971). Rawls writes there that "acting autonomously is acting from principles that we would consent to as free and equal rational beings. . . . They are the principles that we would want everyone (including ourselves) to follow were we to take up together the appropriate general point of view" (516). The appropriate general view, of course, is the original position. Rawls rejects moral autonomy as a basis for generating principles of justice in *Political Liberalism*, arguing that moral autonomy constitutes a comprehensive moral doctrine that cannot serve as the foundation of justice under conditions of moral pluralism. Hence Rawls's retreat to political autonomy; see John Rawls, *Political Liberalism* (New York: Columbia University Press, 1993), xliii, 77 ff.

19. Alexander Nehamas, *The Art of Living: Socratic Reflections from Plato to Foucault* (Berkeley, CA: University of California Press, 1998), 4–5; emphasis in original. For Nehamas, Socrates, Montaigne, Nietzsche, and Foucault are exemplars of self-creation.

20. In Nehamas's view, the art of living a life of self-creation places one in constant tension with Socrates, whose dictum that "the unexamined life is not worth living" simultaneously set the standard for self-creation and beckoned others to follow in his path of Socratic examination, thereby undermining claims to individuality; see Nehamas, *Art of Living*.

21. It is possible to offer some empirical evidence about the low incidence of autonomous persons conceived as Kantian self-creators or authors. Psychologists have developed theories of moral development that permit researchers to measure and assess the kind (and quality) of moral reasoning performed by individuals in response to moral dilemmas. Low-level reasoning is said to involve deference to authority and conformity to social norms; high-level reasoning is said to be abstract and principled reasoning of autonomous agents. The highest level of moral reasoning is akin to Kant's moral autonomy: the generation of abstract moral laws that are universal in scope. In a review of the best-known of these theories (Loevinger's, Selman's, and Kohlberg's), John Hill and Grayson Holmbeck find that "few individuals attain the highest level." They conclude, "It seems clear that attainment of the autonomy stages, as defined by the theorists just cited, is very rare during the adolescent years and beyond" (Hill and Holmbeck, "Attachment and Autonomy During Adolescence," in *Annals of Child Development*, vol. 3, ed. Grover Whitehurst [Greenwich, CT: Jai Press, 1986], 174–75; 180).

22. Isaiah Berlin, *Four Essays on Liberty* (Oxford: Oxford University Press, 1969), 131.

23. I should also note that in using a mid-life crisis as an illustration of minimalist autonomy, I do not mean to imply that autonomy is exercised only at certain stages of a person's life. To the contrary, the importance of autonomy lies in our ability to exercise it across our lives, not merely at moments of crisis.

24. This "split-level" or hierarchical view of minimalist autonomy relies heavily on Dworkin, *Theory and Practice of Autonomy*, and Harry Frankfurt's "Freedom of the Will and the Concept of a Person," in *Moral Responsibility*, ed. John Martin Fischer (Ithaca, NY: Cornell University Press, 1986). For Frankfurt, it is precisely this capacity for reflective evaluation about first-order desires that distinguishes human beings from animals.

25. Eamonn Callan, "Liberal Legitimacy, Justice, and Civic Education," *Ethics* 111, no. 1 (2000): 141–55.

26. Joseph Raz, *Ethics in the Public Domain* (Oxford: Clarendon Press, 1994), 121.

27. See Dworkin, *Theory and Practice of Autonomy*, 29 for a similar point.

28. Dworkin, *Theory and Practice of Autonomy*, 21.

29. For helpful discussion on this point I am indebted to Eamonn Callan.

30. Therefore, though it seems paradoxical, it is not necessarily incoherent to choose autonomously to live a non-autonomous life. This explains the problem in arguments that defend political liberalism over comprehensive liberalism because, it is said, the liberal state must allow its citizens to choose to lead non-autonomous lives. When Martha Nussbaum, for example, writes that a liberal society must respect the choice of a person to live a non-autonomous life, she wrongly concludes that a liberal society acts unjustly if it fosters the capacity for autonomy in the private lives of its citizens. To the contrary, the choice to live non-autonomously can reflect the life of an autonomous person. Nussbaum is mistaken, in my view, to condemn comprehensive liberals who seek to foster the capacity for autonomy in persons across their public and nonpublic lives, for her own view about respecting persons who live substantively non-autonomous lives nevertheless assumes that they have not been coerced or led blindly into doing so. It assumes, in other words, that they are minimally autonomous. See Martha Nussbaum, "A Plea for Difficulty," in *Is Multiculturalism Bad for Women?* ed. Joshua Cohen, Matthew Howard, Martha Nussbaum (Princeton, NJ: Princeton University Press, 1999), 109–11.

31. Raz, Morality of Freedom, 204.

32. Indeed, excessive quantity of choice can in some cases impair autonomy. Gerald Dworkin argues that more choice is not always better because increased choice brings with it, among other things, information costs and the potential to make old sets of choices far more difficult to choose (Dworkin, "Is More Choice Better than Less?" in *Theory and Practice of Autonomy*, 62–81). Take two possible examples, neither discussed by Dworkin. First, given biomedical and technological advances, people may now test themselves for *presymptomatic* genetic dispositions to cancer. The very option to undergo such tests is, in the eventuality of a false positive or a true positive, enough to mark a person as terminally ill before any symptoms arise. This is, arguably, undesirable from the standpoint of leading a flourishing life. Second, consider the new option in Louisiana for future spouses to choose between a "standard" marriage license and a "covenant" marriage license, the latter of which places heavy limitations on the circumstances under which divorce is permissible. A covenant marriage is not simply the addition of a new option for people to choose if they so desire; on the contrary, the introduction of this option alters the very context of choice. Imagine a scenario in which a man desires a covenant marriage while the woman desires a standard marriage. The implications for the man about the woman's frame of mind and depth of feeling for him could be severe. The mere existence of this additional option—it need not be chosen at all—fundamentally restructures the dynamic of choosing.

In a similar vein, Harry Frankfurt argues that "extensive growth in the variety of a person's options may weaken his sense of identity. The task of evaluating and ranking a considerably enlarged number of alternatives may be too much for him; it may overload his capacity to make decisions firmly grounded in a steady appreciation of what he really values and desires"; see Frankfurt, *Necessity, Autonomy, and Love* (Cambridge: Cambridge University Press, 1999), 109.

33. Haworth, *Autonomy*, 43.

34. For a rehearsal of such criticisms, which the author ultimately rejects, see Nedelsky, "Reconceiving Autonomy." Cultural psychologists also tend to view autonomy as a Western ideal that is strongly, if not excessively, individualistic. See, for example, Markus, Mullally, and Kitayama, "Selfways."

35. See, for example, Ryan, Deci, and Grolnick, "Autonomy, Relatedness, and the Self," 648; Richard Ryan and Cynthia Powelson, "Autonomy and Relatedness as Fundamental to Motivation and Education," *Journal of Experimental Education* 60, no. 1 (1991): 51; and Susan Silverberg and Dawn Gondoli, "Autonomy in Adolescence: A Contextualized Perspective," in *Psychosocial Development During Adolescence*, ed. Gerald Adams, Raymond Montemayor, and Thomas Gullotta (Thousand Oaks, CA: Sage, 1996), 14.

36. Harry Frankfurt, the originator of the split-level view of the self I have described here, maintains in his more recent work that autonomy necessarily coexists with constraint. "Unless a person makes choices within restrictions from which he cannot escape by merely choosing to do so, the notion of self-direction, of autonomy, cannot find a grip. Someone free of all such restrictions is so vacant of identifiable and stable volitional tendencies and constraints that he cannot deliberate or make decisions in any conscientious way. If he nonetheless does remain in some way capable of choice, the decisions and choices he makes will be altogether arbitrary. They cannot possess authentically personal significance or authority, for his will has no determinate character"; see Frankfurt, *Necessity, Autonomy, and Love*, 110. Frankfurt appears on occasion to endorse a view that autonomy requires some attachments that are irrevocable (111, 130). My own view is that autonomous persons must never be without some commitments and values that attach them to other persons and projects, but that every commitment and value is ultimately revocable. Autonomy requires constraining attachments, even if these attachments are ultimately the possible subjects of critical examination and revision. Put otherwise, we can never simultaneously throw every aspect of ourselves into question, examining the entirety of our lives from a wholly detached position. There is no unencumbered metaphysical self or naked chooser behind the real and encumbered self of our everyday lives.

37. Brian Barry sarcastically suggests that people who display a high degree of autonomy would be considered psychologically disturbed and deviant by the American Psychiatric Association. Such potshots reflect an unfortunate tendency among skeptics to view autonomy as something that leads to incessant self-questioning; see Brian Barry, *Culture and Equality* (London: Harvard University Press, 2001), 357n. 65. But highly autonomous persons, in my view, do not necessarily engage in constant self-doubt. Highly autonomous persons are secure in their endorsement of their first-order beliefs, values, and commitments, and feel confident that they could subject their lives to critical reflection in the future, revising or rejecting certain values and commitments should they no longer seem worthy.

38. See Thomas Hill, Jr., *Autonomy and Self-Respect* (Cambridge: Cambridge University Press, 1991), esp. 33–34.

39. See Beauchamp and Childress, *Principles of Biomedical Ethics* (Oxford: Oxford University Press, 1994), ch. 3.

40. Jon Elster, for example, challenges traditional social choice theorists who simply take preferences and desires as given, assuming the autonomy of the person. Elster argues for "adaptive preference formation," the idea that social institutions and peers, among other things, affect the generation of our preferences, sometimes in ways that would suggest the preferences no longer be respected as if they were simply given. Elster identifies the phenomenon of "sour grapes"—when persons adjust their second-order preferences to conform with their first-order desires because they cannot get what they want; see Jon Elster, "Sour Grapes—Utilitarianism

and the Genesis of Wants," in Christman, ed., *Inner Citadel,* 170–88. Similarly, Lawrence Haworth argues that utilitarians and libertarians of all stripes simply presume persons to be autonomous; for the utilitarians or libertarians, a life of happiness or liberty is nearly worthless unless each person is autonomous. See Haworth, *Autonomy,* 135–39; ch. 10.

41. Given the usual provisos, of course, that these decisions do not harm others.

42. Galston, "Two Concepts of Liberalism," 525.

43. See Avishai Margalit and Moshe Halbertal, "The Right to Culture" *Social Research* 61, no. 3 (fall 1994), 508; and Chandran Kukathas, "Are There Any Cultural Rights?" in *The Rights of Minority Cultures,* ed. Will Kymlicka (Oxford: Oxford University Press, 1995), 243, 252. See chapter 3 for more detail.

44. The degree to which they promote policies that will enable the exercise of minimalist autonomy is another matter. I have argued in chapters 2 and 3 that the educational consequences of their theories effectively undermine rights of exit and/or minimalist autonomy.

45. Galston, Margalit and Halbertal, and Kukathas may further object that their arguments are not based on respect for *autonomy,* even construed in the minimal way I have outlined, but on respect for *human beings.* What generates rights to non-interference, they might say, is not the exercise of autonomy, however defined, but the mere fact of being human. People are inherently deserving of respect, not only autonomous people. Furthermore, they might continue, respect for humanness is sufficient to yield the conclusions that they reach about prioritizing tolerance over autonomy or a right to one's own culture.

It is true that respect for humanness is important. Simply being a human confers, or ought to confer, a certain dignity and value upon a person that does not require the exercise of autonomy for their recognition. On many arguments, both philosophical and theological, human life is inherently valuable. But the question is, does respect for mere personhood do the work of protecting rights of exit that Galston, Margalit and Halbertal, and Kukathas need it to do? The clear answer is no. Each of them insists upon a right of exit as crucial components of their theories. But obviously, simple humanness cannot guarantee that a person is capable of exiting a group. As I argued above, a necessary element to a meaningful right of exit is minimalist autonomy.

46. In chapter 6, I examine several cases in detail to suggest a new way of thinking about how to balance the respective interests of the state, the parents, and the child in developing appropriate policies.

47. Richard Dagger, *Civic Virtues: Rights, Citizenship, and Republican Liberalism* (Oxford: Oxford University Press, 1997), 17.

48. Several theorists I have examined here would agree. Lawrence Haworth writes, for example, "Securing the child's future autonomy requires positive action . . . and may require coercion. For his capacity to live autonomously to be developed, he needs, among other things, the sorts of formal and informal educational experiences that nurture both an ability to think critically and an ability to act on the results of such thought. And often it will be necessary to require the child to submit to discipline, in the interest of nurturing capacities on which development of the capacity for autonomous life depends" (Haworth, *Autonomy,* 127; see also 60, 81, 132, 214). See also Richard Arneson and Ian Shapiro, "Democratic Autonomy and Religious Freedom: A Critique of *Wisconsin v. Yoder*" in *NOMOS 38: Political Order,* ed. Ian Shapiro and Russell Hardin (New York: New York University Press, 1996), 393 ff.; and Nedelsky, "Reconceiving Autonomy," 10.

CHAPTER FIVE

1. Stephen Macedo reaches a very similar conclusion, arguing that liberalism engages in a transformative project that aims at shaping diversity for civic purposes; see *Diversity and Distrust* (Cambridge, MA: Harvard University Press, 2000).

2. Brian Barry, *The Liberal Theory of Justice* (Oxford: Clarendon Press, 1973), 126.

3. See, among others, Brian Barry, *Culture and Equality* (Cambridge, MA: Harvard University Press, 2001); Macedo, *Diversity and Distrust;* Harry Brighouse, *School Choice and Social Justice* (Oxford: Oxford University Press, 2000); Meira Levinson, *The Demands of Liberal Education* (Oxford: Oxford University Press, 1999); Walter Feinberg, *Common Schools, Uncommon Identities* (New Haven, CT: Yale University Press, 1998); Eamonn Callan, *Creating Citizens* (Oxford: Oxford University Press, 1997).

4. John Dewey, *Democracy and Education* (New York: Free Press, [1916] 1966), 328.

5. I draw here from Rawls's definition of a comprehensive doctrine; see John Rawls, *Political Liberalism* (New York: Columbia University Press, 1993), 13, 175.

6. See Rawls, *Political Liberalism*, xlii–xliv; 199. Because Kantian and Millian conceptions of autonomy describe comprehensive doctrines, Rawls rules them out as possible bases for generating principles of justice in the modern liberal state. The liberal state, he says, can only recommend political autonomy. But as I argued in chapter 2, following Kymlicka, an endorsement of political autonomy, especially in the realm of education, will have inevitable effects on a person's private as well as political identity, making political autonomy much less circumscribed than Rawls would have it.

7. Galston's argument, for example, concludes with this remark: "To place an ideal of autonomous choice at the core of liberalism is in fact to narrow the range of possibilities available within liberal societies. It is a drive toward a kind of uniformity, disguised in the language of liberal diversity" (Galston, *Liberal Purposes*, 329, n. 12). Similarly, Joseph Raz says, "Autonomy is, to be sure, inconsistent with various alternative forms of valuable lives. It cannot be obtained within societies which support social forms which do not leave enough room for individual choice"; see Joseph Raz, *The Morality of Freedom* (Oxford: Clarendon Press, 1986), 395.

8. Criticizing Rawls's pretension to neutrality, Deborah Fitzmaurice makes a similar claim: "Once liberal principles are seen to depend on the claim that autonomy is a good, it is clear that the liberal state is bound to be to some extent inhospitable to traditional ways of life. For the principle of autonomy implies that we, as liberals, have an obligation to sustain a public sphere, accessible to all, which is supportive of autonomy." Reinforcing my own arguments, Fitzmaurice asserts that a crucial part of this public sphere includes "an educational system which nurtures habits of critical reflection"; see "Autonomy as a Good: Liberalism, Autonomy, and Toleration," *Journal of Political Philosophy* 1, no. 1 (1993): 14.

9. Meira Levinson's ringing defense of autonomy yields an even broader conclusion: "[The adoption of personal autonomy] within a weakly perfectionist framework provides a strong and stable justification for the establishment and preservation of liberal freedoms and institutions. If individuals are to be able to reflect upon their values and desires . . . as a means of establishing higher-order preferences with which they identify and upon which they are able to act, citizens must be granted freedoms of speech, association, religion, heresy, apostasy, sexual conduct, property rights, bodily integrity, etc. These freedoms are also needed to produce the kind of community necessary for fostering autonomy; thus, they are justified on a communal as well as individual level"; see Levinson, *The Demands of Liberal Education*, 35. In my view, Levinson goes too far here, for these many freedoms are not justified only, or not justified most strongly, because they conduce to the development of autonomy. Moreover, autonomy is not the only thing of value in society or for individuals, and competing values, such as equality or love, might give rise to reasons to limit on some occasions the freedoms she describes.

10. Raz, *Morality of Freedom*, 391.

11. I build upon, and to some extent follow, the arguments of John Rawls about self-respect and of Thomas Hill and Eamonn Callan about avoiding servility. See Rawls, *A Theory of Justice* (Cambridge, MA: Harvard University Press, 1971), 440 ff.; Hill, *Autonomy and Self-Respect* (Cambridge: Cambridge University Press, 1991), ch. 1; and Eamonn Callan, *Creating Citizens* (Oxford: Oxford University Press, 1997), 152 ff.

12. Rawls, *Theory of Justice*, 440. Rawls defines primary goods as "things which it is supposed a rational man wants whatever else he wants" (92).

13. Rawls, *Theory of Justice*, 440.

14. Ibid.

15. Hill, *Autonomy and Self-Respect*, 4.

16. Ibid., 12–13.

17. Feminist critics might argue that there must be something wrong with a woman's decision, however autonomous, to devote herself to serving her husband. A few comments are in order. First, just as we would forbid people who autonomously choose to enslave themselves on the basis that such a decision forecloses all future possibility of autonomy, it is right to insist in the case of the autonomous deferential woman that she be able to revisit her decision whenever she so chose. Second, it might be argued that in choosing autonomously to serve her husband, the woman is a victim of false consciousness—she is not truly aware of the choices before her because all her previous socialization, from parents, cultural groups, and broader society, has impressed upon her that the proper role of a woman is always to defer to her husband. But this points less to a flaw in the conception of autonomy than to a failure in educating her to be autonomous. A condition of minimalist autonomy is that there be a variety of meaningful options from which a person may choose. A false consciousness points to the need for an education for autonomy that exposes people to widely different cultural norms, so that these may function as possible vehicles of critique for one's own norms, or as norms that one might adopt for oneself. A multicultural education, as I shall argue in the next section, facilitates the development of minimalist autonomy.

18. See David A. J. Richards, "Rights and Autonomy," in *The Inner Citadel: Essays on Individual Autonomy*, ed. John Christman (Oxford: Oxford University Press, 1989), 203–20.

19. Autonomy is also the driving force behind a fair number of perfectionist political theories. Joseph Raz's perfectionism revolves around the centrality of autonomy, as does George Sher's. See Raz, *Morality of Freedom*; George Sher, *Beyond Neutrality: Perfectionism and Politics* (Cambridge: Cambridge University Press, 1997); and Steven Wall, *Liberalism, Perfectionism, and Restraint* (Cambridge: Cambridge University Press, 1998). The fact that autonomy has been marshaled behind both perfectionist and antiperfectionist theories testifies both to the centrality of the concept to political thought generally and to the different and conflictual ways it is understood.

20. Gerald Dworkin, *The Theory and Practice of Autonomy* (Cambridge: Cambridge University Press, 1988), 10.

21. Rawls, *Political Liberalism*, 30–34.

22. The civic imperative of developing the capacity for and exercise of minimalist autonomy can also be seen in Rawls's description of the two moral powers which all citizens are assumed to possess. The first is the capacity for a sense of justice, a capacity "to understand, to apply, and normally to be moved by an effective desire to act from (and not merely in accordance with) the principles of justice as the fair terms of social cooperation." A sense of justice requires, thus, that rather than acting blindly or out of fear of punishment, a person be able to turn his autonomous reflective abilities upon the principles of justice which govern him, and others, and affirm (or reject) them. The second moral power is the capacity "to form, to revise, and rationally to pursue a conception [of the good], that is, a conception of what we regard for us as a worthwhile human life." Forming, revising, and pursuing a conception of the good (particularly revising it) similarly requires the exercise of minimalist autonomy, which enables a person to assess her conception of the good, chosen or unchosen, to revise or reject it, and to evaluate her capacity to realize the good. See Rawls, *Political Liberalism*, 302.

23. To be specific, Rawls says that "being free in these respects enables citizens to be both rationally and fully autonomous" (*Political Liberalism*, 72). The difference between rational and

full autonomy is that rational autonomy is exercised only within the original position, while full autonomy is exercised by citizens in the real world. Recall, however, that neither rational nor full autonomy are the equivalent, according to Rawls, of moral autonomy, which describes a comprehensive doctrine. Full autonomy, in other words, refers only to the character of individuals in their civic roles. As I argued in chapter 2, this distinction fails.

24. See Rawls, *Political Liberalism*, xx, xli.

25. They are guided in their deliberations, as Rawls explains, by the extent to which principles of justice would secure primary goods, and by their interest in developing and exercising a capacity for a sense of justice and a capacity for forming and pursuing some determinate (but in the original position unspecified) conception of the good, allowing for possible revisions or conversions (*Political Liberalism*, 74–75). It is worth noting that Rawls originally saw the original position as "a procedural interpretation of Kant's conception of autonomy and the categorical imperative" (*Theory of Justice*, 256). Because Rawls now rejects the public relevance of Kantian autonomy, he has adjusted his argument to conform with a more limited conception of autonomy, as described here.

26. Rawls, *Political Liberalism*, xlvi.

27. Rawls, *Political Liberalism*, 98.

28. Harry Brighouse, "Civic Education and Liberal Legitimacy," *Ethics* 108, no. 4 (1998): 735. In this article Brighouse also distinguishes between autonomy-facilitating and autonomy-promoting education (733). He argues that the liberal state need only facilitate, not promote, autonomy. This strikes me as a classic case of a distinction without a difference. Even accepting Brighouse's claim that autonomy is character-neutral and just a set of skills, a notion of autonomy I find implausible, it is still difficult to see how the teaching of a set of skills that will be necessarily deployed if the state is to be legitimate can be separated from actually promoting the use of the skills.

29. Brian Barry, *Culture and Equality*, 207.

30. Despite language referring to the exercise of autonomy by individuals and by citizens, it makes little sense to talk of an "individual autonomy" and a "political autonomy." The exercise of autonomy is not an on/off switch which we throw at will; it describes, as I argued in chapter 4, a character, coloring the whole of a person's life. Cultivating its exercise, therefore, for political purposes will enable its exercise with regard to the private commitments, values, and desires of an individual. For this reason, as I have mentioned several times, Rawls's separation of political and individual autonomy fails (*Political Liberalism*, 77 ff.). This fact also reminds us why the liberal state cannot be neutral. For in educating students to be autonomous for civic or political purposes, there are inevitable "spillover effects," as Amy Gutmann puts it. She writes, "The spillovers are unintended by political liberalism, but it is not a coincidence that the political skills and virtues of a liberal democracy resemble the personal skills and virtues of a self-directing or autonomous life"; see "Civic Education and Social Diversity," *Ethics* 105, no. 3 (1995), 576. In the realm of education, then, political liberalism comes to look much like comprehensive liberalism (see Gutmann, "Civic Education and Social Diversity," 558; Callan, *Creating Citizens*, 40).

31. Rawls, *Political Liberalism*, 165.

32. I do not wish to be interpreted here as implying that people in desperate socioeconomic conditions are less capable of autonomy than others in more favorable circumstances. My point is that many elements conducive to the development of autonomy, including equal opportunities in education, are cruelly absent. The development of autonomy, as this observation should make clear, is not merely the province of schools.

33. See, for example, Joel Feinberg, "The Child's Right to an Open Future," in *Whose Child?: Children's Rights, Parental Authority, and State Power*, ed. William Aiken and Hugh LaFollette (Totowa, NJ: Rowman & Littlefield, 1980), 124–53; and Haworth, *Autonomy*, 126.

34. See James Banks, *Educating Citizens in a Multicultural Society* (New York: Teachers

College Press, 1997), 69–70. Among philosophers, Lawrence Blum has perhaps addressed questions of multicultural education most directly. He sees multicultural education as forwarding five moral values in students: antiracism, cultural respect, commitment to cultural pluralism, interethnic or interracial unity or community, and culturally sensitive teaching; see Blum, "Multicultural Education as Values Education," Working Papers of the Harvard Project on Schooling and Children (1997).

35. Mark Brilliant, discussing these ideas with me, once asked which person I thought stood the better chance of becoming minimally autonomous: Student A, who lives in an ethnically, religiously, and socioeconomically homogenous rural town in, say, North Dakota, and who attends a high school whose population is equally homogenous but which nevertheless has an especially vigorous and well-developed multicultural curriculum, or Student B, who lives in an ethnically, religiously, and socioeconomically diverse urban area, say Brooklyn, but who attends a private high school with like-minded and like-looking peers, where the curriculum mirrors the values of his or her parents? By virtue of where he lives, Student A is unlikely ever to socialize or become friends with people who are culturally different from him, though he will learn about cultural diversity in school. By virtue of where Student B lives, however, he can never escape actual personal contact with cultural diversity, as he confronts it daily on the streets of the city. His school curriculum, though, conveys the message that it is only people like him, who believe in what he believes, who share his history, that matter. To put labels on these abstractions, we might ask whether the child of rural farmhands in North Dakota or the child of Hasidic Jews in Brooklyn is more likely to develop minimalist autonomy. My colleague believes that despite an education that would not conduce to autonomy, in my reading, the Hasidic Jew would be far likelier to foster its capacity because of the broader socialization of the city streets from which he cannot escape. I am unsure whether he is correct, for I do not believe that simple exposure to diversity, however prolonged, is a substitute for actual intellectual engagement with diversity. However, my colleague and I agreed that the relationships a young person forms inside and outside school are very important. Personal interaction and friendships with culturally diverse others are probably more powerful lessons about diversity than any textbook lesson could be. This observation also reflects the fact that education for autonomy is not merely the province of the schoolhouse. Social institutions and forces that structure our relationships with other people also play a role in education for autonomy. A complete theory of education for autonomy would take up the role played by civil society and our associational lives in addition to the role played by schools.

36. A case could be made, I suppose, that the fact that a way of life is mine is a legitimate reason to value it, but there are clearly much better ways to assert the worth of something than reflexively referring to the fact that one possesses or espouses it.

37. Martha Nussbaum, *Cultivating Humanity: A Classical Defense of Reform in Liberal Education* (Cambridge, MA: Harvard University Press, 1997), 56, 58, 297.

38. Thomas Nagel, *The View from Nowhere* (Oxford: Oxford University Press, 1986).

39. I follow here a long list of theorists who criticize Michael Sandel for attributing this view to liberals. Sandel's picture of the "encumbered self," as many have shown, is wholly consistent with the exercise of autonomy and efforts to revise one's ends. See Michael Sandel, *Liberalism and the Limits of Justice* (Cambridge: Cambridge University Press, 1982). For critiques of Sandel, see Will Kymlicka, *Liberalism, Community, and Culture* (Oxford: Clarendon Press, 1989), chap. 4; and Stephen Macedo, *Liberal Virtues* (Oxford: Clarendon Press, 1990), 241–50.

40. Of course, identity construction is not a matter of choosing from a menu of cultural options for self-definition; it is an ineluctably social or dialogical process, where we negotiate how we understand ourselves on the basis of how others ascribe to us an identity and how we choose one for ourselves. Some aspects of identity (e.g., racial identity) are exceptionally prone to ascription. Historically, of course, racial ascription has often had a pernicious intent and devastating effects. But as a simple matter of sociology and psychology, ascription affects the self-understanding of

all involved—those who ascribe and those who are ascripted. My point is not that a multicultural education suddenly frees people to create themselves as a matter of their free will and agency (e.g., "Tomorrow, I think I'll become a Native American by identifying with and endorsing their values and traditions) but that multicultural education provides essential resources for understanding and negotiating one's own identity. I agree with Anthony Appiah, who writes, "Contemporary multiculturalists are right in thinking that a decent education will teach children about the various social identities around them. First, because each child has to negotiate the creation of his or her own individual identity, using these collective resources as one (but only one) of the resources; second, so that all can be prepared to deal with one another respectfully in a common civic life" ("The Multiculturalist Misunderstanding," *New York Review of Books,* 9 October 1997, 34).

A similar point is made by Robert Gooding-Williams, inspired by Ian Hacking's view that self-understanding is a function of the names and descriptions we have available to us. "Our sense of ourselves and of the possibilities existing for us is, to a significant degree, a function of the descriptions we have available to us to conceptualize our intended actions and prospective lives. 'What is curious about human action,' Hacking remarks, 'is that by and large what I am deliberately doing depends on the possibilities of description. . . . Hence if new modes of description come into being, new possibilities of action come into being in consequence"; see his "Race, Multiculturalism, and Democracy," *Constellations* 5, no. 1 (1998): 23. Gooding-Williams is acutely aware of the ways in which racial identities are ascribed to persons, but insists on a role for first-person construction of racial identity.

Finally, I am sympathetic to Jeremy Waldron's claim that multicultural education enables cosmopolitan identity construction. I find it unnecessary to claim as a matter of fact, however, as Waldron appears to do, that modern individuals are all cosmopolitans. Waldron writes, "Under modern conditions, boundaries between cultures are permeable, and materials of quite disparate provenance make themselves available for the constitution of individual lives. We need a notion of respect for persons that is sensitive to those conditions, and to the fact that for every man and woman the construction of an identity is a painfully *individual* task. We need, accordingly, a conception of multicultural education that is sensitive to the fact that each *individual's identity is multicultural* and that individuals can no longer be regarded in the modern world (if indeed they ever could) as mere artifacts of the culture of the one community to which we think they ought to belong"; see Waldron, "Multiculturalism and Melange," in *Public Education in a Multicultural Society,* ed. Robert Fullinwider (Cambridge: Cambridge University Press, 1996), 114.

41. Gooding-Williams, "Race, Multiculturalism, and Democracy," 18–41; Walter Feinberg, *Common Schools, Uncommon Identities: National Unity and Cultural Difference* (New Haven, CT: Yale University Press, 1998); Sandra Stotsky, "Multicultural Literature and Civic Education," in Fullinwider, ed., *Public Education in a Multicultural Society,* 231–64.

42. Amy Gutmann and Dennis Thompson write of mutual respect, "Like toleration, mutual respect is a form of agreeing to disagree. But mutual respect demands more than toleration. It requires a favorable attitude toward, and constructive interaction with, the persons with whom one disagrees. It consists in an excellence of character that permits a democracy to flourish in the face of fundamental moral disagreement"; see *Democracy and Disagreement* (Cambridge, MA: Harvard University Press, 1996), 79.

43. For an explanation of what this might look like in practice in a classroom, see Melinda Fine, "You Can't Just Say That the Only Ones Who Can Speak Are Those Who Agree with Your Position: Political Discourse in the Classroom," *Harvard Educational Review* 63, no. 4 (1993): 412–33.

44. Gooding-Williams, "Race, Multiculturalism, and Democracy," 31.

45. Martha Nussbaum, *Cultivating Humanity,* 111.

46. Gary Nash, Charlotte Crabtree, and Ross Dunn, *History on Trial* (New York: Knopf,

1997), especially chaps. 2–3. "To American educators at the turn of the century, Eurocentrism was not an intellectual position but a serene certainty" (48).

47. See Nash, Crabtree, and Dunn, *History on Trial;* see also Nash, "Multiculturalism and History: Historical Perspectives and Present Prospects," in Fullinwider, ed., *Public Education in a Multicultural Society,* 183–202.

48. For a similar comment, see Susan Wolf, "Comment," in Charles Taylor, *Multiculturalism: Examining the Politics of Recognition,* ed. Amy Gutmann (Princeton, NJ: Princeton University Press, 1994), 84.

49. Taylor, *Multiculturalism,* 65.

50. Amy Gutmann, *Democratic Education,* 2d ed. (Princeton, NJ: Princeton University Press, 1999), 305.

51. Arthur Schlesinger Jr., *The Disuniting of America,* 2d ed. (New York: W. W. Norton, 1998).

Chapter Six

1. *Wisconsin v. Yoder,* 406 U.S. 205 (1972); *Mozert v. Hawkins County Board of Education,* 827 F.2d 1058 (1987).

2. For some of the more prominent examples, see Stephen Macedo, *Diversity and Distrust: Civic Education in a Multicultural Democracy* (Cambridge, MA: Harvard University Press, 2000); John Tomasi, *Liberalism Beyond Justice* (Princeton, NJ: Princeton University Press, 2001); Meira Levinson, *The Demands of Liberal Education* (Oxford: Oxford University Press, 1999); Walter Feinberg, *Common Schools, Uncommon Identities* (New Haven, CT: Yale University Press, 1998); Eamonn Callan, *Creating Citizens* (Oxford: Clarendon Press, 1997); Will Kymlicka, *Multicultural Citizenship* (Oxford: Clarendon Press, 1995); Jeff Spinner, *The Boundaries of Liberal Citizenship* (Baltimore: Johns Hopkins University Press, 1994); Nomi Stolzenberg, "'He Drew a Circle That Shut Me Out': Assimilation, Indoctrination, and the Paradox of Liberal Education," *Harvard Law Review* 106 (1993): 581–667; Amy Gutmann, "Civic Education and Social Diversity," *Ethics* 105 (1995): 557–79; William Galston, "Two Concepts of Liberalism," *Ethics* 105 (1995): 516–34; Shelley Burtt, "In Defense of *Yoder*: Parental Authority and the Public Schools," in *NOMOS 38: Political Order,* ed. Ian Shapiro and Russell Hardin (New York: New York University Press, 1996), 412–37; and Richard Arneson and Ian Shapiro, "Democratic Autonomy and Religious Freedom: A Critique of *Wisconsin v. Yoder,*" in Shapiro and Hardin, eds., *NOMOS 38: Political Order,* 365–411.

3. Feinberg and Galston agree about *Yoder,* for example, but differ greatly on the appropriate scope of parental authority. Callan and Tomasi reach different conclusions about *Mozert* on the basis of very different interpretations of the plaintiff's demands.

4. Indeed, one of the reasons to be concerned about the actual outcome of *Mozert* is that, from a strictly practical standpoint, the likely result of the decision is to hasten the exit of Christian Fundamentalists in Tennessee from public schools into private schools or homeschools. If exposure to value diversity is an important element of the civic education required in public schools, the long-term consequence of *Mozert* is almost certain to result in the children of fundamentalist believers receiving less exposure. On this reasoning, it might have been better to permit the exemption the *Mozert* parents requested on the grounds that at least their children would receive the benefits of the public school environment for the remainder of the school day.

5. For a history of the rise of common schools and the spread of compulsory attendance laws, see David Tyack, *The One Best System: A History of American Urban Education* (Cambridge, MA: Harvard University Press, 1974).

6. See Patricia Lines, "Homeschoolers: Estimating Numbers and Growth," U.S. Department of Education, Office of Educational Research and Improvement, 1998, 1; J. Gary Knowles, Stacey E. Marlow, and James Muchmore, "From Pedagogy to Ideology: Origins and Phases of

Home Education in the United States, 1970–1990, *American Journal of Education* (February 1992): 196.

7. Lines notes that "Many families do not file papers, although it is required. . . . Some families are homeschooling under a state constitutional or statutory provision that excuses religious-based homeschoolers from filing requirements" ("Homeschoolers," 2).

8. Lines uses current rates of growth to suggest a number of 1 million in 1997. A cover story in *Newsweek* in 1998 claimed that up to 1.5 million children were being homeschooled. And the National Home Education Research Institute, an advocacy group, offers a high estimate of 1.9 million in 2000. As this book went to press, the United States Department of Education released a study that estimated the number of homeschoolers to be significantly lower: 850,000 in 1999 (Stacey Bielick, Kathryn Chandler, and Stephen Broughman, *Homeschooling in the United States: 1999* [NCES 2001–033] U.S. Department of Education [Washington, DC: National Center for Education Statistics, 2001]). That there is widespread disagreement over the number of children being homeschooled points to the failure of states even to have accurate records of homeschooling. Without regulations that require districts and states to collect information about the numbers of homeschoolers, data about the academic achievement of homeschoolers will be necessarily inconclusive.

9. Mindy Sink, "Shootings Intensify Interest in Home Schooling," *New York Times*, 11 August 1999, B7; Lynn Schnaiberg, "Home Schooling Queries Spike After Shootings," *Education Week*, 9 June 1999, 3.

10. *Digest of Educational Statistics, 1998*, U.S. Department of Education, National Center for Educational Statistics (1999), 24.

11. "Private School Survey, 1997–98," U.S. Department of Education, National Center for Educational Statistics (1999), 12. The categorization "conservative Christian" is not mine, but the Department of Education's.

12. Barbara Kantrowitz and Pat Wingert, "Learning at Home: Does It Pass the Test?" *Newsweek*, 5 October 1998, 64–70; United States Senate Resolution 183, 106th United States Congress (1999). Echoing contested language first found in the *Pierce v. Society of Sisters* case (1925), the Senate declared in the resolution that the "United States recognizes the fundamental right of parents to direct the education and upbringing of their children."

13. James C. Carper, "Pluralism to Establishment to Dissent: The Religious and Educational Context of Home Schooling," *Peabody Journal of Education* 75, nos. 1, 2 (2000): 16. See also Knowles, Marlowe, and Muchmore, "From Pedagogy to Ideology," 227.

14. See, for example, Cheryl Lange and Kristin Kline Liu, "Homeschooling: Parents' Reasons for Transfer and the Implications for Educational Policy," Research Report No. 29, University of Minnesota, College of Education and Human Development, 1999. For the most extensive survey on homeschooling parents, see Lawrence Rudner, "Scholastic Achievement and Demographic Characteristics of Home School Students in 1998," *Educational Policy Analysis Archives* 7, no. 8 (1999).

15. Knowles, Marlowe, and Muchmore, "From Pedagogy to Ideology," 211–12; see also James Tobak and Perry Zirkel, "Home Instruction: An Analysis of the Statutes and Case Law," *University of Dayton Law Review* 8, no. 1 (1982): 1–60.

16. See, for example, Dana Hull, "Home Schooling's High-Tech Wave," *San Jose Mercury News*, 24 October 1999, A1.

17. *Wisconsin v. Yoder*, 406 U.S. at 236.

18. Hull, "Home Schooling's High-Tech Wave," A20. For another example of non-enforcement, see Jeff Archer, "Woman in Maryland Home-School Case Acquitted," *Education Week*, 30 October 1996.

19. James Dwyer, *Religious Schools v. Children's Rights* (Ithaca, NY: Cornell University Press, 1998), 2; see also 10.

20. Christopher Klicka, *Homeschooling in the United States: A Legal Analysis* (Purcerville, VA: Home School Legal Defense Association, 1999). A note of caution: because the HSLDA is an advocacy group, the legal analysis probably interprets state laws in the light most favorable to homeschoolers.

21. Klicka, *Homeschooling in the United States*, v, 105–6. See also Virginia, *Home School Statute* (1984): 22.1–254.1.

22. By using the term *parents*, I do not mean to privilege biological parents over other kinds of parents. A more general, and for my purposes synonymous term, would be *guardians*.

23. Eamonn Callan, *Creating Citizens* (Oxford: Clarendon Press, 1997), 142. Callan's point in the book, however, is not to make parent-centered claims about education.

24. There are some plausible alternatives, of course, most famously the communal child-rearing described in Plato's *Republic* or, more recently, the communal parenting on kibbutzim. But such possibilities are highly unlikely ever to be implemented on a wide scale in modern society.

25. In a defense of the decision in *Yoder*, Shelley Burtt has argued that parents' authority over their children's education cannot be justified in the religious free exercise claims of the parents, nor in the satisfaction of parental conceptions of the good life. Instead, Burtt argues parents are best situated to meet the "developmental needs" of their children. Burtt defines "developmental needs" as including emotional, physical, and cognitive needs, as well as moral, spiritual, and cultural needs. With the addition of these latter three, however, Burtt sets a standard that is ethically contestable, which in turn undermines, in my view, her claim that parents are entitled to state deference in determining the educational environment of their children (Burtt, "In Defense of *Yoder*").

26. This approach is taken, for example, by Jon Elster in *Solomonic Judgments: Studies in the Limitations of Rationality* (Cambridge: Cambridge University Press, 1989), 134ff.

27. *Wisconsin v. Yoder*, 406 U.S. at 213.

28. *Brown v. Board of Education* 347 U.S. 483, 493 (1954).

29. See, for example, Arneson and Shapiro, "Democratic Autonomy and Religious Freedom," 376 ff.

30. See, for example, John Rawls, *Political Liberalism* (New York: Columbia University Press, 1993), 194–200; Stephen Macedo, *Liberal Virtues* (Oxford: Clarendon Press, 1990); and Macedo, "Liberal Civic Education," 486 ff.

31. Galston, "Two Concepts of Liberalism," 525, 528.

32. Evidence of the importance of educational attainment can be seen in the booming rates of high school attendance and graduation in only the past fifty years. In 1960, 41 percent of adults had a high school degree; in 1998, 82 percent did (*Statistical Abstract of the United States 1998* [Washington, DC: U.S. Census Bureau, 1998]).

33. It is tempting to think that when parents and the state clash with respect to ensuring the development of children into independent adulthood, it is because the state is acting in its backstop role, intervening in the face of negligent or abusive parents. But the reverse is more likely. Parents often allege that the state is negligent or abusive in providing schools of such low quality that their children are effectively disabled from acquiring the necessary competencies to become independently functioning adults in society. Parents routinely and justly decry public schools that fail to teach their children to read and write, that fail to keep their children physically safe, that evince a callous disregard for or ignorance of their children's distinctive needs and interests, and so on. It is not only the state which seeks to hold parents responsible for helping to develop their children into healthy adults; parents also seek to hold the state responsible for providing good schools in the service of the same goal.

34. On this question, the available empirical evidence seems to indicate that Catholic schools, for example, can be very successful, perhaps more successful than public schools, in developing

citizenship. See Anthony Bryk, *Catholic Schools and the Common Good* (Cambridge, MA: Harvard University Press, 1993).

35. As many commentators have noted, United States courts have rarely recognized independent interests, much less rights, of children; see, among others, Hillary Rodham, "Children Under the Law," *Harvard Educational Review* 43, no. 4 (1973): 1–28; Martha Minow, *Making All the Difference: Inclusion, Exclusion, and American Law* (Ithaca, NY: Cornell University Press, 1990); and James Dwyer, "The Children We Abandon: Religious Exemptions to Child Welfare and Education Laws as Denials of Equal Protection to Children of Religious Objectors," 74 *North Carolina Law Review* 1321 (1996).

36. This underscores the weak perfectionism inherent in my argument. Education is necessary not only for civic reasons related to the cultivation of citizenship. To the extent that education is necessary to foster minimalist autonomy, education equips people to lead good lives. For a similar claim, see Harry Brighouse, *School Choice and Social Justice*, 69 ff.; and Eamonn Callan, "Autonomy, Child-Rearing, and Good Lives." Brian Barry also endorses the notion that education is in the eudaemonistic as opposed to civic interest of the state and individuals, though he rejects autonomy education; see his *Culture and Equality*, chap. 6.

37. In *Pierce v. Society of Sisters*, for example, the Court established the principle that a law compelling parents to send their children to public schools "interferes with the liberty of parents and guardians to direct the upbringing and education of children under their control" (*Pierce v. Society of Sisters*, 268 U.S. 510, 534–35 [1925]). Similarly, in *Yoder* the Court opined, "This case involves the fundamental interest of parents, as contrasted with that of the State, to guide the religious future and education of their children. The history and culture of Western civilization reflect a strong tradition of parental concern for the nurture and upbringing of their children. This primary role of the parents in the upbringing of their children is now established beyond debate as an enduring American tradition" (*Wisconsin v. Yoder*, 406 U.S. at 232). On the other hand, Yael Tamir has argued that there can be no right to educate, only a right to be educated ("Whose Education Is It Anyway?" *Journal of Philosophy of Education* 24, no. 7 [1990]: 161–70). See also James Dwyer's argument in "Why Parents' Rights are Wrong" (Dwyer, *Religious Schools*, (62–101).

38. I'd endorse Bertrand Russell's observation that "the question of home versus school is difficult to argue in the abstract. If ideal homes are contrasted with actual schools, the balance tips one way; if ideal schools are contrasted with actual homes, the balance tips the other way. I have no doubt in my mind that the ideal school is better than the ideal home, at any rate the ideal urban home, because it allows more light and air, more freedom of movement, and more companionship of contemporaries. But it by no means follows that the actual school will be better than the actual home"; see *Education and the Social Order* (London: Unwin Books, 1967), p. 41.

Several recent arguments answer the balancing question very differently. For a view that gives predominant weight to children's interests and wholly cancels parental interests, see Dwyer, *Religious Schools v. Children's Rights*. Dwyer argues that religious and private schools should be heavily regulated because without such regulation they frequently cause harm to children. For a view that divides educational authority between parents and the state, see Shapiro, "Governing Children," in *Democratic Justice* (New Haven, CT: Yale University Press, 1999), 64–109. Shapiro argues that parents should be responsible for the education of children for their best interests, as the parents understand them, and that the state should be responsible for the education of children for their basic interests, which include security, nutrition, health, and citizenship. In the event of conflicts, the state's basic interests trump the parents' assertion of best interests. And for a view that gives almost exclusive authority to parents, see Stephen Gilles, "On Educating Children: A Parentalist Manifesto," 63 *University of Chicago Law Review* 937 (1996): 937–1034. Gilles argues that "the deference we extend to parental educational choices should approach (though not necessarily equal) the deference we give to the self-regarding choices of adult individuals" (939). In addition, Amy Gutmann's recently reissued *Democratic Education* (Princeton, NJ: Princeton University Press, 1999) addresses this question of educational authority directly, arguing that such authority "must be shared among parents, citizens, and professional educators" (42).

39. Hull, "Homeschooling's High-Tech Wave," A20. Hull quotes another student who says, "School isn't about learning. It's about writing 'Metallica' on your notebook and wearing the right clothes and trying to be popular" (A1).

40. Rudner, "Scholastic Achievement and Demographic Characteristics of Home School Students in 1998."

41. The 1997 Individuals with Disabilities Education Act mandates that the state provide appropriate services for even the most disabled students. These services are to be provided in "the least restrictive setting," which is often judged to be the school rather than the home. But because as a matter of purely practical constraint every school district cannot provide a complete array of all special education services, parents of children with rare or severe disabilities, and who have sufficient skills and/or resources, sometimes prefer to educate in the home.

42. Levinson, *Demands of Liberal Education*, 58.

43. Levinson, *Demands of Liberal Education*, 61.

44. Both Levinson and Callan reach similar conclusions. Callan writes, for example, "The essential demand is that schooling properly involves at some stage sympathetic and critical engagement with beliefs and ways of life at odds with the culture of the family or religious or ethnic group into which the child is born" (*Creating Citizens*, 133).

45. For a sympathetic and illuminating account of one Christian homeschooling family whose motivation was, in the author's words, to "encapsulate themselves in a culture of their own making" and to provide "a parallel world" apart from the popular, secular society, see Margaret Talbot, "A Mighty Fortress," *New York Times Magazine*, 27 February 2000, 40.

46. bell hooks, *Teaching to Transgress* (New York: Routledge, 1994), 3.

47. *Wisconsin v. Yoder*, 406 U.S. at 240.

48. Psychologists as well as lawyers have pointed to research indicating that the decision-making competence of late adolescents does not differ significantly, if at all, from that of adults. One psychologist notes that "in so far as denial of autonomy has been based on assumptions of incompetence (in decision-making, related to matters such as psychotherapy, abortion, medical treatment, and contraception), current psychological research does not support such an age-graded distinction" (G. Melton, as cited in John Hill and Grayson Holmbeck, "Attachment and Autonomy During Adolescence," in *Annals of Child Development: A Research Annual*, vol. 3, ed. Grover Whitehurst [Greenwich, CT: Jai Press, 1986], 148). Similarly, in a literature review, Susan Silverberg and Dawn Gondoli conclude that "the evidence available to date suggests that adolescents—at least once they reach age sixteen—have acquired a host of critical decision-making skills that are comparable to those of adults" ("Autonomy in Adolescence: A Contextualized Perspective," in *Psychosocial Development During Adolescence*, ed. Gerald Adams, Raymond Montemayor, and Thomas Gullotta [Thousand Oaks, CA: Sage: 1996], 50). Noting that judges rarely use cognitive development studies to assess the competence of minors, Walter Mlyniec nevertheless concludes that studies show that "as a matter of cognitive functioning, adolescents possess a capacity equal to adults for making decisions about significant life events"; see "A Judge's Ethical Dilemma: Assessing a Child's Capacity to Choose," 64 *Fordham Law Review* 1873, 1882 (1996). Such studies lend support to the claim that the preferences of adolescents, if expressed in a legal context, should not be assumed to be immature or unreasonable.

49. Mark Walsh, "Court Sends Girl to Public School Against Parents' Wishes," *Education Week*, 25 November 25, 1998, 1; Maria Glod, "An Education in the Courts; Couple Fights Order on Teen's Schooling," *Washington Post*, 7 November 1998, B1.

50. Writing in his dissent, Justice Douglas opined, "If an Amish child desires to attend high

school, and is mature enough to have that desire respected, the State may well be able to override the parents' religiously motivated objections" (*Wisconsin v. Yoder*, 406 U.S. at 242).

51. See Randy Kandel, "Just Ask the Kid! Toward a Rule of Children's Choice in Custody Determinations," 49 *University of Miami Law Review* 299 (1994).

52. Mlyniec, "A Judge's Ethical Dilemma," 1892.

53. Mlyniec, "A Judge's Ethical Dilemma," 1895.

54. Mlyniec, "A Judge's Ethical Dilemma," 1889. The key case establishing a minor's right to an abortion is *Bellotti v. Baird*, 443 U.S. 622 (1979). The Court held there that lower courts should not interfere with the choices of a mature minor, even if judges believed that an abortion would not be in the child's best interest.

55. Mlyniec, "A Judge's Ethical Dilemma," 1907. Randy Kandel holds the less persuasive position that in custody cases, the choices of children should be dispositive as of the age six (Kandel, "Just Ask the Kid!").

56. Emily Buss argues, for example, that while courts may often have solid grounds to accord children rights of religious exercise that are independent of their parents, the state will do more harm than good if it actively seeks to elicit children's religious views in order to protect them; see "What Does Frieda Yoder Believe?" 2 *University of Pennsylvania Journal of Constitutional Law* 53 (1999).

57. Minow, *Making All the Difference*, 293. I agree with Minow's claim that the attribution of rights to children does not undermine community but makes possible ongoing conversations about boundaries and membership in communities. She writes, "The language of rights thus draws each claimant into the community and grants each a basic opportunity to participate in the process of communal debate" (296).

58. Mlyniec notes the frequency with which judges are faced with the task of evaluating the competence of a child to make a choice regarding some important aspect of her life, and how little has been written about it. He rejects the largely idiosyncratic judgments made by courts today and seeks to rest a judge's assessment of a minor's competence on social scientific evidence about cognitive development (Mlyniec, "A Judge's Ethical Dilemma," 1875 ff.).

59. Mlyniec recommends a procedure called an "informed consent dialogue" in which a judge, or some third party, attempts to assess the cognitive competence of a child and whether a child voluntarily and knowingly agrees to a certain course of action (e.g., medical or mental health treatment, the waiving of rights in delinquency cases, etc.). This might also have some purchase in conflicts over educational authority; see Mlyniec, "A Judge's Ethical Dilemma," 1907.

60. *Mozert v. Hawkins County Board of Education*, 827 F.2d at 1073.

61. According to a recent news article, Pennsylvania Congressman Bill Goodling, who chairs the House Committee on Education and the Workforce, has called homeschoolers "the most effective education lobby on Capitol Hill" (Daniel Golden, "Home Schoolers Learn How to Gain Clout Inside the Beltway," *Wall Street Journal*, 24 April 2000, A1).

62. Cass Sunstein, "Paradoxes of the Regulatory State" in *Free Markets and Social Justice* (Oxford: Oxford University Press, 1997): 271–97.

63. Comment, "The Latest Home Education Challenge: The Relationship Between Home Schools and Public Schools," *North Carolina Law Review* 74 (1996): 1913–77; Patricia Lines, "When Home Schoolers Go to School: A Partnership between Families and Schools," *Peabody Journal of Education* 75, nos. 1 and 2 (2000): 159–86.

64. See Luis Huerta, "Losing Public Accountability: A Home Schooling Charter," in *Inside Charter Schools: The Paradox of Radical Decentralization*, ed. Bruce Fuller (Cambridge, MA: Harvard University Press, 2000), 177–202. See also Rebecca Weiner, "Kansas Educators Turn to the Web to Create a Unique 'Virtual' School," *New York Times*, 16 August 2000.

65. Paul Hill, for example, believes that as more and more people homeschool, most home-

schooling families will form networks that will come to resemble regular schools ("Home Schooling and the Future of Public Education," *Peabody Journal of Education* 75, nos. 1 and 2 (2000): 20–31.

CHAPTER SEVEN

1. For a concise history of this tradition, see David Tyack and Larry Cuban, *Tinkering Toward Utopia: A Century of Public School Reform* (Cambridge, MA: Harvard University Press, 1995).

2. Just as policymakers have long recognized the yawning gap between educational policy and actual educational practice, political and educational theorists should confront the likelihood that a similar gap may exist between educational theory and educational policy. To the extent that educational theory provides the framework within which policymakers work, who in turn craft policies that set the framework within which administrators and teachers work, theorists should resist the temptation to prescribe precise educational policies or practices. The task of the theorist, in my view, is to provide arguments for the aims of education and define the general terrain upon which educational policymakers and practitioners perform their own work and exercise their own discretion.

3. Other main figures in the field include Geneva Gay, Sonia Nieto, Christine Bennett, and Christine Sleeter, from whose work I also draw in the following pages.

For Banks's scholarship, see James Banks, ed., *Handbook of Research on Multicultural Education* (New York: Macmillan, 1995); James Banks, *Educating Citizens in a Multicultural Society* (New York: Teachers College Press, 1997); James Banks, ed., *Multicultural Education, Transformative Knowledge, and Action: Historical and Contemporary Perspectives* (New York: Teachers College Press, 1996); James Banks, *Multiethnic Education: Theory and Practice*, 3d ed. (Boston: Allyn & Bacon, 1994); and James Banks, *Teaching Ethnic Studies: Concepts and Strategies* (43d Yearbook) (Washington DC: National Council for the Social Studies, 1973).

4. Arthur Schlesinger Jr., *The Disuniting of America: Reflections on a Multicultural Society* (New York: W. W. Norton, 1992); Dinesh D'Souza, *Illiberal Education: The Politics of Race and Sex on Campus* (New York: Free Press, 1991). Though Schlesinger and D'Souza both are critical of multiculturalism, they are by no means intellectual bedfellows. Schlesinger is a lifelong liberal scholar who was an advisor to President Kennedy and advocate of civil rights policies, while D'Souza is a conservative polemicist whose screeds are supported by a coterie of right-wing think tanks.

5. Molefi Asante, *The Afrocentric Idea* (Philadelphia: Temple University Press, 1987). Banks, for example, calls Asante an Afrocentrist rather than a multiculturalist (James Banks, "The Canon Debate, Knowledge Construction, and Multicultural Education," in *Multicultural Education, Transformative Knowledge, and Action*, ed. Banks, 4).

6. Banks, *Educating Citizens in a Multicultural Society*, 5.

7. Sonia Nieto, *Affirming Diversity*, 2d ed. (White Plains, NY: Longman, 1996), 345.

8. That statements about avoiding cultural assimilation and inclusive civic participation seem uncontroversial and commonplace is not meant to trivialize them. Multicultural educators have struggled for decades against racist, mainstream educational practices, and the acceptance by educators of antiracist educational aims is due in part to their labor.

9. Author Paul Beatty offers the best parody I know of a multicultural education given over to token ornamentalism in his scathing *The White Boy Shuffle* (New York: Henry Holt, 1997). For example: "Everything was multicultural, but nothing was multicultural. The class studied Asian styles of calculation by learning to add and subtract on an abacus, and then we applied the same mathematical principles on Seiko calculators. Prompting my hand to go up and me to ask naively, 'Isn't the Seiko XL-126 from the same culture as the abacus?'" (29–30).

10. Banks, *Educating Citizens in a Multicultural Society*, 78.

11. Geneva Gay, *Culturally Responsive Teaching: Theory, Research, and Practice* (New York: Teachers College Press, 2000), 29.

12. Gay, *Culturally Responsive Teaching,* 44.

13. See also Sonia Nieto, *The Light in Their Eyes: Creating Multicultural Learning Communities* (New York: Teachers College Press, 2000); Jacqueline Jordan Irvine and Darlene Eleanor York, "Learning Styles and Culturally Diverse Students: A Literature Review," in *Handbook of Research on Multicultural Education,* ed. Banks, 484–96.

14. For comments on this phenomenon, see Lawrence Blum, "Multicultural Education as Values Education," Working Paper, Harvard Project on Schooling and Children, Harvard University (1997), 10. It is important to note that recognizing the tendency of some southeast Asians to avoid direct eye contact does not mean that teachers should simply respect and accept the tendency. On the contrary, as multicultural education scholar Lisa Delpit has argued, teachers should encourage students to learn the habits and language that will enable them to navigate and succeed in mainstream society. Teachers should build upon and expand, rather than denigrate, the linguistic and behavioral repertoire that students bring with them into school. See Lisa Delpit, *Other People's Children: Cultural Conflict in the Classroom* (New York: New Press, 1996).

15. See John Rickford and Russell Rickford, *Spoken Soul: The Story of Black English* (New York: John Wiley & Sons, 2000).

16. John Ogbu, "Understanding Cultural Diversity and Learning," in *Handbook of Research on Multicultural Education,* ed. Banks, 582–93.

17. Signithia Fordham, *Blacked Out: Dilemmas of Race, Identity, and Success at Capital High* (Chicago: University of Chicago Press, 1996).

18. Claude Steele, "A Threat in the Air: How Stereotypes Shape Intellectual Identity and Performance," *American Psychologist* 52, no. 6 (1997): 613–29; Claude Steele and J. Aronson, "Stereotype Threat and the Intellectual Test Performance of African Americans," *Journal of Personality and Social Psychology* 69, no. 5 (1995): 797–811.

19. Gay, *Culturally Responsive Teaching,* xvi, 9, 10.

20. Gay's asserted link between ethnic affiliation and cultural personality is a prime example of the danger of what Anthony Appiah calls a cultural script. In Gay's view, it appears that people could not claim to be highly ethnically affiliated without exhibiting, and indeed valuing, the appropriate core cultural characteristics of their ethnic group. But when cultural identities come along with specific behavioral and value scripts, they compromise the autonomy of individuals to revise their ends without simultaneously forsaking claims of cultural membership. They also compromise the ability of individuals to contest the cultural norms and values of their group, because to do so would be to risk charges of inauthenticity or betrayal. As Appiah writes, "Demanding respect for people as blacks and as gays requires that there are some scripts that go with being an African-American or having same-sex desires. There will be proper ways of being black or gay, there will be expectations to be met, demands will be made. It is at this point that someone who takes autonomy seriously will ask whether we have not replaced one kind of tyranny with another"; Appiah, "Identity, Authenticity, Survival," in Charles Taylor, *Multiculturalism,* ed. Amy Gutmann (Princeton, NJ: Princeton University Press, 1994), 162–63.

21. For assertions about the ethnic coding of field dependence and independence, see Gay, *Culturally Responsive Teaching,* 93, 147; Nieto, *Light in Their Eyes,* 63; Banks, *Educating Citizens in a Multicultural Society,* 56–57; and Irvine and York, "Learning Styles and Culturally Diverse Students: A Literature Review," 487 ff.

22. Gay, *Culturally Responsive Teaching,* 152.

23. The claim about brain differences between racial groups is made by A. Pasteur and I. Toldson in *The Roots of Soul: The Psychology of Black Expressiveness* (New York: Anchor Press,

1982) and is reported without comment in a chapter of Banks's *Handbook of Research on Multicultural Education* (Irvine and York, "Learning Styles and Culturally Diverse Students: A Literature Review," 490).

24. Irvine and York, "Learning Styles and Culturally Diverse Students: A Literature Review," 490–91.

25. See Gay, *Culturally Responsive Teaching*, 156, 176; Christine Bennett's widely used text in teacher education, *Comprehensive Multicultural Education* adapts from the claims of Asa Hilliard, a popular figure in professional development and teacher training programs (I encountered his work in my own professional development programs while teaching in Houston), asserting among other things that "Afro-Americans respond to things in terms of the whole picture instead of its parts. The Euro-American tends to believe that anything can be divided and subdivided into pieces and that these pieces can be added up to a whole. Therefore, art is sometimes taught by numbers, as are dancing and music. That is why some people never learn to dance. They are too busy counting and analyzing"; see Bennett, *Comprehensive Multicultural Education* (Boston: Allyn & Bacon, 1990), 158.

26. Nieto says, for example, that "categorizing students' learning styles based on race or ethnicity can veer dangerously close to the racist implications drawn from distinctions on IQ tests" (Nieto, *Light in Their Eyes*, 64).

27. Nieto, *Light in Their Eyes*, 67.

28. Gay rejects ethnic-centered classrooms and schools as a policy directive but also notes the supposed academic benefits in schools that have adopted ethnocentric approaches (Gay, *Culturally Sensitive Teaching*, 150, 173 ff.).

29. Nieto, *Light in Their Eyes*, 17.

30. For the positive effects of cooperative learning, see, for example, the highly regarded work of Robert Slavin and Uri Treisman. Gay herself notes the power of cooperative learning with the seemingly apologetic comment that "for the most part, this instructional technique has similar positive effects for students across ethnic, gender, and ability groupings, achievement measures, and intervention scales (classroom or school, short- or long-term)" (Gay, *Culturally Responsive Teaching*, 159).

31. Heath is cited by Gay (95–96), by Nieto (*Light in Their Eyes*, 66; *Affirming Diversity*, 143–44), and Banks ("The Canon Debate, Knowledge Construction, and Multicultural Education," 13). The quote from Heath can be found in an essay written for a volume on Afrocentric schooling, "Island by Island We Must Go Across: Challenges from Language and Culture among African-Americans," in *African-Centered Schooling in Theory and Practice*, ed. Diane Pollard and Cheryl Ajirotutu (Westport, CT: Bergin & Garvey, 2000), 180. She expresses her skepticism about cultural categorization in several other essays as well: "Current enthusiasm over 'multiculturalism,' 'plural cultures,' and 'cultural competence' often proceeds from essentialist categorizations of entire groups with labels based on racial or ethnic membership"; see Shirley Brice Heath, "Culture: Contested Realm in Research on Children and Youth," *Applied Developmental Science* 1, no. 3 (1997): 113; see also "Race, Ethnicity, and the Defiance of Categories," in *Toward a Common Destiny: Improving Race and Ethnic Relations in America* (San Francisco: Jossey-Bass Publishers, 1995).

32. Banks, *Educating Citizens in a Multicultural Society*, xi. Banks has also written that through multicultural education, "students should be helped to develop accurate self-identities"; see National Council for the Social Studies, "Curriculum Guidelines for Multicultural Education," *Social Education*, no. 55 (September 1992), 281. Another example of this cultural fixity can be found in Gary Howard's argument that white students should not appropriate other cultural identities, customs, or values because to do so would be inauthentic in light of the fact that "any of us who choose to look more deeply into our European roots will find there a rich and diverse experience waiting to be discovered"; see Gary Howard, "Whites in Multicultural Edu-

cation: Rethinking Our Role," in *Multicultural Education, Transformative Knowledge, and Action*, ed. Banks, 332.

33. Nieto, *Light in Their Eyes*, 52.

34. Heath, "Race, Ethnicity, and the Defiance of Categories," 47, 48. The increasingly multicultural identity of youth is reflected in a U.S. Department of Education survey of school district policies, part of the Census Bureau's consideration of whether or not to change the ways in which people could identify themselves on the census, in which 41 percent of all public schools reported that the racial categories used by the government did not accurately describe their school populations; see "Racial and Ethnic Classifications used by Public Schools," National Center for Education Statistics (NCES 96–092, March 1996).

Paul Beatty captures nicely the trouble with multicultural education's simplistic cultural categorizations. "After a long schoolday of moralistic bombardment with the aphorisms of Martin Luther King, John F. Kennedy, Cesar Chavez, Pocahontas, and a herd of pacifist pachyderms, my friends and I were ready to think about color on our own terms. We'd make plans to spend the weekend at the beach, sunning in the shoreline's warm chromatics and filling in childhood's abstract impressionism coloring books with our own definitions of color, trying our hardest not to stay inside the lines" (Beatty, *White Boy Shuffle*, 34).

35. Richard Bernstein, *Dictatorship of Virtue: How the Battle over Multiculturalism Is Reshaping Our Schools, Our Country, and Our Lives* (New York: Knopf, 1995), 9.

36. For more on the unwillingness or reluctance of teachers to initiate moral discourse, see Katherine Simon, *Moral Questions in the Classroom* (New Haven, CT: Yale University Press, 2001).

37. See Gadamer's *Truth and Method* (New York: Continuum, 1989), 306–7, 374–75.

38. Charles Taylor, *Multiculturalism: Examining the Politics of Recognition* (Princeton, NJ: Princeton University Press, 1994), 67.

39. Michael Rabinder James, "Critical Intercultural Dialogue," *Polity* 31, no. 4 (1999): 590. James's very interesting work examines the limitations and possibilities of intercultural dialogue, concentrating specifically on communication and understanding between Native Americans and non–Native Americans.

40. James, "Critical Intercultural Dialogue," 67.

41. Gadamer, *Truth and Method*, 379.

42. Thomas Hill, Jr., *Respect, Pluralism, and Justice* (Oxford: Oxford University Press, 2000), 83.

43. Jay Lampert, "Gadamer and Cross-Cultural Hermeneutics," *Philosophical Forum*, 28 and 29 (summer and fall 1997), 359.

44. Robert Gooding-Williams makes a similar remark in his endorsement of multicultural education as fostering cross-cultural dialogue and mutual understanding and respect: "Indeed, the ideal of mutual understanding invites *increasing* complexity by suggesting that cross-cultural educational insights, since they can effect changes in the self-understandings of persons who have benefitted from a multicultural education, may alter and further complicate those person's identities, perhaps making them more multicultural"; see "Race, Multiculturalism, and Democracy," *Constellations* 5, no. 1 (1998): 32.

45. Lampert, "Gadamer and Cross-Cultural Hermeneutics," 357.

46. Melinda Fine, *Habits of Mind: Struggling over Values in America's Classrooms* (San Francisco: Jossey-Bass, 1995).

47. Fine, *Habits of Mind*, 63; emphasis in original.

48. Fine, *Habits of Mind*, 95; emphasis in original.

49. A substantial philosophical literature on cosmopolitanism has accumulated in recent years. Contributions most relevant and influential for multicultural education include Taylor, *Multiculturalism*; Hollinger, *Postethnic America* (New York: Basic Books, 1995), chaps. 4–6;

Martha Nussbaum, "Patriotism or Cosmopolitanism?" *Boston Review* 19, no. 5 (1994): 3–6; Jeremy Waldron, "Minority Cultures and the Cosmopolitan Alternative," *University of Michigan Journal of Law Reform* 25, nos. 3 and 4 (spring and summer 1992): 751–93; Mitchell Cohen, "Rooted Cosmopolitanism," in *Toward a Global Civil Society,* ed. Michael Walzer (Oxford: Berghahn Books, 1995), 223–34; and Bruce Ackermann, "Rooted Cosmopolitanism," *Ethics* no. 104 (1994): 516–35.

50. Nussbaum, "Patriotism or Cosmopolitanism," 4.

51. In a critique of the American obsession with multiculturalism, K. Anthony Appiah notes that "one of the most pious of the pieties of our age [is] that the United States is a society of enormous cultural diversity," but that, "coming, as I do, from Ghana, I find the broad cultural homogeneity of America more striking than its much vaunted variety" (Appiah, "Multiculturalist Misunderstanding," New York Review of Books, 9 October 1997, 30, 31).

52. Nussbaum, "Patriotism or Cosmopolitanism," 6.

53. Václav Havel, "The New Measure of Man," *New York Times,* 8 July 1994, A27. Havel comments further on the dire need to find measures of human commonality and cause for human solidarity in the light of global threats: "In today's multicultural world, the truly reliable path to peaceful co-existence and creative cooperation must start from what is at the root of all cultures and what lies infinitely deeper in human hearts and minds than political opinion, convictions, antipathies or sympathies: it must be rooted in self-transcendence" (27).

54. For a more detailed discussion on the need for cosmopolitanism in the light of global threats, see Hollinger, *Postethnic America,* 108–110; and Nussbaum, "Patriotism or Cosmopolitanism," 4–6.

55. For an argument about construing citizenship as shared fate, see Melissa Williams, "Citizenship as Shared Fate," in *Education and Citizenship in Liberal-Democratic Societies,* ed. Kevin McDonough and Walter Feinberg (Oxford: Oxford University Press, forthcoming).

56. See Richard Rorty, *Contingency, Irony, Solidarity* (Cambridge: Cambridge University Press, 1991), ch. 9.

57. Amy Gutmann, "The Challenges of Multiculturalism in Democratic Education," in *Public Education in a Multicultural Society,* ed. Robert Fullinwider (Cambridge: Cambridge University Press, 1996), 175 ff.

58. I adopt the phrase "connected criticism" from Michael Walzer, who advanced it as an effort at internal critique upon a society that fails to abide by its own proclaimed ideals and standards; see Walzer, *Interpretation and Social Criticism* (Cambridge, MA: Harvard University Press, 1987).

59. Meira Levinson, *The Demands of Liberal Education* (Oxford: Oxford University Press, 1999). Levinson writes, "All told . . . there would be in practice little if anything to distinguish private schools from state schools—which is exactly the way it should be. Given the extent of these regulations, individuals and organizations may have little incentive to open private schools, and a state which implements the above requirements or principles may in practice include few private schools" (145). On the question of religious schools: "As a result of religion's place in the individual, social, and political lives of Americans, I suggest that it would be inappropriate for liberal schools in the United States to differentiate themselves on religious grounds. Because of religion's status as both a fundamental and a socially divisive conception of the good, religious schools would violate the liberal educative aims of commonality, autonomy, and citizenship" (158).

60. James Dwyer, *Religious Schools v. Children's Rights* (Ithaca, NY: Cornell University Press, 1998). Of the regulations Dwyer defends, he writes, "The changes would certainly be radical for Fundamentalist schools and substantial for most Catholic schools. That Fundamentalist and Catholic schooling as presently constituted would no longer exist should not, however, be cause for mourning, at least not for anyone who respects the personhood of children. It should

rather be cause for celebration" (180). While I am sympathetic to much of Dwyer's arguments about the significance of children's rights and interests, and to his conclusion that Fundamentalist schools would change dramatically as a result of this significance, his regulatory scheme hinges on the implausible conclusion that Catholic schools in their current form cause irreparable harm to their students' ability to lead a good life, to become decent citizens, and to experience meaningful freedom. The empirical evidence about the effect of Catholic schooling suggests the opposite; see Anthony Bryk, Valerie Lee, and Peter Holland, *Catholic Schooling and the Common Good* (Cambridge, MA: Harvard University Press, 1993).

61. See Rawls, *Political Liberalism* (New York: Columbia University Press, 1993), 4, 36 ff.

62. Mill wrote: "That the whole or any large part of the education of the people should be in state hands, I go so far as anyone in deprecating. All that has been said of the importance of individuality of character, and diversity in opinion and modes of conduct, involves, as of the same unspeakable importance, diversity of education"; see Mill, *On Liberty*, ed. David Spitz (New York: W. W. Norton: 1975), 98.

63. The power of the U.S. state to regulate all kinds of schools was recognized by the Supreme Court even as it exempted Amish parents from two years of compulsory school attendance: "There is no doubt as to the power of a State, having a high responsibility for education of its citizens, to impose reasonable regulations for the control and duration of basic education" (*Wisconsin v. Yoder*, 406 U.S. 205, 213 [1972]).

64. Eamonn Callan, *Creating Citizens* (Oxford: Clarendon Press, 1997), 158.

65. Callan, *Creating Citizens*, 181.

66. Martha Nussbaum, *Cultivating Humanity* (Cambridge, MA: Harvard University Press, 1997), 62.

67. An unlikely pair of organizations, the National Bible Association and the First Amendment Center, recently released a joint report on teaching about the Bible in public schools without running afoul of the First Amendment. The report counsels that "the school's approach to religion [be] academic, not devotional," that "the school may expose students to a diversity of religious views, but may not impose, discourage, or encourage any particular view" and that "the school may inform the student about various beliefs, but should not seek to conform him or her to any particular belief." It concludes with the sensible admonition that "as in secondary schools, a balanced and fair curriculum in the elementary grades would not limit study about religion to Judaism and Christianity, but would include a variety of the world's major religious faiths" (First Amendment Center, "The Bible and Public Schools: A First Amendment Guide" [Nashville, TN: Freedom Forum, 1999]).

68. The relatively recent phenomenon of private donations to public schools is understudied, though its inegalitarian implications are absolutely clear. In Silicon Valley, for example, PTAs have essentially turned into fund-raising machines for public schools, drastically exacerbating the funding inequalities among public schools in the area and greater state. David Kaplan describes the annual fundraising auction in Woodside, California for the single public elementary school (enrollment: about four hundred) in the town: by selling opportunities to lunch with high-tech CEOs, vacations to Hawaii, and so on. The PTA raises more than $400,000 a year, adding more than $1,000 *per pupil* to the school expenditures in the small town; see *Silicon Boys* (New York: William Morrow, 1999).

69. Thus Brian Barry, for instance, believes "that it is essential for the maintenance of even rough equality of opportunity to make it illegal for any private school to spend more per head on its students than the average amount spent by the state system, unless the school can show that it has disproportionate numbers of children with special physical, psychological, or educational needs"; see *Culture and Equality* (New York: Harvard University Press, 2001), 206. For an incisive argument about educational equality and its policy consequences on funding, see Harry Brighouse, *School Choice and Social Justice* (Oxford: Oxford University Press, 2000).

70. Jonathan Kozol, *Savage Inequalities* (New York: Harper Perennial, 1992).

71. See Eric Hanushek, "The Impact of Differential Expenditures on School Performance," *Educational Researcher* 18 (May 1989): 45–51, and "Assessing the Effects of School Resources on Student Performance: An Update," *Educational Evaluation and Policy Analysis* 19, no. 2 (summer 1997): 141–64; and Larry Hedges, Richard Laine, and Bob Greenwald, "Does Money Matter? A Meta-Analysis of Studies of the Effects of Differential School Inputs on Student Outcomes," *Educational Researcher* 23 (April 1994): 5–14.

72. It would be irresponsible to claim that simply reducing funding disparities in schools would suffice for autonomy cultivation. I agree with Harry Brighouse's insistence that liberal states do far more: "The state should do a great deal (far more than the U.S. government currently does) to ensure that all children enjoy good health care, circumstantial stability, and physical security, both because these are prerequisites of autonomy and because they are, independently, important for well-being"; see "Civic Education and Liberal Legitimacy," *Ethics* 108, no. 4 (July 1998): 744–45.

73. Friedman's 1955 essay found wide circulation in his *Capitalism and Freedom* (Chicago: University of Chicago Press, 1962). Vouchers received a powerful boost with the publication of John Chubb's and Terry Moe's *Politics, Markets, and America's Schools* (Washington, DC: The Brookings Institute, 1990).

74. Phi Delta Kappa and the Gallup Organization conduct an annual poll on education. When asked "whether students and parents should be given the choice of selecting a private school to attend at public expense," the percentage in favor rose from 24 percent in 1993 to 44 percent in 1998; see Lowell Rose and Alec Gallup, "The 32nd Annual Phi Delta Kappa/Gallup Poll of the Public's Attitudes toward the Public Schools," *Kappan* 82, no. 1 (2000): 41–66.

75. The primary support for voucher success comes from Paul Peterson and his colleagues (see Jay Greene, Paul Peterson, and Jiangtao Du, "Effectiveness of School Choice: The Milwaukee Experiment," Occasional Paper 97–1, Program in Education Policy and Governance, Harvard University, 1997; and William Howell, Patrick Wolf, Paul Peterson, and David Campbell, "Test Score Effect of School Vouchers in Dayton, Ohio, Washington DC, and New York City: Evidence from Randomized Field Trials," paper prepared and delivered at the annual meeting of the American Political Science Association, September 2000). The primary criticism of voucher effects comes from John Witte in *The Market Approach to Education* (Princeton, NJ: Princeton University Press, 2000).

76. In the 1960s, Christopher Jencks forwarded a leftist voucher proposal for poor children; see "Is the Public School Obsolete?" *Public Interest* 2 (winter 1966): 18–27. In the 1990s, the best-known radical liberal voucher proposal came from Samuel Bowles and Herbert Gintis, "Efficient Redistribution: New Rules for Markets, States, and Communities," in *Recasting Egalitarianism* (New York: Verso, 1998). Harry Brighouse's proposal owes much to Bowles's and Gintis's work (Brighouse, *School Choice and Social Justice*). By contrast, Milton Friedman's 1955 and John Chubb's and Terry Moe's 1990 voucher proposals stem from an essentially libertarian position; see Friedman, *Capitalism and Freedom*; Chubb and Moe, *Politics, Markets, and America's Schools*.

77. Brighouse, *School Choice and Social Justice*, 53, 206.

78. For more on the Florida voucher plan, see Jessica Sandham, "Florida OKs First Statewide Voucher Plan," *Education Week* 18, no. 34 (May 1999): 1, 21; Jessica Sandham, "Schools Hit By Vouchers Fight Back," *Education Week* 19, no. 2 (September 1999), 1, 20–21. As of 1999, fifty-eight students had received vouchers.

79. To be fair, the state's efforts at reforming schools in order to improve student achievement may be unsuccessful less as a function of the reform itself than of the dismal socioeconomic conditions of the children's families. As Amy Gutmann, who opposes vouchers, rightly comments, "The unfairness of our present [school] system resides not in the absence of choice per se

but in the presence of poverty and an inadequate school system. . . . The truly bold reform—and one that is also clearly constitutional—would be for the public to support decent-paying work and a real safety net for everyone, including good child care, public schools, and health care"; see "What Does 'School Choice' Mean?" *Dissent* [summer 2000]: 20.

80. Harry Brighouse provides a compelling argument for a universal voucher program designed to ensure an autonomy-facilitating education and to promote educational equality in *School Choice and Social Justice.*

81. Excluding religious schools, it must be admitted, would severely restrict the available choices to parents, for religious schools in the United States constitute the overwhelming majority of private schools. In 1987, for example, fully 84.3 percent of all private schools had some religious affiliation; see National Center for Education Statistics, *Digest of Education Statistics, 1992* (Washington DC: Government Printing Office, 1992), table 57.

82. As I am not a Constitutional scholar, I cannot say whether public support of religious schooling is in violation of the First Amendment. A series of inconsistent rulings in state courts in the United States makes it a virtual certainty that the Supreme Court will address the issue sometime in the future.

83. Office of Educational Research and Improvement, "National Study of Charter Schools: Fourth Year Report" (Washington, DC: OERI, 2000).

84. According to a recent and comprehensive review of charter schools, "It appears that between 37 and 41 percent of charter students come from low-income families, almost the same percentage as among regular public school pupils" and that "charter schools are serving at least 'their share' of disadvantaged youth"; see Chester Finn, Bruno Manno, and Gregg Vanourek, *Charter Schools in Action: Renewing Public Education* (Princeton, NJ: Princeton University Press, 2000), 80.

85. Finn, Manno, and Vanourek, in an otherwise upbeat assessment of charter schools, "acknowledge that some charter schools do not meet all their students' special needs. Part of the reason may be stinginess, malfeasance, or insensitivity, but mostly it is due to lack of experience, expertise, or resources" (*Charter Schools in Action,* 159). Howard Gardner, a renowned educational innovator, has criticized charter schools for their questionable survival rates: "Many [charters] are started by people with unusual energy and appealing ideas. Such efforts are sometimes sustained for a time by the charisma of exceptional leaders. . . . However, pioneers usually move on. In the absence of a group of first-rate teachers, a hefty endowment, or, perhaps most important, a sustained tradition of excellence supported fiscally and ideologically, the schools will eventually have a hard time competing with other schools, public or chartered"; see "Paroxysms of Choice," *New York Review of Books* 47, no. 16 (October 2000), 46–47.

86. Even optimistic charter school exponents concede that with regard to evaluations, "definitive data are scarce, particularly concerning pupil achievement" (Finn, Manno, and Vanourek, *Charter Schools in Action,* 74). They also report some preliminary evidence that charter schools are catalysts for systemic change and have district-level effects (pp. 203–209).

87. Robert Putnam, *Bowling Alone: The Collapse and Revival of American Community* (New York: Simon & Schuster, 2000).

88. Finn, Manno, and Vanourek, *Charter Schools in Action,* 222. Howard Gardner, more of a charter school skeptic, also remarks that "the charter school movement seems a quintessentially American enterprise, one that would not have surprised Alexis de Tocqueville when he visited America in the 1830s" (Gardner, "Paroxysms of Choice," 45).

89. National Commission on Civic Renewal, *A Nation of Spectators: How Civic Disengagement Weakens America and What We Can Do About It* (College Park, MD: National Commission on Civic Renewal, 1998), 16.

90. Bruce Fuller, ed., *Inside Charter Schools: The Paradox of Radical Decentralization* (Cambridge, MA: Harvard University Press, 2001), 30.

91. These charter schools are described in Finn, Manno, and Vanourek, *Charter Schools in Action*, 161, 232.

92. The median size of charter schools in 1999–2000 was 137 students, and the majority of charters enroll fewer than 200 students (Office of Educational Research and Improvement "National Study of Charter Schools: Fourth Year Report," 1).

93. Fuller, *Inside Charter Schools*, 10.

94. Finn, Manno, and Vanourek, *Charter Schools in Action*, 164. Because of the importance of age-appropriate practice, as described earlier, elementary schools would have a greater claim on being more insular or exclusive communities while high schools should bear a greater burden for striving for diversity and inclusivity.

95. Indeed, small schools were once the concern of educational policymakers, but today are looked upon as an all-important reform, especially in large urban districts. The success of the consolidation of districts and the creation of larger schools can be seen in the fact that in 1940 there were 114,000 one-room schools, and in 1970 only 2,000. Larger schools were said to be able to provide more specialized instruction, more and better opportunities for students, and a more attractive and professional work environment for educators. Perhaps the most influential champion of larger schools was James Conant, the former President of Harvard University, who published *The American High School Today* in 1959, which recommended expanding schools so as to permit ability grouping and increased academic, vocational, and extracurricular opportunities. See James Conant, *The American High School Today* (New York: McGraw Hill, 1959). For a history of the modern American high school and incisive commentary on Conant's role, see Robert Hampel, *The Last Little Citadel: American High Schools Since 1940* (Boston: Houghton Mifflin, 1986).

96. For four comprehensive reviews of and recommendations in favor of small schools, see William Ayers, Michael Klonsky, and Gabrielle Lyon, eds., *A Simple Justice: The Challenge of Small Schools* (New York: Teachers College Press, 2000); Michelle Fine and Jan Somerville, *Small School, Big Imaginations: A Creative Look at Urban Public Schools* (Chicago: Cross City Campaign for Urban School Reform, 1998); Patricia Wasley et al., *Small School: Great Strides* (New York: Bank Street College of Education, 2000); and Evans Clinchy, ed., *Creating New Schools: How Small Schools Are Changing American Education* (New York: Teachers College Press, 2000).

97. Among the earliest and strongest supporter of small schools was Debbie Meier, the innovative founder of a successful school in Harlem; see *The Power of Their Ideas: Lessons for America from a Small School in Harlem* (Boston: Beacon Press, 1995). The University of Illinois at Chicago has a "Small Schools Workshop" which supports and carries out research on the small schools in Chicago. And Oakland, California, has created a "Small Schools Incubator" designed to support and encourage the creation of small schools.

98. National Center for Education Statistics, *Digest of Education Statistics, 2000*, table 95.

99. Arthur Powell, Eleanor Farrar, David Cohen, *The Shopping Mall High School: Winners and Losers in the Educational Marketplace* (Boston: Houghton Mifflin, 1985), 4.

100. Valerie Lee and Susanna Loeb, "School Size in Chicago Elementary Schools: Effects on Teachers' Attitudes and Students' Achievement," *American Educational Research Journal* 37, no. 1 (spring 2000): 3–32; Wasley et al., *Small Schools: Great Strides*.

101. Fine and Somerville, *Small School, Big Imaginations*.

102. Linda Powell, *Small Schools and the Issue of Race*, Occasional Paper Series, 3.4 (New York: Bank Street College of Education, 2000), 10.

103. The Small Schools Workshop in Chicago, for example, lists as the first guiding feature of small schools that they "have a maximum population of 250–300 students, in a heterogeneous mix that represents the local school community": see Michael Klonsky, "Small Schools:

The Numbers Tell a Story" (Chicago: The Small Schools Workshop at the University of Illinois at Chicago, 1996).

104. Macedo, *Diversity and Distrust*, 233–4.

105. Powell, Farrar, and Cohen, *The Shopping Mall High School*, 4. They later say that "schools settle for the absence of conflict as the definition of community" (58).

CONCLUSION

1. As cited in Robert Putnam, *Bowling Alone* (New York: Simon & Schuster, 2000), 186–87.

2. National Commission on Excellence in Education, *A Nation At Risk: The Imperative for Educational Reform* (Washington, DC: GPO, 1983). For the argument that the report ushered in an era of focus on economic purposes of education, see, among others, David Tyack and Larry Cuban, *Tinkering Toward Utopia: A Century of Public School Reform* (Cambridge, MA: Harvard University Press, 1995).

3. Benjamin Barber, "Thomas Jefferson and the Education of the Citizen," in *A Passion for Democracy* (Princeton, NJ: Princeton University Press, 1998), 161.

4. Tyack and Cuban, *Tinkering toward Utopia*, 140.

5. Center for Civic Education, *National Standards for Civics and Government* (Calabasas, CA: Center for Civic Education, 1994).

6. The NAEP civics assessment was last administered in 1998, and found that two-thirds of the test-takers in each of the three grade levels achieved at the "basic" level or above, but that relatively few, less than 5 percent in any grade level, reached the "advanced" level. See David Hoff, "Beyond Basics, Civics Eludes U.S. Students," *Education Week* (24 November 1999).

7. Richard Niemi and Jane Junn, *Civic Education: What Makes Students Learn?* (New Haven, CT: Yale University Press, 1998). In their words, "The most important message to come out of our study of the political knowledge of high school seniors is that the school civics curriculum does indeed enhance what and how much they know about American government and politics" (147).

8. According to Center for Civic Education materials, more than 20 million students have participated in We the People programs. See www.civiced.org.

9. One evaluation by Richard Brody found that the We the People program had significant impact on the cultivation of political tolerance in students (Richard Brody, "Secondary Education and Political Attitudes: Examining the Effects on Political Tolerance of the We the People ... Curriculum," [Calabasas, CA: Center for Civic Education, 1994]); another evaluation by Kenneth Tolo found that the We the People program for middle school students promoted a host of desirable civic knowledge, attitudes, and behaviors (Kenneth Tolo, "An Assessment of We the People ... Project Citizen: Promoting Citizenship in Classrooms and Communities," Policy Research Project Report Number 129 [Austin, TX: Lyndon Johnson School of Public Affairs, University of Texas, 1999]).

10. For more on service learning, see Timothy Stanton, Dwight Giles, and Nadinne Cruz, *Service-Learning: A Movement's Pioneers Reflect on Its Origins, Practice, and Future* (San Francisco: Jossey-Bass, 1999).

11. National Center for Education Statistics, "Service Learning and Community Service in K–12 Public Schools" (NCES 1999043), 1999.

12. Rogers Smith, "American Conceptions of Citizenship and National Service," in *New Communitarian Thinking*, ed. Amitai Etzioni (Charlottesville, VA: University Press of Virginia, 1995), 256.

13. John Dewey, "My Pedagogic Creed," in *Dewey on Education*, ed. Martin Dworkin (New York: Teachers College Bureau of Publications, 1959), 32.

INDEX

Adams, David Wallace, 29
American Bar Association, 221
Americanization, 4, 15, 17, 24–28, 29, 31, 39, 136, 195
Amish, 7, 72, 73, 87, 109, 208; and parental authority over education, 142–44, 146, 163; and *Wisconsin v. Yoder*, 9, 47–48, 68, 119, 142–44, 146, 163
Appiah, Anthony, 12, 72
Arab Israelis, 60
Aristotle, 4, 115
Asante, Molefi, 12, 176
autonomy: and choice-making beyond culture, 77–81; and cosmopolitan identity, 78, 83–85; definition of, 9, 46; and Galston's Diversity State, 51–54; history of, 90–91; importance to other disciplines, 91; Kantian interpretation of, 96, 99; Kymlicka's defense of, 46–47, 49, 73, 74; moral, 48–49, 96–99, 109, 119; moral vs. political conceptions of, 46–50, 89–90, 91; personal vs. group, 90–91; political, 48, 52, 74, 89, 91, 125; and political virtues, 46; respect for vs. exercise of, 93, 107–11; and right of exit, 54, 58, 61–64, 66–69, 88, 110, 163 (*see also* right of exit); as self-creation, 97; as sovereignty or self-determination, 98–99; and the worth of liberties, 50–51. *See also* minimalist autonomy

Banks, James, 131, 175–78, 181, 183
Barber, Benjamin, 218
Barry, Brian, 114, 127
Bennett, Christine, 181
Berlin, Isaiah, 100
Bernstein, Richard, 184
Bible, 4, 18, 19, 20, 21, 47, 162
bilingual education, 21–24, 27, 28, 31, 40, 198
Bourne, Randolph, 27

Boykin, Wade, 182
Brighouse, Harry, 126, 203
Brown v. Board of Education, 113, 152, 217

Callan, Eamonn, 4, 5, 51, 102, 103, 149, 197, 219
Catholics, 4, 17–21, 23, 27; and Catholic schools, 182, 192, 201
Center for Civic Education, 220
charter schools, 10, 174, 206–10
child's interests in education, 143, 148, 155–57; and autonomy, 156–57, 165–67; best interest standard, 150–51; boundaries of in liberal multicultural education, 195; clashes with parents' and state's interests, 155, 158–59; in control over education, 164; and homeschooling, 159–63; independence of, 155; and independent functioning, 156; in legal disputes, 164–68; and relational considerations, 165; representation of, 155, 170. *See also* interests in education
Christian Fundamentalism. *See* Fundamentalism
civic virtues. *See* political virtues
Columbine High School, 145
communitarianism, 56
community service, 221–22
Constitutional Rights Foundation, 221
Corporation for National Service, 221
cosmopolitanism, 27, 102, 118, 190–92; and identity, 78, 84, 132, 135; and liberal multicultural education, 174, 184, 190–92; and Waldron, 61, 78, 84
Covello, Leonard, 27
Cremin, Lawrence, 25
Crevecoeur, Hector St. John, 16
Cuban, Larry, 218
Cubberley, Ellwood, 25, 26

Index

Date Due
